CULTURAL THEORY
THE KEY CONCEPTS

'Thorough, well-written and accessible, this text should be an indispensable part of every library.'

Professor Douglas Kellner,
University of California at Los Angeles

Here is an up-to-date and comprehensive survey of over 350 of the key terms encountered in cultural theory today. Each entry provides clear and succinct explanations for students in a wide range of disciplines, including literature, cultural studies, sociology and philosophy.

Topics include:

- Deconstruction
- Hermeneutics
- Postmodernism
- Epistemology
- Holism

- Semiotics
- Feminism
- Culture
- Sociobiology
- Consumption

Major entries are accompanied by suggestions for further reading, and the book also includes a bibliography of essential texts in cultural theory.

Andrew Edgar and **Peter Sedgwick** are lecturers in the philosophy department of Cardiff University.

ROUTLEDGE KEY GUIDES

Routledge Key Guides are accessible, informative and lucid handbooks, which define and discuss the central concepts, thinkers and debates in a broad range of academic disciplines. All are written by noted experts in their respective subjects. Clear, concise exposition of complex and stimulating issues and ideas make *Routledge Key Guides* the ultimate reference resources for students, teachers, researchers and the interested lay person.

CULTURAL THEORY
THE KEY CONCEPTS

Edited by
Andrew Edgar
and Peter Sedgwick

London and New York

First published, as *Key Concepts in Cultural Theory, 1999*
by Routledge
11 New Fetter Lane, London EC4P 4EE

Simultaneously published in the USA and Canada
by Routledge
29 West 35th Street, New York, NY 10001

This edition first published 2002

Routledge is an imprint of the Taylor & Francis Group

© 1999, 2002 Andrew Edgar and Peter Sedgwick

Typeset in Bembo by Florence Production, Stoodleigh, Devon

Printed and bound in Great Britain by Biddles Ltd,
Guildford and King's Lynn

British Library Cataloguing in Publication Data
A catalogue record for this book is available from the British
Library

Library of Congress Cataloging in Publication Data
A catalog record for this book has been requested.

ISBN 0–415–28426–0

CONTENTS

KEY CONCEPTS

A

absence
Abstract Expressionism
Absurd (Theatre of the)
action theory
aesthetics
agency and structure
agriculture
alienation
allegory
analytic philosophy
année sociologique l'
anomie
archetype
architecture
articulation
artworld
attitude
author
authoritarian personality
authority
avant-garde

B

Baroque
base and superstructure
Bauhaus
beauty
behavioural ideology
behaviourism
binary opposition
Birmingham Centre for Contemporary Cultural Studies
body
bourgeoisie
bricolage
bureaucracy

C

canon
capital
capitalism
Cartesianism
cinema
citizenship
civic humanism
civil society
class
class consciousness
code
comics
commodity
commodity fetishism
communication
communitarianism
conceptual art
conflict theory
conscience collective
consciousness
conservatism

consumption
content analysis
continental philosophy
contradiction
conversation analysis
counterculture
critical theory
cultural anthropology
cultural capital
cultural relativism
cultural reproduction
cultural studies
culture
culture industry

D

Dada
dance
deconstruction
determinism
deviance
diachronic *see* synchronic/diachronic
dialectical and historical materialism
dialectics
dictatorship of the proletariat
difference/*différance*
discourse
division of labour
dramaturgical model
drive

E

écriture féminine
elaborated and restricted codes
elite
empiricism

ontology
organic analogy
organic solidarity
Orientalism *see* Other
Other

P

paradigm
parole
participant observation
patriarchy
phenomenology
philosophy of language
philosophy of science
photography
pluralism
political economy
Pop Art
popular culture
popular music
positivism
post-colonialism
post-industrial society
postmodernism
post-structuralism
power
pragmatism
praxis
prejudice
production
progress
proletariat
propaganda
property
psychoanalysis
punk

Q

queer theory

R

race/racism
rationalisation
rationality
realism
reference
reflexivity
reification
relations of production
relative autonomy
religion
repetition
representation
reproduction *see* cultural reproduction
rhetoric
rites de passage
ritual
role
Romanticism
rule

S

self
semiotics/semiology
serialism
sexuality
sign
signifier/signified
simulacrum
social contract
Social Darwinism

theology
transference

U

unconscious
underclass
urbanism
uses and gratifications
use-value
utilitarianism
utopia/nism
utterance

V

value
value-freedom

W

worldview

Y

youth culture

CONTRIBUTORS

Gideon Calder (GC)
Richard Cochrane (RC)
Stephen Horton (SH)
Gordon Hughes (GH)
Christa Knellwolf (CK)
Kevin Mills (KM)
Christopher Norris (CN)
Jessica Osborne (JO)
Nadira Regrage (NR)
Shiva Kumar Srinivassan (SKS)
Alessandra Tanasini (AT)
Robin Wackerbarth (RW)
Christopher Wraight (CW)

INTRODUCTION

If we ask what the word '**culture**' means we are inevitably able to think of a diversity of possible answers, often depending upon the ways in which we pose such a question. Cultural theory takes as its domain of enquiry the study of all aspects of culture (if not in fact, then at least in principle). To this extent, this domain is delineated at once in the clearest and vaguest of ways. For 'culture' is immanent to human experience, yet this very immanence makes the term difficult to define in a univocal sense. Cultural theorists have, in turn, generally held the word 'culture' to have a polyvocal sense, i.e. a plurality of meanings (a view which has, in recent years, frequently taken its point of departure from some of the central tenets associated with **postmodernism**). This plurality has, in turn, often been cited as the distinctive feature of cultural theory. Doubtless, the assertion of **pluralism** with regard to the meaning of the word 'culture' has a **genealogy** which may be traced back to the immediate post-war period: to the demise of European imperialism, the rise of multiculturalism, increased geographical and social mobility and the diversification of social roles in modern western societies. Equally, work in **cultural studies** (associated with the writings of such figures as Stuart Hall) has sought to draw attention to issues of **race**, **class** and **gender** in the cultural domain. In doing so, it has exerted an important influence upon the form and content of debates within cultural theory as well as in other disciplines. Such

1

developments have brought with them, amongst other things, the perceived need to re-examine what have traditionally been regarded as normative or naturalised realms, such as those issues of human **identity** which fall under the rubrics of 'race' and 'gender'. In place of attitudes that hold these to be a matter of mere fact, cultural theorists generally argue for the view that these are constructed. They argue, in short, that naturalised concepts are in fact social constructions which can be questioned in the wake of a burgeoning knowledge of the pluralism of social forms. 'Culture', in this context, becomes both a space and object of debate about questions which centre not only on issues concerning the constitution of **subjectivity** but on such matters as those of **power**, **representation** and **discourse**, rather than signifying a pre-determined subject-matter with a pre-established and naturalised sense.

Because of this, the question of 'theory' equally becomes an important one, for the constitution of a theory is intimately bound up with what it is about. Although it is perhaps obvious, it is worth mentioning that cultural theory does not merely discuss or catalogue instances of 'culture', it *theorises* it. A theory is a schema of explanation according to which a diversity of phenomena are accorded a significance. The practice of cultural theory therefore implies the elucidation and explanation of cultural forms according to criteria afforded by some schema or other. There are numerous methodologies applicable or relevant to the study of culture which have been developed in the contexts of a wide range of disciplines and approaches. These offer a variety of possible accounts of its meaning and significance (for example, **analytic** and **continental philosophy**, **cultural anthropology**, **Marxism**, **psychoanalysis**, **sociology**). Cultural theory has, traditionally, drawn upon these in two ways. First, through an appropriation of these approaches by way of adopting a theoretical framework derived from aspects of them – for example, through drawing upon approaches to **meaning** within the domain of **philosophy of language**, principally in conjunction with developments within **post-structuralism**. Second, in reacting against some of the concepts which have formed the subject-matter of these disciplines. A case in point would be the debates within philosophy about truth, a notion which critical and cultural theorists have sought to criticise in the light of the work of thinkers such as Foucault. The range of theories available, it follows, likewise reflects the purported pluralism of cultural theory, for there is no theoretical perspective which can be exclusively associated with it. Indeed, this theoretical diversity reflects the multiplicity of possible meanings that can in turn be associated with the word 'culture'.

Cultural theory, then, starts from the self-proclaimed assertion of a plurality of meanings associated with the word 'culture'. That said, the activity of talking and theorising about culture is not new. Although often a maligned figure within the cultural theory scene, the writings of Plato (428–347 BC) deal with a range of questions which necessarily encompass cultural considerations; for example, ontological questions concerning the constitution of human **identity** and the nature of human relations, or questions about politics, ethics and **aesthetics**. Thus, when one asks about the meaning of human culture, one also raises issues that are related to the political, the aesthetic, or the ethical spheres of human life with which Plato's philosophical texts, too, concerned themselves. Equally, any attempt to construct an account of culture presupposes modes of knowledge adequate to the task (a problem related to **epistemology**) and likewise encounters other philosophically delineated problems, such as those associated with the problems of **language**, **representation** and **metaphysics**. Cultural theory need not, of course, take as its starting point a purely 'philosophical' range of problems. As already mentioned, perspectives have also been offered within other disciplines (for example, anthropology, economics, psychoanalysis or sociology) which take on relevance for cultural theory. Like philosophy, such disciplines can offer distinctive models of explanation with regard to questions with which cultural theorists concern themselves. It is not surprising, therefore, that cultural theory has connections with these fields, too, not only with regard to some of its key concerns, but also methodologically.

To return to our opening point, where cultural theory is usually held to differ from such disciplines is in its espousal of a multidisciplinary approach. This approach seeks to transcend the traditionally constituted boundaries of these different **discourses** and their associated subject-matter. In turn, the range of concerns which cultural theorists address are often articulated with a view to posing questions about the adequacy of such boundaries. For example, in certain forms of **Marxism**, which aimed at an investigation of the structure of society through an analysis of the **dialectical** relationship between its economic and ideological elements, 'culture' was open to being regarded as a peripheral concern, as something derivable from the primacy of economic relationships, cultural theory foregrounds the view that the construction of the meaning of the word 'culture' itself is at stake within any such account of human society. Equally, in the sphere of **literary criticism**, cultural and **critical theory** has sought to overturn accepted definitions of 'literature', and thereby redefine the reading of such texts in terms of social or historical factors (an approach linked to **historicism**), or through the advocacy of particular conceptions of language and meaning (a case in point being the espousal of a view of language derived from the writings of Jacques Derrida). Work in cultural theory, it follows, is typically highly self-reflective, which is to say it is acutely aware of the part that a methodology or academic discipline can play in constructing its subject-matter. Thus, the very process of selection found in the critical disciplines, and which leads to the construction of a seemingly self-evident canon of great works, is itself a legitimate, and indeed central, object of enquiry. Great art works are not simply assumed to be out there, awaiting recognition and analysis. Rather, they are actively validated as great, and the **values** imputed to them, or held to be expressed through the analysis and celebration of them, are seen to have implications for the legitimation of **power** structures throughout society. To complement the critical attention given to 'high' art, therefore, serious academic attention can also be paid to such seemingly illegitimate objects of enquiry as comic books, popular music or other popular **genres**.

The engagement in cultural theory, therefore, cannot begin from assuming the predominance of a determinate methodology and a simply defined subject-matter, from which one then may proceed to engage in analysis according to a given set of **rules**. Since culture exists in the everyday world of experience, its subject-matter and its methods must be adequate to reflect the diversity inherent in this; hence its need for self-reflexivity. However, while such reflexivity is laudable, it can serve to make the positioning of cultural theory between, for example, English literature, philosophy and sociology uncomfortable. Indeed, a number of characteristics of cultural theory lead one to the suspicion that it may, albeit unwittingly, be setting up its own disciplinary boundaries by defining itself in terms of what it is not, and doing so only by presenting a superficial understanding of other disciplines, and therefore of its own reflexivity. This thought begins to raise questions as to what exactly is distinctive about cultural theory. Thus we might ask whether the mere assertion of plurality is sufficient justification for asserting this distinctiveness and, more precisely, whether cultural theory may not be more properly understood in terms of the radical components of cultural anthropology and the sociology of culture on the one hand, and literary and art criticism, musicology and philosophy on the other. A number of observations may illustrate this point.

First, there is some danger in assuming that cultural theory, in its spurning of traditional academic boundaries, necessarily brings with that gesture a radicalism which is both methodological and political. Nevertheless, it does not necessarily follow that the criticism of institutional boundaries of itself signals a radical methodological break with institutional forms of thought. A case in point is the treatment of subjectivity within much contemporary cultural theory. The postmodern 'critique of the **subject**', it has often been assumed, brings with it a radical move away from more traditional forms of discourse, such as that of **liberalism**. It is not, however, clear that the simple advocacy of a politics of multiplicity brings with it any radical move away from at least one of the central tenets of liberal thought, namely the principle that social diversity and multiplicity is a public good (a view put forward by John Stuart Mill in *On Liberty* (1859)), nor that it escapes from some of the problems

5

inherent in liberalism. Neither does it follow that the methodological break which signals a re-thinking of normative conceptions of subjectivity, and the institutions that accompany it, of itself offers the basis for a political radicalism (thinkers associated with **fascism**, after all, were also committed to criticising liberal and **humanist** views of subjectivity and pursued their own 'radical' agenda in this regard). Moreover, there is a danger that the conviction of one's own radicalism can bring with it its own naiveté, which in certain respects can be as stifling as the naiveté one seeks to overcome. In celebrating its own multi-, or even anti-disciplinary character, cultural theory can offer mere caricatures of other disciplines – a conversation with a fairly prominent literary critical theorist springs to mind here, in which they espoused the view that *all* philosophers accept the notion of a universal and unconditional 'Truth' (something which is manifestly *not* the case) and then went on to claim that contemporary theory represents a radical and progressive break from such outmoded forms of thought.

To suggest that cultural theory is distinctive as an 'anti-discipline' in that it lacks a dominant unifying **paradigm**, is merely ill-informed. By way of comparison it is worth recalling that Thomas Kuhn, in originally articulating the concept of the scientific paradigm, argued that sociology was not a science, precisely because it did not have one dominant paradigm. While one may argue with Kuhn's definition of a 'science', his characterisation of sociology, in terms of a complex series of overlapping and contradictory approaches to its subject-matter, cannot reasonably be disputed. For within sociology, approaches derived from **positivism**, concerned with quantifiable data, were embraced alongside others grounded in **hermeneutics**, **phenomenology**, **conversation analysis**, **Marxism**, **feminism** and so on. Precisely because such a plurality of approaches jostle each other, sociologists, too, are acutely self-reflective and aware of the status of sociology as itself a distinctive, politically embroiled social practice. Likewise, it would harm the discipline of philosophy to hold that it operates according to one unifying paradigm. It may therefore be suggested that cultural theory can only claim a monopoly on reflexivity at the cost of trivialising the complex and dynamic nature of existing disciplines, and in doing so it jeopardises precisely the possibility of the informed, multi-disciplinary borrowings, that it would seek from them.

One further point may be sketched in, in defence of these suspicions. Even though cultural theorists have frequently engaged in criticising positivism, and the model of scientific investigation from which it was derived, as being inadequate to understanding important questions, it does not follow that a thorough-going criticism of the positivist scientific **division of labour** is unique to cultural theory. Marxists, and particularly the Hegelian Marxists of the **Frankfurt School**, drawing on a variety of influences (from Marx, German idealist philosophy and psychoanalysis) had made extensive and politically sensitive criticisms of scientific specialisation back in the 1930s. Indeed, Max Horkheimer's formulation in this period of critical theory, in opposition to 'traditional theory', anticipates much for what is now the orthodoxy of contemporary cultural theory. Paying attention to the dangers of a failure to engage fully with these developments is not simply the wasted effort of reinventing the wheel. Doing so is, rather, to recognise the fact that what should be available to the exponent of cultural theory as a philosophically rigorous justification of his or her position, is in fact held as a more or less ill-articulated expression of discontent with how things are done in the traditional disciplines. Without such recognition, there is always the risk that the advocacy of disciplinary pluralism becomes little more than a fashion statement, a stylistic posturing akin to the critical theorist's tendency at one time to place brackets in and around words, thereby purportedly revealing something interesting about them but in fact all too seldom doing so.

The point of such observations is by no means to dismiss the achievements of cultural theory to date. Rather, we are arguing for the importance of situating cultural theory more profoundly in its own historical and intellectual context. In so doing, it may be possible to facilitate a more thorough-going reflexivity and opposition to orthodox, postivistic approaches to academic study. It is, perhaps, to pose again the question of exactly what sort of discipline cultural theory is, and to suggest that it may merely mark the current dynamism in a number of diverse disciplines (including sociology, anthropology, philosophy, musicology and literary criticism) rather than being a distinctive (anti-)discipline. Cultural theory may, then, more properly, be understood as marking the accumulation of doubts and criticisms that have been posed against orthodox approaches to academic study throughout the twentieth century. These doubts have culminated in the criticisms of modernity and the project of **Enlightenment**, and oblige us to acknowledge that such intellectual changes are intimately linked to other social, economic and political processes, including the shift to mass education and increased sensitivity to political pluralism since the Second World War.

As a consequence of these reflections, in compiling this dictionary we have not confined ourselves to the key concepts that have come to prominence in cultural theory alone. Additionally, we have sought to extend our coverage out into the conceptual and cultural tools that give deeper foundations and intellectual rigour to those concepts.

Inevitably, in a work of this sort, there will be omissions and gaps. Judgement as what to include and what to exclude often seems a somewhat haphazard affair, and it is unlikely that anyone (even ourselves) will be wholly satisfied with the selection we have made. However, a few broad guidelines, as to exclusions or gaps, may be noted. This book seeks to be as general in its approach as possible, and to explore concepts that have a broad, and often multi-disciplinary, relevance to the study of culture. We have therefore attempted to avoid the space occupied by existing or planned books in the Key Concepts Series. Thus, there are few specific entries on forms of popular music or cinema, for these are much better covered in the existing Key Concepts volumes on popular music and the cinema. Similarly, we would hope that a Key Concepts volume on Colonialism would appear sometime in the near future, and complement the relevant entries we have offered here. Two disciplines that have largely, and perhaps arbitrarily, been excluded are history and archaeology. For the former, interested readers could do worse than turn to E.H. Carr (1987) or Hayden White (1987), while those with an interest in archaeology might usefully be referred to Ian Hodder (1992).

Andrew Edgar
Peter Sedgwick

absence   In **semiotics**, a term is absent from a meaningful sequence of **signs** if it could potentially occupy a position in the sequence, and if its exclusion affects the meaning of the signs which are present. [AE]

Abstract Expressionism   Originally a term used to describe Kandinsky's painting between 1910 and 1914 (see **Expressionism**), but coming into popular use in the 1950s as a description of the work of Jackson Pollock, Mark Rothko, Willem de Kooning and other **avant-garde** New York painters. The artists' personal styles differed considerably, but they shared some elements of a common philosophy (influenced by existentialism). They rejected traditional styles and technical skills, and the priority of a finished product, in order to emphasise the physical act of painting and creation. Harold Rosenberg suggested the term 'action painting' as a more suitable label. Pollock's paintings, produced by splashing, pouring and dripping paint on to the canvas, thereby creating complex and vital patterns, are possibly the most familiar representatives of abstract expressionist works. In contrast, Rothko's vast canvases were composed of superimposed fields of typically subdued colours. [AE]

Further reading: Polcari 1991; Shapiro and Shapiro 1990.

Absurd (Theatre of the)   A term applied to the work of a number of European and American dramatists in the 1950s and 1960s. Influenced by existentialism, and especially Camus' essay *Le Mythe de Sisyphe* (1942), the writers sought to express a pervading sense of futility, loss and bewilderment. Dramas are characterised by disjointed and repetitious dialogue, meaningless behaviour and a lack of logical development in the plot, but also draw on elements of traditional popular drama, including mime, clowning and acrobatics. Key works included Beckett's *En attendant Godot* (1952) – about two tramps waiting for the mysterious Godot, who never appears – and Ionesco's *Rhinoceros* (1959) – that explores individuality in the face of the dehumanising force of totalitarianism. Dramatists to whom the term has been applied include Edward Albee, Harold Pinter and Jean Genet. Alfred Jarry's *Ubu-Roi* (1888) – originally a marionette play about the vicious and cowardly Pere Ubu – represents a seminal influence on the theatre of the absurd. [AE]

Further reading: Esslin 1980.

action theory   In social theory, a distinction is usually made between action and behaviour. While behaviour is purely physical (or instinctual) movement on the part of the agent, action is intentional and meaningful, and more precisely, social action is oriented to the behaviour and action of others. Weber (1978) distinguishes four **ideal types** of action. Traditional actions are performed because they have always been performed so, and thus provide a limiting case of action, being little better than behaviour. Affectual actions are expressive of an emotion. More significantly, *zweckrational* (goal rational or instrumental) action entails the choice of that which is perceived to be the most instrumentally efficient means to the achievement of a goal. (The goal itself may be assessed in terms of the desirability of the consequences of pursuing and achieving it.) An instrumental action is comprehensible in so far as one recognises or shares the agent's view of instrumental or causal relationships in the world. In

11

wertrational (value rational) action, the action is oriented to the achievement of a positively valued, and thus taken for granted, goal. Such actions are understood through recognising the importance of the appropriate values to the agent.

Two broad responses to Weber's account may be identified. On the one hand, emphasis may be placed upon the meaningfulness of the action, and the generation of meaning within the community and within the process of social interaction. For Schutz (1962, 1964), the attributing of motivations to actions (and thus the explication of goals, means or values) is the exception rather than the rule. Mundane social interaction is grounded in taken-for-granted responses to the actions of others, and of others' responses to one's own actions. (In effect, most action is unreflective, habitual behaviour.) Should this taken-for-granted **life-world** break down,) motivation can be attributed, either retrospectively (with 'because motives', explicating the immediate motives of past actions), or prospectively (with 'in-order-to motives', that work effectively to explicate the goals of a forthcoming action), for example, in order to defend one's actions, or orient the actions of others. The meaning of an action ultimately rests upon its negotiation by all participating agents, rather than by an unproblematic appeal to the intentions of the original agent. This approach was developed, to something of an extreme, by **ethnomethodology**.

On the other hand, within a **positivist** tradition, the actions of individual agents are subordinated to an overarching social order. Thus, for Parsons (1937, 1951), the complexity of social interaction, in which there is such a range of interpretations (in terms of intentions, motives or goals) that one will never be able to predict with any certainty how another may react, entails that some prior social mechanism must exist in order to reduce complexity and increase predictability. Thus, interaction agents appeal to **norms** that are **institutionalised** in society, and internalised by individual agents in the process of **socialisation**. Norms do not merely codify the rules pursued by each agent and their evaluation of potential goals, but rather serve to direct their actions. In

Parsons's system, the social action of the individual is thereby integrated into the social system as a whole. While Schutz's agents actively draw upon cultural resources to make sense of action as necessary, Parsons's agents more or less passively follow determining rules of conduct. [AE]

Further reading: Habermas 1984; Joas 1996.

aesthetics Aesthetics is that sub-discipline within philosophy that deals with questions of art and **beauty**. While it is in many respects an ill-defined and highly disputed area of philosophy, its principal concerns can be seen as those of defining the concept of 'art', or at least, providing an account of how we come to recognise art works as art works; questioning the relationship of art to the non-art or 'real' world (and thereby raising questions about the role of representation (or mimesis) and expression in art, and also of art's relationship to moral and political activity); and providing a philosophy of criticism (that explores how works of art are interpreted and evaluated).

The discussion of judgements of taste occurs throughout the history of philosophy, from the ancient Greeks. Plato's *Hippias Major* contains a discussion of the concept of beauty, and Aristotle's analysis of the structure of drama (and particularly tragedy) had a prolonged, if at times stultifying, influence on art and art criticism. While diverse reflections on art occur throughout the history of philosophy, it is not until the eighteenth century that aesthetics begins to emerge as a well defined, and self-confident, division within the discipline. It is not coincidental that this follows on, and may thus be seen to respond to, the separation of works of art from craft works. There is little need to justify or explain the existence of craft works. In contrast, art works, increasingly divorced from political, ceremonial or religious uses, are problematic. In 1746, Charles Batteux coined the term fine art (*beaux arts*), arguing that such works shared the common property of beauty. The term 'aesthetics' is coined by Alexander Gottlieb Baumgarten, publishing his *Aesthetica* in 1750. However, Hume's essay 'Of the Standard of Taste'

(1757) raises a fundamental problem that serves, periodically, to undermine confidence in aesthetics. The problem is whether or not a judgement of taste is purely **subjective**, for if it is, then rational debate about aesthetic objects is rendered pointless. Kant's *Critique of Judgement* (1790) provides a complex and masterful response to initial doubts about the viability of aesthetics. By appealing to the resources developed in his theory of knowledge and in his moral philosophy, he is able to provide an account of aesthetic judgement that is grounded in the universal structure of the human mind (so that a genuine judgement of beauty is such that all ought to agree with it); and he separates aesthetic experiences from experiences of merely sensual pleasure, principally in terms of the disinterestedness with which the spectator engages with the aesthetic object, and the lack of any practical purpose that can be attributed to the object. Hegel and Schopenhauer are able to build aesthetics confidently into their grand philosophical systems largely on the back of Kant's achievement.

If the nineteenth century saw aesthetics flourish, the twentieth century saw a renewal of doubts and assaults. In lectures delivered in 1907, Edward Bullough confronted doubts as to the utility of aesthetics (1957). Aesthetics does not obviously help either the artist create new work (and indeed the definition of general and universal rules defining 'art' or 'beauty' actual hamper the artist), or the audience to make sense of art (philosophical accounts being too general to illuminate the particular artefact that is before the audience). More bluntly, in the 1960s, the American artist Barnett Newman declared that: 'Aesthetics is for art what ornithology is for the birds', meaning that birds have coped perfectly well in ignorance of ornithology, and artists have coped just as well in ignorance of aesthetics.

The sociological criticisms of aesthetics are perhaps more damning than those arising from within philosophy, and it may be suggested that cultural studies grows out of a reaction to the implicit **elitism** of aesthetics (and more particularly, of the approach to literary criticism defended by Leavis). The development of the **sociology of culture**, for example in the work of Pierre Bourdieu (1984, 1993), throws into question, not merely the **ideological** basis of art (i.e. the distinction between high and **popular culture** that is taken-for-granted by so much writing in aesthetics), but also the role of aesthetics in perpetuating that ideology, and thus in failing to explore its own cultural and political roots. This is to say that aesthetics may be little more than the illusory justification and glorification of a middle-class leisure pursuit. The main purpose of aesthetics would be that of sustaining the economic (and not the mysterious 'aesthetic') **value** of art works.

Within philosophy, recent developments within aesthetics have demonstrated a greater sensitivity to the social and cultural context within which art is produced and consumed. The American philosopher Arthur C. Danto has suggested that with the rise of **modern** and **postmodern** art, and thus of art forms which self-consciously reflect upon their status as art (and which are most dramatically exemplified by Duchamp's exhibition of a urinal as a work of art ('Fountain') in 1917), that art itself now poses philosophical questions. Art asks exactly what art is and what the limits and purposes of art might be. Danto therefore recognises that what art is, and the way in which a particular work of art is interpreted, will depend heavily upon the particular historical, cultural and even political conditions within which it is created (Danto 1981). The institutional theory of art, through its key term **artworld**, has brought about a recent convergence with the sociological account of art, albeit without the political criticism implied by Bourdieu and others. Thus, for example, Dickie (1984), in recognising the diversity of art forms that have proliferated in the twentieth century (and not least in the development of **conceptual art**), argues that the criteria for defining and recognising an object or activity as art emerges within those **institutions**, such as galleries and the journals, which deal with art. An art work is an art work because it has been 'baptised' as such through its recognition in the artworld of critics, connoisseurs, gallery proprietors, artists and audiences.

In Germany, the paradox and strength of Adorno's *Aesthetic Theory* (1984), perhaps the last grand theory of art following in the tradition of Kant and Hegel, is that it vehemently embraces the criticisms of aesthetics and art posed by sociology and **Marxism**, while maintaining that art (and especially the **avant-garde** art of the twentieth century) still has a role in resisting ideology. Adorno accepts that art is a product of a particular society (and thus that the production and consumption of art will be intimately bound up with the production of any other artefact and commodity within that society). But art, for Adorno, can still have a moment of autonomy or freedom from that social determinism. It can therefore allow the artist and audience to think in ways that are not condoned by the dominant culture of the day. As such, art keeps alive the hope of resistance to ideology and political oppression. [AE]

Further reading: Cooper 1992, 1997; Eagleton 1999; Graham 1997; Maynard and Feagin 1997.

agency and structure   A central problem in social theory is the relationship between the apparently autonomous actions of individuals, and an overarching and stable social order. Durkheim provides a graphic presentation of the problem in his study of suicide (1952), by observing that while the act of suicide must typically occur in isolation from society and is an action that cannot be repeated, the number of suicides that do occur in a particular society are highly predictable from one year to the next. The problem may be seen in terms of the questions as to whether (or how) structures can determine the actions of individuals; and as to how such structures are created. The most successful and generally accepted solution to these problems may exist in economics, in Adam Smith's account of the free market. The self-interested action of many individual agents, each acting independently of all others, results in the co-ordination of the quantity of goods supplied with the quantity of goods demanded. Superficially the market appears to be the result of some guiding 'invisible hand', akin to the actions of a puppet master perhaps. Smith's analysis of the role of the price mechanism dispels this illusion. (The success of Smith's analysis in economics has misled certain political philosophers, especially in the **social contract** tradition to apply it beyond its true scope.)

In social theory, attempts to resolve the tension between agency and **social structure** have involved various approaches. At one extreme, structural **functionalists** (following in a tradition from Durkheim) and structural Marxists have tended to belittle the freedom of the individual, reducing social agents to (what Dennis Wrong called) 'judgmental dopes', or mere bearers of a structure, who passively follow rules that they have internalised during **socialisation**. At the other extreme, the reality of the social structure is denied altogether by ethnomethodologists, or at best, for methodological individualists, is acknowledged as a heuristic, providing a short-hand for what are ultimately multiple individual actions, and thus as having no determining power over the individual. Between these extremes various attempts have been made to understand social structures as the sedimented products of competent human agency, that in turn must be both actively (if unwittingly) sustained or reproduced by such agency, and that provide delimiting (rather than determining) conditions within which action is understood, given meaning, and pursued. In this light, the tension between agency and structure may be seen in Habermas's (1987) analysis of system and **lifeworld**, and in Anthony Giddens's (1984) theory of **structuration**. [AE]

Further reading: Callinicos 1983; Giddens 1979; Sztompka 1993.

agriculture   Given its central concern with urban life in industrial societies, and with everyday life as experienced by large proportions of the population, cultural studies has relatively little to say about agriculture (in contrast, say, to **cultural anthropology**). However, it is worth noting that agriculture is a fundamental form of **culture** (as its name suggests), and as such a key site at which humanity confronts and transforms

nature to its own ends. Agriculture is therefore relevant as the subject-matter of much high and **popular culture** (from Virgil's *Georgics* of the first century BC, through Thomas Hardy's Wessex, to that quintessentially English (radio) soap opera, *The Archers* ('an everyday story of country folk'). Yet also, it continues to be a boundary where the inter-relationship of culture and nature is negotiated – as is indicated, for example, by contemporary concerns about the genetic manipulation of crops and farm animals. Such concerns may conceal the fact that existing agricultural products are themselves already the outcome of centuries of cultural manipulation. [AE]

Further reading: Newby 1988.

alienation　Theory developed in the early writings of Marx, that seeks to characterise and to explain the estrangement of humanity from its society, and its essential or potential nature. In the *Economic and Philosophical Manuscripts* of 1844 (1975), Marx attributes alienation (a term that had previously been current in philosophical and theological writings, and most significantly in Hegel), to the **division of labour** under **capitalism**. For Marx, humanity is distinguished from all other animal species by its ability, not merely to transform its environment, but to transform the environment through conscious (rather than merely instinctual) activity. The resultant conscious re-engagement with an environment that is no longer merely natural, but is itself the product of the labour of previous generations of humans, gives humanity, uniquely, the ability to shape not only its environment, but also itself. **Production** is, in summary, a process of objectification, such that subjective human creativity is given objective form in the product. This in turn allows a new self-consciousness on the part of the subject. Alienation is the corruption of this objectivity, and the stifling of humanity's self-understanding.

The capitalist division of labour is characterised, not merely by the specialisation of labourers in manufacturing, so that no individual works on the whole product but only upon an isolated fragment, but further by divisions between manufacture

18

and distribution, manual and mental labour and between labourer and capitalist. These structural features lead to four manifestations of alienation (Lukes 1969). First, the worker is alienated from the product, in so far as he or she has no control over its subsequent fate. Second, the worker is alienated from the act of production, so that it ceases to have any intrinsic satisfaction. The ability to labour itself becomes no more than one more **commodity**, having **value** only in so far as it can be exchanged for any other. Third, the worker is alienated from other workers and from society as a whole. The worker is treated as an isolated individual, and is judged by his or her ability to fulfil a pre-existing function within the production process. Production therefore ceases to be a genuinely co-operative or communal process. Finally, the worker is alienated from humanity's 'species being'. The term 'species being' was developed by philosopher Ludwig Feuerbach (1804–72), and is developed by Marx to refer to humanity's potential to determine, collectively and freely, its own destiny.

In **sociology** and social psychology, alienation has more recently been taken to apply to the subjective experience of modern life (particularly in the urban environment and in work). Thus, Robert Blauner (1964) identified four empirically measurable forms of experience of alienation, powerlessness (the experience of being unable to influence one's environment), meaninglessness (from the inability to identify one's contribution to the product), isolation (the lack of any sense of belonging to the work organisation) and self-estrangement (the lack of any psychological reward from the work). This differs from Marx's analysis precisely in so far as Marx's account of alienation was an analysis of the structure of capitalism and the labourer's position within that structure, independent of any subjective perception of it.

A less precisely defined use of 'alienation', albeit one that makes full use of the metaphorical association of being a foreigner, outsider or stranger in one's own land, occurs in much philosophical and cultural commentary on the condition of modern society. Alienation may readily be associated with the experience of exile as in some sense paradigmatic of the experience of the twentieth century. Thus existentialism may tempt parallels to be drawn between alienation and such ideas as anxiety and inauthenticity. Similarly, alienation may be associated with Durkheim's concept of **anomie**, or with Weber's confrontation of the modern individual with the iron cage of **bureaucracy**. [AE]

Further reading: Mészáros 1986; Rotenstreich 1989.

allegory A drama, poem, picture or other work of art in which characters and events portrayed are used to represent or personify a deeper or veiled meaning, typically a moral or spiritual meaning. Abstract qualities are thus given human or other concrete shape. Monteverdi's opera *Orfeo* (1607), for example, is introduced by a soprano as 'La musica'. Allegory is fundamental to medieval morality plays, where virtues, vices and temptations are personified in the depiction of the struggle for a human soul, as in William Langland's *Piers Plowman* (second half of the fourteenth century). In Edmund Spenser's *The Faerie Queene* (1590–96) the Queen is an allegory of both Glory and Elizabeth I, her knights are allegories of specific virtues, such as Holiness, Temperance and Justice, Prince Arthur is Magnificence, and so on. John Bunyan's *The Pilgrim's Progress* (1678 and 1684) is populated by such characters as Christian and Christiana, Mr Worldly Wiseman, Faithful and Mercy, and allegorical places such as the Slough of Despond, Vanity Fair and the Delectable Mountains. Similarly, allegory provides a key to the interpretation of much Renaissance painting, state imagery and pageantry (see Yates 1975), albeit that the allegorical relationships may be obscure and highly disputable. The exact interpretation of images (and acknowledgement or otherwise that they are indeed allegorical images) within Jan van Eyck's *Arnolfini and his Wife* (1434) fundamentally affects the understanding of the painting as a whole. Albrecht Dürer's engraving *Melencolia I* (1514) provides a particularly intense example of the use of allegorical images. The role of allegory in **Baroque** music has been explored by Bukofzer (1939), indicating how a conventional meaning can be attributed to specific musical figures (so that, for example, in a Bach cantata reference to the 'cross' in a text may be linked to a sharpened note in the accompanying music, 'sharp' being 'Kreuz' in German). Walter Benjamin's *Origin of German Tragic Drama* (1977) provides an extensive analysis of the role of allegory in Baroque drama. Allegory is understood in terms of conventional and thus interchangeable images, having little or no relationship to their hidden meanings. A parallel is thereby implied with **commodity** exchange. More specifically, allegory is implicated in the encoding, reproduction and exposure of political **power** (manifest, not least, in the image of the melancholy prince). Allegory is cryptically summarised as the authority of power and the power of authority (Benjamin 1977). [AE]

Further reading: Kelley 1997.

analytic philosophy   As a school of philosophy, it is typically characterised by its interest in the logical analysis of **language**. The purpose of this analysis is to enhance our understanding of how language maps on to the natural world. The assumption behind this project is that the primary use of language is to communicate facts about that world. This assumption also explains the interest of analytic philosophers in questions relating to the referential relationship between language and reality (see the entry for **reference**) and how it is that words mean what they do (see the entry for **meaning**).

This tradition of philosophy has been particularly influential in Britain and North America. Its roots can be traced back to the work of Gottlob Frege, through the works of Bertrand Russell (see the entry for **meaning**), Ludwig Wittgenstein, the 'Vienna Circle' (see the entries for **meaning** and **metaphysics**), Peter Strawson (see under the entry for **reference**), W.V.O. Quine and through to the present day in the works of Saul Kripke (see under the entry for **reference**) and Donald Davidson.

As a result of the work of Quine, Davidson and the later Wittgenstein in particular, the assumption that the primary

21

function of language is to refer to or communicate about the natural world has come into question. Indeed, Davidson ultimately rejects this notion of reference altogether (Davidson 1984). However, there are still many analytic philosophers who support the project of analytic philosophy in its original guise (Kripke 1980). [SH]

année sociologique l'   Journal, edited by Durkheim between 1896 and 1913, that became the main publishing outlet of the research of Durkheimian sociologists, significantly contributing to the dominance of that group in French sociology. [AE]

anomie   Key term in Durkheimian sociology, referring to the loss, on the part of an individual or group, of **norms** to guide social interaction. The concept serves to illuminate the relationship of individual behaviour and experience to the social structure. Norms mundanely constitute a framework that restricts the aspirations and goals of individual members of a society, so that they are coherent with the means available for their realisation. For Durkheim (1952, 1984) this coherence is a pre-condition of human happiness. The collapse or erosion of this framework (for example through increasing individualism), or the expansion of available means (for example through rapid economic growth and prosperity), lead to a discrepancy between means and goals. 'The scale is upset; but a new scale cannot be immediately improvised. Time is required for the public conscience to reclassify men and things.' (Haralambos 1985: 238, citing Durkheim). The term was further developed by R.K. Merton (1968), as a general theory of **deviancy**. Certain groups may experience a conflict between the goals positively valued by a wider society, and the means available within their particular group. The dominant normative framework of the wider society is therefore abandoned, and theft, for example, is adopted as a deviant means to achieve normal goals. [AE]

Further reading: Lukes 1969; Orrù 1987.

archetype   Term from Jungian analytic psychology. Archetypes are the processes that universally structure symbols and imagery in all cultures (and as such are part of what Jung calls the 'collective unconscious', which itself may be understood either as an account of a genetically determined structuring of human experience and understanding, or, more mystically, as a point of communion with the divine). Strictly, archetypes determine the form of imagery, rather than the content. They are, however, inferred from the vast range of concrete images and symbols found in mythologies, religions, dreams and art, across history and space. A number of archetypes are identified by Jung, although the most significant are, perhaps, the anima (the female archetype, and as such the inner face of man), the animus (the male archetype and inner face of woman), and the shadow (the undeveloped 'animal' instincts, and thus the darker or negative side of human personality). [AE]

Further reading: Gray 1996.

architecture   The concept of architecture can cover all types of construction (housing, temples, office blocks and so on), or it may be used in opposition to building, in order to focus upon construction that is intended to be more prestigious or impressive. In its more inclusive sense, it may be argued that an understanding and engagement with architecture is fundamental to any comprehensive understanding of culture. One of the most extreme explorations of this idea may be found in Heidegger's reflections of the relationship between Being and dwelling (1993). By relating dwelling to building, Heidegger presents dwelling as the fundamental form of human existence. Buildings express the human capacity to organise the environment within which they live, in terms of locations that are meaningful, and thus to articulate and bound their cultural world. It may then be suggested that it is through architecture that particular **cultures**, as well as humanity as a whole, come to express and understand themselves. It is through confrontation with the buildings of

23

another culture that we can recognise their otherness. The narrower definition, however, highlights the important point that the built environment is the product of political hierarchies and is expressive of these hierarchies. The environment one encounters is typically one reflecting the differential power of groups to build as they please. Taken further, as the work of Foucault and Deleuze for example has shown, architecture can also be understood as a means of controlling populations.

Despite architecture's importance, cultural studies have perhaps dealt only obliquely with it. On the one hand, architectural theory and practice has influenced cultural studies as an early source of the concept of **postmodernism**. On the other hand, cultural studies renews the response to architectural space that is fundamental to modernist experience, either through consideration of **urban** existence and the city in general, or through specific spaces, such as those of the hotel lobby and the shopping mall.

The concept of postmodernism has been developed in architectural theory to mark a response, in both theory and practice, to the perceived crisis and failure of the modernist architecture that had dominated twentieth-century building (represented for example by the work of the **Bauhaus**, Le Corbusier, Mies van der Rohe, and at a slight tangent, Frank Lloyd Wright). The history of modern architecture can, perhaps all too easily, be summarised in series of slogans. Le Corbusier's 'the house is a machine for living in', or that architecture is 'the masterly, correct and magnificent play of masses brought together in light' are indeed well worth quoting. Yet of all these, the first and most fundamental is Louis Sullivan's maxim that 'form follows function' (coined in 1896). Like most architectural slogans, including Le Corbusier's, it has been as influential by being misunderstood as it has by being understood. It does, however, mark Sullivan's position in founding modern functionalism. Any part of a building is to be so designed as to express the function that it performs within a building. A weight-bearing beam is to look like a weight-bearing beam. This expresses a shift in architectural thinking, away from ornament (at its most dramatic in Adolf Loos's association of ornament and crime (1966)), and towards a renewed rationalism.

Architectural rationalism, especially in its European form, tended to articulate an explicit political (and typically socialist) programme, and thus to reflect upon the relationship between architecture and society. Crucially, this development, for all its actual diversity, represents what may be understood as an **Enlightenment** appeal to a universal reason, for the solution of all social problems. Rationalism thus led to an emphasis upon the technical possibilities of building (exploited in the use of steel, concrete and glass in high-rise building) and mass production. Partly in response to the need for cheap housing in the inter-war years, architects explored the possibilities of pre-fabrication. However, underpinning this is a tendency to sunder the building, planned according to a universal rationality, from the particular environment or habitat within which it was erected. Beyond this, reason was also applied to the design, not simply of individual buildings, but of the housing estate, and even the city as a whole in urban planning. The Athens Charter, published after the fourth Congrès Internationaux d'Architecture Moderne in 1933, and deeply indebted to Le Corbusier's thinking at the time, presented a rational approach to the 'functional city'. Despite its benign intent, the inhabitants of a city are reduced to little more than the passive occupants of a plurality of rationally administered functional spaces. Robert Jan van Pelt's argument that Auschwitz fulfilled the classical functions of a city (veneration of the dead, celebration of the future, government, dwelling, sustenance or trade) provides an ironic and disturbing comment on this conception of urban planning.

Robert Venturi may be placed as at least one of the first key critics of modernism. More polemically, the likes of Christopher Jencks and Tom Wolfe popularised the resultant alternative conception of architecture. Postmodernism emphasises a restoration of meaning to the built environment, through the use of a plurality of conventional design elements. Ornament is most emphatically reinstated in Venturi's analysis

25

of the place of commercial signs (not least in Las Vegas casinos) as expressive of modern American culture. Postmodernism is thus 'multivalent', rejecting the idea of a single universal and ahistorical reason. An increased playfulness and ambiguity, alongside the use of metaphor or the pastiche of historical styles (used without reflection upon their historical specificity), challenges the most severe modernist structures. Michael Graves's Public Services Building in Portland, Oregon (1980–2) with its diverse lines and textures, is as typical of postmodernism as the monumental steel and glass of Mies's Seagram Building, New York City (1954–8) is of modernism. Similarly, urban planning comes to be challenged by a community architecture, that would seek to involve residents in the planning process, and uses vernacular styles that are sensitive to a local environment.

Outside the confines of architectural theory, the urban experience, as a characteristically modern experience, has had a central place in the development of the social sciences. In the work of authors such as Simmel, Weber and Benjamin, the nineteenth and early twentieth century experience of the city came under scrutiny, either directly, as for example in Simmel's account of the metropolis (1950b), or indirectly through reflection of the place of the city in literature, as in Benjamin's study of Baudelaire and Paris (1973a). Williams's seminal study of the tension between the urban and the rural was published in 1973. Again, the debate over postmodernism has renewed interest in the urban, not least in the work of Berman, Baudrillard and Jameson, Cixous and Virilio. Despite the diversity of this writing, a common concern may be that of how to make sense of and to articulate the urban experience, and the plurality of its meanings. This may further mark the neglect of the issue of meaning by modernist architectural theory, thanks to its over-emphasis on a technologically oriented functionalism. In addition, the development of the city in the late twentieth century exemplifies a number of core postmodernist themes, for example in terms of the shift from production to consumption, increased gentrification and the role of tourism in defining and reshaping the city. Leach has expertly brought together key representative texts in the cultural theory of architecture in his *Rethinking Architecture* (1997). [AE]

Further reading: Kolb 1990; Watkin 1977, 1992.

articulation   The joining together of two social forces in a structured and hierarchical relationship. The term emerges in Marxist, and particularly Althusserian, analyses of the **mode of production**. At any given historical moment, one mode of production is dominant. It does not, however, exclude other modes, but rather forces their adaptation to its own needs. Thus, the **feudal** monarchy may survive in **capitalism**, but only in so far as it is adapted to the needs of capitalism (see Anderson 1979). The concept has been developed in analyses of **race**, **gender** and **nationalism**. [AE]

artworld   Term in **aesthetics**, originally coined by Arthur Danto (1964), but developed by George Dickie as the key concept within the institutional theory of art. Certain modern works, notably by Duchamp (especially *The Fountain*), and **conceptual art**, pose problems for traditional approaches to aesthetics, in so far as they claim the status of works of art, yet seemingly have none of the characteristics traditionally attributed to art. Institutional theory attempts to resolve this problem by arguing that there are no properties inherent to an object which serve to determine it as art. Rather, the status of art work will be conferred upon the object by the artworld. The artworld is defined, by Dickie, as 'a loosely organised, but nevertheless related, set of persons including artists . . ., producers, museum directors, museum-goers . . ., critics . . ., philosophers of art, and others' (Dickie 1974: 35–6). In summary, it is a largely self-defined group of people, who express an interest in art, and thus negotiate the current status of particular artefacts. According to institutional theory, artefacts that were not originally created as works of art (e.g. medieval or antique works created before the modern concept of 'art' had been formulated) may be accorded the status of art now, and similarly, objects once considered to be art may have that status removed from them. The question may legitimately be asked as to whether institutional theory may not more properly be understood as an approach within the **sociology of culture** than within aesthetics. [AE]

attitude   Relatively stable sets of beliefs and evaluations. Such beliefs may develop through direct experience or through **socialisation**. That strongly held beliefs and value judgements about objects and social groups can exist independently of direct experience makes the study of attitudes of central relevance to the understanding of **stereotyping** and prejudice. The eliciting of attitudes through questionnaires is fraught with difficulty, as replies may conform to what the respondents perceive to be expected of them, and so avoid socially unacceptable responses. [AE]

author   The author is superficially understood to be the creative, and individual, source of a written **text**. The idea that there is a unique creator of a text, and that the task of reading is, in consequence, a more or less passive process of recovering his or her intentions and meanings, has been variously challenged. Nineteenth-century **hermeneuticians**, notably Wilhelm Dilthey, challenged the assumption that the author had any privileged insight into the meaning of his or her text by critically examining the active process entailed in reading, and thus the need to construct rather than merely to recover meaning from a text. In effect, the author's self-understandings are exposed as merely one more interpretation of the text amongst many others. In **aesthetics**, criticism of the 'intentional fallacy' holds that interpretation of a work of art cannot claim to be definitive or authoritative by having recovered the author's intentions. (Within **post-structuralism**, Barthes most spectacularly declared the 'death of the author' (1977c).) Challenging the author's status thereby pushes aesthetic reflection towards the intrinsic qualities of the art work or text, and at the extreme undermines the possibility of there being a single, definitive or correct reading. It may be noted that only certain texts typically have authors attributed to them. Thus private and functional texts, such as shopping lists, exercises, advertising copy and much journalism, are not credited to an author, or the authorship is not perceived as significant to the understanding of the work. Similarly, many texts (such as folk songs, jokes, urban myths) emerge in an oral tradition, where again, conventional ideas of authorship are inappropriate. Conversely, any text (such as provisional drafts, letters and diaries) written by someone considered to be an author (such as an established novelist) may acquire additional significance precisely because of this authorship. Individual authorship may also, paradoxically, be attributed to products of co-operative work, so that a film may be attributed to the director (or possibly the producer), although rarely to the writer of the screenplay. [AE]

Further reading: Biriotti and Miller 1993; Burke 1992.

authoritarian personality   Concept associated with the study conducted by Adorno *et al.* (1950), and emerging from the work of Erich Fromm and Wilhelm Reich. Certain personality structures are posited as predisposing the self to the acceptance of anti-democratic political beliefs, and are characterised by hierarchical and authoritarian parent-child relationships, the formation of **stereotypes**, rigidity and repressive denial. [AE]

Further reading: Christie and Jahoda 1954.

authority   Concept in **sociology** and political philosophy indicating the **legitimate** use of **power**. An agent thus submits willingly to, or is obedient to, the commands of another agent if that agent is perceived to be in authority. Obedience to authority is not induced through coercion and the threat of violence. In social theory, the analysis of authority is first developed by Weber. He focuses on the question of why certain agents have authority. He offers three **ideal types** in explanation. Authority may be legal-rational, in which case authority is bestowed on rules or laws, typically through some regular and public process of law formation or a demonstration of the necessity and efficiency of the rules (as in the case of **bureaucracies**). Traditional authority again follows more or less well defined rules, but such rules are grounded in traditional practices, customs and cosmologies, rather than in recent, public processes of formation. Charismatic authority rests, not in rules, but in the personality (and sanctity or heroism) of a particular leader, and thus in that person's teaching and example.

In political philosophy, the question of authority may be seen to receive a crucial modern formulation in the work of Hobbes. Hobbes effectively addresses the question of the need for authority (contingently in the face of the social disorder of civil war), and the grounds upon which individuals should submit to it. In Weberian terms, Hobbes's account is a legal-rational one. It is, for Hobbes, rational to form a free **social contract** with a sovereign, providing that the sovereign maintains the social order and delivers peace. This approach is developed in the **liberal** tradition. A state is perceived to have authority in so far as its rules and laws would be acceptable to all rational citizens, independently of any particular interests they may wish to pursue. John Rawls's (1972) thought experiment of an 'original position', in which potential citizens plan a society in ignorance of their own talents and interests, is the most sophisticated contemporary version of such social contract accounts. In contrast, **communitarian** political philosophy suggests the primacy of traditional authority. In contradistinction to liberalism, agents are understood as already embedded in a particular community and culture. The agent's judgement of authority will thus depend upon values taken-for-granted in their community.

Political 'realists', such as Vilfredo Pareto and Gaetano Mosca, reject the distinction between authority and power, arguing that all submission and obedience is ultimately imposed upon the mass of social members. The distinction between authority and power is questioned more subtly by certain accounts of **ideology**. Within **Marxism** particularly, the possibility that agents may be coerced, not merely by the use or threat of physical violence, but also by the control that a dominant group or class can exercise over ideas (for example, through control over education, **mass media** and **religion**) is broached. A state may have authority in the eyes of its citizens, only because those citizens are denied the relevant cultural resources and information necessary to recognise that it is not acting in their best interests. The increasing difficulty that states find in maintaining authority has been analysed by Habermas (1976b) within the theory of a legitimation crisis. [AE]

Further reading: Barry 1989; Hampton 1997.

avant-garde   Metaphorical term used in art theory and political philosophy. The French 'avant-garde', or English 'vanguard' literally refers to the foremost part of an army. Metaphorically, since the beginning of the twentieth century, it has been taken to refer to the political or cultural leadership by an elite. Implicit in this idea are assumptions of political or cultural progress, which the avant-garde pursues. The mass of society will be more or less indifferent to, or ignorant of, their interest in this progress, and will resist or be hostile to the avant-garde. As a key aspect of cultural **modernism**, the avant-garde typically expresses itself through obscure and innovative techniques, deliberately resisting easy assimilation into popular or mass culture (see Adorno 1984). In political theory, the avant-garde is seen as a necessary intellectual elite, leading a mass that remains afflicted by **ideology** and thus by a **false consciousness** that blinds it to its own best interests (see Lukács, 1971). With the increasing questioning of modernism, and indeed of **Marxism**, the validity of the avant-garde has itself come into question (see Bürger 1984). [AE]

Baroque Term identifying the dominant aspects of the visual arts (including architecture), music and (to a lesser extent) literature in Europe between the late sixteenth century and the mid-eighteenth century. The term, the etymology of which is obscure, was initially used in a derogatory sense. Only in the middle to late nineteenth century did it acquire its current meaning.

In **theological**-political terms, the Baroque is closely associated with the counter-reformation, and thus with a reassertion of the values and political presence of the Roman Catholic Church. The Baroque thus emerges most strongly in Rome, and flourishes in Catholic, as opposed to Protestant, countries.

In the visual arts and architecture, the Baroque style is characterised by a fusion of the flowing movement and emotional expression of Mannerism and the discipline and solidity of the high Renaissance. Complex but well structured parts are thus brought together in an equally complex but unified whole. Architecture, sculpture and painting may typically be integrated, as in Bernini's Cornaro Chapel in the church of Santa Maria della Vittoria in Rome (1645–52). While there is a marked concern with verisimilitude – found in the emphasis on observation from nature found in Caravaggio's art (1573–1610), but culminating in *trompe l'œil* ceiling paintings that aspire to deceive the eye into being drawn up into a skyscape – the Baroque is also spectacular. The role of the spectacular can be readily related to the reassertion of church (and also secular) power, seen not least in the grand building programmes of seventeenth-century Rome, and Louis XIV's France. This is also a period of spectacular theatre designs and stage engineering. It may be suggested that reflection on the place of the spectator, in order to stimulate not merely emotional but also bodily participation in the realisation of the work, is a core element of the Baroque aesthetic. The most familiar visual images of the Baroque include *The Rapture of St Teresa* by Bernini (1645–52), much of the work of Rubens (1577–1640), and Velazquez' *Las Meninas* (1656) (not least because of Foucault's analysis in the introduction to *The Order of Things* (1970)). Perhaps the most familar examples of Baroque work in England are the later churches of Wren (including St Paul's Cathedral (1675–1710)), and the churches and houses of Hawksmore and Vanbrugh.

In European high music, the Baroque style is dominant from the beginning of the seventeenth century (where the major exponent is Monteverdi), through to the middle of the eighteenth (culminating in Handel and J.S. Bach). Spectacle is as fundamental to Baroque music as it is to Baroque painting, and the opera is in many respects the most typical Baroque musical art form. Baroque music marks a radical break from the *stilo antico*, or first practice (exemplified by the complex polyphonic music of Palestrina), to a music composed in terms of a melodic line and figured bass (such that the composer would write out only the melody and the bass line of the music, with figures indicating the chords to be played, but leave the precise realisation of the inner lines to the performers). In theory, this approach allows the words (e.g. of the opera or madrigal text) to be heard clearly. In practice, a much greater emphasis is placed upon the rhythmic structure of the music (as opposed to the more subtle pulse that governed the *stilo antico*), and thus to a rearticulation of music time. The opening fanfare to Monteverdi's opera *Orpheus* represents a most spectacular introduction to the Baroque.

The concept of the 'Baroque' has its deepest resonance in cultural studies thanks to Walter Benjamin's complex study of *Trauerspiel* (1977). The 'mourning play' is exemplified by Shakespeare's tragedies (and Benjamin directs much attention to *Hamlet*), but also to the work of the Spanish dramatist Calderón (1600–81), and a multitude of German dramatists. Benjamin's analysis explores both the aesthetic form of the drama (and thus Baroque style itself), in the tension between discipline and licence – above all in the core role of **allegory** as a means of Baroque expression – and its grounding in, and articulation of, the political. Ultimately, Benjamin's analysis suggests the intimate association of the Baroque aesthetic form with the rise of capitalism (not least through an association of allegory and commodity form). [AE]

Further reading: Hauser 1962; Palisca 1991.

base and superstructure   Metaphor (from architecture) used in **Marxism** to indicate the relationship between the economy and the rest of society. Just as the size and shape of the superstructure of a building will depend upon the extent and depth of its foundations, so the characteristics of the non-economic spheres of human social life will depend upon the nature of economic activity. For Marxism, the economic base is composed of the **forces of production** and the **relations of production** (crudely, the application of technology and the relationships established between those who carry out the productive work and those who control the process of production). The **capitalist** base will therefore encompass industrial production techniques and the markets in **labour** and **commodities**, the **feudal** economic base will encompass pre-industrial production and serfdom. The superstructure is most simply defined as referring to all other spheres of society, but specifically including the state, law, the family and cultural or ideological spheres such as **religion**, the arts and the **mass media**.

The model of base and superstructure leaves open two questions, the response to which depends upon the precise way in which Marxist social theory is interpreted. The first and more pressing question focuses on the nature of the determinism involved. The explanatory mechanism that relates the base to the superstructure centres on the manifestation of **class** conflict and power. The promotion and exploitation of a given set of forces of production is held to be in the interests of one class (e.g. early industrial production and the **bourgeoisie**). The economic power of the dominant class (manifest as political power in the state) will allow it to influence the development and shaping of superstructural institutions so that they provide the most advantageous conditions for the exploitation of the forces of production. Legal systems will therefore facilitate the refinement of the relations of production (e.g. by allowing a free labour force for capitalism), while other superstructural institutions will tend to legitimate the existing economic and political order (as natural, God-given or just), and carry out the socialisation of new members of society. A strict determinist model would grant the superstructure little or no autonomy of the base. This would allow, in principle, a Marxist social science to generate strict, deterministic laws that would facilitate the prediction of the structure and the historical development of a society from knowledge of its economy. More flexible models suggest that superstructural institutions will have a greater or lesser degree of autonomy from the base, and thus will be able to develop independently of the immediate or overt interests of the dominant class. The relationship of causality need not then be one-way, giving scope for superstructural developments to influence economic development. The economic base may then merely be determinant in the last instance, or may set broad limits within which the superstructure may take shape.

The second question asks for a precise definition of the boundary between the base and superstructure. This is not easily given, because of the ambiguous status of the legal system. Superficially, the legal system is confined to the superstructure, yet the labour law, or any form of commercial law serves in large part to define the relations of production. As such it is part of the economic base. It is not clear whether or not the relations of production can be defined in non-legal terms. The ambiguity does, however, serve to emphasise the dangers of placing too much theoretical weight on an unconsidered metaphor. The base-superstructure model is a useful image, but it cannot serve as a substitute for rigorous theorisation of the relationship between the economy and the rest of society. [AE]

Bauhaus   A school of architecture and design, founded in 1919 in Weimar, moving to Dessau in 1925, and then to Berlin in 1932 (due to opposition from the local Nazi party) and being closed in 1933. The School represents a key institution in the development and propagation of modernism in archi-tecture. The founding director was Walter Gropius, whose staff included a number of artists closely associated with **Expressionism** (including Kandinsky and Klee). The philos-ophy that Gropius brought to the Bauhaus concerned the relationship between design and industrial production, between art and engineering, echoing some of the ideas of William Morris. Craft-based design was seen to be capable of making a vital contribution to industrial mass production. The tubular steel chair, perhaps, typifies the impact that the Bauhaus has had on the design of everyday artefacts. In accord with a functionalist approach to architecture, whereby the purpose of the object is held to determine its design (to the exclusion of ornament), the Bauhaus style manifests an impersonal, geometric and severe refinement of line and shape. [AE]

Further reading: Whitford 1984.

beauty   A key term in **aesthetics**, where it may crudely be taken to refer to that property that makes works of art (and even natural objects) worthy of contemplation. Since Plato, beauty has been seen as a core human value, alongside truth and goodness, and the association of beauty to one or both of these concepts has been subject to various analyses in diverse aesthetic theories well into the twentieth century. Modern aesthetics responds crucially to the presentation of the problems of beauty and aesthetic enjoyment given in Kant's *Critique of Judgement* (1987). In the Kantian tradition, a beautiful object is valued independently of any practical interest that the observer might have in that object, and judgements of beauty are held to be analogous to moral judgements.

The centrality of 'beauty' as an aesthetic concept comes into question due to two problems. On the one hand, in ordinary language, 'beauty' may not be the exclusive or even dominant concept in evaluating works of art. Thus the relationship of 'beautiful' to such terms as 'graceful', 'elegant' or 'exciting'. On the other hand, works of art may be valued despite the fact that they are concerned with events or objects that would not be considered 'beautiful' in the ordinary language usage of the word. This problem dates back at least to Aristotle and his discussion of tragedy (asking why we derive pleasure at the sight of destructive and immoral events and characters). Furthermore, in the twentieth century, many artists have ceased to value beauty (or indeed have overtly challenged it). 'Ugliness' may therefore have a status equivalent, or even be superior to that of beauty, for example, in **Expressionism**. There is a danger that the continued use of beauty in aesthetics serves to reduce it to a technical term, divorced from ordinary langauge usage, and having little precision, beyond being synonymous with what is of value in art works. In recent debates on aesthetics, and particularly those associated with **postmodernism**, the centrality of beauty has been challenged by consideration of the **sublime**. [AE]

behavioural ideology In V.N. Voloshinov's thought behavioural ideology is distinguished from official ideology. The latter consists of 'stable, formulated' verbal systems such as those comprising law, ethics, religion, the sciences and the arts (1976: 88; see also 1973: 91). Behavioural ideology by contrast consists of those verbal expressions and inner verbal experiences which do not fall within such systems, a highly inclusive definition made possible by Voloshinov's identification of ideology with the **sign**, of which the word is an instance (1973: 10). The name Voloshinov gives to this type of ideology is connected to his view that it 'endows our every instance of behaviour and action with meaning' (1973: 91).

A number of points on the relationship between the two types of ideology are forwarded or implied by Voloshinov (1973: 19–20, 91–3), amounting to an outline of the relationship between language in everyday, practical life and in its elaborated, theoretical formulations. Official ideology is founded upon behavioural ideology inasmuch as ideological systems are crystallisations of ideas present in behavioural ideology. Yet behavioural ideology is subject to a reciprocal influence by official ideology, often having its 'tone' set by the latter, and, in cases of ideological struggle, partly incorporating 'forms' and 'practices' of ideological systems which it seeks to alter or displace. Behavioural ideology is the more sensitive of the two, as demonstrated by its ability to register barely noticeable aspects of emergent social change. And, once formed, an official ideology is dependent for its continued vitality and existence upon renewed interpretation from within behavioural ideology, which draws it into a 'particular social situation' and enables it to be regarded as meaningful. Behavioural ideology, additionally, serves to connect a society's economic **base** with its official ideology and thus its superstructure (1973: 14, 18–19). As such it is of interest to **Marxism** and, Voloshinov indicates, his concept of it, through its emphasis on verbal interaction, promises a more materialist account of the transitional link between base and superstructure than some Marxists, employing the concept of 'social psychology', have traditionally been able to offer.

Within behavioural ideology, Voloshinov (1976, chapter 9) distinguishes between an official conscious and an unofficial conscious 'corresponding', respectively, to Freud's concepts of the conscious and the **unconscious**. Whereas the official conscious closely converges with the official ideology of a society, the unofficial type differs greatly from and 'contradicts' it. The latter type, additionally, is less easily communicated. Implying nevertheless that, like the official conscious, the unofficial conscious may comprise a type of social consciousness, Voloshinov suggests that these concepts make possible a macrosocial, as well as ideological, account of those conflicts affecting the person which Freud allegedly regards as individual and 'psychical'. The concepts are also employed in a reflection on social change in which Voloshinov posits that the presence of an unofficial conscious within behavioural ideology, such that the latter is marked by two contradictory forms of consciousness, may signal the disintegration of an official ideology and of a **class** or some of its groups. Inasmuch as Voloshinov considers these remarks to be related, behavioural ideology appears as having the promise to play a central, mediating role in a project linking psychology with pressures for and against social and historical change. However, whilst the realisation of such a project might well benefit psychology, an arguable weakness in Voloshinov's thinking lies in its implication that the sort of psychological ailments which **psychoanalysis** seeks to treat occur only when a society's behavioural ideology is marked by **contradictions**.

The great breadth of Voloshinov's concept of ideology, and his related identification of ideology with the sign, have been subjected to criticism (Rossi-Landi 1990: 238–47; Ponzio 1993: 83–4). But Eagleton (1991: 47–50) indicates that in extending the concept of ideology beyond its usual limits and positing the notion of behavioural ideology, Voloshinov provides the conceptual means which enable the theorist to account for that translation of ideological systems and doctrines into practical activity which is necessary for their success. [RW]

behaviourism   An approach to psychology that argues that the discipline can only be genuinely scientific if it concerns itself with publicly measurable phenomena, such as muscular and glandular responses. The approach may therefore be seen as a response to the problems inherent in a dualist account of the human being (where the human being is understood as a mind or soul within a body), and with the status of any claim to knowledge of the mental states of another human being.

The introduction of behaviourism into psychology is usually credited to J.B. Watson in the 1910s. Watson reacted against introspection as a technique in psychology, ridiculing the demands that were put upon psychologists to be trained supposedly to distinguish and classify their own mental states. Influenced by the research that Pavlov had carried out on the reflexes of animals (demonstrating that if a dog was presented with the sound of a bell prior to food, it could be conditioned to salivate upon the sound of the bell alone). From this, Watson was able to argue that an appeal to mental states in the explanation of human action was unnecessary. Explanation could proceed, on positivist lines, by identifying law-like associations between external stimuli and the subject's observable response to them. Thus, a mental state, such as 'being hungry' could be understood, or operationalised, purely in terms of the behaviour that one expects of the person or animal in that state. (Crudely, 'being hungry' is manifest in, or in stricter forms of behaviourism, exhausted by, the behaviour of seeking food.) A subject's behaviour will not then depend upon (inwardly and privately experienced) mental states (such as intentions, purposes or emotions), but rather upon the 'recency' and frequency with which partic-ular stimuli have been encountered. In line with this, Watson adopted a position of strict environmentalism, to the effect that little if anything is innate (or genetically determined) in human behaviour. Humans learn in response to the stimuli provided by their environments.

Watson was forced to retire from academic life in 1920 (after his scandalous divorce), but behaviourism became a dominant force in American psychology up to the 1960s, being developed most significantly by Edward Guthrie, Clark Hull and B.F. Skinner. Guthrie remained close to Watson's concept of behaviourism, although he dropped frequency as a significant determinant of behaviour. Hull aspired to a systematic and mathematically expressed account of human behaviour. Skinner's behaviourism moved away from Watson, and particularly from the centrality given to the concept of the reflex, in order to focus on the effect that behaviour has upon the environment. What matters about behaviour, for Skinner, is that it strives to adapt to the animal's environment. For example, a laboratory animal changes the position of a switch, and thereby causes food to become available. Crucially, Skinner argues that the animal's behaviour cannot be explained in terms of its intention or purpose to acquire food. Rather, the intention or purpose of the action lies not in some anticipation of the future, but rather because this was the effect of the behaviour in the past. Thus, animals (including humans) are argued not to act because they have a purpose, but rather because of past consequences.

Skinner distinguishes between 'methodological behaviourism' and his own 'radical behaviourism' (again marking a break from Watson). The methodological behaviourist simply accepts that mental events are publicly unobservable, and so cannot play a legitimate part in a publicly verifiable scientific explanation. The radical behaviourist recognises the existence and role of mental events, and attempts to come to terms with (rather than merely side-step) their privacy, by arguing that they are governed by the same forms of (stimulus-response) conditioning that govern public behaviour, and that they lie in discoverable causal relations to overt behaviour. Skinner's behaviourism therefore attempts to embrace even mathematical and logical reasoning and introspection within the same explanatory framework as that applied to the conditioned behaviour of laboratory animals.

The controversial nature of behaviourism rests not merely upon what may appear to be an excessively mechanistic account of human being, and the challenges it poses to the supposed dignity of human freedom, but also in the fact that, at least in the hands of Watson and Skinner, it was intended to have a practical application in mundane social life. The extreme prospect of this is given by Skinner in his novel *Waldon Two* (1976), describing the community where behaviourist techniques are used to condition a population into co-operation, love and even creativity. More mundanely, behaviourist psychology lies behind behaviour therapy and various techniques that allow individuals successfully to overcome phobias or neuroses. [AE]

Further reading: Skinner 1973, 1974; Zuriff 1985.

binary opposition Concept in **structuralism**, rooted in Saussure's linguistics but also Radcliffe-Brown's (1977) **cultural anthropology**, serving to explain the generation of meaning in one term or **sign** by reference to another mutually exclusive term. The two terms may be seen to describe a complete system, by reference to two basic states in which the elements in that system can exist (e.g. culture/nature; dark/light; male/female; birth/death). One side of the binary opposition can be meaningful only in relation to the other side. Each side has the meaning of not being its opposite. A term may therefore appear in more than one binary opposition, with its meaning being modified accordingly. (Thus, death may be understood as an event as 'not birth'; or as a state as 'not life'.) Binary oppositions structure perception and interpretation of the natural and social world.

In any system of signs, certain binary oppositions may be seen to stand in determinate relationships to each other. One binary opposition may be open to transformation into another, therefore enriching the meaning of all the terms concerned. Thus, for example, in western cultures, the opposition between birth and death may be transformed into an opposition between white and black (for example manifest in white christening robes and black hearses). Put differently, white is to black, as birth is to death. In addition, the binary opposition may contain an implicit evaluation, so that, for example, birth and white are associated with good, death and black with bad. The analysis of such series of oppositions provides a crucial insight into the working of **ideology**. Consider, for example, the following series: male/female; public/private; culture/nature; reason/emotion. Ideology may therefore work precisely to the degree that such series of binary oppositions are taken for granted, appearing to reflect rather than to structure the world. The critique of ideology entails the explication of a series of binary oppositions as a culturally specific interpretation, selection and privileging of elements from the ambient world.

A further implication of the theorisation of binary oppositions focuses upon the status of ambiguous categories. Anything that shares characteristics of both sides of the opposition is suspect or otherwise problematic. Anthropologists have therefore suggested that the importance given to human hair or nail clippings in magic and folk law rests in their ambiguous status. They are at once part of the body, for they grow from the body, but have no feeling and are easily cut from the body without pain or damage. Similarly, **rites de passage** mark ambiguous stages in a human's development between childhood and adulthood. Magic, ceremony and the sacred are thus seen to be concerned with ambiguous categories. [AE]

Birmingham Centre for Contemporary Cultural Studies Founded in 1964, as a postgraduate research centre at the University of Birmingham, UK, the Centre for Contemporary Cultural Studies has had a pivotal role in the development of cultural studies in the UK. (A significant number of the leading figures in British cultural studies have passed through the Centre at some stage in their careers.) Initially under the directorship of Richard Hoggart and Stuart Hall from 1968–1979, the Centre developed much that is now typical of the subject-matter of cultural studies, and the techniques of analysis. Under Hall, research topics developed from an initial interest in the 'lived' culture of different classes (stemming from Hoggart's own work in *Uses of Literature* (1957)), to the centrality of the **mass media**, and associated areas of youth and **subcultures**, education, **race** and **gender**. The Centre was interdisciplinary from its inception, drawing most notably on **sociology** and **literary criticism**, but also importantly on history (for example, through the influence of

E.P. Thompson (1963)). The Centre's theoretical development may be seen in part as a response to American approaches to the study of mass media. Drawing on the intellectual resources of contemporary Europe, including both Althusser and Barthes' **structuralism**, the Centre approached the media as ideological and hegemonic institutions. **Popular culture** is therefore understood as the site of the resistance and negotiation of marginal and disempowered groups within **society**. The Centre's work may also be characterised by the collaborative nature of its research. The Centre's series of working papers became a key medium of publication, both for its staff and its postgraduate students. Under the directorship of Richard Johnson and then Jorge Lorrain, some shift in the focus of the Centre's research away from textual analysis of the media, and towards the history of everyday life has been identified by some commentators. In 1988, the Centre became a Department of Cultural Studies, offering undergraduate courses in addition to postgraduate research. [AE]

Further reading: Turner 1996.

body   Until recently, the body has been either ignored or made marginal in philosophical, political and cultural theory. Thus, in philosophy, human agency and the **identity** of the person were traditionally seen to lie in the mind. The mind (or soul) was permanent and in its rationality, was the source of all our knowledge. A key philosophical problem (for example from the writings of Descartes in the seventeenth century onwards) was the relationship of the mind to the body. A few thinkers, especially within the seventeenth- and eighteenth-century empiricist tradition of British philosophy (such as David Hume), could be seen to be making something of the human body, by recognising that our experience of the world entirely depends upon our bodily sense organs. However, even this potential was stifled, by emphasising sight and hearing as the sources of knowledge. The more obviously bodily senses of smell, taste and touch are side-lined, and so too are the implications that they have for our practical engagement with the world through our bodies. At the end of the eighteenth century, Kant demonstrates the problematic status of the senses in his *Critique of Judgement* (1987). On the one hand he argues that it is only as both rational and sensual (or embodied) creatures that we can experience the pleasure of beauty (as opposed to the purely rational delight in the morally good, or the purely physical agreeableness of food and drink). On the other hand, beauty rests in sight and hearing, not in touch, smell and taste.

In the mid-nineteenth century, Marx's view of human beings as fundamentally beings that transform and create their own environment through **labour**, offers some awareness of embodiment. It is perhaps only in American **pragmatism**, at the end of the nineteenth century, that the importance of the embodied, practical experience of the world is given thorough and rigorous treatment in philosophy. It is here that the importance of taken-for-granted knowledge of the world, carried in the habitual skill and competence with which we use our bodies to manipulate and test the world, comes to the fore. In the twentieth century, this perspective is developed in Heidegger's work, for example in his concepts of 'present to hand' and 'present at hand' (1962: 102–7). Normally, objects are used unthinkingly. While a tool works, we do not worry about it. When it fails, we step back and question and examine it. Thus, we acquire conscious, theoretical knowledge of the world, only when the world trips us up practically. Against Descartes' assumptions, we cannot gain knowledge through merely reflecting on the world. We need a reason to reflect upon it, and that reason comes only through a bodily engagement. Thus Heidegger, like the pragmatists and even David Hume, introduces the body into philosophical thought, by directly criticising the way in which Descartes does philosophy. Heidegger further emphasises the necessity of the body – along with all its contingencies – to our self-understanding as human beings, in the demand that we must accept that we are mortal. The Heideggerian approach was influential on the development of French **phenomenology**, particularly in the analysis of 'flesh' by Maurice Merleau-Ponty (again beginning from the argument that consciousness

45

is embodied in a particular world) (1962), and Jean-Paul Sartre (not least in his spectacular analysis of torture, as the attempt to capture and possess the freedom of the victim within his or her flesh) (1958: 303–59).

In western political theory, the body is again ignored until recently. **Liberalism**, for example, adopts a model of human being that stresses rationality. As such, it is the human intellect that matters. Indeed, the unrestrained pursuit of bodily desires may be theorised as a threat to political order. In addition, liberalism tends to assume a series of more or less implicit dichotomies. Reason is set against unreason, mind against body, and male against female. Liberalism's traditional blindness to gender difference, and to the exclusion of women from politics, may in part be understood through this association of reason, mind and masculinity.

In the late 1970s and early 1980s, with the revival of liberal theory through the work of John Rawls (1972), there also came a new criticism of liberalism from the **communitarians**. In this line of argument, Michael Sandel (1982) is critical of Rawls (and thus contemporary liberalism) precisely because the Rawlsian model of human beings is disembodied and disembedded. That is to say that Rawls artificially abstracts human beings from the bodily and cultural experiences that form them as the particular beings they are. In effect, Rawls is accused of assuming that the human being, as a rational personality capable of choice, exists prior to its embodied life in a particular community. Sandel argues that the very ability to choose and to hold **values**, and to be aware of ourselves as individuals, comes only from bodily experience, and cannot exist prior to it.

In cultural theory, there is a significant literature on the nude as a core subject-matter of western art. In part, this literature comes from the orthodox approach of a cultural historian, such as Clarke's analysis of the idealisation of the body according to historically varying cultural norms (1956). More recently **feminists** and others (such as John Berger (1972)) have placed the nude in a political context, in order to question the ascription of intrinsic **aesthetic** value to it, as part of the **patriarchal** or **ideological** structure of power in western culture (Diprose 1994; Grosz 1994; Irigaray 1985a).

The understanding of the body develops in cultural studies through the recognition of the body as a site of meaning. A **semiotic** approach may be taken to the body. Umberto Eco's characterisation of the body as a 'communication machine' is telling (1986). The body is not simply there, as a brute fact of nature, but is incorporated into culture. The body is indeed a key site at which culture and cultural **identity** is expressed and articulated, through clothing, jewellery and other decoration and through the shaping of the body itself (through tattoos, hair styles, body-building and dieting, for example). It is through the body that individuals can conform to or resist the cultural expectations imposed upon them. Sociology has thus been able to turn to the analysis of 'body-centred practices' (see Turner 1984). Foucault's analysis of the development of the prison system and state punishment focuses on the body as the subject of discipline (1977a). Crucially, the body is shaped and disciplined through systems of surveillance, either actual surveillance or surveillance that is imagined to be occurring. Analysis of the body can there-fore increasingly see it as a product of social constraint and construction (which is a theme also found in Goffman's work), or of the languages and **discourses** within which it is discussed and analysed (as for example, in the languages of medical science, psychiatry, or criminology). [AE]

bourgeoisie Much used, but often poorly understood term, referring to the dominant **class** in capitalist society. In Marxist theory, it is most strictly employed in opposition to '**prole-tariat**', where it refers to the owners of productive **capital** (and thus to mercantile, industrial and financial entrepreneurs). What distinguishes the bourgeoisie is that they have no need to sell their labour in order to survive. While such a bold contrast may be effective in the analysis of early **capitalism**, it fails to grasp the role and status of the administrative and managerial classes that have emerged with the development

47

of high and late capitalism. Thus, 'bourgeoisie' is frequently used to refer to the 'middle classes' of contemporary capitalism. While such classes may still need to sell their labour (as does the working-class), their higher financial reward, and higher status, entails that the continuation of capitalism is as much in their interests as in the interests of any class of owners. The role that the middle-classes have in shaping culture, has led to the frequent use of the adjective 'bourgeois' as a derogatory term. [AE]

Further reading: Gay 1984, 1986; Habermas 1989a.

bricolage   Engaging metaphor developed from Lévi-Strauss's structural anthropology. The French word 'bricoleur' refers literally to the sort of worker capable of mending or maintaining any machinery and installation by re-using items from elsewhere, typically improvising new uses for these items. So, in cultural theory, and especially the analysis of **subcultures**, the term refers to the processes by which elements are appropriated from the dominant culture, and their meaning transformed, for example through ironic juxtapositions, to challenge and subvert that culture. [AE]

Further reading: Lévi-Strauss 1966.

bureaucracy   As the term is understood in contemporary **sociology**, bureaucracy is that form of administration in which decision-making power is invested in offices, rather than in identifiable individuals. While bureaucracies have existed in pre-industrial societies (including feudal China), it is the fundamental role that bureaucracy plays in the organisation and control of twentieth century **capitalism** that has received greatest theoretical and empirical study.

The classic source for the theory of bureaucracy is Max Weber, published in the 1920s. Weber proposed a six part model (or **ideal type**) of bureaucracy, that served to specify its distinctive characteristics (even if these characteristics need not all be present in any particular empirical example of a bureaucracy) (Weber 1946b). Weber's characteristics are as follows: a high degree of specialisation, with complex tasks broken down and clearly allocated to separate offices; a hierarchy, with chains of **authority** and responsibility clearly defined; activity is governed by a consistent system of abstract rules; officials work impersonally, without emotional or personal attachment either to colleagues or clients; personnel are recruited and promoted on the grounds of technical knowledge, ability and expertise; the official's activities as an official are wholly separate from his or her private activities (so that a professional position cannot be used for personal advantage). For Weber, this structure is the most efficient (and therefore most instrumentally rational) way in which to organise the complex activities of a modern industrial society. As such, bureaucracy is an unavoidable feature of advanced society, not merely in industry, but in almost every area of social life. Mommsen has thus written of the total bureaucratisation of life (1974). Weber himself predicted, not just the growing influence of bureaucracy in capitalism, but also a convergence between capitalist and Soviet communist societies, in terms of the dominant role played by bureaucracy in both.

While bureaucracy is technically efficient, for Weber, it also has undesirable consequences for democracy. Precisely because nearly all social activities must proceed through stages that are pre-determined by bureaucracies, and given that those bureaucratic structures are themselves inflexible and possibly unresponsive to change, innovative activity, or activity that does not make sense within the narrow parameters of the bureaucracy, is inhibited. Further, technical expertise is concentrated within the democratically unaccountable offices of the bureaucracy, so that bureaucratic decisions and procedures are not easily challenged. Bureaucracy thereby becomes a 'steel-hard cage' that encloses us all.

Marxism has perhaps contributed little to the theory of bureaucracy. Bureaucracies were less extensive when Marx and Engels were writing, and they may be seen to be generally antipathetic to bureaucracy. The classic Marxist writings notably underestimate the significance that administrative structures have in capitalism (and thus have little to say on the significance of the managerial **classes**). The Marxists who have had most to say about bureaucracy tend to be those who seek to fuse Marxist and Weberian theories. In *History and Class Consciousness* (1971), the Hungarian Marxist Lukács began to use Weberian accounts of bureaucracy and rationalisation to extend Marx's theory of **commodity fetishism** into an account of the reificiation of the social totality (and thus to explain the distinctive **ideological** forms of contemporary capitalism, in so far as society confronts the individual as an autonomous, quasi-natural object, rather than as a product of human agency and choice). This in turn influenced the **Frankfurt School**, and especially T.W. Adorno, in developing a characterisation of late capitalism as a totally administered society. [AE]

Further reading: Beetham 1996.

canon Typically, the term is used to encompass what are generally recognised as the most important works in a particular artistic tradition (most usually of literature or music). It is derived from its original use, dating from the fourth century, to refer to the authoritative and definitive books of the Christian Bible. Defenders of the notion of a canon would argue from the position that there are universal **aesthetic** values (albeit that these values may unfold over time, with the development of the tradition). Individual works are therefore included in the canon on the grounds that they best express these universal values. The canonical works are therefore the finest expression of a particular language, and may indeed be taken as the expression of a culture's or a nation's identity. The idea of a canon has come under increasing criticism, not least with the emergence of Marxist and feminist criticism in the 1960s, and **post-structuralist** and **post-colonial** accounts of culture. With increased sensitivity to cultural **pluralism** and to the economic and political conditions of artistic production, the canon appears less as an expression of universal values than as an expression of power relations. The canon may be seen to exclude subordinated groups at a number of levels. First, the canonical works may represent certain groups (non-whites, the poor, women) according to culturally dominant **stereotypes**. Second, the canon may exclude works produced by those groups, or not recognise the media within which those groups have traditionally expressed themselves. Finally, the manner of expression celebrated within the canon (including preconceptions of the nature of human subjectivity and creativity) may be inappropriate in articulating the experience of subordinated groups. [AE]

Further reading: Eagleton 1984; Kermode 1975.

capital   Concept from economics, referring most obviously and intuitively to the machines, plant and buildings used in the industrial manufacturing process. More technically, capital is one of four factors of production. A factor of production is a resource that is valued, not for its own sake, but for its function in the production of other goods or services that are of intrinsic value. The other factors of production are land (including all natural resources prior to their extraction, the land surface, sea and space), **labour** (being the ability of human beings to engage in productive work), and entrepreneurship (being the ability to organise together the other three factors in the production process). Capital is any resource or item used in the production process that has already been subject to some form of productive labour. [AE]

capitalism   A form of social and economic organisation, typified by the predominant role played by **capital** in the economic production process, and by the existence of extensive markets by which the production, distribution and consumption of goods and services (including **labour**) is organised. The development of capitalism may most readily be linked to industrialisation, and thus has its purest manifestation in nineteenth-century Britain and USA. However, a more limited form of (mercantile) capitalism, characterised by limited markets in commodities, and thus by the existence of a small capitalist class of merchants, but without industrial production or free labour markets, existed in medieval Europe.

Different theories of capitalism exist, especially within social theory, providing different explanatory models of the origin of capitalism and of its predominant features. In **Marxism**, capitalism is theorised in terms of the organisation of production and the resultant relationship between economic **classes**. The emergence of capitalism is thus explained in terms of the development of industrial technology (or the **forces of production**). A capitalist society is structured through the antagonism of two dominant classes: the **bourgeoisie** which owns and controls the means of production, and the **proletariat** that owns only its ability to work (and therefore survives by selling its labour power). At the surface, there appears to be a fair and free exchange of commodities, including labour power, through the market mechanism. In Marx's analysis, beneath this surface lies a systematic exploitation of the proletariat, in so far as the price of labour set on the free market is less than the value of labour's product. The bourgeoisie are therefore seen to appropriate **surplus value** akin to the discrepancy between the costs of producing a commodity and the total revenue received from its sale. While Max Weber's analysis of capitalism shares much in common with Marx's, Weber places greater emphasis on the surface organisation of capitalism, and thus on capitalism as a system of exchange and **consumption** (1964 and 1979). The link between capitalism and rationalisation is central to this account. For Weber, a precondition of capitalist development is the development of double entry book-keeping (and thus the possibility of rational control and prediction of the capitalist's resources).

At the beginning of the twentieth century, European and American capitalism developed in a number of key areas. Weber's analysis of rationality responded to the increasing **bureaucracy** of capitalism, as more complex production required ever more sophisticated forms of administration and control. This in turn leads to the rise of a white-collar middle class that is distinct in its interests and allegiances from either the working class proletariat or the bourgeoisie. Furthermore, banks and other financial organisations became more significant, as the day-to-day control of production was increasingly separated from ownership. A distinctive form of finance capital was identified, for example, by the Austro-Marxist Rudolf

Hilferding (1981) around 1910. Linked to this development is both the increasing concentration of capital, so that production is controlled by fewer, larger, corporations (leading to monopoly capitalism), and the expansion of capitalism into colonial markets. Increasing state intervention, not merely in the regulation of capitalist production, but also in the ownership of the means of production, leads to a further deviation from the 'pure' model of free-market capitalism. A period of organised capitalism thus begins to emerge after the First World War, and continues, with the increasing multi-national consumption and production bases of major corporations, under the rise of welfare state capitalism and Keynesian economic policies, at least into the 1970s. All these developments may be seen to obscure the basic lines of class conflict identified by Marx. The proletariat is increasingly differentiated within itself, and through greater job security and real income, is more integrated into the capitalist system. The economic crises predicted by Marx are at worst managed and at best avoided by interventionist governments.

Recent developments, in technology, with the decline of traditional manufacturing industries and the rise of communications or knowledge based industries; in consumerism, with increasingly affluent working and middle classes; and in the political shifts of the 1980s away from state intervention, demand new theories of the organisation of contemporary societies. Thus theories of late capitalism (Jameson 1991), post-industrial **society** (Bell 1973), disorganised capitalism (Lash and Urry 1987) and various accounts of **postmodernism** suggest a more or less radical break from capitalist modes of organisation. [AE]

Further reading: Bottomore 1985; Giddens 1973; Mandel 1972; Sayer 1991.

Cartesianism   A term which, strictly speaking, means 'of, or bearing some relation to, the thought of philosopher René Descartes' (1596–1650). However, 'Cartesianism' has also come to signify a **metaphysical** viewpoint that bears upon issues of personal **identity**, the nature of the **self**, and also questions in **epistemology**.

In reply to the writings of contemporary sceptics who questioned whether we can have any certain knowledge, Descartes' writings seek to show that there is at least one certain piece of knowledge we are in possession of. Arriving at this view, he argues, involves employing what is termed the 'sceptical method'. Thus, Descartes resolves to 'demolish' all his beliefs, and afterwards attempts to construct the foundations of knowledge as stable and lasting science. In order to do this, it is sufficient merely to bring into question all one's opinions, i.e. to show that they are *not certain*, rather than that they are false. For instance, what we often accept as true are beliefs derived from experience (from the senses). But, the senses can deceive us, so many beliefs derived from them can be doubted. But some beliefs cannot be doubted: 'for example, that I am here, sitting by the fire, wearing a winter dressing-gown holding this piece of paper in my hands, and so on'. However, taking his scepticism one step further, Descartes asks how can we distinguish between being awake and asleep? Having sensations could be a product of the imagination; nevertheless, even if the sensation of having a body is merely a dream, there are some things ('simpler and universal', of which bodies are made up) which are real, i.e. notions of quantity, shape, size and number.

Thus, we can distinguish between the physical sciences (physics, astronomy, etc.) which depend upon composite notions (they conceive of objects as having specific sizes, shapes, etc.), and other forms of knowledge (e.g. geometry, mathematics) which do not. Whether we are asleep or awake $2 + 3 = 5$ and a square has four sides. Some might argue that the existence of an omnipotent God guarantees that these beliefs are true. But suppose that 'I am so imperfect as to be deceived all the time'. Then, even these beliefs are doubtful. Suppose that 'not God [. . .] but rather some malicious demon of the utmost power and cunning has employed all his energies to deceive me'. I might think $2 + 3 = 5$, but I am being fooled. What then?

According to Descartes, one thing remains true: even if I am being deceived, I am still thinking: 'I must conclude that this proposition, *I am, I exist*, is necessarily true whenever it is put forward or conceived by me in my mind'. This is most famously expressed in the phrase 'I think, therefore I am' (*cogito, ergo sum*). But, what is this 'I' that thinks? (1) There is the mechanical structure of the human body. (2) There are the activities which humans pursue: they walk about, eat, have perceptions from their senses, etc. On Descartes' view, these activities are the actions of a 'soul' or 'mind', which is a different kind of substance from physical stuff.

The properties of a body are physical: it can be seen, moved, occupies a particular space, etc. The 'power of self-movement', however, is not a property we can attribute to a physical body. Given the presence of his malicious demon, Descartes thinks that the existence even of the body can be doubted. But the self that thinks cannot: 'At present I am not admitting anything except what is necessarily true; that is, I am a mind, or intelligence, or intellect, or reason [. . .] a thinking thing'. Descartes thus holds that he is a mind, 'not that structure of limbs which is called a human body'. In this way Descartes' mind-body (or 'Cartesian') dualism is thereby set firmly in place. What is essential about him, he contends, is that he is a mind, not a body. In other words, he is essentially a thinking thing, and mind is essentially different from body.

From the standpoint of epistemology, what is notable about Descartes' argument is that it is **subjectivity** (the 'I think') that forms the foundation of knowledge. Moreover, the conception of subjectivity that Descartes proposes is thus one that is not constrained by the social world. Indeed, it is (at least purportedly) derived independently from the social/material realm. Hence, the relationship between the human subject and the external world which it experiences is accounted for by way of a model which places the subject 'outside' the world, as a kind of observer who is not implicated in it. There have been a number of criticisms of this view. For instance, the German philosopher, Martin Heidegger (1889–1976), offers an account of the subject that is directly opposed to this central presupposition of Cartesianism. For Heidegger, the subject (or, more properly Dasein) is not a passive observer of experience, but is actively engaged in its own world. Thus, on Heidegger's view, human subjects are not 'in' the world in the same sense that a match might be said to be 'in a match box'. Rather, we are 'in the world' in a concrete sense that cannot be divorced from our actual Being. Hence, our world cannot be viewed from an 'objective' perspective that is external to it, as a spectator sitting in the stalls of a theatre might be said to view the events that unfold in a play. Rather, we actively relate to our world, and this relationship is constitutive of that world. Thus, for example, in addition to our ability to conceptualise objects we can also relate to them as things we can grasp in a practical sense (in Heidegger's parlance, they are not merely 'present-at-hand' but 'ready-to-hand'). On Heidegger's view, Cartesianism cannot provide us with an adequate account of how this latter form of relationship to the objects in our world is possible because it has driven an irreconcilable wedge between cognition and what is conceived.

The Cartesian thesis has important cultural ramifications, in so far as traditional scientific forms of **discourse** presuppose a notion of subjectivity which has much in common with this model (i.e. the notion of a passive or neutral observer). Equally, the history of modern philosophy (by which is usually meant philosophy after Descartes) is marked by a critical (and sometimes not so critical) engagement with many of the central tenets of Cartesianism. [PS]

Further reading: Descartes 1986; Heidegger 1993; Mulhall 1996.

cinema Motion pictures emerged from slide shows displayed at fair grounds and vaudeville theatres in the late nineteenth century. By the beginning of the First World War, films had developed from shorts of a few minutes to performances of ninety minutes or more. The period after the war saw, at once, the establishing of Hollywood as a global centre for film production, and the development of a more sophisticated means of narration, not least through the work of German

Expressionists and of Soviet film-makers such as Eisenstein and Pudovkin. In the late 1920s the first sound films were produced and Technicolor was introduced in the 1930s. During this early period, writing about film focused on the status of film as an art form, and thus the aesthetic experience associated with film, and on the development of cinematic techniques, such as the handling of the camera, the length and nature of shots, and the process of editing (not least in the role of montage). Such technical and aesthetic analyses were complemented by reflections on the social function of cinema. The neo-Marxists of the **Frankfurt School,** along with Walter Benjamin, focused on the relationship of cinema to **ideology** (for example in the theorisation of the **culture industry**), and the impact that art forms based in mechanical reproduction have on traditional conceptions of art and the aesthetic experience.

In the 1940s and 1950s, German Marxist analyses of cinema continued, most notably, in the work of Siegfried Kracauer (1947). The French review *Cahiers du Cinéma*, founded in 1951, began to develop a new and distinctive approach to film criticism, not least through the writings of the review's editor, André Bazin (1967). The group associated with *Cahiers* developed an account of the film director as **author**, in part by recognising how Hollywood directors, who were otherwise part of a highly controlled production process, could mark a film with signs of their authorship through the distinctive style with which they constructed scenes. Bazin further developed . an account of the role of the spectator as an active interpreter of the film. He argued that realist cinema, that eschewed Eisenstein's emphasis on montage in favour of what is termed 'deep focus' editing, gave greater scope for ambiguity of expression, thereby at once reproducing the ambiguity of real life, and requiring a greater interpretative effort from the spectator.

The 1960s saw a fundamental challenge to the *Cahiers* group, crucially in its celebration of the director as author. This challenge came through the application of **structuralist** and **semiological** approaches to cinema. Within structuralism, the film is treated as a text. The task of the structuralist critic, exemplified by the work of Christian Metz (1974), is to expose the hidden meaning of the text and the grammatical structure that underpins it by determining the range of meaningful combinations of the significant cinematic elements (treated as **syntagm**). Will Wright (1975) analysed Westerns, for example, in terms of the way in which a series of **binary oppositions** (inside society/outside society; good/bad; strong/weak; civilisation/wilderness) common to all Westerns are variously articulated, principally through the positioning of the hero in relation to society. In a classic Western of the 1930s to 1950s, the hero is aligned with a good society, against a threat from the wilderness. In Westerns of the late 1950s, this opposition is reversed, with an all powerful society now being set in opposition to the good hero.

While structuralist accounts disrupted the preconception about the author, and thus the interpretation of the film through the author's intentions and style, they still tended to assume that there was a single fixed meaning to be extracted from the film. At worst, the film was also considered as a text in isolation from the historical and material conditions of its production. Structuralism was thus itself challenged by the rise of **post-structuralism**, and its associated plurality of approaches (not least through the influence of Derrida and **deconstruction**, of Lacanian **psychoanalysis**, and of **feminism**). The film ceases to be seen as a text in isolation from others, but in terms of a plurality of possible relations to other texts (including material production processes). The meaning of the film is therefore fluid, being a result of the interaction of texts. At its core, the poststructuralist approach may be seen to raise the question of the construction of both the author and the spectator by the film-text. The spectator's gaze, and the voyeuristic pleasure gained from viewing, become crucial to this analysis. Cinema presupposes, or constructs, a certain viewing subject. Initially, for example in the work of Metz, this spectator is assumed to be male. Women display 'to-be-looked-at-ness', both to the hero within the film and to the male spectator in the audience.

The pleasure from viewing is thus seemingly constrained within male fantasies (and hence the 'Oedipal trajectory', in which a male protagonist overcomes difficulties in order to find, and settle down with, a woman). Laura Mulvey (1975 and 1993) explores this further. The male gaze leaves no obvious scope for female pleasure. Mulvey argues that the female spectator must therefore either identify with the passive position of the women on screen (a position of unpleasure), or adopt a male position. The possibility of a non-patriarchal cinema would, in consequence, demand a radical challenge to traditional cinematic forms.

A final, important, component in a cultural studies approach to cinema rests in the use of **ethnographic** studies. The poststructuralist reduction of the audience to products of the cinema's textuality, so that the nature of the spectator can be deduced from the text, is challenged by empirical questioning of cinema goers about their experience of and attitudes to film. Thus, Jackie Stacey's (1994) work is grounded in the interviewing of women who identified themselves as keen cinema goers in the 1940s and 1950s. Through categories of 'escapism', 'identification' and 'consumerism', she explores the utopian aspect of cinema-going (not least, following Dyer (1985) in so far as the cinematic text provides solutions for real social problems experienced by the audience, but also in recognising the real luxury experienced within the cinema as a building), but thereby emphasises the self-consciousness which the audience has of its relationship to the film, the film star and the products associated with films. [AE]

Further reading: Cavell 1971; Deleuze 1991; Dyer 1979; Kracauer 1960; Metz 1982.

citizenship A human agent who is endowed with particular social characteristics which have a legally codified political significance (such as rights, duties and obligations, the freedom to make decisions which are a matter of their own private interests and to participate in matters of public interest, to participate in the life of **civil society**) is generally said to have citizenship. Such citizenship is sometimes termed 'substantive citizenship', in contrast to the possession of 'formal citizenship', which is now usually taken to signify merely the fact of being a member of a nation-state. The possession of citizenship in the first of these senses implies that an individual is part of a socio-political body, and that the rights, duties, and so forth which that individual has are possessed both concretely and in virtue of their being a member of that body. Thus, for instance, a French citizen is granted a particular political status (citizenship) as a result of being both (i) subject to and (ii) able to appeal to the rule of French law. Whether the possession of a particular right necessarily entails obligations is, however, unclear. Such a view would be disputed by, for instance, advocates of **libertarianism**, who tend to conceive of rights as being the fundamental issue accompanying questions of political freedom. Likewise, whether the legal codification of rights is commensurable with the satisfactory articulation of the interests a subject may have, has been questioned by the philosopher Jean-François Lyotard. [PS]

Further reading: Marshall 1950; Mead 1986; Turner 1986; Turner and Hamilton 1994.

civic humanism An approach to questions of political **authority** and **power** which can be traced back to the writings of the Ancient Greek philosopher Aristotle (384–322 BC), civic humanism has a conception of power, authority and the civil agent which is markedly different from those of either **liberalism** or **Marxism**. Most famous amongst exponents of civic humanism is Niccolò Machiavelli (1469–1527), although other thinkers have offered accounts of political power which embrace civic humanist thought (e.g. James Harrington (seventeenth century) and, in the twentieth century, the exponent of 'Guild Socialism' G.D.H. Cole, while certain elements of **Enlightenment** thinker J.J. Rousseau's *The Social Contract* could be said to exhibit attitudes in common with this tradition). Both Machiavelli's *The Discourses* (a work that in many ways stands in stark contrast to his *The Prince*) and Harrington's

The Commonwealth of Oceana (influenced by Machiavelli) give a good idea of the civic humanist attitude to politics. They advocate a politically active citizenry which is endowed with a strong sense of civic duty (Machiavelli terms this sense 'civic virtue'). Central to civic humanism is the contention that the legislature which governs a community must consist of laws which ensure the reproduction of the conditions necessary to the survival of that community, namely civic virtue (hence Harrington's maxim that 'good laws make good men'). The civic humanist thus conceives of the political agent not, as with liberalism, in terms of an individualism which expresses its identity by making choices unhindered except by the minimum of justifiable state interference, but as an extension of the identity and governing principles underlying the community itself. There is, in other words, no rigid distinction between the so-called 'public' and 'private' spheres. In turn, the citizen is conceived of as an autonomous being to the extent that he or she performs an active role in the political and cultural life of the community (the model here being that of the Ancient Roman Republic). Both Machiavelli and Harrington sought to produce a 'balanced' political legislature, i.e. one in which both the interests and talents of the wealthy few (nobles) and the plebian majority were exploited and played-off against each other in order to arrive at a model of government that prevented the worst political consequences of the three different forms of government (i.e. absolute monarchy, aristocratic rule or democratic rule – deemed capable of degenerating into tyranny, oligarchy or anarchy respectively). [PS]

Further reading: Harrington 1992; Machiavelli 1983; Pocock 1975.

civil society Before the work of the philosopher Hegel, the term 'civil society' was roughly equivalent in meaning to the term 'state' (see Allen Wood's introduction to Hegel's *Elements of the Philosophy of Right*: xviii). Hegel, in using this term, was alluding to the social domain of market exchange (the market economy – a notion derived from such texts as

Adam Smith's *Wealth of Nations*) in which individual civil agents freely engage in the pursuit of financial wealth, and the ownership and exchange of goods. Civil society is contrasted by Hegel with the realm of the family, in which the ties between members are based on mutual affection (the bonds of love). In contrast to the family, civil society is defined as a realm of engagement in which an individual pursues their own private ends, and in so doing encounters others primarily as means for the satisfaction of subjective needs (in other words, the relationship between individuals is an instrumental one). In civil society the individual thereby gains a sense of identity derived from his or her relative independence from others. Yet, for Hegel, this dependence contains within it a shared characteristic, for through the active pursuit of their subjective ends individuals also develop a sense of mutual interdependence. Civil society, therefore, is not for Hegel merely to be understood as the outcome of individuals engaged in the free pursuit of their own desires (a domain purely of the market economy in Adam Smith's sense), but as bringing with it a sense of shared interests in which individuals recognise both the duty they have to support themselves *and* their duties toward one another (for instance, within civil society, Hegel argues, individuals can claim certain entitlements such as the right to job security, the right to education and to protection from such social hardships as poverty). Because of this, civil society is characterised by Hegel as constituting a 'universal family', which is composed of groups or 'corporations' of individuals who are affiliated by means of a common craft or profession. On Hegel's account civil society is contrasted with the state, which is ultimately concerned with the ethical good of the whole and takes the principle of the universal family to its logical fruition by functioning as a means of mediating between the competing claims of differing interests (both of individuals and corporations) with the aim of achieving the well-being of the whole of society (in Hegel's terms, the 'ethical life').

The young Karl Marx inherited Hegel's conception of civil society, and displayed a more or less uncritical attitude toward it. In his later writings, however, Marx came to adopt the view that civil society and the state are intimately connected, contending that the apparent freedom of individual association and pursuits in civil society is in fact a masked manifestation of an underlying structure of state power, the latter being in the hands of a wealthy capitalist minority whose aim is the exploitation of the majority in the interests of enhanced profit. On a marxian view, therefore, the realm of civil society is intimately connected with issues of **power** and **ideology**. Some recent commentators (see Keane 1988) tend to adhere to the Hegelian view, namely that civil society is a sphere of individual association which may be contrasted with the domain of state power. The meaning of the term has not, therefore, been exhausted by Marx's attempted revaluation of it. [PS]

Further reading: Hegel 1991; Keane 1988; Smith 1986.

class   Classes may primarily be understood as economic group-ings, although the relevant economic factors that serve to identify a class may be disputed. Thus, in the Marxist tradition, classes are defined in terms of the ownership of productive wealth, while other traditions look to differences in income or occupation. Class divisions are typically seen as funda-mental to the stratification of society, and as such may be associated with differences in power and culture. Crucially, classes are not typically understood as aggregates of individ-uals, where class analysis would be concerned with classifying some common attribute shared by these individuals. Rather, classes are understood as social entities that have a reality that is independent of the individuals that make them up. As such, class may be a crucial causal factor in explaining the consti-tution of the individual human subject.

Marx and Engels' famous, if slightly glib, comment that all preceding history has been the history of class conflict (1985), expresses much that is fundamental to the Marxist approach to class. The analysis of any given society, at any moment of history, can focus on the latent or explicit conflict that exists between two major classes. The subordinate class will be active economic producers in the society. However, the members of that class will not have control over the production process, and thus will not be able to retain the full value of what they produce, or otherwise determine the allocation and distribution of that product. This is because the dominant class will own and control the society's stock of economic resources (or **means of production**), and will thereby control the fate of whatever is produced with these resources. The relationship between the dominant and subordinate classes will therefore be one of exploitation, although the precise nature of exploitation will depend upon the particular historical stage, or **mode of production**, in which it occurs. In **capitalism**, for example, the dominant class is the **bourgeoisie**, which owns **capital**, while the subordinate class is the **proletariat** (the members of which have only their ability to labour, which they must sell in order to survive). Exploitation occurs through the appropriation of **surplus-value**, which is to say that the proletariat's reward for selling its labour is worth less than the **exchange-value** of the product when it is sold. While the bourgeoisie and proletariat are recognised as the major historical players within capitalism, Marx recognised that other classes will exist. At any moment in history, these classes can be the remnants of earlier historical stages (so that, for example, a **feudal** aristocracy survived into capitalism), or may be the early form of a class that will subsequently become significant (such as the mercantile capitalists who existed in late feudalism). Other groups may have ambiguous class positions, such as the small, petit-bourgeois producer (including the shop keeper or independent entrepreneur) in capitalism, who own insufficient productive property to free themselves from the necessity of labour (see Marx 1976).

Class conflict, within **Marxism**, is understood in terms of the conflicting interests of classes. It is in the interests of the dominant class for the existing economic relations to continue. It is in the interests of the subordinate classes to see the ending of those relations. Overt class conflict, in the form of revolution, is however inhibited, at least in large part, through

ideological mechanisms (such as educational institutions, **religion** and the **mass media**) existing in the society. A theory of ideology suggests that the dominant class does not maintain its position purely through the exercise of physical force (or control of the means of violence). Rather, the threat of violence is complemented, and possibly in the short-term rendered redundant, by structures of belief that appear to give legitimacy to the dominance of the ruling class. Thus, under the influence of ideology, the subordinate classes will hold beliefs that are against their own objective long-term interests. The issue of ideology becomes a core issue for cultural studies when more sophisticated theories of ideology (not least those centring around the concept of **hegemony**) suggest that the subordinate classes do not simply accept, passively, an account of the world that is in the interests of the dominant class, but rather more or less successfully negotiate and resist that account, in the light of their own experience. **Culture** thereby comes to be seen as fundamentally structured in terms of class inequalities.

While the Marxist tradition tends to explain all social inequalities through reference to economic differences (so that the dominant economic class is also expected to be dominant politically and culturally), in the tradition of sociological analysis that arises from the work of Max Weber, a more layered account of social inequality is favoured (1946c). Weber complements an economic analysis of class by analyses of differences in **power** and social **status**. Weber's approach to the economic determinants of class is itself more varied than that of Marx. Firstly, Weber does not presuppose that all social differences can be collapsed on to economic differences (noting, for example, that the aristocratic Junta in late nineteenth century Germany held political power, in spite of the existence of an economically powerful bourgeoisie). Further, for Weber, at least with respect to contemporary capitalism, an individual's class position does not depend exclusively upon his or her relationship to the means of production, but is realised through the market. Weber thus talks of market opportunities, such that an individual brings various resources, including ownership of stocks of capital, the ability to labour and crucially, high levels of skill, to the labour and capital markets. Different resources will earn different levels and kinds of material and symbolic reward (or **life-chances**). This allows the Weberian to make differentiations within Marxism's proletariat class, in order to explain the higher levels of material reward and status accorded to intellectuals and managers or administrators over those of manual workers. This in turn throws light on the ambiguous class position of those groups, in that while they are to be strictly defined as labourers, their short-term or apparent class interests, self-understanding and cultural identity may accord more closely with those of the property-owning bourgeoisie. (Analyses of these groups have been a key part of E.O. Wright's (1985) class theory, for example.) In addition, analysis of differences in the social status, or the prestige and respect, that is associated with different social positions, can lead to an analysis of the distinctive **lifestyles** that are associated with different classes (so that class is again seen as a cultural, rather than purely economic, phenomenon).

There is a danger that the Weberian approach to class analysis can be reduced to an account of class purely in terms of occupational difference and thus to something akin to the Registrar General's classification of Socio-Economic Groups (of professional; employers and managers; intermediate non-manual; skilled manual and self-employed non-manual; semi-skilled manual; unskilled manual) found in the UK. Without a rigorous underpinning in class theory, such classifications tend to do little more than label, for administrative purposes, aggregates of diverse individuals, rather than to describe and account for classes as real social entities and to explain the constitutive role that they have in our lives. A further problem with all class analysis, that its reduction to Socio-Economic Groups serves to exemplify, is its failure to take account of the position of women. Precisely because class analysis is conducted predominantly in terms of economic activity, women have either remained invisible or been allocated to the class of their male partner, on the grounds that they were not active as wage earners, or if they were wage earners, their wage (and associated economic position) was secondary to that of their partner. Socialist feminists have attempted to analyse the relationship between men and women as itself analogous to a class relationship, by focusing on the male expropriation of female labour (for example in unpaid housework, or in the differential that continues to exist between male and female wages) (Barrett 1980). (See also **social mobility**.) [AE]

Further reading: Bennett *et al.* 1981; Eagleton 1991; Edgell 1993; Giddens 1973; Giddens and Held 1982.

class consciousness Within Marxist theory, class consciousness refers to the self-understanding that members of the **proletariat**, in particular, have of themselves as members of a **class**. Marx distinguishes between a class in itself and a class for itself. A class in itself is a social group that is determined by a common economic position. A class for itself is collectively aware of that determination, of its place within the economic and social structure, and in consequence of its real interests in social change. A class for itself, and thus a group in possession of genuine class consciousness, will have thrown off the illusions of **ideology** and **false consciousness**. For Marx, this transformation was to be achieved through the increasing collectivisation of production under capitalism, so that dominant ideas of individualism would no longer make sense to an oppressed proletariat.

In non-Marxist sociology, the term 'class consciousness' may be used, but is less well defined or focused. It may refer to the perception that individuals have of their class position and the way in which they articulate that awareness. Thus, for example, elements of class consciousness may include one's self-identification as belonging to a particular class, and thus accepting the label 'working class'), or one's awareness of another class (owners and managers) as constitutive of one's opponents.[AE]

Further reading: Lukács 1971; Marx 1968; Marx and Engels 1985.

code   A signifying code is a set of culturally recognised rules that guide the way in which a **text** may be read. The code will determine the material from which significant units can be selected (see **paradigm**) and the manner in which selected units can be meaningfully combined (see **syntagm**). [AE]

comics   Cartoons, comic strips and comic books have, perhaps, been relatively neglected, not merely by orthodox **aesthetics** and criticism, as might be expected, but also by cultural studies (especially in comparison to the amount of attention devoted to other aspects of **popular culture**, such as **television** and **popular music**). Apart from the interest in the comic (and its close relative, the cartoon) as a complex **text**, developing its **narrative**, at best, through the interplay of visually image and literary text, the comic and cartoon have played an important role in youth culture, **subcultures**, and political resistance throughout the twentieth century.

The comic may be seen to have an important precursor in the political cartoon. The term 'cartoon' was not transferred from the sphere of high art (where it refers to a preparatory drawing) until the nineteenth century (when the humorous magazine *Punch* parodied designs submitted for House of Commons frescoes – and not a lot of people know that). However, what may be recognised as political cartoons emerged in late eighteenth century England, notably in the work of Gillray and Rowlandson. Their images commented upon and ridiculed public personalities (including the Royal family, military leaders and even Lady Hamilton). The French artist Henri Daumier was imprisoned in 1832, for his caricatured attacks on Louis Philippe. While the political cartoon remains a popular and important feature of mainstream newspapers throughout the world (and as such an important source of political comment, criticism and **ideology** within democracies), the 1960s saw the emergence of the 'underground' comic. Robert Crumb's *Zap* linked the comic to the values of the **counterculture**, articulating the issues of drug use and sexual expression.

The comic strip, as something that is generally amusing rather than politically pointed, became established in America in the last decade of the nineteenth century, with Richard F. Outcault's 'Hogan's Alley' being published (with significant commercial success) in the newspaper *New York World*. The strip cartoon emerged as an attempt to exploit new colour printing techniques, with Outcault's main character (the Yellow Kid) being presented in a bright yellow night-shirt. In 1893, Outcault's separate strips were gathered together into a comic book, and published by William Randolph Hearst as a supplement to the *New York Journal*. Original comic books began to appear in the 1930s. Shortly afterwards, the move from purely humorous to adventure and fantasy based comics occurred in the US, most famously with Jerry Siegel and Joe Shuster's *Superman* (published by DC Comics), rapidly followed by *Batman*, *Captain America* and *Captain Marvel*. In the post-war period the subject matter of comic books diversified, to include westerns, romance and science fiction. In the 1960s, the comic book image (including its method of printing through Ben Day dots) was appropriated as a core element of **Pop Art** by Roy Lichtenstein.

In Britain the development of the comic was quite distinct from, and earlier than, that in America. While the American comic strip is associated with newspapers, in Britain the comic emerged as a separate publication for children. *Ally's Sloper's Half-Holiday*, a comic in the modern sense, with regular characters, was first published in 1884. This was followed by *Comic Cuts* and *Chips* in 1890. If American comics were motivated by new technology, British comics were motivated by the rise of mass literacy, as a result of the 1870 Education Act. The late 1930s saw perhaps the most distinctive development in the British comic, with the publication of the *Beano* and *Dandy*. The humour of these, and many subsequent comics, was far more anarchic and less respectful to authority than that of their predecessors. Even if authority figures did occasionally get the better of their young tormentors, they expressed their authority through unseemly ferocity.

The British understanding of the comic as a magazine marketed for children also widens the coverage of the term to include a range of magazines marketed for children and adolescents (whether the comic strip is their core component or not). Magazines, such as *Jackie* (that significantly retained a variant on the comic strip, in the photo story) were amongst the first cultural artefacts to receive sustained attention within cultural studies (McRobbie 1989, 1991), not least in terms of the part they played in the **articulation** of **gender** and **sexuality** within contemporary **ideology**.

The comic book saw a significant revival in the 1980s, with the emergence of the 'graphic novel'. Typically, these took on the themes of the super hero comics, but now with a new realism, irony and depth. Thus, Frank Miller's *Batman: The Dark Knight Returns* (1986) reflected on the prospect of a middle-aged Bruce Wayne coming out of retirement. Alan Moore and Dave Gibbons' *Watchmen* (1987) worked through the implications of super heroes being real, and highly fallible men and women in the real world. Art Spiegelman's *Maus: A Survivor's Tale* (1987) and *And Here My Troubles Began* (1992) used the comic strip conventions of anthropomorphic animals to tell the story of a survivor of Auschwitz. [AE]

Further reading: Barker 1989; McCloud 1993; Pearson and Uricchio 1991; Sabin 1993.

commodity A commodity is an object (or service) that is produced for exchange (or a market) rather than for **consumption** or use by the producer. 'Commodity' is the most basic category in Marx's economics, for it opens up his analysis of **capitalism**, and specifically of the part that the commodity and commodity exchange play in the exploitation of the **proletariat**. (See **commodity fetishism**.) [AE]

commodity fetishism 'Commodity fetishism' encapsulates much of Marx's criticism of the **capitalist** economy (which is to say, an economy grounded in the ownership of private property and in the exchange of **commodities** through markets). Marx argues (1976: 163–77) that in the exchange

71

of commodities, the social relationships between human beings take on the appearance of a relationship between objects. Indeed, this relationship between things takes on a phantasmagorical appearance, such that the things confront us as if they themselves were a strange and obscure crowd of persons. Interpreted slightly differently, properties (such as price) that are ascribed to objects through **cultural** processes, come to appear as if they were natural or inherent properties of the objects.

Commodity fetishism occurs because, in a capitalist economy, producers only come into contact with each other through the market. As such, they relate to each other, not as substantial, complex and unique human beings, but as producers of commodities, and these commodities are made comparable to (and therefore interchangeable with) any other commodities through the common standard of money. Thus, that which is qualitatively unique and distinctive, both in producers and product, is concealed by transformation into a pure quantity.

The theory of commodity fetishism therefore suggests that capitalism reproduces itself by concealing its essence beneath a deceptive appearance. Just as quality appears as quantity, so **objects** appear as **subjects**, and subjects as objects. Things are personified and persons objectified. Ultimately, market exchange becomes the appearance of the real essence of production, so that humans falsely understand themselves as consumers rather than as producers. This, in turn, conceals the process of exploitation inherent to capitalism (expropriation of **surplus-value**).

The theory of commodity fetishism was fundamental to the development of theory of **ideology** within western **Marxism**, in the account of reification offered by Lukács and members of the **Frankfurt School**. [AE]

Further reading: Burke and Moore 1979; Carver 1975; Dant 1996.

communication   In many respects, communication, as the exchange of information between two or more agents, is the most fundamental concern of cultural studies. A number of different approaches to the analysis of communication may be identified.

In **structuralism** and **semiology**, communication is analysed in terms of the **codes** or rules and conventions that determine the meaningfulness of any message, in terms of the selection and combination of meaningful elements (or **signs**). This approach, in turn, leads to an interest in **texts** (be these written and spoken texts, or other carriers of meaning and significance, such as clothing and social actions) and the process of producing and reading them, as well as problems of how (if at all) the sign can refer to a world that is external to the text. In **hermeneutics**, the processes of reading and interpretation are treated less systematically. Emphasis here rests upon the competence that ordinary people and readers have in developing interpretations by working with the relationship between the particular meaningful unit before them, and the larger whole (or horizon) that provides the context in which the unit makes sense (and crucially, where the meaning of the unit reciprocally modifies the meaning of the context). Within **sociology**, analysis of communication comes to prominence with the rise of those schools of sociological inquiry that emphasise the social skills and competence that members of society possess. Thus, the **symbolic interactionists** and **ethnomethodologists** show an interest in how a meaningful and stable social reality is created and maintained through skilful interaction, and thus through the exercise of forms of communicative competence.

The wider implications of a study of communication, that are suggested by the interest that sociology has in communication, are to be seen through the etymological link between communication and community. For Aristotle, a state is a community held together by the communication of the diverse perspectives within it. Communication is what holds a community together. The political and moral worth of the community can therefore be analysed in terms of the communication that is possible within it. Thus, the philosopher of science, Charles Sanders Peirce, projected an ideal scientific

community, in which there would be free and open communication between all participants. Open communication (or
democratic participation) is therefore presented as a precondition of good science. Jürgen Habermas has developed this
idea in his notion of the 'ideal speech situation' (McCarthy
1978: 306–10). This is again a projection of perfect communication, in which all participants are able to question others
as to the sincerity, factual accuracy and meaning of what they
say, as well as their moral entitlement to say it. Actual communication will fall short of this ideal, as political and
ideological structures distort it, inhibiting participation or
understanding by specific groups or individuals. The degree
to which it falls short is a measure of the justice of any particular society. [AE]

Further reading: Habermas 1970a, 1970b; Williams 1962.

communitarianism   An approach primarily to questions of
ethics and politics (although its ramifications extend also into
the domain of **epistemology**), which holds that the norms
which function in any particular cultural community are the
only sources of what is to count as ethically or politically
right. In other words, communitarians reject any standpoint
which seeks to provide forms of justification for conceptions
of morality or politics which transcend cultural contexts (such
as Rawls's formulation of an 'original position' as providing
a rational justification for basic principles of political justice
– see **liberalism**).

The key thinkers who have been associated with a communitarian approach are Alasdair MacIntyre, Michael Sandel,
Charles Taylor and Michael Walzer. MacIntyre's approach to
questions of ethics holds that if we are to offer a coherent
account of what a human subject (conceived of as a moral
being) is, then we must recognise the fact that individuals are
embedded in social practices and traditions. This shared (i.e.
communal) nature of the meaning of ethical action is, in
MacIntyre's view, a necessary precondition of it, and thus an
essential property of any conception of what we mean by a

'human good'. Sandel's work has tended to focus on criticising Rawls's conception of the self. Rawls, Sandel argues, constructs a metaphysical account of the self in order to ground his liberal politics, and in turn ignores the social dimension of individual identity in his account of what constitutes a political subject. Likewise, Taylor has adopted a similar approach, taking as his point of focus the shared linguistic preconditions which, he holds, are necessary to the articulation of personhood, morality and reasoning ability. Thus, in Taylor's view, community (understood as being constituted out of a shared structure of linguistic norms) is necessarily presupposed by conceptions such as subjectivity, agency, ethical rightness, etc. Walzer, too, has adopted the position of arguing that the nature of what constitutes a good is dependent upon a shared realm of meanings, and that it must therefore follow that any conception of justice must be dependent upon the communal structure of meanings which a political community has. Communitarians thus take the position of foregrounding the social dimension of ethical language. In light of this, it is possible to claim that the approaches adopted by these thinkers have features in common with those of some advocates of **postmodernism** (e.g. Michel Foucault, Jean-François Lyotard, Richard Rorty), although it is worth noting that, for Charles Taylor at least, the issue of whether we are obliged to adopt a postmodern anti-epistemological attitude (rather than overcoming the transcendental epistemology outlined by Kant in other ways) is one which is far from settled. [PS]

Further reading: Avineri and De-Shalit 1992; Bell 1993; MacIntyre 1981, 1988; Mulhall and Swift 1996; Sandel 1982; Taylor 1990, 1997; Walzer 1983.

conceptual art   The term 'conceptual art' can cover a multitude of different approaches to creation of art in the second half of the twentieth century. The term was first coined in the early 1960s, to refer to art that saw its material as ideas (or concepts) rather than any physical or sensual material. As such, it has much in common with **minimalism**, in that it questioned the traditional emphasis in western **aesthetics** on the attractive or at least interesting sensual stimuli provided by art works. Conceptual art is about an idea, and the materials used to articulate or explore that idea could either be purely conceptual (so that verbal instructions or a description replace an artefact) or be destroyed in their use. The only record of a conceptual art work might then be photographic or other documentation of its design and construction. (Claus Oldenburg's *Placid City Monument* entailed gravediggers excavating and then filling a large hole in Central Park.) At its best, by focusing on the processes that underpin the construction and presentation of art work, conceptual art has much to offer cultural studies (and indeed, at its best, it *is* cultural studies). For example, the installations of Christo (to stretch the definition of conceptual art a bit) typically involve wrapping public monuments or buildings (most famously, the Reichstag). The point of this lies less in the ephemeral finished product, however spectacular that is, than in the engagement with the political and **bureaucratic** planning processes, the commercial implications (a wrapped Reichstag is a tourist attraction) and the logistics that are the pre-conditions of its achievement. Art is thus understood and created within an explicitly social, political and cultural context. Similarly, the work of the British group Art & Language is intensely self-aware of the political nature of the gallery space traditionally used for exhibitions. However, at its worst, conceptual art is either banal (e.g. Kosuth's display of *One and Three Chairs*, being a real chair, a photograph of a chair and a description of a chair), or developed in a self-indulgent private language that excludes the spectator. [AE]

Further reading: Harrison 1991; Lucie-Smith 1995.

conflict theory In **sociology**, 'conflict theory' refers to a diverse group of theories that emerged in the 1950s and 1960s to challenge the orthodoxy of structural **functionalism**. Functionalists tended to assume that stable societies are generally harmonious, with conflict being seen as undesirable and aberrant. Functionalism therefore rejected the possibility that societies could be characterised in terms of long-term structural conflict between different groups. The sources of conflict theory may be traced back to the political philosophies of Hegel and Marx and to Simmel, to **Social Darwinism**, and to **elite** theory. Conflict theories may be broadly classified into two forms. **Marxism** is typical of those theories that see social conflict as occurring along a single, all important axis. In Marxism, this is **class** conflict, and as such is conflict over control of the economy and the means of production. Such accounts suggest that conflict will ultimately undermine social stability (leading according to Marxism to a class based revolution, and in elite theory, to the succession of an old and exhausted elite by a new and vital one). In contrast, the version of conflict theory that was developed by Lewis Coser (1956) from Simmel's work, suggested that conflict may also occur along a wide range of axes, and that such conflict is advantageous to the stability and growth of an open, pluralistic society. (The precise significance of conflict is therefore seen to depend upon the sort of social and political structure within which it occurs. Open societies can tolerate and benefit from conflict in a way that closed or authoritarian societies cannot.) Coser's account suggests that all conflicts cannot be mapped onto a single axis, such as class division. Thus, any individual protagonist could be one's ally in one dispute, and one's enemy in another. Such pluralistic conflict serves to bind society together, for conflict is typically worked out within commonly accepted and approved social institutions, generating new ideas and motivation for gradual reform. [AE]

Further reading: Collins 1975.

conscience collective Term in Durkheim's sociology, indicating the reality of society over and above that of the individual. Individual consciousness and moral conscience is derived from a normative order which coerces social members into thinking, judging and acting according to certain, socially desirable, **norms**. [AE]

consciousness   The notions of 'consciousness' and 'mind' are often taken as interchangeable. Consciousness is the awareness by an individual (human or animal) of its environment and, if self-conscious, of its place in and relationship to that environment. Humans, higher primates and certain other creatures, e.g. dolphins, are usually regarded as self-conscious. Some philosophers, e.g. Jonathan Glover (1990a: 46–50), have conjectured that there exists a progressive spectrum of consciousness starting with lower, mere conscious animals and ending with self-conscious human beings.

The stance one adopts regarding the nature of consciousness and on what can possess this property, depends upon one's view of the nature of mind. A dualist such as René Descartes would view 'souls' (minds) and bodies as two radically different substances. **Bodies**, according to Descartes, have shape, mass and location both in time and space. Minds, on the other hand, although containing thoughts that have duration, do not share any other properties with bodies. This radical separation of minds and bodies led to the infamous mind/body problem. This is the problem of how two substances, so totally different in their natures, can causally interact, granted that minds do in fact affect bodies and vice versa. Descartes would not agree that animals are conscious since he held only humans have souls.

In modern philosophy of mind the attempt to answer the mind/body problem usually results in the adoption of materialism. Materialists attempt to explain the mind in physical and biological terms. Behaviourists suggest that the mind is nothing more than a series of dispositions to behave in various ways given certain sorts of environmental stimuli. Most behaviourists reject all talk of inner psychological processes. Supporters of the mind-brain identity theory take a reductionist approach, holding that the mind is nothing more than the brain. Functionalists argue that mental phenomena or psychological states can be understood in terms of the causal relationships that exist between causal stimuli, other mental states and the behaviour that results. Eliminativists suggest that all our common-sense talk of psychological states, such as beliefs and desires, is wrong. In fact eliminativists, such as Paul Churchland, hold that science will ultimately generate a much better model than the one we have now for explaining consciousness. This new model will result in a wholly different view of what minds are and how they work. [SH]

Further reading: Churchland 1988, 1995; Crane 1995; Descartes 1968; Ryle 1949.

conservatism   Conservatism is perhaps better described as constituting an attitude toward politics and society rather than a political ideology. Its origins can be traced back to Edmund Burke's *Reflections on the Revolution in France* (1790), which was inspired by the events of the French Revolution into articulating the basic characteristics underlying conservative thinking. As such, modern conservatism may well be said to have drawn its first inspiration from a reaction to the rationalist ideals of the **Enlightenment**, which found (albeit rather distorted) expression in the French Revolution. These reactions are: (i) a negative attitude toward social change; (ii) a tenaciously held faith in the moral and political rightness of traditionally held attitudes and beliefs; (iii) a generally bleak and pessimistic view of human nature, i.e. conservatives tend to think that individuals left completely alone to pursue their own goals will generally descend into an at best immoral, and at worst amoral, lifestyle (a view which stands in direct contrast to the more optimistic conception of the individual held by both **liberalism** and **socialism**); (iv) the view that society is an interconnected structure of relationships constituting a community.

In the twentieth century there have been a number of significant (or at least well-known) exponents of conservatism. Michael Oakeshott has frequently been cited in this connection, although his political thinking, as well as owing a significant debt to such philosophers as Aristotle, Thomas Hobbes and G.W.F. Hegel (the latter two of which display 'conservative' tendencies), also has features which might equally be described as having features in common with the

79

thinking of **communitarianism** and is, in any case, far more complex than such a label might imply. Leo Strauss and, most recently, Roger Scruton, might both be taken as better examples of modern conservative thought.

More recently the German philosopher Jürgen Habermas has provided an account of conservatism which links it to the writings of **postmodernism** (e.g. Jacques Derrida, Michel Foucault, Jean-François Lyotard). Postmodern thinking, Habermas argues, in articulating its criticisms of the Enlightenment (i.e. of the Enlightenment faith in reason and science) is in effect the expression of a resurgent conservatism which takes its inspiration from the writings of those 'darker' thinkers of the bourgeoise tradition, Sade and Nietzsche (although it may well be equally germane to connect the thought of a thinker like Lyotard with the liberal tradition, with which his later work shares some common features). [PS]

Further reading: Burke 1982; Oakeshott 1975; Scruton 1984.

consumption   The idea that **capitalism** had become a 'consumer society' arose, at least in western Europe, in the 1950s, in response to increased affluence and changes in the economic and industrial structure (a move away from traditional heavy industry and towards new technologies and service provision) after the Second World War. This awareness gradually led to an increased interest in consumption as a culturally significant activity. However, important theories of consumption can be found from the late nineteenth century onwards.

Social theorists such as Thorstein Veblen and Georg Simmel were amongst the first to begin to articulate the significance of consumption to urban existence. Veblen's (1953) account of the 'conspicuous consumption' of the new **bourgeois** leisure **class** suggested that class identity could rest, not upon occupation, but upon patterns of consumption, that served to construct distinctive **lifestyles** and express **status**. Similarly, Simmel's essays, including those on 'The Metropolis and Mental Life' (1950b) and on 'Fashion' (1957), analyse the manner in which consumption may be used to cultivate, what for Simmel is a sham individuality. Such sophisticated, and indeed blasé, consumption allows the consumer to differentiate him or herself. Fashion is thus seen to work through a curious interplay of conformity and dissension, of familiarity and strangeness, in so far as fashion-conscious consumers at once consolidate their membership of the fashionable as they distinguish themselves from the mass. Fashion, for Simmel, represents an attraction to the exotic, strange and new, and yet, thanks to its continual historical change, an opportunity to ridicule the fashions of the past (and thus paradoxically one's own once fashionable self).

Marxists typically demonstrate a similar, or even more pronounced, scepticism as to the value of consumption, not least in so far as Marxist social theory is grounded in the view of human beings as primarily **producers**. An emphasis on humans as consumers suggests an **ideological** distraction from the essence of economic and political struggle, or at best a manifestation of the unfulfilling or **alienating** nature of production within **capitalism**. Perhaps the most sustained Marxist engagement with consumption came from the **Frankfurt School**. The account of the **culture industry** proposed by Horkheimer and Adorno (1972) holds that twentieth-century capitalism is a distinct **mode of production**, at least in comparison with the high capitalism of **Marx's** own time. For Marx, nineteenth-century consumers could freely choose between **commodities** on the grounds of the utility (or **use-value**) that they would derive from them. A useless commodity would be rejected, and thus the consumer retained some vestige of power with high capitalism. Horkheimer and Adorno argue that in late capitalism, use-value has been brought within the control of the capitalist producers, thanks to the power of advertising and the mass media. The consumers buy, crudely, what capitalism wants them to buy. The model of the culture industry is, however, more subtle than this. The consumers are not, on Horkheimer and Adorno's account, passive dupes of the capitalist system. Rather, the most efficient way of surviving and gaining some pleasure within the constraints of a highly bureaucratic and instrumental society, is to accept the goods offered, and that consumption may serve to express a deep awareness of the damage that capitalism is inflicting upon them. Adorno imagines a 'shop girl' who visits the cinema, not because she believes that the fantastic events of the cinema could happen to her, but because only in the cinema can she admit that they will not happen to her (Adorno 1992b: 49–50). This vignette expresses a side of Frankfurt theory that is often lost to its less sensitive readers.

More recent approaches to consumption recognise the **utopian** element inherent in shopping. An ideology of shopping may be analysed, where shopping or consumption are perceived as solutions to the discontents of one's life. In Lacanian terms, shopping promises to make us whole again. Yet, as with Freud's analysis of dreams, the pursuit of consumption may be interpreted as an illusory solution to the real problems of social life. In effect, this returns the analysis to the Frankfurt position. The continual round of consumerism is rejected as a short-term and ultimately illusory solution to one's problems. The task of theory would be to expose the real (social and psychological) problems that cause this discontent in the first place. Jacques Attali (1985) has lamented upon this theme, suggesting that when we purchase music (in the form of records), what we do is exchange our own labour (and thus involvement in the pressures and necessities of working life) for a commodity. But, unlike most other commodities, we carry out this exchange only in the utopian expectation of some day having the leisure time to enjoy it. (We work, in effect, for the promise of a work-free future.) This time, of course, never comes, and the use-value of the music lies forever unrealised.

More positive accounts of consumption, not least in that they suggested the potential of consumption as a form of political resistance, first emerged in association with **sub-cultural** theory. Youth subcultures, from the 1950s onwards, were seen as consuming the products of capitalism, but not in a manner that accorded with the expectations of the producers. The consumer is thus credited with the ability to make his or her own use-value from the commodity. Michel de Certeau (1984) thus describes consumption as 'secondary production'. While the products may be imposed by capitalism, the ways of using them are not. The shopping centre itself (as well as a number of key contemporary commodities, such as the 'Walkman' (du Gay *et al.* 1997) and 'Barbie' dolls (Rand 1995)) has become the focus of much analysis from cultural studies. Shopping is recognised as a highly popular leisure activity (and not simply the means to other leisure activities). The shopping centre becomes one focus of this activity, not least in so far as the shopping centre may well offer attractions other than shopping (including restaurants, cinemas and other leisure facilities). Yet, again, different groups will consume the centre itself differently. The young, unemployed, elderly and homeless, despite the fact that they are overtly excluded from consumerism due to lack of economic resources, will still find use within the centre (for example as a source of shelter, warmth and entertainment, or as a meeting place) (Morris 1993).

The theoretical issues in the analysis of the political and social significance of consumption perhaps revolve around the conceptualisation and understanding of human autonomy and individuality. Empirical evidence (for example that 80 per cent of all new products are rejected by consumers) is, in itself, of little value in establishing whether or not consumers have exercised active and autonomous choice. Simmel's pseudo-individualism, and even Horkheimer and Adorno's culture industry are not incompatible with such statistics. Yet, consideration of consumption does indicate much about how humans find scope for self-expression (however glorious or impoverished this expression is ultimately judged to be) within the close restrictions of their everyday life. [AE]

Further reading: Bocock 1993; Corrigan 1997; Falk and Campbell 1997; Miller 1995.

content analysis Content analysis is a specific approach to the analysis of **communication**. It strives to avoid subjective bias, and to generate quantifiable (statistical) results. Content analysis is most appropriate to the analysis of large samples, rather than to individual **texts**. The statistical occurrence of key units within this sample is of significance. For example, the content analysis of television news reports of strike action might focus on the proportion of reports (or the proportion of all broadcast time devoted to strike action) which cover a particular industry, and compare these to the actual proportion of all industrial action that this industry represents. Thus, if 50 per cent of all strike reports concern the car industry, and yet only 5 per cent of all strikes (or days lost through industrial action) are from the car industry, this would suggest some form of selective reporting. The claim of content analysis to avoid subjective bias rests heavily upon the possibility of using clearly defined and thus unambiguously applicable units of analysis. [AE]

Further reading: Weber 1990.

continental philosophy   The term 'continental philosophy' is generally applied to the work of philosophers who come from the mainland of the European continent. However, there is within the range of thinkers who might be thus described such a diversity of approaches to a wide variety of philosophical questions that it is really quite difficult to categorise them in a homogeneous manner as 'continental philosophers'. Nevertheless, it is true that during the last one hundred years or so there has been a split between, on the one hand Anglo-American **analytic philosophy** and, on the other, philosophy as it has been practised by the continental tradition. This might be best described as a division which occurred at an institutional level (i.e. within the university systems of mainland Europe, the UK and the US). If there was a key moment which served to define this split, it might be located within the work of philosophers within the analytic tradition rather than the continentals (e.g. that of Bertrand Russell and Gottlob Frege). Thus, for example, Russell, a philosophy student in Britain at a time when Hegel's philosophy was dominant in the university system, and himself a youthful devotee of it, came to regard what he saw as the excesses of metaphysical speculation and idealism in the thought of not only Hegel but also such thinkers as Schopenhauer and Nietzsche, with a distinct air of suspicion (see his *A History of Western Philosophy* (1946) for a good impression of his attitude). In the place of such speculation Russell and other analytics propounded a rigorous analytical discourse which concentrated upon, for example, elucidating definitions of key philosophical notions (e.g. **meaning**, **reference**, **language**). Above all, one might characterise analytic philosophy's rigour in terms of its commitment to a primarily logical form of **discourse**, and an accompanying commitment to a primarily metaphysical understanding of the meaning of terms such as 'necessity'. Analytics have generally sought to clarify issues of meaning, and have usually avoided what many of them have considered (even until quite recently) to be the vague idealistic speculations characteristic of thinkers within the continental tradition (Gilbert Ryle's famous dismissal of Heidegger's *Being and Time* as not worth reading is perhaps the most notorious expression of this attitude). Continental philosophy, if one indeed ventures to define it, might better be understood by situating it within the context of specific debates about questions of knowledge, rather than characterising it in terms of its purportedly 'speculative' character. Such an approach is especially useful since the question of knowledge is a concern common to both the analytic and continental traditions, and some comparison and contrast is thereby rendered possible. Naturally, there are exceptions to the account offered below, but it is certainly the case that what is discussed under the rubric of a 'continental' approach embodies something markedly different from the analyses of many analytic philosophers.

Where analytic philosophers have tended to treat the investigation of questions about knowledge in what may be called logical–metaphysical terms (see, for example, Ludwig Wittgenstein's early text, *Tractatus Logico-Philosophicus* (1921)), a significant number of continental philosophers have conducted their research with an additional emphasis on the material/

temporal factors that may be significant to knowledge. Thus, for example, Nietzsche's account of the generation of knowledge is one which concentrates upon an analysis of the material conditions that are fundamental to its possibility. Indeed, for Nietzsche, 'knowledge' is thereby rendered the consequence of a series of contingent eventualities, while the logical preconditions of thinking are often taken to signify *not* an ontological proof of how the world is (and a criterion, therefore, of objectivity and truth) but an indication merely of a human incapacity to think about the world differently. That we must think logically, on Nietzsche's view, does not entitle us to the further claim that the world itself ought to conform to the strictures of logical form (see Nietzsche's notebooks, as published in *The Will to Power* (1968b), which contain many versions of this kind of argument) but rather pays testimony to the material conditions in which the human species developed.

This point can be further illustrated by the approach of analytic and continental commentators to Kant's project, in the *Critique of Pure Reason* (1964), of elucidating the *a priori* conditions required for the possibility of knowledge. By the phrase *a priori* Kant means independent of all empirical experience. Although, for Kant, all knowledge is knowledge about experience, it does not follow that the conditions for the possibility of having experience are themselves derived from experience. Analytic commentators (e.g. Stroud 1984: 153ff.) have generally taken this independence to have a metaphysical significance. For Stroud, *a priori* always means independent of experience and concerns the subjective conditions (i.e. those features a **subject** must have in order to know something) which are to be found 'in' us. On Stroud's view, such conditions are those properties which a mind must have in order to be capable of knowledge (1984: 160). For Stroud, the subjective conditions are 'characteristics' or properties of human beings. They are what must necessarily be true of a mind in order for knowledge to be possible for it. The kind of necessity involved here is metaphysical, i.e. it concerns those conditions in virtue of which knowledge is possible for us. Necessary conditions, taken in this sense, need not exist prior to (i.e.

before) what they are conditions for. Hence, the possibility that the sense of *a priori* might also be taken as meaning preceding experience is ignored within Stroud's account. In contrast, a thinker like Michel Foucault takes a rather different view of the meaning of Kant's notion of the *a priori*, which reflects how it has been articulated within the continental tradition (see Foucault's *The Order of Things* (1970; discussed below, and *The Archeology of Knowledge* (1972)).

Foucault takes Kant's critical enterprise to constitute a turning point in the history of European philosophy (as initiating the period of modernity), and considers the legacy of Kant in the French and German traditions. He therefore attempts to provide an account of what he believes to be the received (continental) interpretation of this legacy. On Foucault's view, the classical conception of theory of knowledge can be characterised as taking the search for its conditions as being a matter of the relationship between representations (i.e. the question of how our representations of experience map on to reality). Kant's modern account, in contrast, does not seek to locate these conditions at the level of representation (Foucault 1970: 241, 254), but instead side-steps the issue of representation in order to address the question of those conditions 'on the basis of which all representation, whatever its form, may be posited' (ibid.: 242, 254–5). On Foucault's account, such a starting point is equivalent to analysing 'the source and origin [*la source et l'origine*] of representation' (ibid.: 243, 256). On this view, Kant's interest in the conditions of knowledge is one which concentrates on the matter of its prior (i.e. preceding) conditions. This point can be highlighted by turning to Foucault's implicit attribution to Kant of a view of the subject as an 'empirico-transcendental doublet' (ibid.: 318, 329). This view, Foucault argues, has given rise to two kinds of analysis of human knowledge: (i) a reductivist empiricism, which is interested in the 'anatomo-physiological conditions' of knowledge; (ii) a form of transcendental, dialectical analysis, which examines the historical conditions of knowledge (ibid.: 319, 330). Foucault sees both kinds of analysis as explaining the genesis of knowledge, not its logical/metaphysical conditions of possibility. The first seeks to elucidate the historical development of knowledge after the fact (**positivism**), the second to provide an account of those conditions of knowledge which history must fulfil (**dialectics**) (ibid.: 320, 331). In both cases, what is analysed are the antecedent conditions of knowledge. Thus, Foucault takes the Kantian notion of the necessity which grounds the validity of our knowledge to be a matter of its antecedent conditions. The *a priori*, taken in this sense, is what is prior (in a temporal sense) to experience.

From this comparison, it is evident that the two traditions tend to depart from one another not with regard to the kind of questions they ask (in this case the question concerns the necessary conditions of knowledge), but in terms of how the question is dealt with. The emphasis on the significance of the temporal or material mode is not merely present in Nietzsche and Foucault (both of whom also treat ethical and political questions with an eye on the problem of **power** which is itself generated from an investment in a material analysis of social relations). In Martin Heidegger's *Being and Time*, likewise, temporality is seen as being fundamental to the success of any interpretation of the ontological question of the meaning of Being. Equally, for Gilles Deleuze temporality is taken to form the basis for the construction of an account of an ontology of 'becoming'.

Of course, as already mentioned there are exceptions to the account offered above, and it is worth emphasising again that it would be incorrect to read 'continental philosophy' as an all-embracing term which indicates a set of doctrines with regard to how philosophical enquiry ought to be conducted. Jacques Derrida, for example, has pursued an approach which does not embrace the material mode, but offers an account of processes of signification which problematises a metaphysical attitude to questions of knowledge whilst at the same time remaining both firmly within the domain demarcated by metaphysical thinking and highly suspicious of the historicised project Foucault engages in (see his criticisms of Foucault in the essay 'Cogito and the History of Madness' in *Writing and Difference* (1978)). Likewise, Jean-François Lyotard should really be described as a thinker who employs a range of strategies common to both the analytic and continental traditions (and indeed constructs his arguments in the light of his knowledge of the works of Russell, Frege and Wittgenstein as well as Hegel, Nietzsche and Heidegger). [PS/AE]

Further reading: Foucault 1970; Hylton 1990; Kearney and Rainwater 1996; Silverman and Welton 1988; Stroud 1984; West 1996.

contradiction   In the case of a proposition (*p*) which makes an assertion (*f*) (for example, concerning a state of affairs) which is denied by another proposition (*q*), the two propositions are said to be in contradiction. The assertion of the truth one of the propositions (*p*) necessarily implies the falsity of the other (*q*). Thus, in logic, the *principle of non-contradiction* states that two mutually exclusive states of affairs cannot simultaneously be asserted to be the case, e.g. it is impossible for something to exist and at the same time not to exist. The principle of non-contradiction thus serves as a rule for the construction of arguments that have *validity*. In the work of Hegel and Marx contradiction performs an important function. Hegel's conception of **dialectic**, for instance, is dependent upon the notion of contradiction for its force. For Hegel, contradiction is a principle fundamental to the nature of existence, which is overcome in the dialectical process.

   In the social and political spheres, the notion of contradiction has been used to articulate a range of problems basic to the relationships that exist between civil agents. In **civil society**, for example, contradictions may arise from the fact of individual civil agents pursuing their own particular purposes (*x*'s purposes may not be commensurable with *y*'s purposes) or from their having mutually incompatible interests. [PS]

conversation analysis   Conversation analysis emerged in **sociology**, specifically through **ethnomethodology**. Conversations are highly organised social events, with participants typically able to tell when they must or are able to speak, when they may legitimately interrupt, or when they must respect another participant's silence and not speak. In conversations, participants therefore manifest their competence in managing social interaction. Conversation analysis is primarily concerned with the description of conversations. Class studies have been carried out on the first five seconds of telephone conversations. [AE]

Further reading: Atkinson *et al.* 1984; Moerman 1988; Sacks 1992.

counterculture   The term 'counterculture' was coined in the 1960s, largely in response to the emergence of middle-**class** youth movements (such as the hippies), to refer to groups that questioned the **values** of the dominant culture. While centring on an opposition to the Vietnam War, the hippie counterculture also expressed its dissatisfaction with the values and goals of capitalism, such as consumerism, the work ethic and a dependence on technology. In general, the concept of counterculture may now be extended to the values, beliefs and attitudes of any minority group that opposes the dominant culture, but more precisely, does so in a relatively articulate and reflective manner. Thus, at its emergence, the Christian **religion** was a counterculture, in opposition to the dominant Jewish and Roman cultures. In the early period of British **capitalism**, the Quakers and the Methodists represented countercultures in opposition to the dominant values of Anglicanism. (See also **subculture**, **youth culture**.) [AE]

Further reading: Hill 1975; Roszak 1968; Yinger 1982.

critical theory   'Critical theory' is something of an umbrella term, and has come to be associated in the Anglo-American academic world with a brand of textual analysis which has taken root predominantly in university English Literature departments. The term itself, however, was first linked to the work of the **Frankfurt School** (e.g. Horkheimer, Adorno, Benjamin and Marcuse). In the hands of these thinkers, critical theory was envisaged as a rigorous critical engagement with social and philosophical issues which aimed at the cross-fertilisation of research methods derived from the social sciences with a Marxist theoretical framework for conceptualising social relations. However, as exemplified by Horkheimer and Adorno's book *Dialectic of Enlightenment*, there always existed in the work of the Frankfurt School a tendency to question certain ideas that were central to **Marxism** (for instance, the traditional Marxist confidence in the politicisation of the proletariat leading to revolution, or an unproblematic affirmation of the **Enlightenment** ideal of **rationality** as providing the key to social progress).

Since the 1980s, the term 'critical theory' has come to be associated with an approach to textual criticism which draws upon the writings of thinkers linked with **structuralism**, **post-structuralism** and **postmodernism** (for example, Foucault, Derrida, and Lyotard). Some exponents of critical theory have also found room for the adoption of approaches derived from new **historicism** or from the writings of psychoanalyst Jacques Lacan. From this it is apparent that any simple or clearly circumscribed definition of 'critical theory' in this sense is not possible. However, a number of characteristics might be cited as a means of arriving at a rather broad description of certain significant features of this form of critical theory.

In the wake of French structuralism, a brand of textual analysis evolved during the 1970s which concentrated on elucidating readings of literary texts in the light of Ferdinand de Saussure's linguistics. Thus, a text was conceived of as a structured network of signs, the meanings of which are determined not by what each sign refers to, but (i) through their differential relationship to one another, and (ii) through a relation of **binary opposition**. Structuralist analysis sought to provide an objective/scientific description of the structural economy of meaning present within texts. Recent critical theory was developed in the wake of the move from structuralism to post-structuralism initiated by the work of such figures as Paul de Man and the French philosopher Jacques Derrida. Derrida's advocacy, in *Of Grammatology* (1976), of a strategy of **deconstruction**, in which the analysis of texts is undertaken with the object of interrogating oppositional structures of meaning so as to allow for the identification and questioning of hierarchically organised conceptual orders, forms the basis of much of the more recent work undertaken in critical theory. Perhaps the most influential of Derridean notions in this context is that of *différance*, which for him represents the continual deferral of the possibility of a closure of meaning within language. Language, on this account, is not merely a system of differences (as with the model of language derived from Saussurean linguistics), but a 'system of *différance*' (Derrida 1981: 28), which may be provisionally arrested so as to produce key conceptual orderings (such as those of '**objectivity**' and '**subjectivity**', '**self**' and '**other**') as its effects. In critical theory, this view of language has resulted in the production of readings of literary and philosophical texts which concentrate upon elucidating the hierarchies present within them, and then attempt to suspend or destabilise those hierarchies by way of invoking the *différance* hypothesis. Unfortunately, this strategy has been repeated so often that one is inclined to suspect that Derrida's notion of *différance* has, in practical terms, been reduced to a form of 'magic lexicon' by those critics who seem inclined to adopt it uncritically as a key to unlocking the 'hidden' meanings present within texts. Such critics thereby seem content to let the work of critical engagement be reduced to the mere invocation of a meta-rule.

This latter fact is perhaps ironic, given the avowed commitment on the part of many critical theorists to a form of epistemic relativism. The roots of this relativism can be traced to two primary influences. First, to the recuperation of the writings of Michel Foucault, whose analysis of discourses of power has led some to stress the importance of power-relations in the construction of meaning within texts (perhaps in this context the most productive effect of Foucault's influence is the work of E.W. Said, which has exerted an influence in furthering the critical awareness of colonial and post-colonial issues in contemporary **culture**). Second, Jean-François Lyotard's advocacy of a postmodern pluralism with regard to questions of ethics and knowledge, in works such as *The*

Postmodern Condition has also left its mark upon the work of literary critical theory (although their reading strategies sit less comfortably with Lyotard's more recent work, in texts such as *The Differend* (1988) which demonstrates a notably ambivalent relationship to postmodernism). Likewise, Jean Baudrillard's writings have also exerted some influence on the attitudes and ideas of critical theorists (see Norris's account of this in his *Uncritical Theory* (1992)). To this extent, and in spite of the fact of its frequently having been practised by academics ensconced within literature departments, critical theory of this type has, in effect, ceased to be a primarily literary discourse – if, indeed, it ever was. In its dealings with literature it has exhibited a tendency to question the received literary canon, and at the same time has demonstrated a strong commitment to intervening in issues which have, in general, hitherto been of sole interest to philosophers (something which, indeed, one might expect, given that many of the key influences upon critical theory have been thinkers, like Derrida and Lyotard, who work within the philosophical tradition). Thus, questions about the nature of identity, of meaning, of the relationship between language and experience (i.e. the realism versus anti-realism debate), have all been identified as being important to the practice of critical theory by various exponents.

More recently, a number of key problems have been identified within critical theory, most notably by Christopher Norris, whose attitude toward it has undergone some radical revisions since he first espoused it in the early 1980s (see *Deconstruction: Theory and Practice* (1986), the most recent edition of which contains a postscript which pays ample witness to its author's disillusionment). Whereas, in his earliest work, Norris displayed a confidence in the radical possibilities of a critical theory committed to an ethical and epistemological relativism, in his later writings (i.e. those dating from the late 1980s onwards) he has come to regard critical theory as embodying and embracing a form of uncritical relativism which has divested itself of the possibility for a radical engagement with contemporary political and ethical concerns. For instance, Norris's book *Uncritical Theory* attacks the anti-realism of Baudrillard, citing as a case in point his articles on the Gulf War which appeared in various French and English newspapers just prior to and immediately after the conflict. Baudrillard's claim that the Gulf War would not (and indeed his assertion subsequently that it did not) ever happen, are seen by Norris as the excesses of an antirealism which has overstepped the boundaries of reason and ethical responsibility. Likewise, the postmodernism espoused by Lyotard's book *The Postmodern Condition*, and taken up by many critical theorists, has been met by Norris with some strong, and often perceptive, passages of criticism.

Whether or not one accepts the tenets of literary critical theory, its development within literature departments must be viewed as significant. Attempts on the part of critical theorists to render all human experience in terms of 'textuality', their criticisms of the realist thesis as it is put forward by some philosophers within, for instance, the analytic tradition, and indeed some of their attacks on philosophy itself may well come to be viewed primarily as being symptomatic of a bid to debunk and thereby take control of the academic 'high ground' of ontology, metaphysics, ethics and epistemology which has traditionally been the domain of philosophers. Ironically (and, indeed, tellingly), however, one of the figures who has exerted an influence on critical theory, Lyotard, was and remains committed to the view that philosophy does and ought to have some privileged claims with regard to these issues (Lyotard's distinction in *The Differend* and elsewhere between the 'philosopher' and the 'intellectual', for instance, pays ample testimony to this fact). This demonstrates the existence of a deep tension within critical theory, between its avowed aims and its philosophical/theoretical heritage which has, at least as yet, not been resolved. For if the proponents of critical theory follow Lyotard's example, and move toward a more Anglo-American philosophical orientation, many of its basic precepts and arguments will require careful scrutiny and, perhaps, radical revision. [PS]

Further reading: Derrida 1976; Harland 1987; Norris 1986, 1992.

cultural anthropology   Anthropology, that literally means the study of man or humankind, is divided into two branches: physical (or biological) and cultural. Physical anthropology is concerned with the physical variation in human form. While in the nineteenth century, this variation was understood in crudely evolutionary terms, and was frequently used to justify the superiority of the white European form over other, supposedly more primitive, forms, now physical anthropology stresses only the diversity of human form (as adaptation to diverse environments), not any progress. A similar shift occurs in cultural anthropology, as it matured into a respectable (and indeed fundamental) social science at the beginning of the twentieth century. Thus, an initial concern with the progress of human society and culture (still reflected in the occasional use of 'primitive' society), was replaced by a recognition of the diversity of human culture, and the different, but none the less equally complex and valid structures and logics that underpinned these cultures.

Perhaps the first great anthropologists, at least in the modern development of the subject, were Marcel Mauss (in France) and Franz Boas (in the United States). Mauss, the nephew and pupil of Emile Durkheim, developed a comparative approach to anthropology. Working with **ethnographic** (which is to say, descriptive) data, compiled by others, from a wide range of pre-industrial and small-scale societies, he sought to find common patterns in the organisation of social and cultural life. In *The Gift* (1966) he analysed the exchange of gifts. Mauss understood that the gift carried with it a reciprocal moral obligation. The gift had to be returned, in some form, at a later date. Gift exchange could therefore be explained as a 'total **social fact**'. That is to say, it is an activity that has implications throughout society, in the economic, legal, political and religious spheres. (Hence, political power might be secured through the potential leader's ability to make gifts, thereby binding the recipients of these gifts to him, for they would repay the gift in political allegiance.) If Mauss developed a theoretical side of anthropology, not least in that he recognised the complexity of other cultures, and the cognitive aspects of a culture (in that one's culture provides the human agent with the resources to make sense of and to classify the natural and social worlds (Durkheim and Mauss 1963)), Franz Boas promoted the empirical side of anthropology. After living amongst the Inuit (during work on a meteorological expedition), Boas stressed the importance of describing the finest detail of everyday life in cultures, and thus the importance of **field work** and ethnographic techniques.

Bronislav Malinowski's study of the Trobriand Islanders of New Guinea (1922) provided a model for sound anthropological research for many years. It combined meticulous ethnographic descriptions of the society, with a **functionalist** explanatory framework. In effect, Malinowski sought to explain the various features and institutions of the society in terms of the functions they fulfilled, which is to say, the needs they satisfied, in order to maintain and reproduce the culture. The functionalist approach was dominant in anthropology prior to the Second World War, with the British anthropologist E.E. Evans-Pritchard (1951) and A.R. Radcliffe-Brown (1952) pre-eminent. However, in the United States, important work was being carried out by, amongst others, Ruth Benedict and Margaret Mead (1928). Benedict's work (1935) produced remarkably elegant interpretations of cultures in terms of their articulation of a dominant theme (or, in the case of Japanese culture, the clash between two themes, the military (the 'sword') and aesthetic (the 'chrysanthemum') (Benedict 1989)). Benedict and Mead's work, like that of Mead's teacher, Boas, explicitly focused on the role that culture has in shaping human personality. In the **nature**-nurture debate – that is to say, the debate over the respective influence of cultural acquisition and genetic inheritance in the shaping of human personality and other traits – cultural anthropologists have typically supported the 'nurture' side of the argument. At the extreme, suggested by Benedict's work, the new-born human may be presented as a blank slate, upon which culture can write whatever traits it chooses (thus placing great emphasis on the importance of **socialisation**).

In practice, this approach may lead to difficulties in explaining the behaviour of those who do not conform (the **deviant**).

The work of Mauss and Radcliffe-Brown had a major influence on Claude Lévi-Strauss, and the development of structuralist anthropology in the immediate post-war period. His *Elementary Structures of Kinship* (1969), treated marriage rules broadly in the manner of Mauss's total social fact. The rules that governed marriage (for example, the widespread custom of preferring first cousins as spouses), were seen to underpin meaningful exchanges between male-dominated clans. Women are the 'messages' transmitted between clans, as they give away daughters and receive wives. The influence of Saussure's **semiology** on Lévi-Strauss was combined with work already done by Radcliffe-Brown on the structures found within **myths**, and especially on the use of **binary oppositions** (such as black-white) to articulate the meaning of the myths. Lévi- ' Strauss's magnum opus, the four-volume *Mythologies* (1970, 1973, 1977, 1981), along with *The Savage Mind* (1966), explore not simply the ways in which human cultures organise classificatory systems (and indeed integrate their understanding of the natural world with an articulation of the social world), but rather present these structures, including particular mythological narratives and classificatory systems, as manifestations of a deep structure that is grounded in the working of the human mind as such. The diversity of particular mythologies and beliefs is seen to employ a relatively limited set of meaningful units (or symbols). The combination of these elements is determined by rules that are akin to grammatical transformations. (In effect, particular mythologies are akin to Saussure's **parole**, while the underlying structure is **langue**.)

If Radcliffe-Brown's work influenced **structuralism**, Evans-Pritchard's work was instrumental in stimulating debate over **cultural relativism**. The British, Wittgensteinian philosopher Peter Winch took up Evans-Pritchard's accounts of witchcraft practices amongst the Azande in order to explore the incommensurability of different cultures (Winch 1958). That is to say, Winch developed the relativist position that all **values** and all knowledge claims were valid and meaningful

only relative to the particular culture (or in Wittgenstein's terminology, 'form of life') within which they emerged. If so,
this entails that one cannot understand these values and beliefs
except in their own terms. The anthropologist was therefore
required to immerse him or herself in the culture studied,
and not to try to translate their findings into the values and
beliefs of his or her own western European culture. The
Winchian approach works against the type of comparative
and explanatory work carried out by Mauss or Lévi-Strauss,
for that would be seen to violate the uniqueness of each
culture, and the requirement to understand and interpret it
in its own terms (not those of an alien scientific culture, such
as that of functionalism or structuralism). At a less extreme
position, cultural anthropology continues to celebrate the
diversity and validity of other cultures as cognitive systems,
leading to the rise of series of sub-disciplines within cultural
anthropology, concerning the way in which cultures organise
their knowledge of various phenomena – hence 'ethno-
medicine' is concerned with the way in which non-western
cultures articulate their knowledge of medicine; or 'ethno-
botany' with the knowledge and classification of plants. [AE]

Further reading: Ingold 1996; James *et al.* 1997; Leach 1982; Strathern
1995.

cultural capital   **Class** membership is defined, at least within
the Marxist tradition, in terms of the individual's access to
and control of economic **capital** (such as industrial machinery,
raw materials and also finance). Pierre Bourdieu (1973) drew
an analogy to an individual's access to cultural resources in
order to explain the workings of the educational system in a
class-divided capitalist society. Children will have differing
degrees of cultural competence (including information and
skills), acquired prior to school within the family. The education system will not then overtly discriminate in favour of
the children of the dominant class. Rather, all children will
be assessed 'neutrally', in terms of their ability to perform
according to the same criteria of excellence. These criteria

will, however, be derived from the dominant **culture**. The children of the dominant class will do better, so yielding interest (in terms of 'symbolic power') on their parents' investment in cultural capital. [AE]

cultural relativism   The view that fundamentally different standards of morality, practices and belief systems operate in different cultures and cannot be judged with regard to their worth from a standpoint exterior to them. Cultural relativism thus holds that there is a fundamental incommensurability between the value-systems of different cultures. Whether or not such a view commits one to a relativism with regard to questions of knowledge (see **epistemology**) is a further issue which depends upon whether or not one is inclined to hold that the rules of validity which apply with regard to the construction of knowledge claims (for example, the principle of non-**contradiction**) are culturally constructed. However, it is difficult to see how a cultural relativist can defend any notion of epistemic validity from the charge of being likewise culturally produced, and therefore incommensurable with conceptions of validity that are generated within different cultures or contexts. It is possible to define more recent cultural relativism in terms of its commitment to a particular model of language and meaning derived from (or having strong parallels with) the work of the later Wittgenstein. Thus, Richard Rorty's espousal of a **liberalism** and **postmodernism** which is relativistic about the practices and procedures that constitute interpretative communities owes a debt to the Wittgensteinean 'meaning is use' thesis. Although it has often been claimed that the cultural relativist is interested in giving voice to the perspectives of marginalised interests and cultures, it is by no means clear that this is the case. Some have argued (cf. Christopher Norris, *The Contest of Faculties* (1985)) that Rorty's espousal of cultural and epistemic relativism brings with it the spectre of cultural imperialism. (See also **cultural anthropology**.) [PS]

Further reading: Hollis and Lukes 1982; Margolis 1991; Norris 1985; Rorty 1991.

cultural reproduction   The term 'cultural reproduction' was coined by Pierre Bourdieu (1973), to refer to the process by which the **culture**, and thus political power, of the dominant **class** is maintained from one generation to the next, through the education system. More generally, the term may be seen to highlight the problem of how societies continue to exist and remain relatively stable over long periods of time. This continued existence requires more than just physical reproduction, in the sense of sufficient births to replace those who have died or left the society. The culture of that society must be transmitted to the new generation. Cultural reproduction is thus intimately linked to the role that **socialisation**, or the process through which individuals internalise the culture of their societies, plays in this stability. As Bourdieu's definition highlights, part of this problem of cultural transmission is not simply the stability of the manner in which society is organised, or the stability of the key values and beliefs of its culture, but rather the stability of the political structures and the structures of domination and exploitation within the society. As such, it may be seen as a process by which political structures are given legitimacy or **authority**.

In the Marxist tradition, social reproduction refers to conditions necessary for the renewal of **labour**. Again, this is not simply a matter of physically replacing labourers, but more centrally involves the place of social and cultural institutions, such as housing, education and health care in that process. [AE]

Further reading: Jenks 1993b.

cultural studies   While the term 'cultural studies' may be used, broadly, to refer to all aspects of the study of **culture**, and as such may be taken to encompass the diverse ways in which culture is understood and analysed, for example, in sociology, history, **ethnography** and **literary criticism**, and even **sociobiology**, it may also, more precisely, be taken to refer to a distinctive field of academic enquiry. In this second use, its historical roots can be traced back to the work of

Raymond Williams and Richard Hoggart in the late 1950s and early 1960s, and thus to the formation of the **Birmingham Centre for Contemporary Cultural Studies** in 1964, originally under the directorship of Hoggart and then of Stuart Hall. From this body of work there emerged a multi-disicplinary approach to culture, drawing not merely on the orthodox approaches derived from the social sciences, but also on more radical approaches suggested by, for example, **feminism**, **Marxism** and **semiotics**. This miscellany of approaches facilitated the asking of new questions, and thus to a reconceptualisation of exactly what was entailed by the term 'culture'. In particular, cultural studies can be seen to have set itself against the preconceptions about culture found in the traditional critical disciplines, such as literary criticism, **aesthetics** and musicology. While such traditional disciplines predominantly treated cultural products as objects or texts that could be legitimately, or even exhaustively, studied in isolation from the social and historical context of their **production** and **consumption**, the exponents of cultural studies sought to situate cultural products explicitly in relation to other social practices, and particularly in relation to political structures and social heirarchies, such as **race**, **class** and **gender**. An implication of this approach was that the cultural products to be studied could not merely be those selected and celebrated by an intellectual and artistic elite, but would rather be the material and symbolic products encountered in all strata and sections of society.

Cultural studies can therefore be seen to be situated between an approach to culture that is explicitly opposed to the celebration of high or elite culture, as represented, for example, in the canonical texts studied in English Literature, or the subject-matter of traditional musicology, and an approach that is more positively derived from the social sciences, and particularly from cultural anthropology and the sociology of culture. [AE]

Further reading: Grossberg *et al.* 1992; Hall 1980, 1996; Inglis 1993.

culture   'Culture' is not easily defined, not least because it can have different meanings in different contexts. However, the concept that lies at the core of cultural studies, it may be suggested, is very much the concept that is found in **cultural anthropology**. As such, it avoids any exclusive concern with 'high' culture (which is still found, for example, in the writings of Arnold, Leavis and **elite** and **mass society** theories). It entails recognition that all human beings live in a world that is created by human beings, and in which they find meaning. Culture is the complex everyday world we all encounter and through which we all move. Culture begins at the point at which humans surpass whatever is simply given in their **natural** inheritance. The cultivation of the natural world, in **agriculture** and **horticulture**, is thus a fundamental element of a culture. As such, the two most important or general elements of culture may be the ability of human beings to construct and to build, and the ability to use **language** (understood most broadly, to embrace all forms of sign system).

Gillian Rose's use of the Jewish myth of the Tower of Babel is illuminating in this context (1993). At Babel, humans attempted to reach heaven by building a tower. God did not merely destroy the Tower, but in order to prevent a further attempt, He prevented **communication** by imposing a multiplicity of languages. This story is often seen as an **allegory** of language. Rose, however, takes it further, as an allegory of language and **architecture**. It is therefore seen to comment upon key themes of cultural studies, including the community, the conflict of diverse cultures, **power**, law and morality, and knowledge. A few of these themes may be outlined. Rose's argument is that Babel represents, not simply an architectural project, but also the building of a city. Cities are a crucial cultural watershed, for in the city, diverse cultures (customs, beliefs and **values**) come together. In a city, people become aware, perhaps for the first time, that they have a culture, for there is always someone who disagrees with what you have always taken for granted. Our self-awareness as cultural beings is grounded in this confrontation, and thus in the exercise of power (as we struggle to sustain our own values against an assault from **others**). The point of Babel, and perhaps of all human culture, is that in the architectural achievement of the tower-city, humans gained a sort of immortality. While the individual may die, the buildings of his or her generation will live on and become part of the future. Cultures endure even though the individuals who built them die. So, at the very least, our understanding of time is transformed, and our understanding of history created. Yet this 'reach', as Rose calls it, entails the loss of a naïve self-certainty. The unity and universality of the isolated, nomadic early Jewish tribe is confronted and questioned by its encounter with a plurality of other cultures and their claims to universality. Paradoxically, at the very moment in which we become aware of ourselves as cultural beings, we are both enabled (we can do new things, and in principle, do anything we like), but can no longer ever be certain what is the right thing to do, and so in doing anything, we fall into conflict with others.

Thus, cultural studies is necessarily concerned with artificiality, and the political struggle to find and defend meaning. [AE]

Further reading: Jenks 1993a; Williams 1986.

culture industry   The term '**culture** industry' was coined by the **Frankfurt School** theorists Horkheimer and Adorno in *The Dialectic of Enlightenment* (1972), to refer to the production of mass culture. This deliberately contradictory term (setting the culture against its apparent antithesis in industry) attempts to grasp something of the fate of culture in the highly instrumentally rational and bureaucratic society of late **capitalism**. The account of the culture industry may be seen, at root, as economic, and as such an integral part of the reinterpretation of dialectical materialism that is a central theme of *The Dialectic of Enlightenment*. The culture industry, embracing advertising as much as radio and **cinema**, serves to transform **use-value** (the utility that consumers derive from a **commodity**) into something that is produced by the capitalist system. It may be suggested that the combination of advertising and the **mass**

media promotes less particular products, and more a capitalist **lifestyle**.

This account of the absorption of use-value into production goes hand in hand with Adorno's analysis of the fate of the relationship between the **forces** and **relations of production** in twentieth-century capitalism. The independence of use-value in nineteenth-century capitalism gave the human subject genuine autonomy and thus potential for resistance (thereby destabilising capitalism). This autonomy is now increasingly lost. Similarly, administrative techniques, that developed as part of the forces of production (to increase the efficiency of industry), now become fundamental to the relations of production (so that market exchange and property ownership are subordinated to bureaucratic organisation, and the employed and the unemployed alike become claimants for welfare payments). The contradiction between the forces and relations of production, that for Marx would bring about the fall of capitalism, is removed in this totally administered society.

The account of the culture industry has frequently been trivialised by its critics (not least those within cultural studies). Horkheimer and Adorno do not, for example, obviously assume that human subjects are passive victims of the culture industry, and nor is the culture industry an instrument of **class** rule. The total administration of contemporary capitalism embraces and constrains everyone, so that although the property-owning **bourgeoisie** may continue to benefit materially from the system, they are as powerless before it as the non-property owning classes. Yet these powerless subjects continue to struggle with the system, and to survive within it. Horkheimer and Adorno hint that **consumption** of culture industry products is diverse. The radio ham, for example, attempts to retain some autonomy and individuality by building and operating his or her own radio, rather than accepting what is given, ready made. Others use the cover of culture industry institutions, such as the cinema, to admit the unhappiness that would paralyse them in the real world. Even within the culture industry, not all of its products are homogeneous. Orson Welles (and later Michelangelo Antonioni) demonstrate that cinema has the critical and self-reflective potential that Adorno attributes to all autonomous art; Bette Davis keeps alive the tradition of great acting; and if the nuances of the text are to be believed, Warner Brothers cartoons do not share the simple minded capitulation to **authority** that is the hall-mark of Disney. [AE]

Further reading: Adorno 1991a; Cook 1996; Held 1980.

Dada   A movement in modern art, emerging more or less simultaneously in Zürich and New York around 1916. It may be seen in part as a nihilistic and anarchic reaction to the First World War. It emphasised irrationalism, and a determination radically to challenge existing artistic conventions and institutions. Its buffoonery, irony and irreverence was aimed to shock, but more significantly, it was one of the first art movements to incorporate some degree of self-reflection on the social, economic and political **institutions** of the **artworld** into its own production. While it is difficult to identify typically stylistic elements in Dada, the use of montage and collage were important (not least in so far as they serve to disrupt the fluency and coherence of traditional artistic representation). Dada's immediate influence was on (the rather tamer) **surrealism**. However, it was perhaps not until the last third of the twentieth century that Dada had its most important impact, when 'ready-mades' by Duchamp (such as 'Fountain' (1914) a urinal displayed as art) and others became important precursors of **conceptual art**, and also of postmodernist approaches to art. (How many Dadaists does it take to change a light bulb? Banana.) [AE]

Further reading: Hedges 1983; Lewis 1990; Lynton 1980; Richter 1965.

dance   Dance has perhaps been rather neglected by the social sciences and by cultural studies. Dance is nonetheless an

106

important activity across society and in very different societies. At one extreme, there is the apparently elitist classical ballet. Within high **culture**, the conservatism of ballet is challenged by the **avant-garde** of 'modern dance'. While such activity may appear to aspire to an **aesthetic** autonomy that serves to divorce it from social and cultural concerns (although there have been a significant number of ballets with political themes and subject matter produced in the twentieth century), modern dance can be seen as a fundamental exploration of the **body**, and the conventions that govern its movement and presentation in contemporary culture. Ballroom, tap and various other dance forms should not be neglected as widely enjoyed leisure activities. The concept of folk dance suggests that dance can represent a community's expression of its **values**, **identity**, or resistance to external pressures, although such folk dance may also be a commercial construction (for example, for a tourist industry).

Angela McRobbie has pointed to dance, not simply as a rich and important part of youth **subculture**, but specifically as a part of feminine youth culture. Its neglect by cultural studies is therefore seen as symptomatic of the general neglect of female involvement in subcultures. McRobbie points to a number of different levels upon which dance can be approached. It is a leisure activity, a source of diffuse erotic pleasure, and form of exercise. Conversely, it may be a form of control of the female body and movement, through its emphasis on grace and beauty. Yet it is also a way in which the dancer can herself take control. For McRobbie, dance can be an extension of the private culture of femininity, into a public space. Dance is a form of evasion and an opportunity for fantasy, as the dancer is both out of control and therefore out of the reach of controlling forces. Dance is 'simultaneously a dramatic display of the self and the body, with an equally dramatic negation of the self and the body' (McRobbie 1991: 144). [AE]

Further reading: Foster 1996; Thomas 1993.

deconstruction   As the term itself implies, deconstruction grew out of **structuralism**. Jacques Derrida coined the term 'deconstruction' and he is the most significant representative of this philosophical and critical movement. As he explains the project of deconstruction in his vastly influential work *De la Grammatologie* (1967), its goal is to dismantle the structures of meaning so as to expose the premises on which they are built and to reveal the concepts of objectivity and linguistic autonomy as constructs. Derrida has always insisted that deconstruction cannot be treated as a clearly defined methodology; the chief reason for this being that deconstruction rejects the idea that there is a controlling intelligence which can recognise and explain the structuring principles of language (especially the system of **binary oppositions** which play such a dominant role in structuralism). In this sense, deconstruction is a development of structuralism which acknowledges that the massively ambitious goals of structuralism could only be envisaged on the grounds of a reductive understanding of language, society, history and cognition.

Because deconstruction is aware of the potential failures of any methodology, it adopts an intensely self-critical stance. First and foremost, it points out that the production of **meaning** at any particular moment is far removed from being a spontaneous expression of ideas and instead involves conventions and preconceptions that are deeply ingrained in language. Meaning is an expression brought forth by an autonomous mind, which explains Derrida's attack on the notion of 'presence', as suggesting control over the full range of meanings of any particular utterance. When deconstruction established itself in the late 1960s, its chief interest was in formulating a critique of language and representation. The contemporaneous claims of a group of intellectuals, notably Roland Barthes and Michel Foucault, concerning the 'death of the **author**' (a catch-phrase by means of which they argued for the subject's loss of control over the production of linguistic meaning) also subverted the view that language was a (neutral) form for the expression of ideas.

The American version of deconstruction was oriented towards a practical analysis of literary texts. Its chief representative, Paul de Man, focused on the rhetorical dimension of language and, together with Geoffrey Hartman and J. Hillis Miller, established deconstruction as a literary critical practice that was to be known as the 'Yale School' and flourished in the 1970s and 1980s.

Derrida's insistence on overturning the order of priority between speech and writing showed that there can be no spontaneous linguistic agency. He emphasises that whatever is said is preconditioned by the structural possibilities of what can be said and he uses the term dissemination to suggest that language possesses a self-regulating rationale. But then, language cannot be equated with the *logos* either and there is no metaphysical instance which guarantees linguistic stability. Or rather, language is affected by a negative force which disturbs order. By revealing logical inconsistencies, deconstruction points towards ideological complicities and disrupts the text's explicit claims. Deconstructive critical practices seek to identify power relations; not only as represented within the text itself but also as they precondition certain responses to the text. That is to say, deconstruction studies works of art through an analysis of the structural logic of the representational medium (language) and the tradition of interpretation associated with a particular kind of text as a means of resisting its ideological outlook.

Because deconstruction rejects any categorical distinction between text and context, it has frequently been accused of being apolitical. However, critics like Barbara Johnson, whose involvement with **feminism** and **Marxism** made a political commitment imperative, showed that deconstruction had to rethink its relation to issues of class, gender and race. In recent years, prominent critics such as Gayatri Spivak have referred to themselves as Marxist feminist deconstructionists. Adherents to this line pursue the goal of a critique of ideology when they engage in an analysis of cultural definitions and distinctions (such as those between male and female; black and white; central and marginal). Even though the play of meaning which characterises all language also applies to the language of the critic of ideology, this should not be understood as incapacitating any kind of intervention but rather as a warning that claims made in an authoritarian manner are particularly likely to be dismantled by language's auto-deconstructive potential. [CK]

Further reading: de Man 1979; Derrida 1976; Holub 1992; Johnson 1980; Norris 1987; Ryan 1982.

determinism   In philosophy, determinism has generally been contrasted with freewill. The latter holds that humans are able to make choices and act upon them, the former that our choices are determined by other forces, and our actions, therefore, can be accounted for in, for instance, causal terms. On a broader 'cultural' level, the concept of determinism is an analogous one: a determinist would be someone who argues that social and cultural activity are causally derived from more immanent forces (for example, the role of **power** relations in the constitution of **subjectivity**). A determinist may hold (as traditional Marxists do) that **ideology** and its accompanying cultural forms are a direct consequence of the base-structure of economic relations; or, as with **Social Darwinism** that there are basic underlying social laws which, as in the natural world, determine which social types are best according to the dictates of 'the survival of the fittest' principle; or that what language you speak determines what thoughts you can have. It might be added that any extreme causal determinism (such as that advocated by psychologist B.F. Skinner) founders on an objection presented by Michael Oakeshott: namely, that the determinist, in order to be making a true claim, must also include the theory itself within their account (i.e. be self-reflexive), and thus an all-out theory of determinism is on its own terms something determined in advance (a problem linked to **epistemology**). At the social level, this view is mainly significant with regard to the question of how much autonomy **individuals** have. [PS]

Further reading: Honderich 1993; Oakeshott 1975; Skinner 1974.

deviance   The concept of 'deviance' may be understood to develop, within **sociology**, in reaction to orthodox criminology. While criminology studies crime, and thus the breaking of law, the sociology of deviance looks to a broader range of activity. The behaviour of the deviant deviates from some generally accepted, or consensual, **norm** of behaviour. The alcoholic may break no laws, but his or her behaviour deviates from society's normal expectations as to what is a reasonable level of alcohol consumption.

This simple definition is problematic in at least two respects. First, it assumes that there is a pre-existing consensus within society as to what is normal. In reply, it may be suggested that this consensus is, in large part, generated through the pursuit and definition of deviance. Cohen's (1980) analysis of 'moral panics' illustrates this. In a moral panic, a group or individual comes to be defined, particularly through extensive **mass media** coverage, as a threat to the **values** and interests of the society. The public are thereby sensitised, not merely to the apparent threat, but also to the values that are threatened.

The second way in which the initial definition oversimplifies the phenomenon of deviance is that it assumes that deviance occurs simply by breaking some norm. There are two problems with this. First, rules and norms are complex, and the precise application of them often depends upon subtle and contextual interpretation. Under certain circumstances, all rules can legitimately be broken. This entails that there is always scope for negotiation and argument, as to whether or not a particular act was deviant. This, for example, is typical of pupils' disobedience of school rules. The second point, that in some respects emerges from this, is that someone only then becomes a deviant through a social process, occurring after the initial violation of a norm. Many members of society break norms, and do so frequently. Only some of these people come to be recognised by others, and by themselves, as deviants. This process is typically theorised as **labelling**. Deviance entails that a person has come to be described according to a value-laden term (so that, for example, the drinker becomes an alcoholic, the gourmet a glutton). Members of certain groups (such as the more affluent and educated **classes**) may have the power and resources to resist such labels (which in turn may partly explain the higher rates of criminality and deviance recorded amongst members of subordinate classes and **ethnic** groups). The public recognition and application of certain labels (such as hooligan, thief, drug taker, child abuser) will serve to isolate the individual from normal society. The individual may therefore take shelter within a deviant subculture, so that the initial, and possibly aberrant act of rule breaking, becomes typical of his or her behaviour. Deviance may therefore be seen to be 'amplified' by the very social institutions (such as the police and courts) that exist to control deviance. (See also **subculture**.) [AE]

Further reading: Aggleton 1987; Downes and Rock 1982.

diachronic   see **synchronic/diachronic**

dialectical and historical materialism   Historical materialism is the theory of social change developed by Karl Marx and Friedrich Engels. History is divided into a series of epochs or **modes of production**. Each is characterised by a distinct economy and a distinct **class** structure. Historical change is fuelled by the progressive expansion of the productive power of the economy (and thus the development of technology, or the **forces of production**) and is manifest in overt class conflict and revolution.

Dialectical materialism encompasses those aspects of Marxist philosophy other than the theory of history, including **epistemology** and ontology. It became the dogmatic official philosophy of the Soviet Union. The term was not used by Marx or Engels, with attempts to develop a coherent dialectical materialist philosophy beginning with Plekhanov and Lenin, building on Engels's *Anti-Dühring* (1947), and *Dialectics of Nature* (1973). Dialectical materialism is characterised by its materialism and its rejection of any form of scepticism.

The material world is held to have primacy over the mental, so that the body is the precondition for consciousness. It is held that this material world is, in principle, knowable through the work of the empirical sciences. In addition, the philosophy is **dialectical**, in that it presents reality as in development. This is to argue, not simply that there is change in the material world, but rather that reality is characterised by the emergence of qualitatively new properties. [AE]

Further reading: Callinicos 1983; Cohen 1978; Cornforth 1971; Ruben 1979.

dialectics In philosophy, the term 'dialectics' originally referred to the argumentative style found in Plato's dialogues. Socrates, Plato's main protagonist, would interrogate other philosophers, thinkers and assorted experts, most typically as to what they meant by a particular concept (such as 'justice', or the 'good'). The Socratic method typically worked by exposing the shallow and ultimately incoherent understanding that others had of concepts, but without Socrates necessarily providing an adequate and coherent definition of his own.

The term 'dialectic' took on a related, but distinctive meaning in German philosophy in the late eighteenth and early nineteenth century, in the work of Kant, Fichte and Hegel. It was Fichte who proposed the common characterisation of the structure of a dialectical argument as thesis, antithesis and synthesis. That is to say, one thesis would be proven. An equally good proof would be provided for an alternative and incompatible thesis. The **contradiction** between the thesis and antithesis would then be resolved typically by a leap to a different way of looking at the problem, so that the initial contradiction is explained away by recognising the limits upon one's reasoning and knowledge that taken for granted presuppositions placed upon the original argument.

Hegel's dialectic is rather more subtle and complex than this. The three terms of Hegel's dialectic may best be seen as universal, particular and individual. The universal is a stage of naïve self-certainty. A single, all-encompassing entity exists.

(For example, the new-born human being knows nothing of the world other than its own existence.) Yet there is no real knowledge here, for that only occurs when there is differentiation or sundering. The entity will only come to know itself if it recognises what it is not (and thus encounters some **other**). The universal is therefore particularised, sundered, or broken up. (The pure subjectivity of the new-born infant encounters an alien object.) This stage of particularisation gives rise to a fruitful period of growth and self-discovery, not merely for the individual human. This is how Hegel characterises human history as a whole. This period ends when the subject recognises itself in the object. The universality of the first stage of the dialectic is then restored, but in a new, profoundly self-conscious form. The subject has returned to itself, but has learnt of itself through the journey. (It is now incidental that many great nineteenth-century novels, such as Goethe's *Wilhelm Meister*, and Dickens' *Great Expectations*, manifest a similar structure (that of the *Bildungsroman*), as the hero discovers himself or herself through a series of adventures in a strange and difficult world.)

Hegel's dialectic is not simply a structure of argument, but is the very structure of the cosmos, manifest from the grandest levels (the development of human history, or the movements of the planets) to the humblest (the growth of a plant). **Marx** uses this model to explain the development of human history through a series of epochs or **modes of production**. History begins as humanity breaks out of the naïve universality of primitive communism, and is forced into class society. Here humans make history, but not under the conditions of their choosing. Which is to say, the products of subjective human action confront humans as alien objects. In communism, this form of history ends, for then humans will have understood themselves as social beings (and will thus have the self-consciousness of the Hegelian individual), and will make history and society as they choose.

In twentieth-century cultural theory, the **Frankfurt School** philosopher, Theodor Adorno, and the French psychoanalyst Jacques Lacan, have, independently, made remarkably similar reinterpretations of Hegel. By claiming to know the final stage of the dialectic, Hegel presumes to know and be able to describe absolute truth. Both Adorno and Lacan reject this authoritarianism of the presumption to know absolute truth. Adorno therefore proposes a 'negative dialectics'. That is to say, the dialectical process is arrested at the second stage. The best that we can then know is the contradictions and inconsistencies, both in the world and in our knowledge of the world, but we cannot presume to escape them. Similarly, Lacan is concerned to analyse the ways in which we spend our lives struggling to restore an 'imaginary' universality, before we were sundered from unity with our mother (and thrown into an empty and incomplete world of selfhood and language). Our lives are the pursuit of substitutes for this lost universality. The idea of a psychoanalytic 'cure', that would restore unity (and thus achieve an Hegelian individual), is rejected. [AE]

Further reading: Adorno 1973b; Hegel 1975a; Lacan 1977a; Mepham and Ruben 1979; Rosen 1982.

dictatorship of the proletariat   In Marxist-Leninism, the dictatorship of the **proletariat** occurs directly after the revolution that brings down **capitalism**, and yet before the achievement of communism. The phrase suggests that state power, that was previously in the hands of the dominant **bourgeoisie**, is transferred to the newly dominant proletariat, in order to manage the transition to communism. Crucially, in communism, there will be no state (for it will have withered away during the preceding period of socialism). The term 'dictatorship' is misleading to a degree. Lenin (1992), in striving to break away from the institutional constraints of the old Tsarist state, conceived of a participatory direct democracy, grounded in workers' councils. [AE]

Further reading: Draper 1987; Ehrenberg 1992.

difference/*différance*   **Difference**: In terms of the **structuralism** advocated by linguist Ferdinand de Saussure, difference

115

constitutes the basis upon which **signs** have **meaning**. Difference in this sense refers to the structurally related phonetic differences between elements of language as they are situated within the system of signs which constitute *langue* (i.e. the fundamental structure of meanings which must be in place at any given time if a speaker is to be able to speak). Thus, meaning is regarded within this model as a system of differences.

Différance: In the work of French philosopher Jacques Derrida, '*différance*', likewise, constitutes the conditions of possibility for meaning in language. As opposed to Saussure's fixed conception of meaning as a structure of difference, however, Derrida's neologism is meant to capture the ceaseless movement of meaning which is a condition of its production, i.e. that meaning is simultaneously 'differential' and 'deferred'. *Différance* is, when spoken, indistinguishable from 'difference', and thereby supplements the Saussurean sense of difference by indicating a semantic slippage (made apparent here only in writing rather than speech) which operates so as to prevent the meaning of a sign achieving a state of self-presence. In other words, meaning on this view is never entirely present within language at a given moment, but is conceived of as a chain of signification that remains incomplete. As such, *différance* is regarded by Derrida as signifying neither a word nor a concept, but as the condition of the functioning of words and concepts. This notion has been deployed by exponents of literary **critical theory**. Derrida's own elaboration of it, however, is situated within the context of a sustained analysis of the western metaphysical tradition, and attempts to use the term as a means of decoding the economy of meaning in a whole variety of texts (i.e. as a kind of meta-concept) run counter to much of the spirit of Derrida's own thinking. [PS]

Further reading: Derrida 1973, 1987.

discourse   There is no single meaning to the word discourse, even if one takes it in a technical sense. Of course, a 'discourse' can mean simply a dialogue between speakers; but it has also come, within linguistics for instance, to mean the way in which linguistic elements are conjoined so as to constitute a structure of **meaning** larger than the sum of its parts. A variant on this sense is also, however, present within conceptions of discourse important to cultural studies. Of the various theories that have been put forward, the conceptions of discourse present within the work of Michel Foucault and Jean-François Lyotard are relevant to cultural theory.

On Foucault's view, various social practices and institutions (for example, those of education and politics, religion and the law) are both constituted by and situated within forms of discourse (that is, ways of speaking about the world of social experience). A discourse, on this view, is a means of both producing and organising meaning within a social context. **Language** is thus a key notion within this view, for it is language which embodies discourses. As such, a discourse constitutes a 'discursive formation', i.e. discourses are conceived of as signifying ways of systematically organising human experience of the social world in language and thereby constituting modes of knowledge. A key function of a discursive formation, on this view, is not merely its inclusive role but also its exclusive role: discursive formations provide rules of justification for what counts as (for example) knowledge within a particular context, and at the same time stipulate what does *not* count as knowledge in that context. On Foucault's account, it follows that the realm of discourse can have a repressive function. Accompanying this notion of discourse is the contention that such concepts as subjectivity cannot be understood as they have generally been within, say, the political tradition of **liberalism**. Whereas, for a liberal, a subject is a more or less unproblematic political entity, from the viewpoint of Foucaultean discourse analysis, subjectivity itself must be constituted by discourse, and hence language. It should be added that if this is the case, then it seems strange to seek to characterise any form of discourse as being 'repressive', for if there is no subject that is not constituted by discourse, then one is entitled to ask about who or what is being 'repressed'.

Lyotard's notion of 'genres of discourse' (see *The Differend: Phrases in Dispute* (1983)) has some similarities with Foucault's conception of discursive formations. However, Lyotard came to propound his views in the light of reading a range of texts from the tradition of **analytic philosophy** (e.g. late as well as early Ludwig Wittgenstein, Bertrand Russell, Saul Kripke) as well as writers from the tradition of **continental philosophy**. Lyotard's notion represents a cross-fertilisation between these two traditions. From the analytics he takes such notions as that of 'rigid designation', which is a term used to describe the function of proper names (this is derived from Kripke's *Naming and Necessity* (1980). Thus Kripke argues that a proper name – note that in his view, even 'gold' counts as a proper name in this sense – has as its function the role of fixing and thereby stipulating the same entity in any number of possible worlds, achieved through an act of 'initial baptism'; in analytic philosophy this has led to the adoption by some of *a posteriori* **essentialism**), and Wittgenstein's conception of 'language games'. From the continental tradition Lyotard takes some of the basic postulates of **post-structuralism** (for instance, the view that the meaning of a term like subjectivity is constituted with language). A (genre of) discourse, on Lyotard's account, is a way of organising reality according to a particular set of rules. These rules tell us how to link together the basic units of language ('phrases'). On this view, genres of discourse have the following distinguishing features: (i) as already mentioned, providing the rules of justification whereby phrases can be linked, (ii) the stipulation of purposes – i.e. one only links phrases with a view to some particular goal or other. A Lyotardean view, therefore, takes discourse as being fundamental in organising meaning, although the basic linguistic units of language are not of themselves 'discursive' in nature (a phrase must be 'seized' by a genre of discourse in order to be codified and thus given a particular meaning).

What is common to conceptions of discourse in the work of figures like Foucault and Lyotard is the notion that language, understood as discourse, is primary when it comes to the issue of how we are to understand questions of culture and society. Moreover, a rational account of social structures is held to be problematised by this approach. Thus, on a Lyotardean view, the plurality of genres of discourse functions to prevent the assertion of any single genre's primacy with regard to establishing what ought to count as true – since all genres are organised according to particular purposes and there are a multiplicity of purposes it follows that no single genre could be said to be adequate to the task of establishing a meta-narrative for this purpose. Forms of this attitude have been criticised by Jürgen Habermas, whose approach is markedly different. For Habermas, discourse can be interpreted in terms of its possibility to take on the form of regulative ideal (an 'ideal speech situation'), which would serve to preserve a critical space for thought which is not subject to the contextualised pressures of particularised interests or **power**. [PS]

Further reading: Foucault 1972; Kripke 1980; Lee 1992; Lyotard 1988; Schiffrin 1993; White 1987.

division of labour 'Division of labour' refers to the differentiation of tasks and occupations within a society. Three distinct forms of, or at least approaches to, the division of labour may be identified. In economics, the division of labour was recognised, in the eighteenth century, by Adam Smith (1976), to be the source of the increased productivity of the industrial capitalist economies. While within a craft economy, a single worker could spend a day making a pin, in a factory, the production of a pin would be divided into a dozen different tasks, with each worker devoted to a single task. For Marx (1975), the division of labour is a key evil of capitalism, in so far as it results in **alienation** (that is to say, the work process becomes meaningless to the workers). In **sociology**, Durkheim (1984), writing at the end of the nineteenth century, identifies the division of labour as central to explaining the difference between pre-industrial and industrial societies, but now in terms of the way in which the societies are held together as stable units. In industrial society, with an extensive division of labour, each individual is dependent upon everyone else for the provision of the bulk of his or her needs. The undesirable correlate of this is **anomie**, or a loss of moral **value** and meaning in social life. More recently, feminist theorists have addressed the problem of the sexual division of labour. The sexual division refers to an allocation of tasks and occupations between men and women, both within the public economy and within the domestic economy of the household. A 'horizontal' division exists in that certain tasks and occupations within the public economy (which tend to mirror domestic activities, such as cleaning and nursing) are predominantly allocated to women, and equally women are excluded from certain supposedly male occupations (such as engineering). Similarly, a 'vertical' division exists, in that women's occupations themselves typically enjoy lower **status**, lower pay and less power than male occupations, and that women are disproportionately employed only in the lower ranks of any profession or occupation. [AE]

Further reading: Gorz 1973; Walby 1986.

dramaturgical model   The dramaturgical model attempts to explain everyday life by drawing an analogy with theatre. The model therefore emphasises the idea that social actors are playing roles, and that a key part of social interaction is the way in which these actors present those roles to each other. Goffman (1959) provides a justly famous account of the different roles that waiters play in the dining room and the kitchen of a restaurant. The polite and deferential behaviour before the customer is replaced by a more relaxed and indeed cynical behaviour before fellow workers. This approach, in practice, perhaps has less explanatory power than it has power in focusing descriptions of face to face social interaction (or 'encounters'). It does, however, raise important questions about the nature of personal **identity** in social interaction. For Goffman, we change not simply roles, but also **selves**, as we move from one encounter to another. [AE]

Further reading: Berger 1963; Burns 1992.

drive   'Drive' is a translation of the Freudian term '*Trieb*' (*treiben*, to push) and not 'Instinkt'. Since there is considerable confusion in the psychoanalytic literature on the difference between these two terms, it is important to differentiate them carefully. Lacan's criticism of Anglo-American psychoanalysis attempts to focus on the theoretical difficulties that have arisen from the mistranslation of the term 'drive' as 'instinct'. '*Instinkt*' appears closer to the behaviour of animals: it is a behavioural pattern that is predetermined genetically and helps the zoologist to sort an animal into a species. On the other hand, '*Trieb*' is less amenable to generic slotting and can take on idiosyncratic forms in the subject. Unlike instinct, which may be seasonal, drive is a 'constant force' that propels the subject. Hence Lacan locates it at the level of the Real – the Real being that which always returns to the same place.

Freud introduced the concept of drive in his *On Sexuality: Three Essays on the Theory of Sexuality* (1905). The drive has a *source*, a *pressure*, an *object* and an *aim*. The source of the drive is an erogenous zone in the body. The pressure is the intensity of the drive. The aim is always satisfaction. The object is that through which the aim is sought to be obtained. Unlike an instinct, the relationship between the drive and its object is arbitrary. Lacan does not hold on to the distinction between the life and death drives that Freud introduced in *Beyond the Pleasure Principle* (1955). For Lacan, all drives partake of the death drive. This results from the paradox that biological life is mediated by **sexuality**. Since sexuality is based in human communities on a system of signification, of representation, it implies the absence, the death of the thing in place of the signifier. [SKS]

Further reading: Freud 1977, 1984, 1991a, 1991b; Jaanus 1995; Lacan 1977a; Laplanche and Pontalis 1988.

écriture feminine A number of French **feminist** theorists, notably including Hélène Cixous and Luce Irigaray, have developed the idea and practice of an *écriture feminine*, a form of writing and reading that resists being appropriated by the dominant patriarchal **culture**. It is argued, developing on the **psychoanalysis** of Lacan, that **patriarchal** culture privileges a hierarchical way of thinking, grounded in a series of oppositions (such as male/female; culture/nature; intelligible/sensitive; active/passive), with the male dominant over the female. The male is active and looks, in comparison to the passive female who is merely observed. Femininity is therefore only present as it is observed by the male, and crucially, while the feminine is the **other** to the masculine, for Cixous, the male is interested in this other only in order to return to itself – that is to say that the masculine desire for woman is ultimately a self-love (1987). The woman is therefore excluded from patriarchal culture, not least in that she is a non-presence even to herself. The woman is separated from her own body and her own desires. The woman simply cannot make sense of herself in a language that is designed to articulate and conceptualise masculinity. *Écriture feminine* appeals back to the bodily experience that is prior to the separation of the child from the mother, and thus to that which is prior to the imposition of the father's law.

Cixous seeks to recover the feminine in terms of its plurality. The relationship of maternity (the 'm/other relation') serves to subvert the masculine concept of **subjectivity**. While the male subject is unified and autonomous, the experience of child birth and nurturing, for Cixous, suggests a disruption of the self and genuine encounter with the other. The relation is a 'gift' economy, where everything is given, but nothing is expected in return. A similar relationship in uncovered in bisexuality (which in turn highlights the masculine denial of its own femininity). Bisexuality, that is seen to be characteristic of women, offers a *jouissance* (or ecstasy) that is distinct from male desire and pleasure, for it entails an interplay of difference and the other. This *jouissance* cannot be described in masculine language. Similarly, *écriture feminine* cannot be theorised, for it attempts to facilitate the return of that which has been repressed by the imposition of the symbolic and its patriarchal law. In Cixous's own writing, this is expressed in the use of pun and wordplay, and a disruption of traditional oppositions, such as those of theory/fiction; or theory/autobiography.

Irigaray's writing has explored the possibility of a feminine writing through readings of the philosophical tradition that exposed what is repressed or passed over in silence (including the **body**, and the elements of water, earth, fire and air) (1991), and the exploration of a 'feminine god' (of multiplicity and flow) that is outside the grasp of patriarchal religion and theology, but also is 'yet to come' (1986: 8). [AE]

elaborated and restricted codes   A pair of concepts referring to different modes of language use, developed by Basil Bernstein in order to explain the correlation between social **class** and academic achievement. An utterance made in a restricted code is highly context dependent. Interpretation of the meaning of the utterance will be dependent upon knowledge of a taken-for-granted stock of values and ideas, inherent to a particular community. In contrast, an utterance in an elaborated code seeks to be independent of any particular context, by explicating the meanings, assumptions and values underpinning it. Basically it is argued that working-class families encourage the learning of language only within a restricted code, while elaborated codes are used in schools, thereby placing working-class pupils at a disadvantage. [AE]

elite   An elite is a small group that has leadership in some sphere of social life (such as a cultural elite), or has leadership of society as a whole. The elite is typically understood to be relatively homogeneous and with a largely closed membership. Modern elite theory developed in the early years of the twentieth century, through the work of Vilfredo Pareto (1963), Gaetano Mosca (1939) and others. This theory was opposed to **socialism**, not least in so far as it argued for the inevitability of the division of all societies into an elite (with superior organisation abilities), and an inferior mass. More significantly, at a theoretical level, elite theory suggested, again in contrast to socialism and **Marxism**, that the power of the dominant group in society did not have to be rooted in economic power. In so far as **classes** are economically defined, elite theory therefore offered an alternative account of **social stratification** and hierarchies than that provided by class theory. In this light, the work of C. Wright Mills (1956) on the 'power elite' is significant. Mills argued that contemporary America was dominated by an elite that unified three key spheres of society: industry, politics and the military. Unlike earlier elite theorists, Mills' concern was to expose the elite, and the adverse effects that it had on democracy, rather than to celebrate its inevitability.

In the study of **culture**, elite theory has had its greatest impact through mass society theory, and in the assumption that there is an inherently superior elite culture. This culture is seen, at worst, to be threatened and eroded by the contemporary **mass media**, or at best, that the mass media are incapable of serving elite culture. As such, elite theory explicitly or implicitly judges **popular culture** by the standards of elite culture, and finds it wanting. It is therefore typically insensitive to the subtleties and complexities of popular culture. [AE]

Further reading: Bottomore 1993; Scott 1990.

empiricism A philosophical approach which stresses the primacy of experience in all human understanding. Empiricism is usually dated from the works of philosopher John Locke, whose *An Essay Concerning Human Understanding* (1690) argued that all of our ideas and concepts ultimately derive from our experience of the world. Locke famously stated that the human mind is something akin to a blank sheet of paper, which is subsequently 'written upon' by experience. Bishop Berkeley and Scottish **Enlightenment** philosopher David Hume are also regarded as key exponents of empiricism, although their approaches differ in some ways from Locke's. The works of Locke and Hume inspired Immanuel Kant (especially in response to the latter's scepticism concerning the possibility of universally valid knowledge) to produce the *Critique of Pure Reason* (1781). Hume's *A Treatise of Human Nature* (1739) (later recast as *An Enquiry Concerning Human Understanding*) famously deployed the empiricist approach to argue that the basis of all human reasoning resides in custom or habit (in other words, that social structures exert a determining effect with regard to our conceptual abilities). [PS]

Further reading: Hume 1990; Locke 1975; Priest 1990; Woolhouse 1988.

Enlightenment, The An intellectual movement which occurred in France (but also in Britain in the form of the 'Scottish Enlightenment') during the latter part of the eighteenth century. Key thinkers associated with The Enlightenment were d'Alembert, Diderot, Hume, Kant, Rousseau, Smith and Voltaire. The maxim propounded by Kant, 'Dare to understand!', sums up well the underlying optimism which spurred much Enlightenment thinking. This thinking was characterised by a number of significant attitudes: a faith in the ability of reason to solve social as well as intellectual and scientific problems, an aggressively critical perspective on what were perceived as the regressive influences of tradition and institutional religion (the latter expressed in Voltaire's famous declaration concerning the Christian religion: 'Crush the infamy!'), a faith in humanism and the ideal of progress, the espousal of a politics of toleration and free thinking. In spite of the generally critical stance towards religion, not all Enlightenment thinkers were, like Diderot, avowed atheists; Voltaire espoused a passionately held belief in a non-Christian deity, whilst Hume was phlegmatically agnostic with regard to such matters, although his famous criticism of the belief in miracles demonstrates a typical Enlightenment commitment to a sceptical view of metaphysical beliefs in the light of advances in the physical sciences after Newton's *Principia*. That said, Hume's thought often cuts against the grain of the Enlightenment faith in reason, while Rousseau's writings are often associated with the development of **Romanticism**.

Commentators such as Habermas continue to adhere to the basic project of Enlightenment as set out by Kant, i.e. an adherence to a critical project of modernity which has as its aim the articulation of a rational basis for discourses of knowledge, and political and social criticism. Lyotard (most notorious for his early (1979) espousal of **postmodernism**) also takes the Enlightenment to signify a key moment in the development of critical reason, namely the initiation of postmodernity (found in the writings of Kant – principally the *Critique of Judgement*). Other thinkers in the nineteenth and twentieth centuries have either reacted against the Enlightenment project, or attempted to rearticulate it in diverse ways. For example, (i) Nietzsche's thinking (in spite of his current association with postmodern anti-Enlightenment thought) without doubt owes a significant debt to the Enlightenment tradition, especially his books of the late 1870s and early 1880s (*Human, All-Too-Human* (1878), for instance, was dedicated to the memory of Voltaire when it was first published, and adopts a methodological scepticism which shows the influence of Enlightenment thought); and (ii) Horkheimer and Adorno's work (c.f. *Dialectic of Enlightenment* (1947)), which seeks to unpack the key methodological presuppositions underlying the Enlightenment conception of rationality while adhering to its critical ideals. [PS]

Further reading: Berlin 1979; Gay 1988a; Habermas 1988.

episteme   A term in the work of Michel Foucault (see *The Order of Things* (1970)). An episteme is a form of knowledge. In modernity, particular forms of **discourse**, Foucault argues, have provided the basic, and limited, concepts which ground the sciences (for example, a particular **epistemological** conception of the **subject**). Together, these constitute the modern episteme. [PS]

Further reading: Foucault 1970; Habermas 1988; Smart 1984.

epistemology   A philosophical term meaning 'theory of knowledge'. Epistemology concerns itself with the analysis of what is meant by the term 'knowledge' itself, and with questions about (i) what we can be said to know (the limits and scope of knowledge), (ii) its reliability, and what constitutes justification or warrant for holding a belief and thereby deeming that belief to be 'knowledge'. Thus, philosophers may ask: 'Is there any difference between knowing and believing something to be the case?' or, 'To what extent does the acquisition of knowledge depend upon reason or the senses?' There have been a wide variety of approaches to this issue. Plato (*c.* 428–348 BC) held that our rational capabilities are an intrinsic property of our minds and are the sole source of knowledge (a view usually placed under the rubric of 'rationalism'). The exponents of **empiricism**, in contrast, argue that human understanding and hence knowledge is a result of sense experience alone. Hence, according to empiricism, what we know is the consequence of our ability to have perceptions of the world via our senses (this view is primarily associated with thinkers such as Locke, Berkeley and Hume).

Against the empiricists, the German philosopher Immanuel Kant argued that there are necessary conditions of knowing that cannot be reduced to mere experience. Thus, Kant offered an account of the '*a priori*' conditions of the possibility of experience. *A priori* judgements can be arrived at independently of experience. On this view, we have a form of knowledge (*a priori* knowledge) which exists prior to, and independently of, any empirical knowledge. Indeed, according to Kant such knowledge (for example, the 'pure intuitions' of time and space) is the precondition of the possibility of our having any knowledge of experience at all. One can best understand Kant's point by way of a comparison with Locke's empiricist conception of the mind. According to Locke, the human mind is like a 'blank sheet' which is then 'written' upon by sensory experience. This view, however, is open to the objection that if the mind is capable of having experiences then this must be so in virtue of some structure that it has prior to having any particular experience. If our minds were simply 'blank sheets' then how would we be able to recognise any experience as an experience in the first place? The ability to have experiences, Kant argues, cannot therefore be derived from any particular experience, hence there must be *a priori* judgements which constitute the conditions of the possibility of experience. Kant holds that there are two kinds of *a priori* knowledge, one based upon 'analytic' judgements, the other upon 'synthetic' judgements. Analytic *a priori* knowledge would include such propositions as 'all triangles have three sides' (i.e. it is true by definition, and we need no experiential data to establish its truth). Thus, in thinking a subject, A, and a predicate, B, the predicate is contained within A as part of it. In contrast, in synthetic judgements the predicate, B, is external to the subject, A (*Critique of Pure Reason*, A7/B11). Synthetic judgements thus involve an act of inference which goes beyond the scope of the analytically derived concepts one has at one's disposal independently of experience (i.e. such judgements involve the empirical or external world). All judgements concerning experience are, for Kant, synthetic, and all knowledge that has any genuine value is knowledge about experience.

In addition to such debates as those listed above concerning where our knowledge comes from, it is worth noting that philosophers also tend to draw distinctions between *kinds* of knowing. For example: (i) 'knowing that . . .', which involves knowledge claims that are factual and capable of being established by way of reference to evidence; (ii) 'knowing how . . .', the kind of knowledge required to do certain kinds of things (such as riding a bicycle); (iii) 'knowledge by acquaintance', which includes such things as knowledge gained through individual experience, or personal knowledge (e.g. memories) and is not necessarily verifiable in the way that the kind of knowledge mentioned in (i) is; (iv) 'knowledge by description', which involves knowledge that is derived from our being informed about certain relevant facts, characteristics, etc. that pertain to something or someone (e.g. 'Shakespeare' is the person who wrote *Hamlet, King Lear* and other plays, was married to Anne Hathaway, and so on). As is often the case with philosophers, there is some considerable disagreement as to the usefulness of these definitions.

Significant amongst other perspectives on knowledge are the views put forward by thinkers such as Friedrich Nietzsche (1844–1900) and, following him, Michel Foucault (1926–84). There are many possible interpretations of Nietzsche's attitude to questions of knowledge (his work has, for instance, certain parallels with some of the ideas central to **pragmatism**). However, one dominant interpretation of knowledge that has exerted an influence upon views associated with **post-modernism** and **post-structuralism** is derived from the manner in which Foucault interpreted Nietzsche's work. For Nietzsche, 'knowledge' is not something which can be analysed properly in the absence of considerations of relations of **power**. This is because, on Nietzsche's view, what we deem 'knowledge' is in fact the expression of an assemblage of drives and interests (see for instance the posthumously published notes which go to make up *The Will to Power*). This attitude parallels Nietzsche's interpretation of the meaning of morality, offered in *On the Genealogy of Morals*

(1887). Here, Nietzsche offers an account of ethical systems which identifies the values they espouse with their genealogical heritage: 'slave' morals valorise the 'meek' because the slave is a victim; 'noble' morality, in contrast, values what is powerful. Both slave and master. in short, in one way or another affirm themselves through their moralities. Foucault developed an argument on the basis of this account which sought to analyse knowledge forms as expressions of determinate social interests (see **discourse** and **genealogy**). Whatever the respective merits and problems with their views one thing is clear: neither Nietzsche (as represented in this way) nor Foucault have an 'epistemology' in the way in which other thinkers, such as Kant, have had. Indeed, if we are persuaded by them, then it is a short step to abandoning epistemology in favour of an intricate analysis of social relations (although what the status of such analyses would be as forms of knowledge is perhaps an awkward issue, especially for Foucault).

However, it is not clear that one can abandon epistemology so easily. Thus, as Nietzsche himself noted at the beginning of *Human, All-Too-Human* (1878–80) providing an analysis of something's origins does not necessarily count as an exhaustive explanation of it. Thus, whatever the conditions or intentions that gave rise to a discourse, it may not be a straightforward matter to reduce its meaning merely to those conditions. Equally, although he certainly did not construct a formal 'theory of knowledge', Nietzsche did not entirely abandon the temptation to pose epistemic questions. Thus, many of his observations remain relevant to the study of epistemology (for instance, it is arguable that from the *Genealogy* one could derive a normative account of justification which could be situated comfortably within the domain of epistemological enquiry). Equally, the genealogical method developed by Foucault can be subjected to various criticisms derived from alternative readings of Nietzsche (a good example is offered by Peter Dews, in Krell and Wood 1988). What is offered by this kind of perspective that is perhaps most significant is its inherently critical attitude to **Cartesian** epistemology, for in so far as power is constitutive of modes of knowledge it is also constitutive of the knower. [PS]

Further reading: Dancy 1985; Dancy and Sosa 1992; Foucault 1970, 1972, 1977b; Krell and Wood 1988; Nietzsche 1968a, 1968b.

essentialism   The view that there are essential properties which define what something is, and without which it could not be what it is. One form of essentialism ascribes these properties in virtue of a definition being given. For example, an essentialist of this kind would hold that there are certain essential properties which define what the term 'gold' refers to (a particular atomic weight, colour, properties of hardness, malleability, etc.). In turn, any piece of gold must have those properties which are included within the definition of 'gold' in order to be designated as real gold. Whether or not adoption of this view commits one to holding that these properties must exist in reality *prior to* the act of naming an object, so that a definition, if it is true is *a priori* true (see Lyotard's criticism of essentialism in *The Differend: Phrases in Dispute* (1988), section 88) is perhaps an open question.

Note also that there is a difference between this form of essentialism and the view which holds that objects must possess a hidden, concrete or 'real' essence which in turn causes us to attribute to them their observable properties (i.e. their 'nominal essence'). This position was first elaborated by empiricist philosopher John Locke. A variant of this view was revived in the 1980s in the wake of American philosopher Saul Kripke's arguments about the nature of proper names. Simply put, Kripke's account implies that since language succeeds in referring to things by means of proper names (Kripke calls such names 'rigid designators', it should be noted that, for him, instances such as 'gold' are proper names), what it refers to must possess properties which make the referent of the name what it is independently of that language. This position is often referred to as '*a posteriori* [i.e. after the fact] essentialism'. This is because on Kripke's account it is only the act of naming and thereby fixing a reference that is necessary *a priori* (i.e. before the fact), whereas the particular properties selected when one names something may be 'accidental' to what is referred to, and it could turn out that what is named does not have all or some of these properties. [PS]

Further reading: Kripke 1980.

ethnic/ethnicity   Generally a word used to refer to different racial or national groups which identifies them in virtue of their shared practices, **norm**s and systems of belief. By terming groups 'ethnic' they are usually implicitly identified as being in a **minority**, and as possessing a different range of attitudes or **traditions** to the ones held and adhered to by the majority of a society's members. In turn, 'ethnicity' denotes the self-awareness on the part of a particular group of its own cultural distinctiveness. As is self-evident, the assertion of ethnic identity can be unifying or divisive in equal measure – often depending upon who is asserting it, of whom, and in which context. In some situations the self-aware possession of an ethnic identity could be a unifying experience (for instance, a point of focus for a given community). In other instances, the attribution of 'ethnicity' might well be regarded as a provocative and injuring form of **stereotyping** embodying **racism**. Thus, the issue turns upon *who* actively designates one particular social grouping as 'ethnic': for to be defined as 'ethinic' and to assert one's own 'ethnicity' are two very different things. In both cases, what is at stake may well be an issue of **power**, in so far as the affirmation of ethnicity can be read as an assertion of identity in the face of a social status quo, whereas to be defined in this way by 'majority opinion' others may well be an oppressive manifestation of the power of more dominant forces and interests within a society. [PS]

Further reading: Foster 1960.

ethnocentrism   The tendency to refer exclusively to one's own cultural **value**s and practices, even if engaged with others who may not share those values. Likewise, the tendency to describe and judge the systems of value and dominant practices of other **culture**s from the standpoint of one's own. Such an attitude has connections with the **stereotyping** of others and can be a feature of **racism** and **prejudice**. [PS]

Further reading: Allport 1980.

ethnography   Ethnography is the approach to research most closely associated with **cultural anthropology**, although it has played a central part in the development of cultural studies, for example, in the work of Richard Hoggart (1957), Phil Cohen (1980), Paul Willis (1977, 1978) and Angela McRobbie (1991). Ethnography entails the close and prolonged observation of a particular social group. The ethnographer is not concerned to describe the behaviour of the members of the group, but rather to understand the **culture** of that group from within. The anthropologist Clifford Geertz characterises this as recognising the difference between a twitch and a wink. A wink and a twitch may look the same as a physical movement, so that photography could not distinguish between them. However, the wink is governed by a social convention, and is therefore meaningful (although this does not prevent twitches being embarrassingly mistaken for winks, and vice versa). As Geertz puts it: 'That's all there is to it: a speak of behaviour, a fleck of culture, and – *voilà!* – a gesture' (1973: 6). Obviously, the ethnographer is not concerned just with isolated gestures, although a crucial part of the ethnographer's task is to record in detail particular events and actions from the everyday life of the group. From this particular material, the ethnographer is ultimately concerned to explicate the whole gamut of **norms**, **values** and **rules** that govern and give meaning to behaviour within the group. The central problem confronting the ethnographer is then that of overcoming the barriers that exist to understanding and interpretation. These will be associated with the difficulty of coming to terms with values and meanings that may be radically divergent from the ethnographer's own, and recognising the danger of imposing one's own values on the culture. (McRobbie (1981), for example, is critical of the exclusion of women from much, male dominated, ethnographic description of youth **subcultures**.) (See also **field work, participant observation**.) [AE]

Further reading: Stanley and Roland 1988.

ethnomethodology The term 'ethnomethodology' was coined by Harold Garfinkel, supposing it to mean 'people's methods', to refer to an approach to the **sociology** of everyday life, that became popular in the 1960s. Ethnomethodology is concerned with the way in which members of society create the ordered social world in which they live. As such, it is opposed to those approaches to sociology (such as **functionalism** and **Marxism**) that presuppose a social reality that is independent of the social agent and that has some quasi-causal influence over him or her. Ethnomethodology claims that members of society in fact have a great deal of skill (or competence) to recognise and continually produce significant and ordered social events, through co-operation with each other. The ethnomethodologist therefore refuses to take for granted any social order. It is never just there, but is always continually maintained in existence by those involved. The competence these lay members of society have is grounded in a recognition of the **indexicality** of all actions and utterances; which is to say, that social actions have unique meaning in unique contexts. The skill of the lay member lies in being able to draw on rather approximate shared, and thus general, understandings and procedures, in order to be able to create these unique meanings and draw on the particular characteristics of the social event. The true sociologist is then, not the scientific expert, who provides an account of social activity and social structure in a language that is largely incomprehensible to that spoken and understood by society's members. The true sociologist, in the sense of the person who has expertise as to how society works, is the lay member him- or herself. Ethnomethodology seeks merely to make us conscious of the competence that we already have, but take for granted.

The two core approaches that ethnomethodologists use to study society are the 'breaching' experiment, and **conversation analysis**. In a breaching experiment, the experimenter deliberately defies a convention taken for granted by other members of society. In a now classic experiment, Garfinkel instructed a class of students to return to their parental homes and to act as lodgers. To the parents, the behaviour of their children was bizarre and disturbing, as the taken for granted (and unnoticed) conventions of how children behave in their home (and thus how parents behave to their children) were unravelled. Conversation analysis seeks to document how particular examples of social interaction are sustained. Classic studies sought to explicate the taken for granted rules that determined the ordering of a telephone conversation, not merely as to turn taking (the person who answers the telephone speaks first – so try answering the telephone, say nothing, and see what happens), but also as to who controls the topics raised in the conversation and when the conversation is acceptably ended.

Ethnomethodology was originally criticised for ignoring many of the traditional issues of sociology, and not least problems of power. However, in the hands of feminist sociologists, ethnomethodological techniques have offered an attractive alternative to increasing statistics based, and positivistic sociological approaches. Issues of power can begin to be incorporated into ethnomethodology, in conversation analysis for example, by simply recognising that men have more power to control a conversation than women. [AE]

Further reading: Garfinkel 1967; Heritage 1984; Hilbert and Collins 1992; Turner 1974.

exchange–value Exchange-value is one of the key concepts in Marxist economics. Marx identifies two forms of **value** in **commodities**. **Use–value** is grounded in the possibility of the object satisfying some identifiable human need or desire. The 'value' of the object, however, lies in the fact that it is a product of human **labour**. According to Marx's version of the **labour theory of value**, the value of a commodity depends upon the amount of labour time that has been spent in its production. Marx qualifies this simple observation, by noting that the actual labour time expended is not relevant (so that the products of a slow, lazy or unskilled worker will not be worth more than those of a fast and efficient worker, simply because the slow worker took longer to produce anything). Rather, Marx refers to 'socially necessary labour-time', which is that required to produce a given amount of a useful commodity, 'under the conditions of production normal for a given society and with the average degree of skill and intensity of labour prevalent in that society' (1976: 129). This value is understood as exchange-value, when different sorts of commodities (that is, commodities with different use-values) are exchanged. Thus, if it takes 5 hours to produce 10 yards of linen, and 20 hours to produce a coat, then 40 yards of linen are equivalent to (or have the same exchange-value as) one coat. Exchange-value is expressed in (although is not strictly identical to) a monetary price. [AE]

Further reading: Cunningham-Wood 1988.

experiment   A situation in which a theory is tested according to rigid methodological criteria, and hence involving empirical analysis. Experiments are associated with the physical sciences (physics, astronomy, biology, etc.). The experimental model, however, has been adopted by various researchers and thinkers within a wide cultural domain of disciplines. Thus, **sociology** seeks to be a science of society, and often has resorted to experimental methods to justify different theories of social behaviour. Equally, in philosophy, **positivism** adopts the experimental **paradigm**. The methodology has wider cultural currency, however. In the media experiments in 'public opinion', or market research by advertisers and political parties, all involve some tacit acknowledgement of the scientific experimental method. It follows that this methodology has a cultural and social significance which goes far beyond the results it produces, e.g. its influence on the way in which we view ourselves and contemporary **society**. (See also **philosophy of science**.) [PS]

Expressionism Label in art theory that denotes the use of distortion and exaggeration, so that the direct expression or communication of emotional states takes precedence over the representation of nature. While applied primarily to the visual arts, and especially to twentieth-century painting, Expressionism has been extended to cover music, theatre, poetry and cinema.

No Expressionist movement has existed as such, and the term has been employed, anachronistically, to describe the paintings of Grünewald (*c.* 1470–1528) and El Greco (1541–1614). Indeed, interest in Grünewald's work revived due to the modern development of Expressionism. The principal figures in the modern emergence are van Gogh (in the Netherlands), Gauguin (France), Ensor (Belgium) and Munch (Norway). (This point, in itself, indicates the pan-European influence of Expressionism.) Van Gogh's paintings deliberately exaggerate colour and line, and the account that he gave of this in his letters typify much Expressionist thinking. Thus, he writes of *The Night Café* that he sought 'to express the idea of the café as a place where one can ruin oneself, go mad or commit a crime', and to 'express the terrible passions of humanity by means of red and green' (Chipp 1968: 36–7). Munch's *The Scream* (1893) has become possibly the best known Expressionist image. Exaggerated colour, so that clouds are painted as 'actual blood', exaggerated perspective and the skull-like face of the central figure serve to express, in Munch's words 'a scream passing through nature'. *The Scream* is part of a series of works, collectively entitled the *Frieze of Life*, which explore emotional extremes, including alienation, sexual jealousies and hatreds.

The Fauves were influenced by the work of van Gogh and Gauguin particularly, developing the use of colour, freed from its traditional representative function. Thus, Matisse held that the primary function of colour was to serve expression. There is, however, a senuous beauty to the Fauves' painting that goes against the darker themes of Germanic Expressionism. In Germany, two groups, Die Brücke (founded in 1905) and Die Blaue Reiter (1911), embody the principal thrust of Expressionist development. The members of Die Brücke were defined in terms of their common opposition to **realism** and Impressionism, and a faith in the art of the future (to which their own art represented the 'bridge' of their title), rather than by any clear positive aims. Most members lacked proper technical training, and their work was characterised by violent or harsh contrasts and crude or simplified forms. However, they did revive certain graphic techniques, and most particularly the woodcut (that itself represented an interest, typical of much Expressionism, in folk and primitive art forms). Die Blaue Reiter included the Russian Kandinsky, the Germans Marc and Macke, and the Swiss born Klee, amongst others. More international in composition than Die Brücke, it was also more outward looking. Its exhibitions included works by Die Brücke's members, by Douanier Rousseau, Picasso, Braque, Derain, Delaunay and Vlaminck. The group published its Almanach in 1912, with Kandinsky's cover illustration (*Le Cavalier bleu*) giving the group its name. Notably a score by Schoenberg was also published in the Almanach. While the aims of the group were again only weakly defined, there was a common reaction to Impressionism, and a concern with the symbolic expression of a spiritual dimension. Kandinsky was influenced by Steiner's theosophy, and Expressionism may be seen to entail a turning away from modern scientific and technological advance, in marked contrast to Futurism.

In music, Expressionism is closely associated with the expansion of, and ultimate emancipation from tonality, that occurred in the later nineteenth century and early twentieth century. Schoenberg's atonal works exemplify Expressionist techniques in music, not merely in the extreme dissonance of the harmonic language, but also in the challenge provided to formal music structures. The breakdown of the traditional tonal language and structure in music therefore corresponds to the breakdown of traditional approaches to colour and composition in painting. Schoenberg's music drama *Erwartung* has no repetition of musical subjects or motifs, and defied musical analysis. Its subject matter is an ambigous dream sequence, in which a woman discovers her murdered lover. Expressionism may be seen as a key aspect of the work of Schoenberg's pupil Berg, but also in the early work of Richard Strauss (including the operas *Salome* (1905, and based on Wilde's play) and *Elektra* (1909)).

In literature and drama, Wedekind's plays, including *Erdgeist* (1895) and *Die Büchse der Pandora* (1904) (together used by Berg as the basis of his opera *Lulu*), and Strindberg's later plays, such as *The Dance of Death* (1901), *The Ghost Sonata* (1907), and the *Damascus* plays (1898–1901) may be seen as the immediate precursors of Expressionism. Again, the term may be applied anachronistically, here to the work of Lenz (1751–92) and Büchner (1813–37) whose play *Woyzeck* provided the libretto for Berg's Expressionist opera *Wozzeck* (1921), although Expressionism flourished between 1914 and 1930. As with painting and music, Expressionist drama (and poetry) is typified by a disruption of traditional form, so that, for example, narrative development is replaced by a succession of episodes (a structure derived in part from medieval drama), characters who are represented by their roles rather than by names, grotesque and satirical elements, and an exclamatory and elliptical style. *Mörder, Hoffnung der Frauen* (1910), by the painter and writer Oskar Kokoschka, concerning the conflict between the sexes, is generally regarded as the first Expressionist play. Other key Expressionist authors include Ernst Toller (especially in work influenced by his experience in the First World War), and Reinhard Sorge (*Der Bettler* (1912)). Expressionism was an aspect of the poetry of Georg Trakl and Gottfried Benn.

An Expressionist cinema thrived, particularly in Germany between 1918 and the rise of the Nazis in 1933. Wiene's *Das Cabinett des Dr Caligari* (1919) is generally acknowledged as the first Expressionist film. A horror film, it introduces stylistic features that are typical of Expressionism, such as disturbing and unnatural sets, and strongly contrasted lighting.

The early films of Fritz Lang continue to build upon this, as does Murnau's reworking of the Dracula story, *Nosferatu* (1922). [AE]

Further reading: Behr *et al.* 1993; Dube 1997; Pascal 1973; Willett 1970.

false consciousness   In **Marxism**, false **consciousness** occurs when a **class** fails to recognise the course of political action and allegiances that are in its real interests. Such a class is under the sway of an **ideology**. (See also, **class consciousness**.) [AE]

fascism   Fascism is not a homogeneous political doctrine, but a collection of unrelated, sometimes contradictory, ideas derived from a number of cultures. Fascist ideology resits definition, exhibiting itself instead as an umbrella-term for a collection of reactionary drives, united only by historical circumstance. Nonetheless, by utilising *via negativa*, one may approach a reasonably coherent impression of the main tendencies active within fascism: in opposition to **liberalism**, fascism upholds a totalitarian state and a claim to socialist principles; whilst in opposition to communism, fascism places emphasis on the importance of nationhood, racial purity and the idea of the elite. Along with these distinguishing criteria, fascist regimes are marked by an identification of the national will with the person of the national leader, militarism and a vague appeal to natural law in order to justify these claims. 'Fascist' also serves as a pejorative term in a more general sense, denoting an institution or authority deemed to exhibit any of the above features; a fact which may serve to illustrate the ill-defined nature of the ideology from which it is derived.

Ernst Nolte has identified six different theories to account for the fascist phenomenon: a Christian account whereby fascism is the result of a secular society; a conservative approach which blames the rejection of the old order; a liberal theory which sees the roots of fascism in totalitarian government; a nationalist theory which identifies fascism with aggressive nationalism; a Marxist interpretation which places emphasis on the contradictory nature of modern industrial capitalism; and Nolte's own, 'non-partisan', theory which stresses the uniqueness of fascism to its particular epoch, independent of sociological trends. Many theorists see the rise of fascism as a direct consequence of the alienation produced by modern industrial societies, while others prefer to emphasise the independence of fascist thought from social conditions. These contrasting approaches have respectively been labelled 'heteronomic' and 'autonomic' theories by Martin Kitchen, who argues that a proper understanding of the fascist urge must take account of both types of theory. Nonetheless, a consensus on the precise origins and nature of fascism remains elusive; Marxist critics tend to identify fascism with capitalism run riot, while liberal theorists may make little distinction between fascist Nazi Germany and Stalinist state-communism.

The extent to which fascism remains a potent force in contemporary societies is a source of contention. Although eminent scholars, such as Hannah Arendt and Carl Friedrich, have argued that fascism is rooted in a specific cultural and historical context, current scholarship often highlights the continuing influence of fascist ideology within modern societies. This may be demonstrated by the proliferation of revisionist histories circulating in Europe denying the severity of the Holocaust and playing-down the unpalatable, racially-selective nature of fascism, together with the presence of fascist parties such as the British National Party and the Italian National Alliance within western democracies. There is, however, agreement within mainstream academia on the fundamental character of fascism: an internally inconsistent, vague and inchoate set of prejudices, distinguished only by a historically proven ability to degrade and destroy the moral and rational character of any culture willing to adopt it. [CW]

Further reading: Laqueur 1988.

feminism   The core of feminism is the belief that women are subordinated to men in western culture. Feminism seeks to liberate women from this subordination and to reconstruct society in such a way that **patriarchy** is eliminated and a culture created that is fully inclusive of women's desires and purposes. There are many different kinds of feminist theory but they all have these goals in common. Where they differ is in the particular visions of what such a reconstructed society would look like and in the strategies they employ to achieve it.

The first well documented feminist theorist in the Anglo-American tradition is Mary Wollstonecraft who produced a social theory of the subordination of women in her tract *A Vindication of the Rights of Woman* in 1792. Wollstonecraft engendered a political activism that has remained at the core of western feminism.

Initially, feminism was primarily concerned with women's political and economic equality with men. It gathered pace in the nineteenth century with political publications cataloguing the injustice of sexual inequality, for example *The Subjection of Women* (co-authored by J.S. Mill and Harriet Taylor Mill in 1869), and through activist organisation of women's suffrage groups such as the Women's Social and Political Union (WSPU) (founded in 1903). The twentieth century saw the proliferation of civil rights movements and groups campaigning for economic equality who focused on the issues of state welfare for mothers, equal education and equal pay. These early feminist issues continue to be a priority for all feminists and are a vital prop for later feminist theory in their emphasis on the importance of economic and political equality as a prerequisite for women's emancipation. They are especially prominent in Liberal Feminism, which has its roots in the civil rights movement and which maintains that equal opportunities and equal rights are the key to full social equality.

Whereas early feminism emphasised political and economic equality with men, the feminism that had its beginnings in the decades after the Second World War aimed to achieve a fuller and more sophisticated understanding of the cultural nature of oppression. To this end 'second wave' feminists look at the ways in which cultural institutions themselves underpin and perpetuate women's subordination. In particular, feminists reject the assumed universality of male values. Instead, they argue, in order to fully emancipate themselves from patriarchy, women must look to their own experience to create their own values and their own identities.

As feminism has developed, different areas of theory have concentrated on different aspects of oppression: Marxist Feminism claims all oppression to be a product of social and economic structures; Radical Feminism locates sexual oppression in the male manipulation of women's sexuality; Psychoanalytic Feminism looks at the construction of women's subjectivity in a sexist culture; Socialist Feminism combines many of these insights in a theory of the systematic oppression and exploitation of women in a patriarchal society, where women's procreative role is co-opted in the service of capitalism.

Moreover, theorists argue that women's oppression is deeply rooted in the very structures of our cultural norms. A particular feature is the existence of **binary oppositions** predicated on the assumed polarity of the sexes which work to undermine the feminine in a variety of instances. For example, in politics the distinction between the public (male) and the private (female) serves to exclude women from positions of social importance and authority; in language, Hélène Cixous (*The Newly Born Woman,* 1987) has argued that gendered binary oppositions are an intrinsic part of grammar and syntax and so affect the possibilities of knowledge; in ethics, Carol Gilligan (*In A Difference Voice,* 1982) has argued that care, traditionally the province of the female, is devalued in opposition to a male idea of justice.

Recently, western feminism has come to the realisation that it is itself a product of a particular cultural tradition, that belonging to the white European/American, rather than a universal expression of women's struggle for emancipation. For black women and women of colour the fight for liberation is as much a racial as a gender issue. They criticise the ethnocentricity of the western feminist tradition at the same time as endorsing the common fight against oppression.

Partly as a reaction to the charge of ethnocentricity, so-called 'third wave' feminism seeks to overcome the difficulties surrounding the question of what or who exactly 'woman' is, and who it is that the feminist movement claims to represent. In common with **post-structuralism**, third wave feminism abandons the concept of a single collective identity. Instead it offers ideas of ambiguity and difference as a means of understanding the unique issues and interests of each woman. This development is a controversial issue within feminism. Its critics argue that the notion of identity is itself fundamental to the analysis of oppression. Its dissolution undercuts the possibility of resistance and change, thus compromising feminism's political commitment. [JO]

feudalism   In Marxist theory, feudalism is the **mode of production** (or historical epoch) that precedes capitalism within western Europe. Feudalism may be characterised by its decentralised structure of authority, and its pattern of land-holding. A feudal lord was linked to a politically subordinated vassal through an oath of fealty. The vassal swore loyalty to the lord, and expressed this loyalty typically through the willingness to supply military services. The vassal would fund this army through large land holdings divided amongst his own subordinates. (This lord–vassal relationship would occur through several levels of the aristocratic hierarchy, with knights at the bottom, in a process called 'sub-infeudation'.) At the base of the feudal economy, serfs were legally tied to work the land owned by their lords. The serf (or peasant) did have some control over the **means of production**, although without any legal ownership (in contrast to the **proletariat** in **capitalism**). Exploitation within feudalism occurred through the payment of rent. Serfs were legally obliged to transfer a portion of their product to the lord, either in kind, in money, or through working on the lord's land. (The Marxist model of feudalism inevitably oversimplifies the actual structure, focusing as it does on the two most significant **classes**, the aristocracy and the serfs or peasants. In practice, from the twelfth century onwards, significant numbers of serfs were able to buy their freedom, and move to the growing towns. The scope of feudal authority was thus increasingly restricted.) The dominant **culture** of feudalism, particularly in so far as culture is understood as an ideology that legitimates the existing political order, centred on the role of the church, in offering a morality of obedience and acceptance of one's place in the social order. [AE]

Further reading: Bloch 1961; Hindess and Hirst 1975.

field work   Field work may broadly be understood as the collecting of empirical sociological or cultural data, generally through participation in a social activity or **culture** (hence **participant observation**) or merely through close observation of that culture ('field observation'), as in the field work associated with **cultural anthropology**. Lévi-Strauss likened the cultural anthropologist's long and intimate association with a particular culture during his or her field work to a would-be psychoanalyst him- or herself undergoing analysis. It exposes the taken for granted assumptions that one has inherited from one's own culture, and that might otherwise make you insensitive to other cultures. [AE]

Further reading: Lareau and Shultz 1996.

folk music   The simplest definition of folk music is music that is orally transmitted between generations, within a culturally homogeneous community. It is typically thought to be of unknown origin. The idea of 'folk' also suggests a rural community, and thus that folk music represents a survival of pre-industrial culture. This simple definition turns out, however, to be somewhat problematic.

The key period in the collecting of folk song is, perhaps, the end of the nineteenth century and the beginning of the twentieth (although an interest in folk culture had been a characteristic of European **Romanticism**, with Herder being an early advocate of the study of folk cultures). The exploration of folk song had several motivations. First, there was a concern to preserve what was perceived to be a rapidly vanishing **culture** (hence, for example, the work of Cecil Sharp in England and in the Appalachian mountains). The collection of folk song rapidly threw into question a number of assumptions about this music. Folk song was discovered not to be a discrete entity, like an art song or a popular song. It will change between performances (even consecutive performances by the same singer). Further, it is not necessarily of anonymous origin. Commercial popular songs were being incorporated in the 'folk' tradition even in the nineteenth century.

A second motivation for folk song study was the recognition, within a number of European societies, that the recovery of a folk tradition could be important to the articulation of a national **identity** (hence, for example, the use of folk song material by Czech, Hungarian and Welsh and English composers in the early twentieth century). These two motivations indicate something of the way in which the very idea of 'folk' is a construction, owing more to political and social dissatisfactions than to the **cultural anthropologist**'s concern to understand pre-industrial society. The aspiration to recover a folk community suggests a critical response to the industrial present, or a way of articulating political tensions. The pioneering work by A.L. Lloyd in the mid-twentieth century extended this response, by questioning the association of 'folk' with a more or less mythical rural past. Lloyd looked at the folk music of urban communities (1967), revealing a rich musical tradition within working-class culture. In certain respects this approach could itself lead to a new myth (of a working-class culture untouched by the corrupting hand of commercial mass culture).

A third motivation for the interest in folk music was as a source of renewal for composers of western art music. The tonal system of western music, that had been dominant since the early seventeenth century, was widely seen to be exhausted. While for most listeners, this system (or musical language) might seem natural, it was in fact very much a product of convention and codification. Much folk music was written in pentatonic or modal scales, and so can sound very different to art and **popular music**. It usefully served to disrupt taken-for-granted expectations of how music should sound. It therefore provided a number of composers (such as Vaughan Williams and Holst in England) with the resources for the revitalisation of their own high art tradition.

The concept of 'folk music', be it in the original sense of the oral tradition of the 'people', or in the more recent sense of a certain **genre** of popular music (albeit one grounded in the styles of anonymous folk music, as is manifest in the tradition of Woody Guthrie, Pete Seeger and Bob Dylan), is a complex construction. It must be treated as much as an expression of political aspiration as a description of the way the cultural world really is. [AE]

Further reading: Harker 1985; Lloyd 1967; Vaughan Williams 1963.

forces of production In **Marxism**, forces of production are the productive capacities available to a society. As such, they include material technology (such as machines, tools and sources of power), and the physical and intellectual skills and capacities of the population. Marx (1971) suggests that forces of production continue to develop, in terms of their productive capacity, throughout history. Social change occurs through the growing conflict between the developing forces of production and the essentially static economic, political and legal organisation of a society (the **relations of production**). Exploitation of a new technology will therefore require the overthrow of the existing social order. (See **mode of production**.) [AE]

Further reading: Balibar 1970; Cohen 1978; Cutler *et al.* 1977.

Fordism/post-Fordism A significant development in the organisation of systems of industrial production in the twentieth century. Fordism, as the name implies, is derived from the name of American factory owner and car manufacturer, Henry Ford. Ford developed a system of production which concentrated all the resources and materials necessary for manufacture on one site – the factory – and which allocated specialised tasks to different workers in a 'production line' in order to ensure the maximum degree of economic efficiency. The products which resulted from this mode of organisation were mass produced and necessarily took on a standardised form with a view to their mass consumption.

The term 'post-Fordism' signals a move away from this model of mass production into diversified sites of production. Thus, the large-scale factory is replaced by smaller industrial units. This is evident even in the case of the production of commodities like cars, where it is often the case that the parts of a product are made in a variety of different places, and then assembled elsewhere. Post-Fordism is often associated with the rise of modern technology, and with the replacement of older, heavy-industry forms of production by it. The significance of this transition is a matter of some debate; as is the relationship between the two forms of production – in so far as post-Fordist models still utilise strategies that are common to the earlier Fordist model and rely upon the same basic commodity-based conception of **value** as **exchange-value**. Aspects of post-Fordism have been related to **postmodernism** – including the implications of technology for cultural and social life. On David Harvey's account of postmodernity, the postmodern era signifies precisely this movement away from large-scale centres of production. Thus, post-Fordism/postmodernism may be characterised in terms of a historical development into a global capitalist culture, which uses and coordinates the efforts of localised workforces in order to deal with a more flexible market. (See also **Taylorism**.) [PS]

Further reading: Amin 1995; Boyer and Durand 1997; Harvey 1989.

Frankfurt School The term 'Frankfurt School' refers to the work of those philosophers, cultural critics and social scientists who belonged to, or were associated with, the Frankfurt Institute for Social Research. (The figures most readily associated with the School are Max Horkheimer, Theodor Adorno, Herbert Marcuse, Erich Fromm and Walter Benjamin, and in the School's post-war 'second generation', Jürgen Habermas.) The Institute was opened in 1924, but began to develop the distinctive approach to **Marxism** with which it is now associated only when the philosopher Max Horkheimer became its director, in 1930. The Frankfurt School approach can be characterised as an attempt to develop an Hegelian-Marxism that is appropriate to the conditions of twentieth-century **capitalism**. A major influence on the Frankfurt School is thus found in the work of the Hungarian Marxist Georg Lukács, not least in so far as his *History and Class Consciousness* (1923) offered a reading of Marx that was grounded in the German philosophical tradition of Kant and Hegel, but also in that it sought to modify Marx's account of capitalism by recognising the importance of the work of the sociologist Max Weber (not least in his analysis of the increasing role that **bureaucracy** and administration play in contemporary industry and government). To this, the Frankfurt School added an interest in **psychoanalysis**, and thus the project of fusing the work of Marx and Freud. Overall, the Frankfurt School, especially under Horkheimer's guidance, sought to pursue multi-disciplinary research projects, in which the empirical social science research would be directed and its results analysed by Marxist theory.

Horkheimer characterised the approach of the Frankfurt School as '**critical theory**'. He drew a distinction between critical theory and what he called traditional theory (1972a). The latter, which had dominated western scientific enquiry since the early seventeenth century (and thus the **Enlightenment**), assumed that the scientist was independent of the object of his or her study. A sound scientific methodology would allow the scientist to observe and describe the world as it really was, and to generate hypotheses and laws to explain it. For Horkheimer this ignored the fact that the scientist (and thus the whole **institution** of science) was a product of social and historical forces. The scientist is not independent of the society and culture within which he or she lives. Scientists are shaped by that culture. Thus, for Horkheimer, the very way in which a scientist sees the world, and the way in which he or she makes sense of what is seen, will be conditioned by society. In addition, at least for the social sciences, the object that the scientist observes is also itself a product of historical change. Critical theory acknowledges these points, and incorporates them in its approach to empirical enquiry and analysis. Crucially, the critical theorist is aware that the way in which he or she sees the world is conditioned, not least by the political and **ideological** structures of society. Critical theory is therefore self-**reflective**. Its enquiry encompasses not just the society that is 'out there', seemingly independent of the observer, but also the way that society shapes and distorts the perception of society. Critical theory is therefore a form of 'ideology-critique' – that is to say that it is not simply an analysis of the social conditioning of knowledge (as is found in the **sociology of knowledge**), but also a recognition of the power structures inherent in that conditioning. Knowledge is therefore seen to play a central role in the **reproduction** of a politically unequal and **class** divided society.

The complexities of this approach become clear if it is compared to the work of Lukács. He was equally aware of the historical development and conditioning of both the knowing **subject** and known **object** in scientific and philosophical enquiry. However, Lukács believed that he had found, in the **proletariat**, and more precisely in the van-garde of the Communist Party, a perspective that was finally free of ideological distortion. The Frankfurt School never made such an assumption, for both empirical and political reasons. Empirically, by the late 1930s most members of the School had abandoned any hope in the revolutionary potential of the working-classes in advanced capitalism. The working-class was seen to be as highly integrated into capitalism as any other class. Developing Weber's account of bureaucracy, it was argued that all groups within society were equally subordinated to the administrative systems of government and industry, and the classes were to be distinguished not by **power**, but material affluence. The proletariat therefore did not represent a privileged perspective on capitalism. In addition, the developmental view of history that Lukács defended (derived from Marx's historical materialism) was also abandoned. History, for the Frankfurt School, was not a gradual emancipation of humanity, but a tightening of the grip of technical and administrative control of all humanity. Politically, the Frankfurt School associated truth claims, be they the truth claims of Enlightenment science or of political leaders, with **authoritarianism**. Those who claim knowledge of (absolute) truth, either ignoring the social conditioning of their position or claiming to have surpassed it, are politically dangerous, whether they are Stalinists, Nazis, or the bureaucratic administrators of the western democracies. This, in effect, is the key thesis of Horkheimer and Adorno's study, *Dialectic of Enlightenment* (written during their war-time exile in the United States (1972)). The Enlightenment emerged as a critical exercise, dispelling **myth** and superstition. As it developed, this critical faculty was blunted, so that in ceasing to be self-critical, it makes its own principles absolute (and thus they become a new myth, accepted without reason). In becoming dogmatic, the Enlightenment itself becomes authoritarian (and finds itself manifest in the brutal but efficient administration of the Nazi extermination camps).

It is worth noting, especially in comparison to recent **postmodernist** criticisms of the Enlightenment, that Horkheimer and Adorno do not simply abandon the Enlightenment. The problem is, as Adorno puts it, that there has been too little Enlightenment (i.e. critical self-reflection), not too much. The Frankfurt School position is thus a delicate (and at times perplexing) balance between a self-critical avoidance of dogmatic truth claims, and a desire to remain politically committed, and not to relapse into what is, for them, the equally undesirable position of **cultural relativism**. A relativist, in arguing that not just knowledge but also judgements of moral goodness and political justice are culturally conditioned, is left unable to challenge the political system within which he or she lives (Adorno 1967). (For the Frankfurt School, the prime example of this is Martin Heidegger's capitulation to Nazism.) It is in the work of the philosopher T. W. Adorno that this problem is most dramatically worked out. Adorno's notion of 'negative dialectics' (1973b) or non-identity thinking, is a reworking of Hegel's **dialectics**. The Hegelian dialectic is in three stages, the last of which is the achievement of absolute truth. Adorno abandons this stage, leaving all thought and reflection at the preceding stage. Here there is a yearning for the truth, and thus for a final state of security and stability. However, that is merely the reaction to a fragmented, particularised or contradictory condition. In order to express and deal with this condition, Adorno argues in contradictions. For Adorno, the only way to grasp contemporary reality is to a describe it always in two contradictory propositions, and to hold both to be simultaneously truth and false. For example, contemporary society is both a product of human action and understood by its members (as Weber argued), and yet also something that stands against its human members as natural and objective (as the French sociologist Durkheim argued). Adorno may therefore be seen to approach the truth critically or 'negatively'. By identifying contradictions in contemporary thought and contemporary society, he identifies the limits of his understanding (and thus the point at which his understanding is conditioned by a contradictory and 'false' society). His grim vision is expressed in the aphorism he borrows from the philosopher Bradley: 'When everything is bad, it is good to know the worst' (1978a).

As theorists of **culture**, the Frankfurt School leave a rich and diverse heritage. There is, for example, the sociology of literature of Leo Lowenthal (1989). Lowenthal was concerned to develop a Marxist reading of literature, explaining how economic and class structures find expression in the form and content of literary works. Horkheimer (1972b) and, in a wide range of writings on music, literature and **popular culture**, Adorno (1991a, 1991b, 1992a, 1992b) attempt to integrate a Marxist sociology of art with more orthodox **aesthetics**. Crucially, they see art (and especially the art of the modernist **avant-garde**) as one of the few sources of resistance that remain in contemporary capitalism (and thus as something from which critical theory can learn – art is a source of political insight). To explain this, recourse is once again needed to one of Adorno's endeavours to think in contradictions: art is at once a **social fact** and autonomous. That is to say that on the one hand, Adorno and Horkheimer acknowledge the validity of sociological explanations of art, that see it as a product of social and economic forces (and especially note the influence that the rise of **bourgeois** markets for art have on its development). On the other, they argue that art can still have aesthetic **value**. The point is that the very material which art uses (be this physical material like paint and sound, or the forms and **genres** that the artist inherits from previous generations) have a social history attached to them. They have a sedimented social content, precisely because, as the sociologist argues, they are socially conditioned. However the artist, thanks paradoxically to the workings of the art market, has a freedom that other economic producers do not have. The art work is not meant to be useful. It is not produced solely in order to make profit (or **surplus-value**) like any other **commodity**. Rather, the artist has the freedom to pursue purely artistic problems, and to create to artistic ends (not economic ones). This is the key, for while the artist is a producer, just like any other producer within capitalism, and he or she is working with the materials given by his or her society, again, just like any other producer, the artist has a unique freedom to play with those materials. The artist can then break out of the taken-for-granted, ideological ways of using materials and thus ways of seeing the world. The importance of avant-garde art, for Adorno and Horkheimer, is therefore that it shatters the illusions of our everyday understanding of the world. (Good art, in its innovation and invention, is also good politics.) As Horkheimer puts it, art breaks away from the usual forms of communication that dominate and deaden social life, so that the **natural** (i.e. what is taken-for-granted), becomes unnatural (i.e. is exposed as problematic and cultural) (1972b: 279). However, both Horkheimer and Adorno readily acknowledge the great problem of contemporary art: the majority of the people shun it, as it fails to say anything to them. In this respect, popular culture is superior to high art. Again, the reader is left with contradictions, rather than solutions, and for Horkheimer and Adorno especially, a political paralysis. While they may be able to theorise what is wrong with contemporary society, and see this expressed in high culture, they are ultimately unable to act or to communicate this knowledge to any popular political movement. (See also: **culture industry**.) [AE]

Further reading: Arato and Gebhardt 1978; Bronner and Kellner 1989; Connerton 1976; Jay 1973; Wiggershaus 1994.

functionalism Functionalism was the dominant **paradigm** within **cultural anthropology** and **sociology** throughout the first half of the twentieth century. At its most basic, it attempts to explain any given social or cultural **institution** in terms of the consequences which that particular institution has for the **society** as a whole. (Functionalism is therefore an alternative to historical accounts of the emergence of institutions or societies.) Functionalist explanation assumes that all institutions ideally participate in maintaining the stability of the society, and thus in reproducing the society from one generation to the next. Society, in accord with a frequently used analogy to a biological organism, is assumed to have the property of homeostasis, which is to say, the various parts of the society work to maintaining the society as a whole. Thus, for example, the functions of the modern family are those of physically nurturing and **socialising** the young. The culture (including the morality, or **norms** and **values** of the society) is thus transmitted, largely unchanged, from one generation to the next, and the economy is provided with a supply of individuals who are capable of playing useful **roles**.

The American sociologist Robert K. Merton (1968) proposed the distinction between manifest and latent functions.

Latent functions of social institutions are those functions of which the social actors are not conscious. Such functions then go beyond any deliberate intentions that the actors may have in carrying out their own particular activities. Thus, the priests or shamen who initiate at a rain dance, may regard themselves as attempting to control the weather. The functionalist sociologist or anthropologist will rather say that the ceremony serves to raise the morale of the group, and thus stabilise and integrate it, perhaps in the face of stresses caused by sustained bad weather.

The most complex version of functionalism was developed largely by Talcott Parsons (1951). He used a systems theory approach borrowed from cybernetics. A system is theorised as maintaining its integrity in relation to an external environment. If a society is treated as a system, then there would be a set of four 'functional pre-requisites' that the social system, like any system, would have to perform in order to maintain integrity and so survive. The first functional pre-requisite that needs to be satisfied is the adaptation to the external environment. This, in effect, is the task of the economy in any society (to make the resources of the external environment available to the society). The second pre-requisite is goal-attainment. Certain institutions in society (such as the political institutions) must be capable of directing the society. Integration, the third pre-requisite, maintains internal order (so can be seen the work of the police and education). The final pre-requisite, pattern-maintenance, entails the motivation of the members of the system to perform the functions required of them. This pre-requisite is met by the cultural sub-system. Culture is thus, for Parsons, itself to be understood as a system (and thus it will have the four pre-requisites of any system). In principle, Parsons' analysis of sub-systems within systems can be carried on ad infinitum, or at least down to the individual social agent, who is, him- or herself, also a system.

Functionalism has been criticised for its inability to deal with social conflict and social change. Functionalists tend to assume that society is a largely homogeneous whole, with a substantial consensus over the core norms and values. In terms of its analysis of **culture**, functionalism gives no scope for a theory of **ideology**, with the implication that a consensus could be manufactured or contested. There is, in addition, little scope to recognise conflict between sub-groups within the society, either as suggested by the Marxist model of **class** conflict, or in terms of the **conflict theorist**'s account of conflict as a sign of a politically vibrant, open society. **Deviance** from the consensual norm is condemned as 'dysfunctional', which is to say disruptive to the social whole. The conservatism inherent in this account of conflict is also seen in the treatment of social change. Societies are seen to change not through revolutionary convulsions, as suggested by the Marxists, but rather through an ever finer differentiation of social functions (and thus, creation of sub-systems). As societies become more sophisticated, new specialist institutions will arise to fulfil functions previously carried out less satisfactorily elsewhere. Thus, the pre-industrial family was largely responsible for a child's education. In industrial society, the school emerges as a specialist educational institution.

Functionalism's greatest fault was perhaps its inability to deal with **meaning**, and to be able to recognise the capacity of social actors actively to recognise and construct a meaningful social world in which they could live and move. For this reason, the first significant challenge to functionalism's supremacy in the social sciences came from **symbolic interactionism**. The more sophisticated versions of functionalism, linked to systems theory, have seen a revival in recent years, not least in the work of the German social theorist Niklaus Luhmann (1982). This version of functionalist theory has also been influential on the work of Jürgen Habermas (1984, 1987). (See also **organic analogy**.) [AE]

Further reading: Giddens 1977; Radcliffe-Brown 1952.

G

gender The concept of 'gender' is typically placed in opposition to the concept of 'sex'. While our sex (female/male)
is a matter of biology, our gender (feminine/masculine) is a
matter of **culture**. Gender may therefore be taken to refer
to learned patterns of behaviour and action, as opposed to
that which is biologically determined. Crucially, biology need
not be assumed to determine gender. This is to suggest that,
while what makes a person male or female is universal and
grounded in laws of nature, the precise ways in which women
express their femininity and men express their masculinity
will vary from culture to culture. Thus, qualities that are
stereotypically attributed to women and men in contemporary western culture (such as greater emotional expression in
women; greater tendencies to violence and aggression in men)
are seen as gender, which entails that they could be changed.
The literature of **cultural anthropology** gives many examples of different expressions of gender in non-western societies
(with the work of Margaret Mead being exemplary in this
respect). The reduction of gender to sex (which would be
to see gender differences as themselves biologically determined) may be understood as a key move in the **ideological**
justification of **patriarchy**. [AE]

Further reading: Butler 1990; Walby 1990.

genealogy   A method of analysis of forms of ethical (Nietzsche) or epistemological (Foucault) discourse. Nietzsche, in *On the Genealogy of Morals* (1887), was the first to outline this approach, and Foucault's work owes much to him. Nietzsche's text argues that the basis of morality and the meaning of value-attributions such as 'good', 'evil' and 'bad' are not derived, as is often supposed to be the case, from either altruistic or utilitarian modes of valuing (nor, it might be added, from any divine sanction). Rather, ethical systems can be understood in terms of their 'genealogy', that is, as being produced by social and historical processes. Above all, morality, for Nietzsche, represents *not* a disinterested conception of what constitutes the 'good', but is rather an expression of the interests of particular social groups. Thus, the notion of 'good' has, he argues, two modes of derivation which signify two very different social perspectives and hence systems of valuing. First, the 'good', in its original sense, expressed the viewpoint of the noble classes who inhabited the ancient world. 'Good', taken in this sense, meant 'beloved of God', and was the expression of the nobles' affirmation of their own identity. 'Bad', in turn, expressed a secondary phenomenon, i.e. the nobles' reaction to those who were their social inferiors ('common', 'plebian', etc.). Noble (or master) morality was thus premised on an affirmation of the identity of the noble as a bestower of values. Second, 'good' in the second sense Nietzsche outlines was a secondary mode of valuing derived from the appellation 'evil' ascribed by slaves to describe their oppressors (the nobles). Slave morality, as Nietzsche terms it, therefore derived its notion of 'good' as a secondary consequence of the negative valuation 'evil'. In this way, negation is the 'creative deed' of the slave. Slave morality, Nietzsche argues, is the morality of both the Hebraic tradition and of Christianity, and is a '*resentiment*' morality, i.e. one whose genealogy is that of the slave's resentment of the nobles'/master's power over them. It is, in Gilles Deleuze's phrase, a 'reactive' morality, rather than an active or affirmative one.

Nietzsche's genealogical method is in fact a variant on a project outlined in one of his earlier works, *Human, All-Too-Human* (1878–80). In the opening sections of that work he argues for the construction of a 'chemistry' of the religious and moral sensations and values. In other words, Nietzsche takes the view that values (and, indeed, feelings/sensations) can be revealingly understood by producing a causal and historical account of them which seeks to unearth their origins. To this extent, the genealogical approach fits in with much of Nietzsche's philosophical thinking, which often expresses the view that what has hitherto been regarded as valuable (or even sacred) can be adequately accounted for within a materialist methodology of explanation. Foucault's genealogical method of investigation, likewise, takes as its point of departure the historical conditions which constitute **discourses** of knowledge. His analysis of, for example, the clinical definitions and treatments of madness since the seventeenth century, emphasises the importance of social relations (above all, relations of **power**) in the construction of knowledge, and seeks to reveal through painstaking historical analysis the influences and interests which underlie and are concealed by discourses which claim to articulate objective knowledge. A key problem, at least with Foucault's application of the genealogical method, is that in applying it to forms of knowledge he opens himself to the criticism that his own discourse is itself a production of historical factors and an expression of interests (see Peter Dews's criticisms listed in the readings below, which provides a Nietzschean criticism of Foucault's methodology). [PS]

Further reading: Dews 1988; Foucault 1977b; Minson 1985; Nietzsche 1968a, 1986.

genre A mode of categorisation. A genre denotes a set of shared characteristics which allows for the grouping together of different forms of artistic expression or cultural production. For example, the genre of the novel denotes a body of texts which all conform to the basic definition of what constitutes a novel (i.e. texts which contain fictional characters, a narrative structure, etc.). Likewise, in the medium of television, 'soap-operas', 'documentaries', or 'situation comedies' all signify particular genres. That said, it is frequently very difficult to provide an exhaustive list of the features which define a particular genre, since any given work that may be situated within a particular genre may well possess features which are not normally shared by other instances of that genre, or lack features common to others. The term 'genre', taken in this sense, might thus be best viewed as a rather loose means of lumping sometimes more or less diverse instances together. Moreover, works ostensibly situated within a genre can express an ironic relationship to the genre itself (for example, a soap-opera which sends up the soap-opera genre, and is therefore a situation comedy).

Amongst philosophers, Jean-François Lyotard's conception of 'genres of discourse' perhaps offers a more rigorous account. On his view, a genre is a way of linking incommensurable linguistic elements together (i.e. a set of rules of linking), and is characterised by its purpose. (See also, **discourse**.) [PS]

grammatology   The first edition of I.J. Gelb's *The Study of Writing*, carried the subtitle: *The Foundations of Grammatology* (dropped from the second edition, 1963). Defining the term, and his project, Gelb wrote: 'The aim of this book is to lay a foundation for a full science of writing. . . . To the new science we could give the name "grammatology."'

The linguist Ferdinand de Saussure had already argued that the study of language in general should be undertaken on a scientific basis (see his *Course in General Linguistics*; French original published in 1916). Rejecting the historical method of previous approaches in order to focus on the state of a language at any given time, Saussure sought to uncover the unchanging principles which form the structural basis of all language. The resultant theory construed language, in the abstract, as a sign-system in which meaning is produced by the contrast between different sound-combinations.

Despite his achievement in the field of general linguistics, Saussure did not deem it necessary to explore writing as a human phenomenon in its own right. He was content to view it as a derived, secondary and instrumental form of language, fraught with various kinds of difficulty and danger.

Gelb's grammatology has been judged a failure precisely because he made no attempt to propound a theory of writing which could rescue its study from the shadow of general linguistics. His approach remained historical and did not break with older, pre-Saussurian, models of study. He simply classified writing systems as belonging to one of three evolutionary forms: logographic (word-based systems), syllabic (syllable-based systems), alphabetic (systems based on units of sound, or phonemes).

In more recent times, Roy Harris has attempted to do for grammatology what Saussure did for general linguistics. In his *Signs of Writing* (1995) he outlines a theoretical framework for the systematic analysis of writing as a 'uniquely complex form of communication'. Unlike Gelb, he does not restrict his analysis to speech-based forms; he includes in the field of study the notation-systems of mathematics and music.

In *Of Grammatology* (French original published in 1967), Jacques Derrida takes a very different, more philosophical tack. He exposes the tendentious privileging of speech over writing in western thought, from Plato (who denounced it as thrice removed from truth, presence and origins), to Saussure (who characterised it as a disease of language). Acknowledging the evolutionary priority of speech, Derrida argues that this historical contingency has been worked up, illegitimately, into a 'metaphysics of presence'. A whole network of evaluative contrasts (presence/absence, interior/exterior, body/spirit etc.), of fundamental importance to western metaphysics, is seen to cluster around the speech/writing hierarchy.

In order to disrupt this tradition of thought, Derrida highlights what he calls *arche-writing*. This refers to the prevenient structures or systems which underlie every human practice, including speech, and which can only be represented by means of inscriptional metaphors such as pre*script*, pro*gramme*, or various words with the suffix -*graphy* (choreography, cinematography, etc.). He observes that even denigrators of writing like Plato, Rousseau and Saussure are continually forced to use such metaphors in order to describe language. [KM]

Further reading: Derrida 1976.

grand narrative A term associated with Jean-François Lyotard's account of **postmodernism**. A grand narrative (or meta-narrative) is a narrative form which seeks to provide a definitive account of reality (e.g. the analysis of history as a sequence of developments culminating in a workers' revolution offered by classical **Marxism**). In terms of Lyotard's later work, meta-narratives (or meta-**genre**s of discourse) founded on the logical aporia (or 'double bind') of class as discussed by **analytic** philosopher Bertrand Russell: 'either this genre is part of the set of the genres, and what is at stake in it is but one among others, and therefore its answer is not supreme. Or else, it is not part of the set of genres, and it does not therefore encompass all that is at stake, since it excepts what is at stake in itself' (*The Differend: Phrases in Dispute*, section 189). [PS]

Further reading: Lyotard 1988, 1989.

hegemony   The term 'hegemony' is derived from the Greek *hegemon*, meaning leader, guide or ruler. In general usage it refers to the rule or influence of one country over others, and to a principle, about which a group of elements are organised. In twentieth-century **Marxism**, it has been developed by the Italian theorist Antonio Gramsci (1891-1937), to explain the control of the dominant **class** in contemporary **capitalism**. He argues that the dominant class cannot maintain control simply through the use of violence or force. Due to the rise of trade unions and other pressure groups, the expansion of civil rights (including the right to vote), and higher levels of educational achievement, rule must be based in consent. The intellectuals sympathetic to the ruling class will therefore work to present the ideas and justifications of the class's domination coherently and persuasively. This work will inform the presentation of ideas through such institutions as the **mass media**, the church, school and family. However, precisely because this hegemonic account of political control entails consent, ideas cannot simply be imposed upon the subordinate classes. On the one hand, the ruling class will have to make concessions to the interests and needs of the subordinate classes. On the other hand, the subordinate classes will not accept hegemony passively. The ideas of the dominant class will have to be negotiated and modified, in order to make them fit the everyday experience of the subordinate classes. (Members of the subordinate classes may therefore have a dual consciousness. They will simultaneously hold contradictory or incompatible beliefs, one set grounded in hegemony, the other in everyday experience.) The theory of hegemony was of central importance to the development of British cultural studies (not least in the work of the **Birmingham Centre for Contemporary Cultural Studies**). It facilitated analysis of the ways in which subordinate groups actively respond to and resist political and economic domination. The subordinate groups need not then be seen merely as the passive dupes of the dominant class and its **ideology**. [AE]

Further reading: Bocock 1986; Fontana 1993; Gramsci 1971; Sassoon 1987.

hermeneutics   The theory of textual interpretation and analysis. The roots of hermeneutics lie in biblical and legal practices of exegesis. However, modern hermeneutics is generally taken as beginning with the work of Friedrich Schleiermacher (1768–1834). Amongst other things, Schleiermacher contended that (i) hermeneutics is an art of interpretation; (ii) that the meaning of a text is a matter of the original readership for which it was intended; (iii) that interpretation is a circular process, since the parts of a text depend for their meaning upon the whole and *vice versa*; (iv) that misunderstanding is a precondition of understanding texts (against the view associated with the **Enlightenment**, which foregrounded the primacy of reason, and thus the clarity of understanding, in interpretation). The most influential aspect of the work of Wilhelm Dilthey (1833–1911) was his postulation of a difference between 'understanding' and 'explanation' as underlying the distinction between the human sciences and the natural sciences. This view, along with Schleiermacher's identification of meaning with authorial intention, was questioned by the later work of Martin Heidegger (1889–1976) and Hans Georg Gadamer (1900–).

   Heidegger's conception of *Dasein* is one which, by implication, questions the role and, indeed, the traditional humanist conception of the subject in interpretation and meaning. *Dasein* is an entity which can, for example, ask questions about its own existence. In turn, Heidegger conceives of *Dasein* as constituting a temporal structure of interpretative understanding, which is thus always already engaged in the activity of intepretation. Since this is the case, meaning and interpretation are fundamental to *Dasein*'s being-in-the-world, and cannot be properly described in terms of an exterior vantage point (the 'hermeneutic circle'). All interpretation, on this view, always concerns what is already 'understood'. Hence, there is no transcendental **subject** in the Kantian sense, functioning to ground meaning according to principles which draw a distinction between the 'form' of the under-standing and its interpretative 'content'. That said, it is not clear that Heidegger is a straightforward anti-realist (either at this stage in his development, i.e. the writing of *Being and Time*, or even later) as critics such as Richard Rorty have claimed.

Heidegger's pupil, Gadamer, is perhaps the most famous recent exponent of hermeneutic theory, in the shape of 'philosophical hermeneutics'. Gadamer takes from Heidegger the contention that the understanding is realised through the activity of interpretation. Interpretation, in this account, is grounded in 'fore-having', 'fore-sight' and 'preconception'. Principal among Gadamer's claims is that interpretation does not proceed, as with the Enlightenment model, on the basis of free and rational criteria, but is in fact grounded in 'prejudice' (a view derived from Schleiermacher). In contrast to Schleiermacher, however, on Gadamer's conception the meaning of texts is not dependent upon their original or intended sense, but on such factors as the language, norms and traditions in and through which subjectivity finds itself constituted. The intersubjective conditions which go to make up a tradition, according to Gadamer, provide the standpoint from which interpretation precedes (hence, we always begin with 'prejudice'), but do not determine it completely. This is because interpretation, in his view, is an engagement which takes the form of a reciprocal relationship between reader and text. Hence, although one starts with pre-judgements in order to engage in interpreting, a text has the ability to transform one's preconceptions, for example, by resisting a reading that is being imposed upon it. Thus, one may move, through the activity of interpretation, to an engagement with the **other**, which is able to re-structure the interpreter's preconceptions, and thereby the basis of their understanding. Interpretation, therefore, is an unlimited, open-ended process.

Critics of Gadamer include Jürgen Habermas, who has sought to argue that there are in fact limits to the scope of hermeneutic analysis. Habermas notes that it is a theory which considers interpretation only in terms of everyday language, and not all forms of social life and the products thereof are a matter of everyday language; rather, they may be constituted by conditions which are independent of this language. [PS]

Further reading: Gadamer 1975; Habermas 1971; Heidegger 1962; Hirsch 1967; Llewelyn, 1985.

historicism   A theory which holds that an historical analysis of human beliefs, concepts, moralities and ways of living is the only tenable means of explaining such phenomena. Thus, an historicist rejects the belief that, for example, there are any a-historical necessary truths concerning the construction of human **identity** (see also **essentialism**), on the grounds that such concepts are the result of historical processes particular to specific **culture**s and cultural forms. Historicism therefore extols a **cultural relativism**. Thinkers associated with the historicist approach include sociologist Karl Mannheim, who (combining an epistemological relativism and a cultural relativism) argued that all knowledge of history is a matter of relations, and that the perspective of the observer cannot be excised from historical analysis. Michel Foucault's work, in turn, argues for the belief that the **self** is historically constructed, rather than a naturally produced and universal structure common to all times and cultures. This position has led to arguments about the construction of aspects of identity in relation to issues of **race** and **gender**.

In the United States, Foucault's work (as well as that of Raymond Williams) has had an influence in initiating New Historicism, which takes as its point of departure a cross-fertilisation between theories associated with **post-structuralism** and **Marxism**. New Historicists are interested in the social and **ideological** effects of **meaning** and its construction. They offer readings of primarily literary texts which, in contrast to the non-historical, text-based approach of traditional criticism, seek to interpret them in the cultural context of their production by way of an historical methodology, and yet spurn the development of **grand narrative**s of history or knowledge. Writers who have adopted this approach include Stephen Greenblatt, who provided a first elaboration of New Historicism in his *The Forms of Power and the Power of Forms in the Renaissance* (1980). [PS]

Further reading: Greenblatt 1980; Hamilton 1996; Mannheim 1972; Veeser 1989.

holism   A contextualist theory of truth, **meaning** and interpretation favoured by some philosophers – notably W.V. Quine – and also by many cultural and literary theorists working in the broadly **hermeneutic** tradition that runs from Schleiermacher to Heidegger and Gadamer. On this view it is impossible to assign meanings or interpret beliefs except in a context wider than that of the individual statement or utterance. Opinions vary as to just how widely this interpretive 'horizon' has to be drawn, or whether – in principle – there is any limit to the range of relevant background knowledge that might be involved. For the most part philosophers in the Anglo-American ('analytic') camp tend to adopt a pragmatic outlook and not worry too much about the demarcation issue while 'continental' thinkers follow Heidegger in espousing a depth-hermeneutic approach that concerns itself centrally with just this issue.

Thus, for Heidegger, the history of 'western metaphysics' from Plato to Husserl is essentially the history of an error, that which resulted when thinking turned away from truth-as-unconcealment (*aletheia*) vouchsafed through language, and instead sought to analyse the structure and content of truth through various theories of knowledge and representation. Only by overcoming that fateful legacy – nurturing a receptive openness to language holistically construed – could philosophy be set back upon the path to authentic, primordial truth. Heidegger's interpreters have differed widely in the extent of their willingness to follow him along this path. For his closest disciples, Gadamer among them, it is the way towards a deeper and fuller understanding of the so-called 'hermeneutic circle', that is to say, the ongoing dialogue between past and present wherein interpretation is always guided – or its 'horizon' already marked out – by traditional meanings and values. Hence, the charge of uncritical conservatism levelled against Gadamer by Jürgen Habermas and other dissenting commentators.

This charge has a bearing on our topic here since the holistic turn in **philosophy of language** and interpretation theory can be seen as lending support to various forms of **cultural-relativist** argument. For if the truth–value of individual statements is a function of their role within the wider context of statements-held-true at any given time, and if these make sense only when construed against the background horizon of communally sanctioned beliefs, then it follows that statements and beliefs cannot be criticised except on the evaluative terms laid down by some existing cultural consensus. Such is the reading of Heidegger proposed by a number of Anglo-American philosophers in quest of alternative ideas from outside the mainstream analytic tradition. Thus, according to Richard Rorty, we can dump all that portentous depth-ontological talk about 'western metaphysics', truth-as-unconcealment, authentic *Dasein*, etc., while taking Heidegger's pragmatist point about language as a way of being-in-the-world which requires nothing more in the way of justifying grounds or epistemological back-up. This goes some way towards explaining the recent (on the face of it unlikely) convergence between a certain strain of 'post-analytic' philosophy and a certain, albeit selective, appropriation of

Heideggerian themes. What unites them across some otherwise sizeable differences of method and approach is the belief that meaning cannot be accounted for by the kinds of logico-semantic analysis that characterised philosophy of language in the line of descent from Frege and Russell.

Quine's essay 'Two Dogmas of Empiricism' is a classic statement of the case and one that has exerted a strong influence on recent Anglo-American debate. Its argument may be stated very briefly as follows. Philosophers have often assumed that there exists a clear-cut categorical distinction between *analytic* statements (such as 'all batchelors are unmarried men') whose truth is purely definitional and hence self-evident to reason, and *synthetic* statements (such as 'water is the substance with molecular structure H_2O') which involve some item of acquired knowledge, and whose truth is therefore neither self-evident nor merely tautological. Such was the position maintained by Kant in his *Critique of Pure Reason* where he also asserted the existence of *a priori* synthetic truths, i.e., those – like the principle of causality – that were always necessarily presupposed in every act of empirical judgement, and which thus provided the transcendental ground (or condition of possibility) for all experience and knowledge. The empiricist Hume also drew a distinction between 'truths of reason' and 'matters of fact', one that was taken up and developed by various twentieth-century thinkers, among them Bertrand Russell, Rudolf Carnap and the Logical Positivists. Where the two traditions converged – despite all their deep-laid differences of philosophic principle – was on the basic point that *individual statements* (judgements or propositions) were the units of meaningful discourse, and moreover that these could be analysed so as to reveal their underlying structure or logico-semantic form.

Such was Russell's celebrated 'Theory of Descriptions', designed to remove certain ambiguities of reference and scope in ordinary (natural) language by providing a clear-cut logical paraphrase in terms of quantifiers, variables, and logical constants. In this respect it paralleled Frege's theory of sense and reference which sought to distinguish genuinely referring

expressions from other (e.g. fictive or mythical) names – such
as 'Pegasus' or 'Odysseus' – that failed to correspond to any
real-world, objective, or historically existent entity. These are
paradigm examples of analytic philosophy in so far as they
assume (1) that the meaning of a statement is given by its
truth-conditions, and (2) that those conditions are definable
in terms of its various component parts. Quine's 'Two Dogmas
of Empiricism' was an attack on this entire programme of
analysis, especially the version of it laid out in Carnap's book
The Logical Construction of the World. According to Quine that
programme ran up against a number of intractable problems.
The most basic of these was its failure to justify the presumed
distinction between analytic and synthetic statements, or
logical truths-of-reason and empirical matters-of-fact. For it
could always be shown that any definition of the term
'analytic' had to rely on other terms – like 'synonymous' or
'logically equivalent' – which themselves relied on the notion
of analyticity, thus falling prey to the charge of circular argument. In which case there is no possibility of holding a firm,
categorical line between logic conceived as the *a priori* basis
of all valid reasoning and those various items of empirical
knowledge that are always open to challenge or revision under
pressure from recalcitrant evidence. That is to say, we might
always be forced to revise some presumptive logical 'law of
thought' – such as bivalence or excluded middle – if it came
into conflict with the best current theories of physical science.
Thus, to take Quine's example: on one interpretation of
quantum mechanics it might be deemed necessary to suspend
the 'law' of excluded middle so as to accommodate otherwise
unthinkable phenomena like quantum superposition or the
wave/particle dualism.

It is in this context that Quine offers his famous metaphor
of the totality of human knowledge at any given time as a
'man-made fabric' extending all the way from a core region
of putative logical ground-rules to a periphery where
observation-statements link up with the data of empirical
experience. His point is that nothing is immune from revision
since we can always save some cherished item of belief or

conserve some pragmatically useful theory by making adjustments elsewhere in the fabric. Hence Quine's argument concerning the holistic character of all interpretation – whether in the natural or the social and human sciences – and the lack of any ultimate (non-scheme-relative) criteria for distinguishing factual from theoretical components in our overall scheme of beliefs. For theories are always 'underdetermined' by the best evidence to hand, while observation-statements are always 'theory-laden' in the sense that they involve a wide range of standing ontological commitments, from the 'posits' of our everyday commonsense object-language to quarks, gluons, muons and other such specialised candidate items. According to Quine there is no good reason – pragmatic convenience apart – for supposing that some of these objects enjoy a privileged ontological status (i.e., that they *really* exist quite apart from our present framework of beliefs) whereas others must be counted theory-dependent or as 'existing' only by virtue of their role in the discourse of advanced theoretical physics. Such distinctions have to drop out if we take his point about ontological relativity and the extent to which *all* our reality-ascriptions are contingent on this or that preferred way of adjusting the belief-fabric.

Indeed Quine is willing to push this argument to the stage of denying that there is *ultimately* any difference between macrophysical 'posits' (such as brick houses on Elm Street), subatomic particles, forces, numbers, mathematical sets or classes, centaurs and the gods of Homer. All these entities 'enter our conception only as cultural posits', even if – as Quine readily concedes – 'the myth of physical objects is epistemologically superior to most in that it has proved more efficacious . . . as a device for working a manageable structure into the flux of experience'. Thus, any choice between them will always turn on 'vaguely pragmatic inclination' (that which leads us to adjust one or another strand in the fabric) plus an empirically informed estimate of 'the degree to which they expedite our dealings with sense experience'. His own inclination is to go with the current best theories of physical science and admit just that range of posits – from brick houses to certain forces, particles, and whatever is required in the way of more abstract entities such as numbers, classes, etc. – in order to bring theory into line with the best observational data. Thus '[f]or my part I do, qua lay physicist, believe in physical objects and not in Homer's gods; and I consider it a scientific error to believe otherwise'. However, 'in point of epistemological footing the physical objects and the gods differ in degree and not in kind', since they are both – along with every other candidate item – imported into various conceptual schemes as a matter of pragmatic convenience or predisposed belief.

It is not hard see why Quine's argument has struck a sympathetic chord not only among 'post-analytic' philosophers like Rorty but also with theorists in a range of other disciplines such as cultural studies, sociology of knowledge, ethnography, literary criticism and the human sciences at large. It is often invoked by way of support for the cultural-relativist (or social-constructivist) thesis that truth and reality *just are* whatever we make of them according to some particular set of linguistic, discursive, or social conventions. Thus, Quine turns up in a range of improbable contexts or allied with thinkers whose arguments he would scarcely find congenial, given his own attitude of sturdy confidence in a physicalist (if not a realist) approach to epistemological issues. Among them are Kuhnian philosophers of science who adopt a holistic theory of scientific paradigm-change; Foucauldian archaeologists (or genealogists) of knowledge who push this doctrine yet further in a sceptical-relativist direction; Wittgensteinian social theorists who view all truth-claims as relative (or 'internal') to some given language-game or cultural 'form of life'; and proponents of a depth-hermeneutical approach who greet Quine's arguments as marking the end of a narrowly analytic or reductionist conception of meaning, knowledge and truth. In one case only – Kuhn's theory of scientific revolutions – can the theory be said to derive directly from Quine's philosophical ideas and to represent a consistent working-out of their further implications for philosophy and history of science. But there is also a plausible link between Quine's argument for a full-fledged contextualist (or meaning-holistic) approach and Foucault's notion that 'truth' is nothing more than a product of historically shifting configurations in the discursively-produced and socially-mediated 'order of things'.

The theory of meaning-holism developed out of a strong reaction against the kinds of logico-semantic approach that took the isolated statement or proposition as their primary object of analysis. In particular it marked a determined break with the philosophy of logical atomism espoused (however briefly) by Russell and carried on in a somewhat different, less overtly reductionist form by logical empiricists like Carnap and Tarski. Thus, according to Quine, 'it is nonsense, and the root of much nonsense, to speak of a linguistic component and a factual component in the truth of any individual state-ment'. Such was the error of logical empiricism and such the mistake of all those philosophers – from Kant and Hume on down – who thought to distinguish analytic from synthetic judgements, or 'truths of reason' from 'matters of fact'. 'Taken collectively', Quine continues, 'science has its double depen-dence upon language and experience; but this duality is not significantly traceable into the statements of science taken one by one.' In which case we should give up the fruitless quest for a theory of knowledge (or philosophy of science) premised on the old-style atomist belief that any statement could be verified – or falsified – by adducing this or that item of empirical evidence. Rather, 'any statement can be held true come what may, if we make drastic enough adjustments else-where in the system'. And again: 'even a statement very close to the [observational] periphery can be held true in the face of recalcitrant experience by pleading hallucination or by amending certain statements of the kind called logical laws'.

It is this aspect of Quine's thinking – his contextualist and (arguably) cultural-relativist theory of knowledge and truth – that has opened a way to the current *rapprochement* between certain strains of 'post-analytic' and 'continental' thought. However, it is a distinctly strained alliance and one that takes no account of Quine's frequent protestations of belief in science as our best, most rational source of guidance in epistemological matters. Nevertheless 'Two Dogmas' lays itself open to just such a sceptical-relativist reading through its adoption of a meaning-holistic approach and – following from that – its doctrine of wholesale ontological relativity. At any rate, cultural theorists should be aware that there exist strong arguments against this approach (see for instance Fodor and LePore (1991)) and in favour of a truth-based propositional account of meaning and belief-content. These arguments have mostly been advanced by philosophers in the Anglo-American camp who seek to avoid what they see as the path leading from holistic theories of interpretation to cultural-relativist or strong-sociological modes of thought. The issue is posed with particular force when Wittgensteinian social theorists such as Peter Winch deny that it is possible to criticise beliefs, language-games or cultural 'life-forms' other than our own without presuming to adopt a stance outside and above the communal practices in question, and hence failing to understand them on their own internally self-validating terms. In which case, as the critics of this doctrine point out, we could never be justified in criticising *any* cultural practice – from witchburning to clitoridectomy, racial segregation or (a good example offered by Mary Midgeley) the samurai custom of chopping off the head of the first stranger one meets in order to test one's new sword – since of course these practices are interwoven with a vast range of other customs and beliefs which we denizens of a late twentieth-century secular culture just happen not to share.

So there are some large issues behind this debate as to whether certain items of belief can be criticised on factual, logical, ethical or other grounds without bringing in the entire background range of associated meanings and values. In philosophy of science likewise it is hard to see how discoveries or progress could ever come about if indeed there were always the possibility – as Quine argues – of invoking some alternative auxiliary hypothesis in order to save appearances, or redistributing predicates and truth-values over the total fabric of belief so as to achieve a workable trade-off between logic, theory and empirical observation. 'Conservatism figures

175

in such choices', Quine remarks, 'and so does the quest for simplicity'. Some statements – those nearest the periphery – may seem especially 'germane' to certain experiences, i.e., strongly supported by the evidence and hence most resistant to challenge. However, 'in this relation of "germaneness" I envisage nothing more than a loose association reflecting the relative likelihood, in practice, of our choosing one statement rather than another for revision in the light of recalcitrant experience'. And, as we have seen, this thesis of across-the-board revisability extends from the logical 'laws of thought' to statements concerning the existence of physical 'posits' like brick houses on Elm Street. So there is clearly a sense – whatever his own more cautious statements on the matter – in which meaning-holism of the Quinean variety consorts readily enough with other sceptical-relativist doctrines such as those promoted by post-structuralists, postmodernists, disciples of Foucault and strong sociologists of knowledge.

As I have said, resistance to this line of thought has come mainly from philosophers trained up in the Anglo-American analytic tradition. However, there are also continental theorists – notably Paul Ricoeur – who have drawn upon various analytic and other (e.g. Habermasian) theories of meaning and truth in order to criticise certain aspects of hermeneutic thinking in the Heidegger–Gadamer line of descent. Ricoeur is himself much influenced by hermeneutic theory and has devoted the larger part of his work to issues in just that sphere. However, he also acknowledges the implicit conservatism – as well as the methodological quandaries – of any theory or philosophy of interpretation which conceives understanding as always caught within the 'hermeneutic circle' of pre-existent values, meanings and beliefs. What is required in order to break that circle is something more than vague Gadamerian talk of the 'fusion' of interpretive horizons or the interplay of past and present cultural perspectives. In brief, it is the capacity of critical thought to analyse its own and other people's presuppositions or acculturated habits of belief, and to do so (moreover) without claiming some impossible vantage-point above and beyond all belief-attachments or value-commitments.

Of course this goes clean against the holistic thesis that statements have meaning or beliefs possess content only when construed in relation to the entirety of what counts as knowledge at any given time. For in that case – as the Wittgensteinians are fond of observing – we could never criticise any item of belief without bringing an entire belief-system into question and thus, in effect, disqualifying ourselves as competent interpreters or critics. Thus the doctrine of radical meaning-holism very often leads on to an outlook of generalised scepticism with regard to the very possibility of interpreting other people's meanings and beliefs while dissenting from them on this or that matter of factual, logical, or ethical-evaluative judgement. Which is also to suggest – in company with various critics of the doctrine – that holism need not (so to speak) be swallowed whole since we *can* assign content and truth-conditions to particular statements while acknowledging the extent to which they are informed by a range of background beliefs and presuppositions. As so often with such debates there is a tendency to polarise the issue so that somehow – absurdly – we are offered what amounts to a straight choice between logical atomism (or something very like it) and the idea of meaning and belief-content as unspecifiable except with reference to the entire circumambient culture. It is, to say the least, an unenviable choice and one that bears no resemblance to what actually goes in our everyday decision-procedures as well as in other, more specialised (e.g., scientific) contexts of enquiry.

Literary critics have mostly got by on some weaker version of meaning-holism, whether as applied to the complex of meanings within some particular text, or to the various kinds of relationship assumed to exist between text and wider historical or cultural context. Thus, formalist critics tend to emphasise immanent structures of metaphor, ambiguity, irony, etc., on the premise that contextualism can be held within well-defined bounds, while New Historicists and Cultural Materialists focus rather on the social dynamics of meaning or the force-field of 'resistance and negotiation' (Stephen Greenblatt) which exceeds all such restrictively work-based ideas of what counts as a relevant context. In this respect they share the holistic approach of a hermeneutic theorist like Gadamer, though reading more often on the look-out for conflicts and instances of ideological tension, and not with a view to some ultimate convergence of interpretive horizons.

Of course it may be said that literary criticism, as generally practised, is not so much concerned with any truth-claims, propositions, or statements to be found in literary texts, but rather with interpreting their meaning or significance in a broadly contextual and non-assertoric sense. To this extent holism – in one or another version – is the default philosophy of most literary criticism. At any rate it doesn't entail the kinds of far-reaching anti-realist or sceptical conclusion that result when similar arguments are applied to philosophy of science or other branches of epistemological enquiry. Nevertheless some critics – including William Empson in his book *The Structure of Complex Words* (1951) – have made a strong case for interpreting literary language in terms of its implicit propositional structures or logico-semantic grammar, rather than some vaguely inclusive rhetoric of paradox, irony, or whatever. Thus, Empson rejects the holistic theory, developed by I.A. Richards, that meanings are somehow 'spread out' over more or less extended passages, and hence that any implied propositional content can only be a matter of associative linkage through a process of gradually emergent contextual definition. On the contrary, Empson argues: what often occurs is the reverse process whereby a whole range of meanings *and the various logical entailment relations between them* are condensed into a single 'complex word' which is then felt to carry a 'compacted doctrine' and to act as a focal point for interpreting the wider context of argument.

Among these keywords are 'wit' in Pope's *Essay on Criticism*; 'sense' in a wide range of texts from Shakespeare to Jane Austen and Wordsworth; 'all' in Milton's *Paradise Lost*; 'honest' in *Othello*; 'fool' in Erasmus's *The Praise of Folly* and *King Lear*; and 'dog' (when addressed to human beings) as a word which runs the whole gamut of meanings from cynical contempt – as in *Timon of Athens* – to a Restoration usage where it serves to convey a kind of proto-Darwinian admiration for those 'rock-bottom' animal virtues (fidelity, stoicism, a straightforward pleasure in the senses) that mark the emergence of a secular-humanist ethos. In each case Empson applies his logico-semantic 'machinery' – developed at length in the book's early chapters – to draw out the various verbal 'equations' (or structures of implied statement) which enable those words to express such a range of complex, ideologically charged, and often conflictual meanings. It was this aspect of his work that inspired Raymond Williams to write his book *Keywords* (1976) where the method is extended – minus much of the machinery – to an analysis of various words that Williams sees as having played a crucial role in the shaping of social and cultural attitudes over the past two centuries.

Empson's main theoretical point, as against Richards, is that we simply could not interpret language – let alone explain its power to communicate across large distances of time and cultural milieu – on anything like the full-scale meaning-holistic account. For on this theory, as Richards describes it, there is nothing more to the business of interpretation than a kind of open-ended contextual adjustment very like the process that Quine describes in 'Two Dogmas of Empiricism'. And from here it is but a short step to the conclusion – eagerly embraced by cultural relativists – that meaning and truth are likewise nothing more than products of pragmatic or interpretive convenience. This is why Empson devotes such efforts to developing an alternative, i.e., a truth-based, propositional theory of complex words with application both to literary texts and to (so-called) 'ordinary language'. Even in the case of 'simple flat prosaic' words such as the deceptively unassuming 'quite' there is room for some quite extraordinary subtleties of tone, meaning and social implication. For it is precisely Empson's point – as against the 'old' New Critics and formalists of various persuasion – that poets communicate in much the same way as everyday language-users, albeit very often at a higher level of semantic complexity. What enables them to do so – and readers to interpret their meaning – is this capacity of language for conveying intentions through structures of implied logico-semantic entailment, structures that are context-sensitive but not entirely context-dependent or (in the Quinean-holistic sense) context-relative. At any rate it seems fair to conclude – like Fodor and LePore in their survey of the field – that an adequate case for meaning-holism has not yet been made and that so far the doctrine has produced more problems than constructive or persuasive solutions. [CN]

Further reading: Empson 1951; Fodor and LePore 1991; Gadamer 1975; Heidegger 1962; Kuhn 1970; Quine 1980, 1981; Richards 1938; Ricoeur 1981; Rorty 1991; Winch 1958.

humanism   A word with a variety of meanings. Usually, a viewpoint which advocates the supreme value of human beings: 'man the measure of all things'. During the period of Renaissance Europe, those who studied the classics (i.e. Ancient Greek and Roman texts) were deemed humanists. They espoused an optimism about human possibilities and achievements. During the twentieth century, being a humanist commonly implies an attitude antithetical to religious beliefs and institutions.

In the post-war period debates have been waged between academics over the term humanism in a variety of contexts (e.g. politics, ethics, philosophy of language). In this context, a humanist has come to signify (amongst other things) someone who advocates a view of human nature which stresses the autonomy of individual agency with regard to such matters as moral or political choice, or one who adheres to the view that human **subjectivity** is the source of **meaning** in language-use. A humanist, on this view, is someone who presupposes that there are essential properties (e.g. autonomy, freedom, intentionality, the ability to use language for the purpose of producing meaningful propositions, rationality) which define what it is to be human. Such a conception of subjectivity has been criticised by way of an invocation of theories of meaning derived from **structuralism** and **post-structuralism**. Following on from such thinkers as Nietzsche, writers within these schools have argued that the production of meaning, and therefore subjectivity, is a matter of relations of **discourse**s of **power** (Foucault) or processes of semantic slippage within language (Derrida) rather than a matter of an extra-linguistic subject who exists 'outside' the domain of language and subsequently 'uses' language to express their intentions. Such views have been taken up by advocates of **postmodernism**, who have claimed, for example, that the politics that purportedly accompanies humanism is susceptible to being undermined by these forms of analysis. Such a view depends upon whether or not one is inclined to accept the claim that the advocacy of a particular **ontology** of the subject commits one to a particular kind of politics. Certainly, many facets of liberalism are not so easily swept away by advocating an anti-humanism. For example, the anti-humanism implicit in philosopher Jean-François Lyotard's conventionalist account of language in *The Differend: Phrases in Dispute* does not circumvent certain key principles of liberal thought as elaborated by J.S. Mill in *On Liberty*, but might rather be said to be compatible with them (see Sedgwick 1998).

Other thinkers who adopt an anti-humanist attitude include Heidegger (whose conception of dasein should not be confused with 'humanist' accounts of subjectivity; indeed, Heidegger explicitly rejected the humanism of Jean-Paul Sartre's existentialism in his 'Letter on Humanism' (1947)); and Louis Althusser, whose 'structural Marxism' opposed Marx's contention that humans were the authors of their own destiny with the view that social relations are instrumental in the construction of identity, belief systems and forms of consciousness. (See **ideological state apparatus**.) [PS]

Further reading: Callinicos 1976; Davies 1997; Heidegger 1996; Sartre 1990; Sedgwick 1998.

hypothetico–deductive method   The hypothetico-deductive method (H-D) is one of a number of attempts to describe the methodology of the physical sciences (see **philosophy of science**). Basically, the methodology of science described by the H–D model is as follows: (i) a hypothesis is put forward; (ii) various statements are then deduced from this hypothesis; (iii) these statements are then tested experimentally. If the hypothesis fails the process of experimental testing, then it is rejected. If, however, the hypothesis can be supported experimentally, then it is tentatively accepted.

This methodology was proposed as a solution to the problem of **induction**. Crudely, this is the problem of how a limited number of observations can be taken to support a theory or law which purports to hold for all members of a class of objects. On the H–D model, we are not committed to accepting any hypothesis as absolutely proven by experiment. Thus, in turn, we are not committed to the derivation of any universal law or theory from a limited number of observations. The best known supporter of the H–D method is Sir Karl Popper. Philosophers of science, such as Lipton, hold that this description of the methodology of science remains popular because practising scientists feel that it closely reflects what they, as scientists, actually do.

There are a number of criticisms of the H–D method, not least of which is the view that it is more a rational reconstruction, rather than a descriptive account of what scientists, in fact, do (Gjertsen 1989: 106–10). However, perhaps the most damaging criticism arises as a result of the work of Pierre Duhem (see entry for **meaning**). According to Duhem, no scientist ever tests a single hypothesis in theoretical isolation. Rather, he or she implicitly employs a whole group of hypotheses. This being so, then it is impossible to know *which* hypothesis is being either rejected or tentatively accepted. [SH]

Further reading: Duhem 1962; Lipton 1991; Popper 1959.

ideal type   Ideal type is a term originating in Max Weber's **sociology**. It is a term that is easily misunderstood. For Weber, an ideal type was an abstract model, usually of some social **institution** or process. The ideal type therefore attempts to identify and isolate the key characteristics of the social institution. It will guide empirical enquiry, drawing attention to the sort of features which the social scientist should be looking for and documenting, and may be modified in the light of empirical research. (See **bureaucracy**, for an example of a Weberian ideal type.) The ideal type is therefore 'ideal' in the sense of being an abstraction. Not all the features of the ideal type will necessarily be manifest in every (or any) empirical manifestation of the type. Crucially, the ideal type is not 'ideal' in the sense of being an account of the perfect or desirable form of the social institution. [AE]

identity   The issue of identity is central to cultural studies, in so far as cultural studies examines the contexts within which and through which both individuals and groups construct, negotiate and defend their identity or self-understanding. Cultural studies draws heavily on those approaches to the problem of identity that question what may be called orthodox accounts of identity. Orthodoxy assumes that the self is something autonomous (being stable and independent of all external influences). Cultural studies draws on those approaches that hold that identity is a response to something external and different from it (an **other**).

In orthodox European philosophy, at least from Descartes' writings in the seventeenth century, it has been assumed that the self (*ego* or **subject**) exists as an autonomous source of meaning and agency. Descartes himself found that the only thing that he could not doubt was that he existed, and that this existence took the form of a 'thinking substance' (Descartes 1968). This notion of the autonomous subject, sure of its own identity and continuing throughout the individual human being's life, was dominant not just in philosophy, but also in political thought (not least as a grounding assumption of **liberalism**) and psychology. The idea was questioned however, not least by the Scottish philosopher David Hume, in the eighteenth century (Hume 1978: 251–63). Hume observed that the contents of his consciousness included images (or sense-impressions) of everything of which he was thinking (either directly perceiving, or recalling in memory). There was, though, no image of the self that was supposedly doing this perceiving and remembering. Hume therefore proffered what was commonly known as the 'bundle theory' of the self, such that the self is nothing more than a bundle of sense impressions, that continually changed as the individual had new experiences or recalled old ones.

In the late nineteenth century, Emile Durkheim posed a fundamental challenge to liberal individualism (Durkheim 1984). The liberal presupposed the primacy of the individual, and thus that society was composed out of individuals (brought together, for example, in a **social contract**). In contrast, Durkheim argued that the individual was a product of society (not that society was a product of individuals). His point was that a modern understanding of individuality (and thus, the self-understanding of humans in modern society) was a product of that particular culture. In pre-industrial societies, with little or no economic specialisation (or **division of labour**), all members of the society would be similar in **attitudes**, **values** and **norms**. Such societies were held together purely because of this homogeneity (see **mechanical solidarity**). In contrast, in industrial society, with its high degree of specialisation, individualism occurs because people live distinctive lives with distinctive experiences. Their values and attitudes can then diverge. Durkheim therefore argues that individual identity is not primary, but is a product of economic organisation.

George Herbert Mead's analysis of the self poses an alternative set of problems for the idea of an autonomous ego. For Mead, the self is constructed through its relations with others. Mead distinguishes the 'I' from the 'me', arguing that: 'The "I" is the response of the organism to the attitudes of others; the "me" is the organised set of attitudes of others which one himself assumes' (Mead 1934: 175). The ego thus collapses into little more than an animal response. The self, and thus self-consciousness, rests rather upon the internalisation of the viewpoint of others. The 'I' becomes self-conscious only in so far as it can imagine how it is seen by others, and responds accordingly. The development of the self therefore depends upon the others it encounters. This line of thought is fundamental to the **symbolic interactionist** approach in sociology. In the work of Erving Goffman (1959) it is taken further. Goffman suggests that the self is a product of particular **interactions**, in so far as the individual's capacities, attitudes and ways of behaving (and possibly, of conceiving of him- or herself) changes as the people around him or her change. Alone, a person is either not self-conscious, and as such does not have, at that moment a self, or is self-conscious, in so far as he or she is aware of how he or she would appear to some more or less specific other. The self therefore has no stability, being almost as fluid as the self proposed by Hume.

Psychoanalysis opens up a further series of questions against the orthodox view of identity. For Freud, identity rests on the child's assimilation of external persons. The self is structured through the relationship of the ego, id and super-ego. While the id is the instinctive substrate of the self, and the super-ego, crucially, is the constraining moral consciousness that is internalised in the process of psychological development, the ego may be understood either as the combination of the id and super-ego, or as an agency separate from these two. The latter interpretation is, in the current context, possibly the more interesting, for it suggests that the ego is never self-identical. Erik Erikson's psychodynamic theory develops upon this. Identity for Erikson is a process between the identity of the individual and the identity of the communal culture. It was Erikson who coined the phrase 'identity crisis' in the 1940s. At first, the term referred to a person who had lost a sense of 'personal sameness and historical continuity' (Erikson 1968: 22). As such, the individual is separated from the culture that can give coherence to his or her sense of self. Later, it came to characterise youth, as a stage in the psychological development of any individual.

In Lacan's reinterpretation of Freud, the problematic identity of the self or subject, is explored further. For Lacan, self-consciousness emerges only at the mirror stage (at approximately six to eighteen months). Here the infant recognises its reflection as a reflection of itself. It therefore comes to know itself, not directly, but through the mirror image. The self emerges as the promise of control in the face of the fragmentation that occurs as the child is separated from the mother. However, as for Freud, the male child's identity depends upon that of the mother (allowing, in English at least, a pun on (m)other). The child enters language through the imposition of the law by the father, with the 'no' that prohibits incest with the mother. The child desires the mother in order to regain a primal unity. This is a desire to disobey the father's prohibition, and yet it must be repressed. Thus, Lacan can argue, the unconscious is structured like language. In effect, this is to argue that the self (or more properly the subject) is positioned by language, which is to say that it is positioned as always repressing its own lack of unity. Althusser's **structuralist** version of **Marxism** offers a parallel account of the subject, albeit now as a product of **ideology**. Social institutions such as the church, education, police, family and **mass media** 'interpellate' or hail the subject, again positioning him or her within society.

The work of Foucault may also be interpreted through the centrality of the question of identity. Thus, in his early work on madness (1971), he analyses how madness is conceived differently in different ages (comparing, for example, the Renaissance view of madness as its own form of reason, with the rationalist seventeenth-century's exclusion of the insane from society). Madness is thus socially constructed and specific, and historically variable social practices exist to constrain it. Yet, crucially for the seventeenth and eighteenth centuries, madness is also the other, in comparison to which the sane and rational define themselves. The identity of the dominant group in society therefore depends upon its construction of its own other. In Foucault's later writings, he turns to the problem of the construction of the 'self' (especially in relation to sexuality) through its positioning within **discourses** (1981). From this, the self may be theorised in terms of the conceptual and other intellectual resources that it calls upon in order to write or talk about itself, and in the way in which it is written about, or written to. The way in which a **text** is composed will anticipate, and thus situate, a certain self as reader.

Structuralist and post-structuralist questioning of the nature of self-identity, as found in the work of Lacan, Althusser and Foucault, may also be linked to an identity politics. The recognition that identity is not merely constructed, but depends upon some other, opens up the theoretical space for marginal or oppressed groups to challenge and re-negotiate the identities that have been forced upon them in the process of domination. Ethnic identities, gay and lesbian identities and female identities are thus brought into a process of political change. (See also **self**.) [AE]

ideological state apparatus   A conception developed by French **structuralist** Marxist Louis Althusser. Althusser developed the notion of ideological state apparatuses (or ISAs) in an attempt to both expand and clarify the meaning of the term **'ideology'** as it is presented in the thoughts of Karl Marx and Friedrich Engels, in line with his revision of traditional Marxist theory. Althusser argued that the traditional Marxist conception of ideology, although in essence correct, is too restrictive and insufficiently subtle as a means of elucidating the structures which underpin Marxist analysis of society. On the traditional model, the term 'ideology' is usually taken to refer to abstracted and illusory forms of thought which serve to naturalise, and thereby legitimise, the dominant social order of capitalism. The system of ideas which function as norms within capitalist society are therefore an articulation of the interests of the ruling class, and hence the base-structure of material relations of production is directly reflected in the ideological superstructure of ideas which serve to legitimise capitalist power. Althusser argued that such an account lacks an important aspect: although the theory of ideology provides an account of the structure of ideas which serve to naturalise the rule of the dominant class, it fails to address the way in which capitalism must at the same time seek to reproduce the conditions of production necessary to its continued survival. This is done, Althusser argued, through ideological state apparatuses.

Thus, the state, which is seen in **Marxism** as consisting of apparatuses of repression (such as a police-force, armed forces, prisons, etc.) has, in addition, ideological apparatuses which carry out the function of reproducing the conditions of production. Such apparatuses include religious institutions, the education system, the system of law, political parties, the media and the family. Through these apparatuses ideology functions to construct the **subjectivity** of individuals, and in so doing it allocates them particular roles within the capitalist system of production. For example, the education system, Althusser argues, functions to satisfy the capitalist demand that a variety of roles be filled by individuals within society. The majority of school children leave school at a fairly early age, equipped with the basic skills required for a future as shop-floor labourers; a smaller number remain within the education system for a longer period, and are equipped with additional skills which suit them to fill the functions necessary to the successful managment of labourers; still fewer are released from the system of education late on to take their place as senior functionaries within the state (and some, i.e. teachers and academics, are never destined to leave the system, but take on the role of educating the next generation). Likewise, the family structure is an ISA which provides the raw material of humanity required before the education system can perform its task upon them. [PS]

Further reading: Althusser 1971.

ideology It can plausibly be suggested that a theory of ideology is fundamental to any critical social or cultural science. However, the exact meaning of the term is often elusive or confused. Its most common use may be simply to refer to a more or less coherent set of beliefs (such as a political ideology, meaning the beliefs, values and basic principles of a political party or faction). 'Ideology' is used in this sense in some branches of political science. In **Marxism** and the **sociology of knowledge**, however, it has taken on much more subtle meanings, in order to analyse the way in which knowledge and beliefs are determined by the societies in which they emerge and are held.

The term was coined at the end of the eighteenth century, by the French philosopher Destutt de Tracy, to refer to a science (*logos*) of ideas. Such a science would be based in analysis of human perception, conceived itself as a sub-discipline of biology, and the *idéologues* sought to reform educational practices on the basis of it. (This origin is more important than it may initially seem, for it presents the argument that ideas depend on some, non-ideational, substrate. For de Tracy, this is biology; for social science it will be the material, economic and political practices and structures of society.) Napoleon's ridiculing of the *idéologues* led to 'ideology' becoming a pejorative term.

It is with Marx that ideology becomes an important critical concept. Marx's approach to ideology may be introduced through the famous observation that, for any society, the ideas of the ruling **class** are the ruling ideas. This is to suggest that our understanding and knowledge of the world (and especially, if not exclusively, of the social world) is determined by political interests. There are certain beliefs, and certain ways of seeing the world, that will be in the interests of the dominant class (but not in the interests of subordinate classes). For example, it was in the interests of the dominant class in **feudalism** to believe in the divine right of kings. The authority of the king and the aristocracy is given by God, and is thus beyond question. It is in the interests of the **bourgeoisie** (the owners and controllers of industry) in **capitalism** to see the social world as highly individualistic and competitive. What for Marx is the genuinely social and collective nature of human life (not least in class membership) is thereby concealed, and the possibilities of effective **proletarian** resistance to capitalism are minimised. The dominant class is able to propagate its ideas throughout society due to its control of various forms of communication and education (such as the **mass media**, the church and schools).

While ideology, in the Marxist sense, is a distorted way of viewing the world, it is not strictly false (and so ideology is not simply a synonym for **false consciousness**). Marx's observation that religion is the opium of the masses (1975: 244) expresses this more complex idea. On one level, religion does distort the subordinate classes' understanding of the social world, not least in its promise of a reward in heaven, for the injustices suffered in this world. Yet, the metaphorical reference to opium is important, not just because opium dulls our experience of pain, but also because opium induces dreams. Heaven is therefore an idea to be taken seriously (although not literally), for it does contain an image of justice – but one that should be realised in this world, not the hereafter. In this sense, ideology is an illusory solution to a real problem (Larrain 1979). The task of the critic of ideology is therefore to recognise this – to recognise the way in which ideology inverts our understanding of real problems – and thereby identify and tackle the real problem.

The Marxist theory of ideology presupposes that ideology is a distortion. It may therefore be set against true knowledge.

In the sociology of knowledge, not least in its development by the German sociologist Karl Mannheim (1960), ideology loses its links to class and to domination, and so challenges this notion of truth. Mannheim retains the link that Marx establishes between ideas and the material base of society, but in order to argue that people from different sections of society will understand the world in different ways. The difference between the bourgeois understanding of the world and the proletariat is not then the difference between the views of a dominant and reactionary class and a subordinated, progressive class, but simply the difference between two, equally valid, **worldviews**. For Mannheim, there is then no single truth against which all ideologies can be judged. Each ideology will have its own standards of truth and accuracy, dependent upon the social circumstances within which it is produced.

The Marxist account of ideology can be seen to have undergone two important revisions in the twentieth century. First, the development of the theory of **hegemony**, by the Italian theorist Gramsci, tackled the problem that the theory of ideology appeared to suggest that ideas could be passively imposed upon the subordinate classes. The theory of hegemony suggests, rather, that ideologies are actually negotiated in the face of contradictory evidence and life experiences. The second revision stems from the work of the French **structuralist**, Althusser. Althusser overturned the emphasis in the theory of ideology on ideas. Ideology need not be about what people think, but rather about how they act – 'lived relations'. Ideological practices, which are taken-for-granted, constitute the human **subject** and his or her **identity** within capitalism, thus allowing him or her to function. (See also **behavioural ideology**.) [AE]

Further reading: Abercrombie *et al.* 1980; Althusser 1971; Barrett 1991; Eagleton 1991; Hall 1982.

indexicality   Indexicality refers to a property of social actions and utterances: that their **meaning** depends upon the particular context within which they occur. This property is of central importance to **ethnomethodologists**' approach to the analysis of social **interaction**. For example, '2 × 2 = 4' is not a self-evidently meaningful utterance. In an elementary maths class, it has meaning. As a reply to the question: 'What's the weather like out there?' it is thoroughly perplexing. Competent members of society have the ability to recognise relevant properties in a context that give meaning to the utterance or action (and thus are said to be 'repairing indexicality'). Thus, generally we can recognise when we are in a maths class and when not. However, it would be an endless task to explain how we recognise this particular situation as a maths class. To give a simple example, Garfinkel (the founder of ethnomethodology) asked students to explain a sentence. Having been given what seemed an adequate paraphrase (or 'gloss'), Garfinkel pointed out that the student had not explained the words used in his or her explanation. The brighter students no doubt rapidly realised that the repairing of indexicality (i.e. the giving of a totally exhaustive account of the meaning of a particular social event) is an endless task. The remarkable thing then is that competent members of society get by perfectly well, most of the time, without being able to articulate fully what they are doing or what it means. However, confusion and 'misunderstandings' can occur when the background assumptions of one person clash markedly with those of another, and thus repair indexicality differently. (You mishear my request about the weather as an invitation to start reciting your multiplication tables.) [AE]

Further reading: Weider 1974.

individual/ism   A person or **self**. Taken in the sense of something which cannot be subject to any further division, an individual is often contrasted with a group. The view that individual selves are (i) irreducible, (ii) endowed with the ability to use their **rationality** according to their own dispositions and desires, and (iii) ought to be free civic agents, is associated with individualism. This conceives of the individual as a free agent in the market place and advocates a view of political and social liberty on these terms. It is a view often linked to the influence of the writings of Adam Smith (for example, in the UK in the 1980s to the impact of his ideas on Margaret Thatcher, who advocated a free-market individualism). [PS]

Further reading: Avineri and De-Shalit 1992; Lukes 1973b; MacPherson 1962; Morris 1991.

induction The method of induction represents the first attempt to give a general account of the methodology of science. This account has a long history which can be traced back to the work of Francis Bacon (1561–1626). On this model, the scientist begins by making a large number of observations. Once the observation stage is complete the scientist then constructs a general law or theory based on the observations he has made. This law or theory can then be used to make predictions about similar phenomena in the future.

A formal definition of this procedure is given by the principle of induction: 'If all observed members of a class of objects possess a particular property, then all members of this class share this property'. There is an obvious fault with this principle as it is stated here, i.e. that not all members of the class being considered have been observed. In other words, what a scientist following the method of induction seems to be doing is to base a claim about all the members of a particular class of objects on their observations of only a limited number of objects in that class. For example, there is the famous case of the black swans of Australia. Until relatively recently, it had been thought that all swans were white because no swans of any other colour had been observed. Following the method of induction, this would amount to the claim that from a limited number of observations, it could be concluded that any swan in any place in the universe, past or present, was, is and will be white. Unfortunately, it was discovered that black swans exist in Australia. Thus, it seems that such a generalisation is unjustified. This is one version of the famous problem of induction.

There have been various attempts at answering this problem. One popular solution was to adapt the principle of induction to say that: 'If all observed members of a class of objects possess a particular property, then probably all members of this class share this property'. However, there are a number of problems associated with the notion of 'probability' and with its application to the inductive method. Alternatively, Karl Popper (see under entry for **philosophy of science**) suggested the abandonment of induction and the adoption of falsification as a description of the methodology of science. This involves the tentative assent to a hypothesis, rather than its outright acceptance. Thomas Kuhn also suggested a rejection of induction. However, Kuhn's motives were rather different to those of Popper. For Kuhn, what the problem of induction indicates is a fundamental mistake in any attempt to give science a fully rational foundation. (See also: **philosophy of science**.) [SH]

Further reading: Chalmers 1982; Kuhn 1970; Popper 1972; Russell 1988.

institution   As a technical term in social science, an institution is a regular and continuously repeated social practice. As such, the term has a wider coverage than in everyday usage, including not merely, prisons, asylums, schools, hospitals and government offices, but also **language**, and moral and **cultural** practices. [AE]

interaction   In interaction, the actions of human beings are made in response to, and anticipation of, the actions of others. Interaction is of importance, for it can be argued that it is only through interaction that social events and situations are given **meaning**, that social reality is itself constructed (Berger and Luckmann 1961), and that personal identity is formed (Mead 1934). (See also **symbolic interactionism**.) [AE]

internalism and externalism   Topics in **epistemology**, but also relevant to issues in cultural theory. One answer to the question 'What is knowledge?' – knowledge is *justified true belief*. (Plato offered this classical definition in his dialogue the *Theaetetus*.) Thus in order for something to count as a genuine item of knowledge it should satisfy the following three criteria: (i) it must be true, (ii) we must believe it to be true, and (iii) our belief should be adequately grounded, i.e. based on adequate evidence, arrived at through a valid process of reasoning, or known as a matter of self-evident (*a priori*) truth. On the face of it this seems a pretty good working definition. Still there are certain problems with it, as shown by counter-examples where the above three conditions are satisfied but where they do not yield genuine knowledge in anything like our usual (intuitive as well as philosophical) sense of that term. Thus we might believe X, and X might be true, and we might moreover have grounds for our belief, and yet it just happens that they are not the *right* grounds in this particular case.

An alternative approach – much favoured of late – is to make justification dependent on the existence of some causal-explanatory link between beliefs and objects-of-belief. This approach is often called 'externalist' since it breaks with the traditional ('internalist') idea that knowledge is a certain distinctive state of mind, one that can be accessed only by the person who knows at first hand what it is to be in that particular state. On the contrary, it is argued: what properly counts as knowledge (– justified true belief) is just what the person is entitled to assert on the basis of their having been exposed to the right sorts of causal stimuli or their having drawn appropriate conclusions from the right kinds of knowledge-conducive learning experience. So an outside observer would be just as well – perhaps even better – placed to judge whether that person's beliefs qualified as genuine knowledge or whether they failed to come up to the required justificatory standard. Externalism is therefore very much a part of the widespread present-day dissatisfaction with **Cartesian** ideas about mind, knowledge and privileged (first-person) epistemic access.

Post-structuralists and postmodernists are likewise keen to disavow any lingering attachment to Cartesian thought. In this they take a lead from various (mainly French) sources, among them Jacques Lacan's psychonanalytic 'decentering' of the subject, Michel Foucault's Nietzsche-derived sceptical **genealogies** of knowledge, and Jacques Derrida's **deconstructive** readings of various texts in the western 'logocentric' tradition of thought from Plato, via Descartes, to Husserl and Heidegger. However, it might be argued (from an externalist standpoint) that these are just the kinds of extreme reactive development that result when a narrowly Cartesian (**subject-centred**) epistemology runs up against the limits of its own internal resources. At any rate, cultural theorists should be aware of alternative approaches, such as that summarised here, which adopt an entirely different approach to issues of knowledge and truth. [CN]

Further reading: Dancy 1985; Gettier 1963; Goldman 1986; McCulloch 1995; Shope 1983.

International Style Term, coined by Henry-Russell Hitchcock and developed by Philip Johnson to describe the new **architecture** that had begun to emerge in the 1920s, and ultimately to promote a unified body of architectural theory and practice by encapsulating the basic principles of modernism, in terms of a functional emphasis on volume, regularity and technical perfection. While rationalistic modernist architecture in Europe tended to be developed in the context of an explicit political project, Hitchcock and Johnson's description of the International Style perhaps more readily fits the apolitical, typically commercially oriented American architecture of the inter- and post-war years. One of Johnson's last summaries of principles of the International Style was: 'structural honesty; repetitive modular rhythms; clarity, expressed by oceans of glass; flat roof; box as perfect container; no ornament'. While this unquestionably, and inevitably, oversimplifies the diversity of modern architecture, it does express something very characteristic of much modern architecture, be it commercial or domestic, found throughout the world. [AE]

Further reading: Hitchcock and Johnson 1966.

intersubjectivity A property is **subjective** if it is only recognised by a particular human being (so that one's experience or susceptibility to pain is subjective, as is the enjoyment one derives from chocolate). A property is **objective** if it actually belongs to the object, exists independently of any observer, and can therefore be recognised by anyone who has the appropriate senses. (Not everyone will enjoy chocolate, but everyone, independently will perceive such properties as its colour and is weight.) The concept of 'intersubjectivity' opens up an important middle ground between these two oppositions. A property is intersubjective if human beings agree upon its existence, and thereby come to perceive it as if it existed in the external, objective world. Thus, **cultural** significance may be understood as intersubjective. A particular sound does not inherently have the meaning it does in a particular language, so it is not objective. Yet, it is not subjective, for (contra Humpty Dumpty) words cannot mean anything that I choose them to mean. Rather, the sound's meaning depends upon the hearer belonging to a particular linguistic community, or at least understanding the appropriate language. It may then be argued that the meaningfulness and significance of all social events is intersubjective. [AE]

intertextuality The term 'intertextuality' was coined by Julia Kristeva to indicate that a **text** (such as a novel, poem or historical document) is not a self-contained or autonomous entity, but is produced from other texts. The interpretation that a particular reader generates from a text will then depend on the recognition of the relationship of the given text to other texts. Thus, for example, a photograph of a politician in a newspaper may yield more meaning, or further levels of meaning, if it is interpreted, not simply as a representation of its subject, but rather through a frame constituted by other photographs of the same person (possibly in widely different situations), speeches made by him/her, newspaper reports and comments on him/her, and even cartoons lampooning the politician. Similarly, our understanding of David Lean's film

197

Great Expectations is influenced by our reading of Dickens's novel, or conversely our understanding of the novel is now framed by having seen the film. Intertextuality may be understood as the thesis that no text exists outside its continuing interpretation and reinterpretation. There can then never be a definitive reading of a text, for each reading generates a new text, that itself becomes part of the frame within which the original text is interpreted. [AE]

Further reading: Barthes 1974; Kristeva 1986a.

irony   The term 'irony' is derived from the Greek *eironeia*, meaning 'simulated ignorance'. Its precise definition is, however, elusive. At its simplest, it is a figure of speech in which what a person says is the opposite to what he or she means (so referring to the tall as short, the cowardly as courageous, and so on). This inversion captures little of the subtlety of irony. A liar or confidence trickster may say the opposite of what he or she means, but the liar is not using irony, for those who understand an utterance as ironic will recognise the inversion of meaning. The point of the inversion is therefore important – why say the opposite of what you mean, unless you are trying to deceive your audience? Two reasons can be offered. First, irony is a form of mockery or critical comment. Ironically to dub the cowardly courageous is to mock their lack of courage. Irony usefully saves the speaker from committing him or herself to a positive position, and to a degree may keep the speaker detached from the issues upon which he or she comments. (A classic example of literary irony is Swift's *Modest Proposal* (1729), in which he advocated eating Irish babies as a solution to the population problem. He thereby ridicules existing solutions to the 'Irish problem', without offering a serious solution of his own.) Second, recognition of irony as irony may serve to distinguish the sophisticated members of an in-group, from the more simple creatures without.

Two special meanings of irony may be noted. 'Socratic irony' refers to the manner of argument employed by Socrates, at least as he is represented in the early dialogues of Plato. Socrates pretends both ignorance and a sympathy with the position of a supposed expert on some topic. This affectation allows Socrates to question his victims, harrying them until their arguments and contradictions collapse into contradiction and incoherence. 'Romantic irony' is especially associated with early nineteenth-century German philosopher-poets, including Hölderlin and Friedrich Schlegel. Such irony, drawing on Socratic irony, is explicitly associated with the ambiguity, uncertainty and fragmentation of meaning. For Schlegel, in irony 'everything should be playful and serious, guilelessly open and deeply hidden'. Or again: 'Irony is the form of paradox. Paradox is everything which is simultaneously good and great' (Simpson 1988: 183). Irony therefore disrupts the taken-for-granted meaningfulness of utterance and writing, exposing its artificiality. It is this emphasis on the problematic and ultimately indeterminate nature of the interpretation of any utterance or **text** that carries irony into contemporary literary theory. Thus, for Barthes, irony is the 'essence of writing', in that it exposes the inability of the writer to control the interpretation of the text. [AE]

Further reading: Kierkegaard 1966.

jazz The word 'jazz' has obscure origins; the most common etymology is that it developed from 'jass', a turn-of-the-century US term for semen. 'Jass music' was hence sexually-charged, dissolute music played in brothels or other dubious establishments and in which musical competence was less important than infectious rhythm and performance gimmicks. Others have claimed, however, that 'jazz' is a word whose origins are North African or even Arabic (a language spoken very widely in North and West Africa) and hence that it predates slavery and the music which is known by that name today. In that case, the link with 'jass' would appear to be rather pernicious.

The music has a long and complex history, and many elements of its early development are still in dispute. What is beyond question is that most of its primary musical innovators have been, and to a lesser extent continue to be, black Americans, including the earliest influential individuals, 'Buddy' Bolden, 'King' Oliver and Louis Armstrong. They played in the New Orleans style (although all three eventually left that city for Chicago), which is characterised by small groups, a regular pulse and group improvisation on simple melodies such as marching tunes. As groups grew larger and audiences became more respectable, the music evolved into 'swing', a dance-hall craze which lasted for over two decades and helped create an audience of more affluent middle-class whites. Duke Ellington is now recognised as the master of swing composition, but the Count Basie orchestra was no less successful and white Paul Whiteman's enormous band was even more so.

Gradually, musicians in swing groups began to experiment. Players such as Coleman Hawkins, Lester Young and Charlie Christian (one of the few guitarists to have an unshakeable place in jazz history) developed a more complex solo style, and sought smaller groupings which would give them the space to develop ideas over a longer period – it is easily forgotten that for the first forty years or so of what is now called 'jazz', individual instrumental statements were not a particularly important feature of the music. In contrast, be-bop groups tend to be small – between three and six players is typical – and to focus on solo statements. Charlie Parker, Dizzy Gillespie and Thelonious Monk are among the most famous innovators in the field, developing the music into a ferociously complex, competitive arena in which technical virtuosity and near-instantaneous reflexes were pitted against intricate harmonic structures and breakneck tempi.

Since the assimilation of be-bop into the jazz mainstream, the music has fragmented into a large number of different schools. Perhaps most significantly, the rigours of be-bop harmony were abandoned by practitioners of 'free jazz', particularly Ornette Coleman and (in his later work) John Coltrane. This music developed, through contact with the European **avant–garde**, into what is today known as 'free improvisation'. Also of very great significance was the move by many musicians into electrified instrumentation in the 1970s, an economically dry time for jazz. In effecting this change, players such as Miles Davis and Herbie Hancock revolutionised the vocabulary of the music, opening the door for genres like fusion, acid jazz and electronic music generally. Jazz from these traditions has had, and continues to have, a strong formative influence on western popular music as a whole, and it would be fair to say that very popular forms of music such as hip hop and electronic dance music are deeply indebted to them.

All of the above is conventional wisdom, but it is also controversial; there are no neutral histories of jazz. Its racially fraught history in particular has led to massive critical distortions both negative (as when early critics denounced it as 'voodoo music') and positive (the primitivist criticism still occasionally produced today, which opposes the supposed instinctive physicality and emotionality of the black musician with the rational approach of white classical players). A useful collection of such distortions is Meltzer (1993). The most influential of studies which thematised its racial origins was LeRoi Jones' *Blues People: Negro Music in White America* (1965) (Jones is now known as Amiri Baraka; his books may be found under both names).

Another tendency in jazz criticism is to compare the music with that of the classical tradition. By far the most important study of this kind was Gunther Schuller's *Early Jazz* (1968), which argued that, if classical analytic standards are applied to jazz, the music may be better understood and appreciated. Famously, Adorno begged to differ, claiming that the comparison showed jazz to be an impoverished form of popular entertainment; on this, see particularly his 'On the Fetish Character of Hearing' (1978b). [RC]

Further reading: Berlin 1980; Berliner 1994; Collier 1977; Gabbard 1995; Jost 1981; Shepherd 1991; Stearns 1956; Wilmer 1992.

labelling Labelling theory is an important explanatory tool within the study of **deviance**. First proposed by Lemert (1951), but most closely associated with the work of Howard Becker (1963), it is grounded in **symbolic interactionism**. The theory argues that an individual does not become a deviant simply by breaking some behavioural norm (such as a law). Rather, 'deviant' is seen as a label that is imposed upon the individual. An initial violation of a commonly accepted behavioural rule becomes significant only if others react to it. Human beings are understood, within the theory, as forming their personal **identity** or self-understanding only through interaction with others. Therefore, if others perceive one's actions negatively, and crucially talk about you and describe your actions in this negative language, then you will begin to think of yourself in those terms. Your personal identity will then be constructed through those terms. Thus, labels, such as junkie or drug addict, lunatic or mentally ill, mugger and child molester, are not neutral. They are inherently critical of the sort of person they describe. In incorporating these labels into one's own self-identity, one learns to live and behave differently. (Goffman (1961), for example, has analysed the processes by which new inmates of asylums for the mentally ill learn to behave as mentally ill.) The deviant may be isolated from 'normal' society, turning to the company of other deviants. The **others** whom the individual encounters on a routine basis, and who are thus responsible for forming the individual's self-identity, change. A relatively minor violation of norms (such as the smoking of cannabis) can then be 'amplified' into more serious forms of deviance (such as the taking of hard drugs) as the deviant shifts from the norms of behaviour and language typical of 'normal' society, to those typical of 'deviant' **subcultures**. It may be added that the process by which the self-identity of the individual is reconstructed is not automatic. The imposition of a label may be resisted. Those with great economic or intellectual and educational resources will have more power to resist the application of a label (for example, by having the resources to provide a more adequate defence of themselves in court). [AE]

Further reading: Fine 1977; Gove 1980.

labour In economics, labour is one of the four factors of production, alongside **capital**, land (or natural resources) and enterprise, which is to say, it is one of the four general types of input or resource required for economic production. In orthodox economics, labour includes the number of people actually employed in, or who are available for, production, or a little more abstractly, the capacity to produce (understood in terms of intellectual and manual skills, and the exertion). In Marxist economics, labour is the source of all economic **value**, (hence the **labour theory of value**). In addition, the **proletariat** (the subordinate **class** within **capitalism**) are characterised by having to exchange their capacity to labour (or labour-power) for the **commodities** that they require in order to live. [AE]

labour theory of value The **labour** theory of **value** is an attempt to explain the value of goods and services in terms of the costs of their production, as opposed to their usefulness (or **use-value**). Elements of the labour theory can be traced back, at least to the seventeenth-century political philosopher John Locke, who analysed the appropriation of private property in terms of a person's ability to 'mix' their labour with natural resources (1980). The British economist David Ricardo (1772–1823) gave the first coherent account of the theory (Ricardo 1951), in part in response to the 'paradox of value'. It was argued that the usefulness of a good could not determine its value, as very useful entities, such as air and water, are generally free or very inexpensive. In contrast, apparently useless luxury goods (gold and diamonds, say) can be very expensive. The labour theory explains this in terms of the amount of labour (or labour-time) that went into their production, either directly, or indirectly through having being stored up by having been expended in the production of machinery and other capital goods. Water is easily found and conveyed to consumers, in contrast to the great amount of time needed to find and extract diamonds. In practice, the actual amount of labour expended in production is of less relevance than a social average labour-time (for otherwise the theory would imply that the products of the lazy would be worth more than those of the efficient). While the theory is fundamental to **Marxist** economics, in orthodox economics, since the late nineteenth century, it has been replaced by more sophisticated explanations of value grounded in usefulness (beginning with Marshall's account of marginal utility). (See also **surplus-value**.) [AE]

Further reading: Meek 1973

language   There are many approaches to language. From a common-sense standpoint, language might be taken as a vehicle for the **communication** of thoughts. Hence, **meaning** and its 'transmission' is essential to a definition of what language is. This view would conceive of a **subject** having thoughts, and in turn expressing them *through* language in the form of speech. Taken in this way, particular languages might be produced by particular cultures, but it would not necessarily be the case that thoughts are culturally specific (the issue of meaning, in other words, might turn on questions of human nature, on psychology, physiology, etc.). In turn, meaning, on this conception, would be primarily a matter of the intentions of speakers. This view is open to question from a number of perspectives, for example, approaches associated with **postmodernism, structuralism** and **post-structuralism**. On such accounts as these, language produces meaning not through the assertion by a language-independent speaker of a proposition which expresses an intention independently of the language used, but it is only in virtue of the existence of language (understood as a system of **signs**, or as a semantic process which is ontologically independent of the constitution of subjectivity) that there are such things as 'speakers' and 'intentions'. In turn, speakers are regarded as being constituted within language, and hence are not taken as ontologically prior to it. The tradition of **analytic philosophy** has offered a number of accounts of language and meaning which simply do not rely upon a self-conscious model of subjectivity as constituting their foundation, but point towards the logical and structural preconditions of languages as being of importance in our understanding of such issues; while Lacan's model of **psychoanalysis** envisages a structural link between the constitution of the **unconscious** and language (i.e. he claims the unconscious is structured like a language).

Equally important to any account of language are the notions of **representation** and **reference**. Thus, we can ask such questions as, 'does language represent the world to us, or construct it for us?' or 'does language succeed in referring to entities which are "non-linguistic"?' Such questions involve the consideration of issues related to the areas of **metaphysics, ontology** and **epistemology**. For example, Derrida's account of the metaphysical tradition of the west conceives of it as embodying a set of presuppositions about the nature of meaning and intention. Such presuppositions include the attitude that meaning is a matter of the 'presence' of speakers and that 'writing', in turn, is secondary to living speech in the hierarchy of meaning: speakers produce meaning, but need writing to preserve the living presence of meaning in their absence. Likewise, the view that subjectivity is the source of meaning presupposes a particular ontology of the **subject** (namely, that the subject is capable, in virtue of what it is, of agency with regard to the generation of meaning); while questions about the nature of knowledge (i.e. epistemological questions) are also questions concerned with language with regard to (i) its capability to refer to 'non-linguistic' experience or alternatively (ii) the linguistic **norms** or conventions which stipulate what counts as knowledge within any given community of speakers. If questions of normativity and community come to the fore, then any account of language must pay attention to the cultural factors involved in the construction of meaning.

Whether it is possible to talk about 'Language' (with a capital 'L') at all in a general sense is perhaps open to question. It has certainly been the case that many theories (e.g. structuralism) have at least an implicit investment in the belief that there are characteristics that can be described which are universally applicable to *all* languages. Only on the basis of such a view was structuralism able to lay claim to its status as a 'scientific' description of language. However, 'Language' in this sense is perhaps a conception which is bound up with problems of **metaphysics**, for what is referred to when one uses the word 'Language' in this way cannot be demonstrated or shown in the way in which the particular referents contained within a proposition can be. Another instance of such a conception would be the phrase 'universe': the referent here is a totality which cannot be shown, not least because the very act of attempting to show it would itself have to be part of what is shown. Likewise, talking of 'Language' at the very least presupposes that one can allude to a totality, of which the proposition which refers to this totality must itself be a part since it is linguistic (a problem related to Russell's aporia – cf. **grand narrative**). [PS]

langue In Saussure's linguistics, 'langue' refers to the under-lying structure and components of a language. It is thus made up of a repertoire of possibilities available to the speaker of the language, along with the rules that determine the meaningful selection and combination of available units of meaning. [AE]

Further reading: Barthes 1967b; Holdcroft 1991.

legitimation   A term in sociologist Max Weber's sociology of politics which means the acknowledgement on the part of a society's **subjects** of the right of their rulers to rule them. In the post-war period the issue of legitimation has become a central issue in social, political and cultural discussion. For Jean-François Lyotard, for example, the question of legitimation is one that is continually suspended within a theoretical double-bind. Questions of legitimation, on this view, are really genre-questions concerning appropriate means to particular ends (see **discourse**), and cannot be divorced from consideration of their social and cultural dimensions. Lyotard argues that there are no universal criteria for legitimation and that, in consequence, the political level is a realm of cultural antagonism between contending purposes rather than goal-oriented. He does, however, reserve a critical space for the study of language: the open-ended philosophical analysis of **rules**. Politics, on a Lyotardean model, would be about competing claims being fought out within the space of cultural life, not in terms of some overall, most desirable state of affairs towards which society should be aiming. Jürgen Habermas, in contrast, has tried to argue against this view (which endorses a politics of conflict or 'dissensus') with a consensual reading of the social language of 'communicative action'. (See also **rationality**.) [PS]

Further reading: Habermas 1976b, 1984, 1987; Lyotard 1988; Weber 1958.

liberalism   A key term within political philosophy, the word 'liberalism' is associated with a large number of thinkers (including Locke, Adam Smith, Malthus, Condorcet, J.S. Mill, Rawls and more recently Richard Rorty). The origins of liberalism can be traced back at least as far as the writings of John Locke (1632–1704). Indeed, Locke's work exhibits many of the key features that have subsequently been used to define liberalism. For instance, in the *Two Treatises of Government* (1690) Locke is concerned to show that the analysis of political power involves the consideration of certain key attributes all human beings possess (in Locke's case this means analysing human beings in their 'natural state', or the **'state of nature'** – a notion derived from the work of Thomas Hobbes (1588–1679)). By taking this approach Locke in effect asserts that there are a number of principles of political right that operate outside the realm of **civil society**, and indeed function to ground it. These principles are (i) freedom of action, and (ii) equality of right. Thus, in the state of nature no individual has the right to transgress another individual's basic freedom. Locke justifies this claim by way of reference to a conception of natural law derived from the claims of reason, 'the common rule and measure God hath given to mankind' (*Second Treatise*, section 11). From a rational point of view, it is claimed, every individual has the right both to self-protection and to claim compensation for suffering a wrong at the hands of another. From this it is clear that a particular conception of the human individual (conceived in a manner which divorces human subjectivity from the constraints of modes of social organisation) forms the basis for Locke's political discourse.

Each individual is, in Locke's view, self-interested. From this it follows that some form of regulative body is required for the impartial administration of these rights. This forms part of the basis of Locke's justification for the existence of government, which constitutes a means of arbitrating between the disputes which necessarily will arise between individuals situated in a state of nature (section 13). Government, in turn, rests on the constitution of civil society, which is voluntarily arrived at through a contract (section 14). Thus, in Locke's view the legitimacy of governmental power should be derived from the consent of those who fall under it. In principle, one is only subject to the power of government if one has agreed to enter into civil society, and thereby become a civil agent.

For Locke, civil society is ultimately derived from one basic principle of natural law which operates within the state of nature: the right to the possession of one's own body and the products thereof. Locke's argument can be summarised thus (sections 25–30): (i) all humans situated in the state of nature have the right to self-preservation; (ii) the earth is the common possession of all human beings equally; (iii) its natural products thus belong in principle to everybody; (iv) however, since these products are available for use it follows that there must be some means whereby they may be appropriated and thereby subsequently owned; (v) there is one piece of property all humans possess, namely their own bodies; (vi) if you own your body, then the products of your labour are also yours; (vii) hence, if you appropriate anything from the state of nature this must, by definition, be the result of your labour and consequently become yours. Once the latter point has been reached, Locke says, it follows that other persons do not have the right to take possession of what is now yours, viz. the products of your labour, for goods appropriated in this manner from the state of nature become through this process a matter of 'private right'. This right is God-given, since God would not have put the world of nature at humanity's disposal if they were not to be taken advantage of. There is, it follows, a 'law of reason', 'an original law of nature', which grounds the ownership of private property and thereby grounds civil society (section 30). In turn, on a Lockean account, the proper function of government is to protect the rights of individuals and of their property (both in the form of the individual's own body and the products of their labour). A limitation to appropriation in the state of nature is set by use: one may only own what can be used without waste (e.g. if one appropriates more apples than one can eat they will go off and be wasted; and the same point goes for land). However, with the invention of money (which is a non-perishable good) this limitation is overcome. For instance, one may indeed own a large quantity of land, the products of which can be exchanged for cash and hence do not go to waste. In turn, it is possible thereby to justify unequal property ownership: 'since gold and silver, being little useful to the life of man, in proportion to food, raiment, and carriage, has its value only from the consent of men . . . it is plain that the consent of men have agreed to the dispropor- tionate and unequal possession of the earth' (section 50). Liberty, it follows, does not guarantee equality. Indeed, the progression from the state of nature to civil society is, for Locke, one which brings with it a necessary inequality with regard to the possession of goods.

Locke's thought exhibits a number of features common to many liberal thinkers. First, a central concern is with the basis of the individual's right to the ownership of goods, including above all their own body. Second, this right is paramount and it is the function of good government to protect it. Third, liberty, in turn, is understood as the freedom to be left alone to pursue one's own goals with the minimum of interference from others. Fourth, the function of the state is articulated and established within this basic assumption concerning liberty: a state should be based on consent (from which it derives its legitimacy and authority), and has as its proper function the protection of the rights of civil agents. Fifth, the state therefore has a limited role in the lives of individuals: it is not there to prescribe particular modes of behaviour which individuals ought to adhere to, but rather ought only to oversee the behaviour of individuals to the extent of ensuring that one person's actions do not infringe the rights of another. It follows that for thinkers within the liberal tradi- tion the individual takes precedence over all other political concerns (i.e. individual liberty has priority over other values, such as equality).

These features are also evident in J.S. Mill's classic text *On Liberty* (1859). Mill's avowed aim in this text is to explore 'the nature and limits of the power which can be legitimately exer- cised by society over the individual' in the context of the social 'struggle between liberty and authority' (1859: 59). There is, for Mill, an inherent political tension which exists between the spheres of liberty and authority, between individual

211

freedom of thought and 'collective opinion' (manifested at its worst in the 'tyranny of the majority'). The individual is for Mill an independent entity with an accompanying right to this independence: 'his independence is, of right, absolute' (1859: 69). An individual exhibits abilities (such as those of reflection and choice) as well as passions, desires and purposes. Taken together, these features allow for the identification of the individual as that which possesses interests. Given a situation in which a diversity of individuals are present in a society, it follows that such a society will also contain a diversity of interests. It is just such a form of society, one which both contains and is an expression of the diversity of human possibility, manifested in the form of the individual, that Mill favours as being the most progressive. Hence, Mill's account of individuality and political authority simultaneously implies an affirmation of a particular conception of cultural life. A more 'progressive culture' is taken to be synonymous with a liberal political culture, i.e. one in which individuality is fostered as the key basic value: 'It is not by wearing down into uniformity all that is individual . . . but by cultivating it and calling it forth, within the limits imposed by the rights of others, that human beings become a beautiful and noble object of contemplation' (1859: 127). As with Locke, then, for Mill the individual has rights which are established by way of reference to a regulative model of negative freedom. Freedom is, in other words, conceived as the freedom to act according to one's individual desires, providing that one does not infringe the liberties of others in the process ('freedom from . . .', as opposed to 'freedom to . . .'). As such, the liberal conception of individuality sets up a normative restriction which tells us what the boundaries of an agent's actions ought to be, even as it asserts the absolute right of individuals to be free from either state or consensual pressures which might impede their basic right to liberty.

More recently, John Rawls (in *A Theory of Justice*, 1972) has rearticulated many of the central tenets which underlie the thinking of both Locke and Mill. As with these two thinkers, Rawls is concerned to demonstrate that political right must be derived from the protection of individual interests, which are anchored within a rational framework capable of providing a normative model for individual agency. In Rawls's case, this framework is articulated through the postulation of the 'original position'. In the 'original position', Rawls says, a group of individuals would be placed behind a 'veil of ignorance' and asked to choose the basic rules which would underpin the society in which they will subsequently live. In such a position, these individuals have no knowledge of such things as what social status they will have, how much money they will possess, etc. Thus, the 'original position' functions as a heuristic device intended to show what choices rational agents divested of individual interest would make about the most favourable form of social order. Rawls's conception of the 'original position' shares common features with Locke's 'state of nature' theory. For example, it envisages that it is possible to describe rational human subjects removed from the constraints of social hierarchy, and in turn to adduce that they would favour a social order which maximises personal liberty. In addition, however, Rawls also argues that such individuals would elect for a society in which the possible injustices they would suffer were they to draw the short straw and find themselves at the bottom of the social pile are minimised (what is termed the 'maximin' principle). Once again, though, it is evident that Rawlsean liberalism envisages the key political issue as being concerned with individual liberty and how best to both maximise and protect it. As with Locke and Mill, individuals have liberty granted to them with the proviso that it ought not to transgress the interests of others.

It is apparent from the work of these three thinkers, however, that liberalism is not a term which may be used to define a particular procedural attitude concerning how to arrive at the best model of social order. Thus, where Locke and Rawls both resort to a model of justification which, in effect, removes the individual from their social context in order to derive the principles of right and liberty which then apply to them, for Mill this move is not necessary. In other words, Mill does not envisage a 'state of nature' theory (or something akin to it) as being necessary to the project of arguing for the primacy of the liberty of individual political agents. Indeed, Mill's conception of the individual is more socially embedded to the extent that individuality gains its meaning, for him, from the social context in which agents engage in their personal pursuits. Nevertheless, Mill is equally committed to the view that the individual's rights are paramount, and that the pursuit of the conditions which maximise individual liberty will lead to the most desirable forms of social organisation and cultural life. With regard to the state, likewise, liberals are not in common agreement. As already noted, a Rawlsean would argue that the maximisation of liberty must nevertheless be compatible with the minimisation of the risks to individual well-being that are present in society. A certain level of wealth redistribution being carried out by government is therefore justifiable in Rawls's view; whereas for a thinker like Locke, the unequal distribution of goods is a necessary consequence of human activity in civil society and one must simply accept this fact.

Along with their emphasis on the importance of individual liberty, liberals also show a commitment to a fairly rigid distinction between the public and private spheres of life. In other words, for a liberal like Mill, what an individual chooses to do with their own goods and even life is not a matter for public concern, so long as any choices that are made do not adversely affect the private rights of others. This line of thinking reflects the liberal emphasis on the individual as the basic unit of political discourse. Putting the matter another way, one might say that liberals are in general committed to an ontology of the individual – a metaphysical conception of the individual as an irreducible entity endowed with an existence that can be taken to transcend the limitations of any particular culture or society.

It may be tempting, in the light of the above, to oppose the thought of liberalism to more recent developments within **postmodernism**. For example, the postmodern critique of the **subject**, if convincing, might be regarded as sounding the death-knell of the liberal conception of subjectivity and its accompanying commitment to its particular conception of liberty. However, this may not be the case. The American pragmatist thinker Richard Rorty, for example, does not shy away from describing himself as both a postmodernist *and* a liberal. Nor, it might be added, is it necessarily the case that certain liberal principles are excised by postmodernist criticism. Amongst the postmodernists, the work of Jean-François Lyotard may be cited as an example of a thinker who, in spite of his commitment to a critique of liberal conceptions of the political, nevertheless retains many features which can with justification be termed 'liberal'. Thus, in his book, *The Differend: Phrases in Dispute* (and indeed elsewhere) Lyotard's advocacy of the pursuit of a plurality of 'genres of discourse' is not incompatible with the liberal's advocacy of a plurality of individual modes of existence. Indeed, it may be more germane to oppose liberal thought to that of the tradition of **Marxism** which, unlike that of the postmoderns, does not tend to regard the pursuit of multiplicity for its own sake in an uncritical light. [PS]

Further reading: Barry 1986; Grant 1987; Gray 1990; Kukathas 1989; Kymlicka 1989; Locke 1988; Lyotard 1988; Mill 1984; Moore 1993; Mulhall and Swift 1996; Rawls 1972; Rorty 1991; Sandel 1982, 1984.

libertarianism   As a political doctrine, libertarianism may be situated as an extreme form of **liberalism**, and like liberalism, it is historically rooted in the work of the seventeenth-century political philosopher John Locke. Libertarianism places a central emphasis upon the moral and political necessity of respecting human freedom, autonomy and responsibility. This freedom is principally expressed through the exercise of the right to own and enjoy property. Humans must be free to acquire property (but not by stealing the property of others) and to transfer property (by giving it away or by selling and exchanging it). The libertarian will therefore argue that state interference in the life of its citizens must be restricted. The state will have a duty to protect the basic freedoms of its citizens (and so will provide a police force and the legal apparatus necessary to support it). The state cannot, however, appropriate its citizens' property (in the form of taxation) for any other purpose. For example, to provide state education or health care would, firstly, require illegitimately appropriating citizens' property (to pay for these services), and secondly would fail to respect the autonomy and responsibility of citizens to organise their own education and health care. In libertarian thinking, the market plays a key role in the organisation of a free society. [AE]

Further reading: Nozick 1974.

life-chances A term used in **sociology** (especially where influenced by Max Weber) to refer to the opportunities that members of social groups have for acquiring positively valued goods and rewards, and avoiding negatively valued goods. Thus, life-chances encompass not just overtly economic goods (such as wealth, income and material possessions), but also cultural goods (including the opportunities for education and consumption of or participation in the arts), health and criminality. Typically, life-chances will be correlated with a person's economic **class**, so that the higher up the class hierarchy one is, the greater one's chances to enjoy a high income, a long and good quality education, and to avoid illness and premature mortality, and to avoid criminal prosecution. [AE]

Further reading: Dahrendorf 1979.

lifestyle As developed in the **sociology** of the 1960s and 1970s, 'lifestyle' referred to the patterns of consumption and use (of material and symbolic goods) associated with different social groups and **classes**. As developed in cultural studies, lifestyles may be understood as a focus of group or individual identity, in so far as the individual expresses him or herself through the meaningful choice of certain items or patterns of behaviour, as symbolic **codes**, from a plurality of possibilities. The choice of lifestyle may be seen as a form of resistance to the dominant social order. However, the analysis of lifestyles has also to address the problem of the degree to which choice of lifestyle represents a genuinely free and creative choice, and the degree to which it represents the influence of advertising and other **mass media** over everyday life, and thus the incorporation of the individual into the dominant social order. [AE]

Further reading: Chancy 1996; Giddens 1991.

life–world　The concept of 'life–world' was introduced by the German phenomenologist Edmund Husserl, to refer to the expectations and practical skills that human beings have, prior to any conscious or theoretical engagement with the world. While these beliefs and abilities may once have been consciously acquired, and thus they are the product of theoretical reflection upon the social and physical world, they are now taken-for-granted and largely unnoticed. They have become 'sedimented' in the life–world, which we acquire as we learn to become competent social agents. The life–world is thus composed of 'stocks of knowledge' (according to Alfred Schutz), or skills and expectations that allow us to give meaning to (and indeed to construct) the social world within which we live. The concept has been taken up recently in the social theory of Jürgen Habermas, where the life–world, as the everyday experience of the world as something meaningful and as within our control, is set against the systematic or seemingly objective, meaningless and constraining aspects of social life. [AE]

Further reading: Habermas 1984, 1987; Husserl 1954; Schutz 1962.

literary criticism　Literary criticism encompasses the analysis, interpretation and evaluation of literary texts. It attempts to identify the text's meaning and addresses questions concerning the larger social relevance of a particular work. In its historical development, the original focus was on the author and has gradually moved over to the text, while incorporating some discussion of the role of the reader and the historical period when the text was written.

217

The emergence of literary criticism went along with the desire to become conscious of the meaning of **culture** and **society**. In many ways it is part of an emancipatory project (an inheritance of the **Enlightenment**) which attempts to understand the self in relation to its historical context. A self-conscious attitude towards the capacities of the mind is one of the hallmarks of criticism and detailed investigations of the imagination produce theories of literature which not only leave far behind any simplistic equations between the poet and the liar, but deal interestingly with the complex of questions around **realism**.

The most important debate in literary criticism has always concerned the relation between **text** and historical reality. Literature unquestionably refers to external reality, but it is extremely difficult to gauge what kind of reference this is. By means of representing the experience of social relationships, the text effects a social positioning: however distanced or defamiliarised the fictional narrative may be, the text is always written from a certain perspective and deploys its rhetoric to implicate the reader in its own ideological stance. Because literature which is assumed to have a right to this title critically engages with its own premises, it dramatises a tension between descriptive and prescriptive standards. It is, then, criticism's task to tease out the ways and means by which literature permits certain conventions and stereotypical assumptions to be contested. An important starting-point for such a task is to analyse the text's mode of address and to ask what kind of subjectivity it projects onto its readers. The analysis of **irony**, here, is as significant as the task of seeking to identify contradictions and logical inconsistencies in the text's argument. While New Critical readings claimed that it is illegitimate either to assume that poetry consists of arguments or to produce a paraphrase of its meaning, recent critical theories have insistently pointed out that a meaningful critical methodology concentrates on plural meanings and discusses the ways in which different interpretations conflict with each other.

In its original deployment as a technique of scriptural exegesis, such criticism treated sacred writings as a self-present entity because the text was taken as a direct revelation of the divine spirit. But twentieth-century hermeneutic theories point out that understanding individual textual passages is only possible on the basis of previous knowledge about the fictional rendition of experience. What is referred to by the concept of the 'hermeneutic circle' describes the difficulties with reaching through to a sense of first-hand experience which exactly reproduces the perceptions implied by the literary text. It is the idea of there being an immediate access to an ideational realm that is most sharply contested, especially by deconstructionist critiques of language and ideology.

In its New Critical guise, literary criticism expressed an authoritative view of the text's meaning. But in spite of the idea that an exclusive focus on the objectively present 'words on the page' would reduce the arbitrariness of interpretation, both **New Criticism** and **structuralism** were soon forced to abandon their appeals to objectivity. In the post-structuralist and deconstructionist view of interpretation, the problem of mis-interpretation was circumvented through establishing an aesthetics of literature which hailed the plural text. This is to say that the text itself was no longer viewed as an entity that could be reduced to one singular meaning. The drawback of this view, however, is that a text could be understood as saying almost anything and the task of criticism became that of selecting relevant interpretations from a vast range of plausible or conceivable options.

Other questions belonging to the discipline of literary criticism concern the relation between literature and criticism. Because criticism is itself a textual genre, it has been claimed that no generic difference can be assumed to exist between text and interpretation. Discussions of literary value, which are now topical in relation to discussions of the status of popular fiction, are an old concern which has particular salience at a moment when cinema and other **mass media** have a more immediate impact on the imagination of the late twentieth-century than other, more sophisticated forms of art. These issues in literary criticism make it clear that the attempt to explicate the meaning of literature is a major site of ideological struggle. [CK]

Further reading: Eagleton 1983; Lodge 1972; Rice and Waugh 1989; Wellek 1986.

M

Marxism Marxism refers to those schools of social, economic, political and philosophical enquiry that derive their approach from the work of Karl Marx and Friedrich Engels. The interpretations and developments of Marx's work are extremely diverse. They share an approach to the analysis of society that gives primacy to economic activity, although key debates within Marxism centre on the degree to which the economic **base** determines the nature and structure of the rest of society. Societies are understood as being structured according to the exploitation of subordinate **classes** by a dominant class. Historical change is therefore typically analysed in terms of developments within the economic base, that are manifest as class conflict and revolution. As a political philosophy, Marxism remains committed to the realisation of a non-exploitative society (communism), typically through the liberation of the **proletariat**, the subordinate class within **capitalism**. Again, a central debate, especially in the earlier periods of Marxism, concerned the degree to which the proletariat revolution was an inevitable event, brought about by the forces of historical change, or whether Marxist political parties were obliged to actively bring about revolution. As Marx wrote little directly on **culture**, there is great scope for diverse applications of his work to cultural studies. What is perhaps common to most Marxist approaches to culture is a recognition that culture is entwined with class struggle

221

through **ideology**. That is to suggest that culture is produced within a class divided society, and will participate either in the maintenance and **legitimation** of existing power relations, or in resisting that power. Three broad approaches to Marxism, and thus to the Marxist theorisation of culture, can be identified.

Classical Marxism is derived, by Kautsk and Plekhanov, and later by Lenin and Trotsky, from the work carried out by Engels in the 1870s and 1880s (Engels 1947). It presents Marxism as a scientific account of social change. As such, in a dogmatic form, it became the official Marxist doctrine of the Soviet Union. The theory of culture most closely associated with this Marxism is Plekhanov's reflection theory. In *Art and Society* (1912), he develops a **sociology** of art, in explicit opposition to the doctrine of art for art's sake, that would isolate art from political and economic reality. Culture therefore comes to be seen as 'the mirror of social life'. Under the Stalinist Zhdanov, this becomes the stultifying dogmatism of socialist **realism**. In comparison to Plekhanov's account of art simply reflecting on society, for Zhdanov the artist is an engineer of the human soul, educating the working classes, and portraying reality in its revolutionary development. The finest exponent of socialist realism as a literary theory was Georg Lukács. For Lukács, the nineteenth century realist novel offered the most politically progressive form of the novel. Balzac, for example, is praised (despite his overt political conservatism), in so far as his novels articulate the underlying social forces, rather than merely documenting the surface appearance of society.

Paradoxically, earlier work by Lukács, and in particular his *History and Class Consciousness* (1923), is the key influence on the development of western Marxism. Lukács interprets Marx as the inheritor of the German philosophical tradition, and thus sees Marx's social theory as a materialist reworking of Hegelian idealism. Marxism becomes a humanist philosophy, rather than a science. It challenges positivist approaches to social science, that would attempt to explain society through the methods of the natural sciences. In contrast, western

Marxism focuses on the problem of bringing an objectified society back under the control of its human members. Hence, the theory, and indeed **metaphor**, of **alienation** (and in the work of Lukács and the **Frankfurt School, reification**) is of prime importance. Humanity is not at home in the world that should be its home. Culture can therefore be attributed a complex position within society, and its aesthetic worth intertwined with its political value. Regressive culture, on the one hand, is understood as ideology. It reproduces the categories of thought and reasoning that make the existing social order appear to be natural and legitimate. Walter Benjamin, for example, laments the use that Fascism can make of the core categories of traditional aesthetics, such as 'originality' and 'genius' (1970b). Progressive culture, on the other hand, is interpreted as an expression of alienation and an act of political resistance. The work of the German philosopher Ernst Bloch, for example, explores the utopian aspirations, the yearnings for a better and more just society, that are embedded in the most diverse forms of culture. **Frankfurt School** theorists, including T.W. Adorno and Max Horkheimer, see high culture, especially, as being one of the few spaces in which one can think differently, and challenge the ideological illusions of dominant, economically motivated (and positivistic) thought. Similarly, Bertolt Brecht's theatre, and specifically the notion of **alienation effect**, disrupts the illusions of politically conservative theatre. The theory of **hegemony**, developed by the Italian Marxist Antonio Gramsci, advances the theory of ideology, precisely by recognising that the ruling class cannot simply impose its own interpretation of the world upon the subordinate classes. Any such interpretation will be negotiated, so that culture becomes a site of class struggle.

In the 1960s, the anti-humanist, or **structuralist** Marxism of Louis Althusser, represented a new stage in the development of Marxism. The Hegelianism of western Marxism is rejected, in favour of a scientific approach. Further, the economic determinism of Soviet Marxism is also thrown into question, so that the economic is seen to be determinant only in

223

the 'last instance', thereby giving the other spheres of society **relative autonomy**. Althusser opened a conception of ideology as lived practice (rather than purely intellectual reflection), which in turn offered new approaches to the analysis of everyday culture, that were particularly significant for the newly emerging cultural studies. The implications of these arguments for art and literature were explored most significantly by Pierre Macherey (1978, 1995). Macherey rejects ideas of creativity and the notion of the author, and indeed of criticism as evaluation or interpretation. The **production** of the literary **text** is treated rather as a determinate material practice, working in and on the raw material of ideology. Literature generates an 'implicit critique' of ideology, exposing the relationship between ideology and the material conditions of its existence.

It may be suggested that cultural studies have increasingly moved into a post-Marxist phase. A number of influential thinkers, including Baudrillard and Lyotard, may be seen to have developed away from initial Marxist influences, ultimately to question not merely the understanding of culture found in Marxism, but more specifically the accounts of politics and history that underpin that understanding. [AE]

Further reading: Bottomore 1983; Kolakowski 1978; Lunn 1982.

mass media The mass media of communication are those **institutions** that produce and distribute information and visual and audio images on a large scale. Historically, the mass media may be dated from the invention of the printing press, and thus in the west, from Johann Gutenberg's commercial exploitation of printing around 1450. The early products of printing presses were religious or literary works, along with medical and legal texts. In the sixteenth and seventeenth centuries, periodicals and newspapers began to appear regularly. Industrialisation led to a further expansion in the book and newspaper industries in the nineteenth century. The twentieth century has seen the introduction and rapid expansion of electronic media (**cinema**, radio and **television**), to the point at which they have become a dominant element in the experience and organisation of everyday life.

The first significant attempts to theorise the mass media in the twentieth century began within the framework of mass society theory. Developed most significantly in the second quarter of the century, not least as a response to the rise of Nazism and Fascism, mass society theory typically presented industrial society as degenerating into an undifferentiated, irrational and emotive mass of people, cut off from tradition and from any fine sensitivity to aesthetic or moral values. The mass entertainment media are thereby presented as key instruments in the creation of this mass, precisely in so far as they are seen to appeal to the more base elements of popular taste (thus reducing all content to some lowest common denominator) in the search for large audiences. The media thereby serve to undermine traditional and local cultural difference, and in the emotional nature of their content, to inhibit rational responses to the messages they present. Entertainment is complemented by the use of radio, especially, as an instrument of political **propaganda**, or more precisely in **Marxism**, as one of the core contemporary instruments of **ideology**. Mass society theory may therefore be seen to attribute enormous power to the media, and, as a complementary presupposition, to present the audience as the more or less passive victim of the messages foisted upon it. The **empirical** research that such theory fostered, 'effects' research, tends to look for the harmful effects that the media had, both politically (in inhibiting democracy) and morally (for example in encouraging violence). This assumption of media power was, paradoxically, in the media's own interests, in that it implied that they were a powerful and effective tool of advertising.

A more subtle approach to media research emerged in the post-war period, within the framework of sociological **functionalism**. '**Uses and gratifications**' research attributes greater activity and diversity to members of the audience, in so far as they are assumed to have subjectively felt needs, created by the social and physical environment, that the media

225

can fulfil. The central functions performed by the media include escapism (in so far as media consumption allows a legitimate withdrawal from the pressures of normal life), the establishing of personal relationships (including the use of media programmes as the focus of discussion and other social interaction), and the formation of personal identity (whereby the values expressed by programmes are seen to reinforce one's personal values).

In the 1950s, a Canadian school of media theory emerged, principally in the work of Harold Innis and Marshall McLuhan. The central argument here was that there was a causal link between the dominant form of communication and the organisation of a society. Thus, Innis (1950, 1951) distinguished 'time biased media' from 'space biased media'. The former, such as clay and stone, could not easily be transported, but were durable, thus leading to stable social phenomena, grounded in the reproduction of tradition over long periods of time. The latter (such as paper), are less durable, but are easily transported. They could therefore support the expansion of administrative and political authority over large territories. McLuhan (1994) argued that the development of new media technologies has a fundamental impact on human cognition. The introduction of printing leads to greater compartmentalisation and specialisation of the human senses, as communication comes to be dominated by the printed page (as opposed to oral communication previously). Vision thus becomes dominant, but deals with information that is presented in a linear, uniform and infinitely repeatable manner. Thought thus becomes standardised and analytical. Print also leads to individualism, as reading becomes silent and private. Print culture, which for McLuhan as for Innis is space biased, is challenged by electronic media. Electronic media, in their proliferation and continual presence, annihilate space and time. Confronting us continually, modern media do not have to be sought out. Similarly, the act of reading or consuming various media is no longer confined to particular periods of the day. Information from diverse locations and even periods in history are juxtaposed in a single newspaper or evening's television. The modern experience is thus one of an unceasing relocation of information in space and time, leading to what McLuhan termed 'the global village'. While McLuhan's theories fell from fashion in the 1970s, they bear a resemblance to much recent postmodernist thinking.

New strands of media theory emerged in the 1960s and 1970s, in no small part through increasing interest specifically in **television**. Two extremes may be identified. At one, concern is with the material base that determines cultural production. The political economy of the mass media thus focused on institutional structures that underpinned media production (and thus its contents and value orientations). Murdock and Golding (1977), for example, looked at the structures of share ownership and control that linked media organisations into multi-national **capitalism**. At the other, emphasis is placed upon media content as **texts**, in need of interpretation or decoding. The increasing influence of **semiotics** led to a fundamental re-evaluation of the role of the media audience. They cease to be mere victims of the media, and come to be seen as actively engaging with media products, interpreting them in a plurality of ways that may be at odds with the possibly ideological intentions of the producers. The work of the Birmingham Centre for Contemporary Cultural Studies and Stuart Hall is crucial here. From this, **cultural studies** may be seen to lead, less to theorisation of the mass media per se, than to the development of distinctive theories and accounts of specific media (such as television, **popular music**, and even the Sony Walkman).

Jürgen Habermas (1989a) and Jean Baudrillard offer two distinct, yet general accounts of the place of the mass media in the experience and development of contemporary society. Habermas's theory centres on the concept of the **public sphere**. The **bourgeois** public sphere emerged in Europe in the seventeenth and eighteenth centuries, as critical self-reflection and reflection upon the state, conducted first in coffee houses and salons, and then through pamphlets, journals and newspapers. While in practice this public sphere was

227

exclusive, allowing participation by the propertied, rational, and male bourgeoisie, Habermas finds in it a principle of the open, and thus democratic, use of public reason. Contemporary electronic media are seen to have a complex, **dialectical**, impact on this sphere. Positively, modern production techniques can make complex, critical and culturally demanding material widely available. In practice, cultural consumption has become increasingly privatised, breaking up the public sphere, and dominated by low quality material, designed to have a mass appeal. In politics, this leads to the degradation of political debate and policy formation into an increasingly stage managed political theatre.

Baudrillard (1990b, 1990c, 1993) understands contemporary capitalism in terms of symbolic (as opposed to strictly economic) exchange. The contemporary world is therefore dominated by **signs**, images and representations, to such a degree that the distinction between the sign and its referent, the real world, collapses (so that one can no longer speak to the real needs or interests of the people, for example). The mass media (and particularly television) are central to this production and exchange of signs, and it is to the nature of the consumption of these signs that Baudrillard looks, in order to outline a pessimistic theory of the impact of the mass media on democratic society. Baudrillard's consumer is typically a channel-hopper and couch potato. On the one hand, television transforms the world into easily consumable fragments, and yet does so within the gamut of media that produce more information than any one person could absorb and understand, so that it attracts only a superficial 'ludic curiosity'. On the other hand, the media swallow up private space, for although typically consumed privately, they intrude upon our most intimate moments by making them public. Nothing is taboo any longer, and the immediacy of media coverage inhibits the possibility of critical reflection. An opinion poll, for example, cannot appeal to a genuine public. It does not manipulate the public, for the public (and the distinction between public and private) has ceased to exist. The expression of political opinion is reduced to a yes/no decision, akin to the choice or rejection of a supermarket brand, or a film. Resistance, for Baudrillard, can then rest only in a refusal to participate in this system. [AE]

Further reading: Giner 1976; McQuail 1994; Stevenson 1995.

meaning   Philosophically, there seems little theoretical agreement as to a definition of this term or as to 'where' exactly meaning resides. Indeed, this lack of agreement is so marked that some philosophers would question its very existence. An understanding of this lack of agreement is perhaps best grasped by examining the historical development of the term.

One of the most influential theories of meaning, 'nomenclaturism', dates from philosophical antiquity. This is basically the idea that the meaning of a name or kind term is the object for which it stands. The grounding assumption of the theory is that there is an essential or natural relationship between a linguistic sign and the object it 'stands for' in a language. It was this doctrine that Plato discussed in his *Cratylus*.

A view very much akin to this is still influential today. Perhaps the best known of its modern supporters are Bertrand Russell (1918 and 1924) and the *early* Wittgenstein (1921). This view, which became known as 'logical atomism', dates approximately from the turn of the twentieth century. The idea central to this philosophy is that the sentences in a language can only have a meaning if they are composed of smaller units of meaning which, in turn, derive their meaning from their direct relationship with states of affairs in the world. This view was the precursor of logical **positivism**, which was supported by the members of the 'Vienna Circle'. Perhaps the most concise exposition of this philosophical theory was given by A.J. Ayer (1946). At the core of logical positivism lies the 'principle of verification', which stipulates that the meaning of a sentence or proposition is the method of its verification. In other words, the meaning of a sentence is defined by the observations which would serve to show its truth or falsity. By definition of the theory, if a sentence is not verifiable by these

229

means it is *meaningless*. Thus, for example, the propositions of traditional **metaphysics** would have no meaning because the conditions of their verifiability could not be given.

The opposing view to logical atomism is that of semantic **holism**. This view has its roots in the works of Frege (1892) and Saussure (1916). From the perspective of **analytic philosophy**, Frege opened the door to the view that language plays an active part in the construction of our notion of **reality** (see **reference**). Saussure, likewise from the perspective of **structuralism**, made a similar point. The most influential figure upon modern **philosophy of science** is that of W.V.O. Quine (1953). Quine challenged the notion that there could be a viable theory of meaning couched in terms of any fragment of a language. Instead, language was to be viewed as a holistic structure, the meaning of whose parts were dependent upon the whole. A similar view to this was held by the philosopher of science, Pierre Duhem (1962). This combined view subsequently became known as the 'Quine-Duhem' hypothesis: that a physicist, when performing an experiment, is never testing a single hypothesis but, rather, a whole group of hypotheses.

A more full-blooded version of this approach to meaning in the philosophy of science was developed by Thomas S. Kuhn (1970). Kuhn said that the sciences comprised a number of **paradigms** which supplied the scientists who worked within them with their **worldviews**. These paradigms, in turn, comprised the theories and assumptions which scientists currently held to be true. The meaning of each of the terms in these theories was defined by its relation to the other terms within the paradigm. Consequently, the meaning of any term, sentence or phrase was, by implication, internal to the paradigm. Thus, when a paradigm changed, the meanings of the terms within it also changed; the net result being that members of different scientific paradigms shared different worldviews. The implication of Kuhn's theory leads to the problem of 'incommensurability'.

A similar view, with reference to ordinary language, was supported by the *later* Wittgenstein (1953) and was encompassed by his notion of a 'language-game'. On this view, the meaning of a term is dependent on how it is used within a particular language-game. The implication is that although certain words can share a 'family resemblance' in that they sound or look the same, their meanings will vary across language-games. Although they have many theoretical differences, this view shares certain important similarities with the work of Saussure in that 'meaning' on this model is internal to and dependent upon a language or, for Wittgenstein, part of a language (Harris 1988). Both the views of Wittgenstein and Saussure have had a significant influence on the schools of **postmodernism** and **post-structuralism**.

The holist view of language has certain fundamentally important implications for not only the physical sciences but also the social sciences. If meanings are internal to a particular language or language-game, then communication between one language or language-game and another becomes problematic in that no common medium of communication exist between them. If languages or language-games are concomitant with particular cultures or parts of a culture, then it seems to follow that communication between cultures or parts of a culture become similarly problematical (see under the entry for **cultural relativism**). This being so, then the possibility of making cross-cultural comparisons seems ruled out as a matter of course since, by definition, the social scientist is as trapped within the confines of a particular language or language-game as those she or he professes to study.

A possible route out of this problematic is at least promised by Quine's notion of 'radical translation' and is taken up again, more successfully, by Donald Davidson.

Perhaps the most damaging challenge to meaning comes from the work of Jacques Derrida (1967). One of the central assumptions of any theory of meaning is that a language can remain in a state of equilibrium long enough for meanings to become a possibility. Such an assumption is certainly true, at least at a methodological level, of Saussure's theory of language. At the centre of his theory is the notion that the meaning or value ('valeur') of a linguistic **sign** in any language comes from its **difference** to all the other signs in that language. The stability of meaning for each sign is preserved provided that a rigid distinction can be maintained between 'la **langue**' and '**parole**'. What Derrida does, in effect, is challenge the validity of this distinction as used by Saussure. Derrida mounts this challenge by deconstructing (see **deconstruction**) Saussure's opposition between speech and writing. Saussure views writing as posing a fundamental threat to the stable oral tradition of a language. To avoid this threat he gives the privileged position in this opposition to speech. Derrida not only reverses the polarity of this opposition, but also employs the logic Saussure uses to construct it to create just the kind of linguistic deformations that the latter wishes to prevent. The net result is the loss of the necessary stability required to keep the meanings of individual signs intact.

Generally it is held, at least by analytic philosophers, that there is a close relationship between the notion of 'meaning' and that of reference. [SH]

means of production In **Marxism**, 'means of production' refers to all the material resources used in production. The major class divisions in any society are understood in terms of ownership and control, or lack of ownership and control, of the means of production. Thus, in **capitalism**, the **bourgeoisie** owns factories, raw materials and other productive resources, and is able to control what is produced, and the disposal of that product. The subordinate **proletariat** have only their ability to labour, which they sell to the bourgeois capitalist. [AE]

Further reading: Cutler *et al.* 1977.

mechanical solidarity Term in Durkheim's sociology, explaining the cohesion of pre-industrial societies. Because cohesion cannot be established through a complex division of labour (see **organic solidarity**), a repressive law, embodying commonly shared values (or **conscience collective**), typically embued with sacred qualities, severely punishes any individual deviation from social **norms**. [AE]

mediation Mediation can have two distinct meanings. At its simplest, and its closest to ordinary English usage, it refers to anything that comes between two other things. In the study of **mass media**, mediation is therefore anything which (or anybody who) conveys a message to the audience. A reporter mediated between the event reported and the audience; or a fictional detective mediates between the audience and its understanding of the police and criminality. In German philosophy (for example as found in the **Frankfurt School** and other forms of **Marxism**), mediation has a more technical usage, closer to 'construction'. Thus, in Marxism, to observe that the subject is mediated by the object is to observe that the human subject – the individual or person – is substantially created or constituted by the objective forces – be these biological laws, or more likely, the coercive force of social pressures – that act upon him or her. Similarly, our (subjective) understanding of the social world will be shaped and constructed by ideological and cultural frameworks; these frameworks mediate our experience and perception. [AE]

meritocracy A meritocracy is a society with an occupational hierarchy (see **social stratification**). Different occupations will enjoy different rewards, **power** and **status**. However, in a meritocracy, individuals move up and down this hierarchy (see **social mobility**) on the basis of merit, which is to say, on the basis of the talents and qualifications that they possess, and the appropriateness of these attributes to the tasks required in the given occupation. The most highly rewarded occupations will also be those which are most important to the society, that require rare skills or skills and knowledge that take a long time to acquire, and which carry the highest levels of responsibility. (It is assumed that financial and other rewards are necessary, in order to motivate the most appropriate people to undertake the training necessary to fulfil the occupation.)

The **liberal** philosopher John Rawls has offered a highly influential defence of meritocracy as being fundamental to a just and fair society (1972). He is, however, at pains to distinguish what he calls a 'callous meritocracy' from fair equality of opportunity. In the former, a person's education will depend predominantly upon what his or her parents can afford. Thus, the children of successful parents will be more likely to acquire prestigious jobs, because they are likely to have had a better education. This would lead to wide inequalities in society. Rawls therefore defends an education system to which everyone has equal access, to ensure that the talents a person does have are recognised and cultivated, regardless of one's parental background. [AE]

Further reading: Young 1958.

metaphor Broadly, a trope in which one thing is referred to by a term which literally describes something else – the term derives from the Greek *metaphora*, meaning transfer or carry over. Hence in Aristotle's *Rhetoric*, metaphor is presented as a word used in a changed and illuminating sense: 'ordinary words convey only what we know already; it is from metaphor that we can best get a hold of something fresh.'

More recently too, metaphor's status in the growth and development of language has invited special attention from philosophers and literary theorists. Various, more or less technical, accounts have been given of what metaphors actually are, how they function, and what, if anything, they contribute at a semantic or cognitive level. In Max Black's influential analysis, for example, the metaphorical utterance contains two 'subjects' – primary and secondary – and works by 'projecting upon' the primary subject (e.g. 'Uncle Ted') a set of associated implications (e.g. 'is a low dog') which act as a kind of filter through which a new angle on, and understanding of, the primary subject is achieved. Thus anatomized, metaphor is more than a mere ornament: it has a privileged, specific role in the application of words to world, and particularly in understanding by comparison.

The reverberating influence of Nietzsche's oft-cited description of truth as 'a mobile army of metaphors' suggests that metaphoricity may go deeper still. For if, as he suggested, literal truths are simply 'metaphors which are worn out and without sensuous power; coins which have lost their pictures and now matter only as metal, no longer as coins', metaphor, rather than being an isolable mode of linguistic meaning, becomes its very basis. Simultaneously, the distinction between the literal and the metaphorical becomes a temporal, rather than an abstractly semantic, matter; the former becoming a roughly equivalent to familiar, or normal language use, and the latter to the unfamiliar, or abnormal.

Subsequent developments have pushed metaphor further up the theoretical agenda. Heidegger's interpretation of the Greek word for truth (*aletheia*) as 'disclosure' or 'unconcealment' rather than strict 'representation' of reality lends much to the idea that the creativity of the metaphorical process is central to truth rather than a superficial distraction. In Jakobson's structuralist linguistics, metaphor, along with metonymy, it is one of the two basic poles of the functioning of language. For Jacques Lacan metaphor, as the substitution of one word for another, is central to his linguistification of the Freudian concept of condensation. And much has been made of metaphor's importance to intellectual and cultural progress by those, like Mary Hesse, Hayden White and Richard Rorty, who would extend its pivotal status respectively to scientific hypotheses, historiography and all descriptive writing of any kind. Thus, for Rorty, the first time Copernicus claimed that the earth revolves around the sun he was simply trying out a new, abnormal, way of speaking – a metaphor which, for reasons more cultural and political than strictly veridical, happens to have 'stuck' as the now-normal, commonsense account.

For some, the conceptual prioritisation of metaphor reaches its apogee with Jacques Derrida's apparent refusal to allow any distinction between literal and metaphorical meaning at all, and the efforts of trigger-happy deconstructionists to expose the artifice of all claims to objectivity. Others, though, see Derrida as highlighting the necessity of precisely the sort of philosophical account of metaphor which the demonstrable metaphoricity of even the most mundane language would seem to demand.

In any case there are those, sold on the idea that reality is best viewed as a linguistic or discursive construction, who would extend the Nietzschean line to the point where all claims and propositions, and all forms of cultural discourse, can be read as metaphorical: where metaphor, in other words, goes 'all the way down'. The consequences are many and profound, not least the blurring of distinctions between truth and ideology, science and superstition, or simulacrum and (supposed) real life. This may, however, deny what is particular about metaphor's importance to descriptive practice. Certainly, questions remain about what an adequate definition of metaphor might be, whether and how it might be distinguished from literal meaning, and whether it *creates* meaning or simply *rehearses* it (see Davidson 1984a). Whatever the scope for final answers, few would now dispute its integral role in the functioning of discourse in general. [GC]

Further reading: Black 1979; Cooper 1986; Davidson 1984a; Derrida 1982; Nietzsche 1995.

metaphysics   Metaphysics is traditionally regarded as the study of reality as it is beyond mere appearance. The three-fold purpose of this study is purportedly to find out (i) what the world is 'really' like, (ii) why the world exists, and (iii) what our place is, as human beings, in this world. More recently metaphysicians have tended, in the main, to limit their investigations to (i) and (iii), thereby, in accordance with modern physics, regarding (ii) as largely unanswerable.

As a result of their attempts to answer all three of the questions of metaphysics, traditional metaphysicians have tended towards system building. They have attempted to explain the true nature of reality by constructing a model of that reality which integrates the answers to the three questions of metaphysics into a single, general and complete answer. Perhaps the grandest employment of this methodology was by Hegel, who held that the universe was just one substance ('Mind' or 'Geist') which was in the process of coming to know itself. Examples of other philosophers who have employed this methodology are G.W. Leibniz and, to a slightly more limited extent, Bishop Berkeley. This style of metaphysics has tended to attract philosophers sympathetic to idealism and of a rationalist inclination. The rationalists regard the only reliable tools to discovering the 'True' nature of reality as being the power of reason and the faculties of the intellect. This approach complements the notion of system building in that the key to achieving a good system is to use this power and these faculties to construct a general and suitably coherent theory of the universe which could answer, in an integrated fashion, the three questions of metaphysics.

Perhaps the greatest challenge to traditional idealist metaphysics comes from the work of Immanuel Kant in the form of his 'transcendental idealism'. Kant held that the approach of the traditional metaphysician could never work because it tried to accomplish too much. His view was that although there was a world beyond mere appearance, we can never know what that world is like in-itself because how we come know that world will be restricted by what we, as rational creatures, bring to it. What we bring to the world is what Kant calls the 'categories', which are the conditions of our thinking about the world. Numbered among these categories are the concepts of 'time' and 'space', and 'cause' and 'effect'. Thus, in a sense, although there is a world independent of how we think about it, it is forever beyond our reach and, consequently, we must settle for investigating the world as it appears to us. Granted this point, it was the influence of Kant that first firmly bound the questions of metaphysics to those of **epistemology**.

The most recent debates in metaphysics have tended to centre around the dispute between those who support metaphysical **realism** and those who support anti-realism in its various more or less extreme versions. The supporters of metaphysical realism reflect and are historically rooted in the concerns of those who have traditionally opposed both rationalism and idealism, i.e. the supporters of **empiricism**. Metaphysical realists hold to the view that there is a mind-independent material/physical reality which we can come to know. Thus, not only does it *appear* that there are such things as trees, cats and stones, but these things *actually exist* in the mind-independent world (van Inwagen 1993).

Opponents of metaphysical realism have become known as anti-realists. However, it is important to distinguish here what exactly the anti-realists are opposed to, and whether they are *all* opposed to the same thing. Indeed, some anti-realists are simply opposed to any *straightforward* notion of reality but not necessarily reality per se, and there are those who seem opposed to the notion of reality in toto. The latter group includes analytic philosophers (see **analytic philosophy**) like Richard Rorty (1972) and Nelson Goodman (1978) and post-modernists (see **postmodernism**) such as Jean Baudrillard (1988). In the former group we have philosophers such as Hilary Putnam (1981) and Thomas S. Kuhn (1970) who, claiming to work in the shadow of Kant, seem to want to note the problematics connected with reaching reality rather than rejecting it as a notion out of hand.

Some philosophers have opposed the project of metaphysics altogether. Within analytic philosophy we have the logical positivists who claim that the metaphysicians could say nothing meaningful (Ayer 1946). This is because they could not state the conditions which allow us to judge a metaphysical statement true or false (see **meaning**). More recently, there has been opposition to what Jacques Derrida calls the 'metaphysics of presence'. Derrida has been variously interpreted as either denying anything as being exterior to the **text** or, less radically, simply showing the hopelessness of speaking of **reality** outside of any particular interpretative framework (see Norris 1987: chapter 6). [SH]

Further reading: Kim and Sosa 1994; Walsh 1963.

metonymy　A form of communication in which a part or element is used to stand for the whole. At its simplest, we talk of a head of cattle, or speak of the crown, when we refer to the monarch. However, we also understand many complex **texts** through metonymy. For example, in a news photograph, a single poor peasant farmer may stand for all peasants, or all members of a certain community, nation or continent. As such, metonymy can play a role in **mythology**, as defined by Barthes. In making the interpretative move from the element that is presented to the whole, we draw, unwittingly, upon certain politically and factually questionable, but none the less taken for-granted (and thus apparently natural), assumptions. Thus, the single peasant farmer may reinforce the unspoken belief that all Africans, say, are the impoverished victims of an adverse climate. [AE]

minimalism　'Minimalism' refers to movements in the visual arts and in music, beginning in the 1950s in visual art and the late 1960s in music. There is, however, no simple or readily agreed definition of the term. In visual art, minimalism tends to refer to art works that have little differentiation of content (hence, for example, the all white and all black canvases exhibited by Robert Rauschenberg in 1952 are an important precursor of minimalism), or that are composed of many near identical, mass–produced components (in Britain, the most infamous example perhaps being Carl Andre's Equivalent VIII, an arrangement of fire bricks, that caused public hilarity and outrage when purchased by the Tate Gallery in 1972). In these two forms, minimalism comes to challenge **values** that have dominated western **aesthetics** for over two thousand years. Orthodox aesthetics (even when applied to **modern** art) tends to privilege a sensuously interesting surface to a painting or sculpture (and typically a surface that has been crafted, not manufactured), and to expect the arrangement of a complex set of parts into a harmonious and unified whole. Minimalist art either has no parts, or the parts are so simple that little or no effort or imagination is required to arrange them together into a whole. (Andre's bricks, for example, are neatly stacked two or three layers high.) There is, in effect, nothing to say about a minimalist work. It is just matter arranged in space.

In music, the term minimalism refers to a reaction to the complexities of modernist, high art music (represented for example by Pierre Boulez and other exponents of total **serialism**). Minimalist compositions (for example, by Steve Reich, Terry Riley and Eno) reject the complex (and often audibly imperceptible) interrelationships established between the parts of a 'maximalist' composition, in favour of the repetition of simple elements, with clear rhythms, simple harmonies and little or no dramatic development of the music. In contrast to minimalist visual art, minimalist music is sensually very attractive. It is equally challenging to orthodox aesthetics, in so far as it rejects the concentrated listening demands made by the **canon** of western art music, in favour of a rapturous abandonment to the sound. (Michael Nyman's minimalist sound tracks were an important component in Peter Greenway's **cinema**.) [AE]

Further reading: Lucie-Smith 1995.

minority   Usually, a social group which is in a numerically inferior position to others within a **society**, and consequently is susceptible to suffering at the hands of majority opinion. The term 'minority', therefore, can often signify an inferior social position or marginalised interests in virtue of a lack of power when it comes to having one's views or interests voiced. Likewise, being in a minority (especially, for example, in the context of being an ethnic minority) can lead to states of inequality and misrepresentation (see **stereotype**). However, it is worth noting that an **oligarchy**, for example, is a minority in the numerical sense, although it wields power over other social groups.

The philosopher J.S. Mill (one of the most famous proponents of **liberalism**) diagnosed modern, popular democratic societies as having the greatest potential for infringing on the rights of minorities in the name of popular, majority opinion (Mill's term for this was the 'tyranny of the majority'). According to Mill, minority interests (and principally the right of minority opinion represented by the autonomy of thought which, he argued, was the preserve of the **individual**) needs to be both respected and preserved if a society is to attain its greatest potential. In Mill's terms, the greatest cultural good is synonymous with the maximisation of a plurality of views and **lifestyles** within a society, and hence with the preservation of the rights of expression of minority opinion.

Gilles Deleuze and Félix Guattari have argued that a distinction needs to be drawn between 'majoritarian' and 'minoritarian' systems of representation and the social effects of these systems. To be minoritarian, in their view, means to have marginalised interests within a social order; thus, being minoritarian is not synonymous with being in a minority. Women, for example, may be a majority in terms of sheer number, but are minoritarian if their interests are marginalised by the dominant power structures and signifying systems which operate in a society or **culture** in such a way as to place them in a position of social inferiority. [PS]

Further reading: Deleuze and Guattari 1988; Mill 1984.

mode of production   In **Marxism**, history is understood as the determinate succession of distinct epochs or modes of production (Marx and Engels 1970). Marx identifies six historical epochs: primitive communism; ancient slave society; **feudalism**; **capitalism**; **socialism** and **communism**. Each has a distinctive economic character, analysed in terms of its **forces** and **relations of production**, which is to say, the level of technology within the society and the relationship between producers and the owners or controllers of the resources required for production (the **means of production**). The mode of production is therefore the distinctive inter-relationship of forces and relations of production, and their associated structures of economic exploitation. While strictly no historically specific **social structure** can be fully analysed in terms of a single mode of production, and there has been fruitful debate over distinctions with the capitalist modes of production (for example, as to a break between high capitalism and late capitalism), the basic Marxist account offers a powerful, if abstract model of social change.

This may be illustrated through reference to the transition from feudalism to capitalism. Feudal technology depends on sources of natural power (including animal power, wind power and human strength), while capitalism has machinery powered by the burning of fossil fuels. The relatively low production of feudal technology can be fully exploited through small scale, and predominantly agrarian production methods. The greater power of capitalist technology entails that a single source can provide the power for a large number of workers. The factory therefore emerges as the most appropriate way to exploit this power. However, the factory, and its organisation, are themselves strictly part of the forces of production. To make the factory possible, the feudal relations of production must be broken. These relations are those existing between the feudal lord and the serf, where the serf is bound to a particular piece of land, and to service for a particular lord. The lord can exploit the serf by appropriating a portion of the production of this land, and by requiring the serf to work for a period on the lord's own land. Capitalism, and thus the **bourgeois** or capitalist class that seeks to take full advantage of the new technology, requires a labour force that is free to move between employers (according to the demands and motivations of a free **labour** market). Capitalist relations of production therefore centre upon the market. The labourer is formally free to work for anyone willing and able to employ them, for a wage determined by the market. The capitalist will own, not just the means of production, but also the product of the labour that is exerted within their factories. The capitalist is free to dispose of this product as they wish (again, at a price largely determined by the market in consumer goods). Exploitation of the subordinate class is now concealed within the exchanges made on the labour and commodity market, all of which are superficially fair.

The value paid to the labourer as a fair and mutually agreed wage for a given amount of labour is less than the **exchange-value** received by the capitalist in selling the product. (Exploitation therefore occurs through the appropriation of **surplus-value**.)

The transition between modes of production is violent (brought about through revolutions that are the overt manifestation of class conflict). This violence is necessitated by the inherently conservative or static nature of the relations of production, in contrast to the dynamic nature of the forces of production. Revolution occurs when a contradiction occurs between the forces of production and the relationships of production. This is to say that the existing relations of production are no longer adequate to exploit the productive potential of the forces of production. The dominant feudal class, and thus feudal relations of production, are seen as being incapable of making full use of industrial technology. The rising capitalist class is only able to develop the potential of industrial technology if it can first overthrow the feudal relations of production, in order to remove the feudal inhibitions on the expansion of a mobile and free labour force. Capitalist relations of production are thus seen to be somehow implicit in early industrial technology, and this implicit capitalism is in contradiction to the reality of the old feudal order.

Through appeal to the **base and superstructure** metaphor (and in various forms of twentieth-century Marxism, analyses of **commodity fetishism** and **reification**), Marxists may suggest that the economic elements of the mode of production (the economic base) has a determining influence over the legal and **cultural** aspects of society. If so, then different modes of production are not merely characterised in terms of different economic characteristics, but also in terms of different cultural characteristics (and most importantly, by the **ideological** mechanisms that are used to give legitimacy to the rule of the dominant class). [AE]

Further reading: Balibar 1970; Cutler *et al.* 1977; Marx and Engels 1970; Sweezy *et al* 1978.

modernism   The precise meaning of the concepts of 'modernity' and 'modernism' depend, very much, upon the context in which they originate and are used. Thus, the concept of 'modernity' typically implies an opposition to something, and particularly to an historical epoch that has passed and has been superseded. Thus, as derived from the Latin 'modernus' (and 'modo', meaning recently), modernity comes to characterise the Christian epoch (from the fifth century, in the writings of St Augustine), in contrast to a pagan past. This distinction is revised at a number of points throughout the European middle-ages and into the Renaissance. (The Renaissance, for example, as a modern age, was initially understood in opposition to the preceding 'middle' ages, but not to the now revalued pagan epoch (or antiquity).) In the seventeenth and eighteenth centuries, modernity came to be associated with the **Enlightenment**. This entailed a revision of the historical understanding of the present. The understanding of time and history in the Christian middle-ages, and even in the Renaissance, was shaped by the expectation, on the part of Christianity, of the immanent end of the world. The more secular Enlightenment presupposes that history will unfold into an open, possibly limitless future. In addition, technological and industrial development, with associated social change, became visibly more rapid during this period. As such, modernity ceases to be merely that which is most recent or new, and now becomes that which is most progressive. Thus, the contemporary social theorist Jürgen Habermas (1983) can still defend the 'unfinished project' of modernity. Such a project suggests that modernity has not merely technological, but more importantly political and moral goals (particularly in the emancipation of humanity from the superstitions and unquestioned **authority** of the past). In this context, 'modernism' in its contemporary meaning, can be seen to emerge in the political revolutions of 1848.

In sociological thinking, modernity is typically placed in contrast to traditional, and therefore pre-industrial, societies. **Sociology**, as a discipline, emerges in the theorisation of modernism in this sense. In the work of Emile Durkheim, at the close of the nineteenth century, contemporary modern society is contrasted, in terms of its complex division of labour and greater sense of individual identity and separateness, from the **mechanical solidarity** of pre-industrial societies. The German social theorist Tönnies similarly distinguished the integrated and homogeneous 'community' of pre-industrial society, from the fragmentation, isolation and artificiality of modern 'society'. In the work of Max Weber, the development of modernism is linked to increasing **rationalisation** in all aspects of social life. This rationalisation entails that all social activities (from the economy, through law and political administration, to **architecture** and music) are subject to scrutiny in order to determine the most instrumentally efficient means of achieving their goals. In these accounts, modernity is never a purely good thing. The idea of modernity as simple, unambiguous progress, is thrown into question, as the problems and tensions of existence in modern society are thrown into relief (from Durkheim's **anomie**, through Marxist theories of alienation, to Weber's iron cage of bureaucracy that curtails individual and political freedom and spontaneity).

In the arts and other areas of **culture**, modernism may be taken to refer to the development of more self-reflective art forms towards the end of the nineteenth century. Thus, in 1845, the poet Baudelaire writes of the French painter Constantin Guys in an essay significantly entitled 'The painter in modern life'. However, modernism in painting is typically tied to Edouard Manet (1832–83), and under his influence, the development of Impressionism. Crucially, in this work, the conventions of **realist** art are thrown into question. The artist's concerns therefore shift away from the overt subject matter of the painting, to the process of painting itself. (As the composer Schoenberg once remarked, painters do not paint trees, they paint paintings.) Similar shifts can be seen in music (with the break from the conventions of tonality at the beginning of the twentieth century, for example in the work of the Second Viennese School) and in literature (as the conventional **narrative** of the realist novel is questioned

245

by such figures as Proust and Joyce). Yet it may be suggested that an increasing interest in the techniques of the artistic medium itself, or in form, is only one aspect of modernist art. This emphasis on form serves to separate the art work from anything outside art (culminating, not merely in the practice of **Abstract Expressionist** painting, for example, but also more importantly in the way in which that work is theorised and defended by such critics as Clement Greenberg (1992) and Michael Fried (1992)). In contrast, much art that can be fairly described as modernist shows a greater commitment to political and social change, or an engagement with the project of producing an art that is appropriate to contemporary (modern) social life. Thus, futurism, for example, sought to celebrate the achievements of an industrial age, and the power and speed of modern technology. Modern **architecture**, for example in the work of Le Corbusier and the **Bauhaus**, sought a building design and urban planning that was appropriate to a rational age, stripped of the conventions and ornaments of the past.

Modernism in art and architecture tended to be characterised by an **elitism** and insularity that made it unpalatable to a wider public. The crisis of modernism comes as its aspirations to universalism (and thus its tendency to dictate, from a privileged position, what culture and architecture should be) are revealed as concealing a closure against the many alternative voices that had in fact been excluded from modernist developments (see **postmodernism**). [AE]

Further reading: Berman 1983; Bradbury and McFarlane 1976; Giddens 1990; Habermas 1988.

multiaccentuality In Voloshinov's thought (1973: 21–4), multiaccentuality refers to the capacity of a **sign** to have different meanings attached to it by different **classes**. This capacity is attributable to the fact that meanings ascribed to signs comprise 'evaluative accents' expressive of social **values**, and that different classes, in connection with their conflicting economic and social interests, have divergent social values.

Multiaccentuality, as Voloshinov notes, is made possible by the fact that a 'sign community', the aggregate of individuals using a particular set of signs, does not coincide with a particular class, but rather is comprised of various classes.

For Voloshinov, multiaccentuality entails that the sign is an 'arena of class struggle'. In saying this, he is to be read as seeking to indicate not only that mulitaccentuality is a factor which enables the sign to be a medium of class struggle, but also that struggles over the meanings of particular signs, which may involve the innovation of concepts of the sign, or language itself, are a part of class struggle. Thus he suggests that a dominant class, as a part of its overall struggle with a subordinate class, attempts to portray signs as having single, unalterable and 'supraclass' meanings and, through so doing, to secure the meanings it attaches to signs which are articulated in a dominant **ideology**. The relative success of this endeavour explains why an actual attachment of different meanings to signs by different classes is generally not manifest. It only becomes so in periods of social crisis or revolutionary change.

Voloshinov's account of mulitaccentuality is linked to other aspects of his concept of the sign. His portrayal of the sign as polysemic and the implication that the sign's representations of the world are mediated by social values and interests are allied to his view (1973: 23) that the sign, rather than reflecting 'existence' in a straightforward way, may refract it (see Weber 1985: 95–6; Gardiner 1992: 70). And through portraying the sign as subject to different accenting by different classes, and allowing that the meanings attached to it may vary with the historically changing values of classes, his discussion may be seen as helping to account for the mutable character of the sign which, for him (Voloshinov 1973: 68–9), distinguishes it from a signal (see Gardiner 1992: 15; Williams 1977: 35–41).

Stuart Hall (1982) has drawn attention to affinities between some developments in thinking about ideological struggle in critical media studies since the 1960s and positions implicit in Voloshinov's account of multiaccentuality, such as the view that the class struggle in language, rather than occurring between two different sets of signifier, may take the form of a different accenting of the same set; and that the meanings which members of a class attach to signs may be the result of the success of an opposing class in an ideological struggle and, as such, diverge from those which would be suggested by the economic circumstances of the class in question. Hall's essay also serves to show that Voloshinov's concept is applicable to the analysis of ideological struggle in the context of race and gender relations. However, it also shows that there are important aspects of 'struggles over meaning' which Voloshinov's concept cannot help to illuminate, notably struggle over access to the means of signification. [RW]

myth 'Myth' is a term that has a number of subtly interrelated meanings. At its most fundamental, a myth is a (typically anonymous) **narrative** about supernatural beings. The importance of the myth lies in the way in which it encapsulates and expresses beliefs and **values** that are shared by, and definitive of, a particular **cultural** group. Thus, a myth may explain the origin of the group (or of the world in general), the place of that group in the world, and its relationship to other groups, and illustrate or exemplify the moral values that are venerated by the group. Mythology has been subject to various theoretical approaches.

In **psychoanalysis**, mythical themes are typically treated as expressive of universal psychic conflicts (with the **Oedipus Complex** being the most famous example). Through an extensive study, not just of mythologies, but also dreams, religion and art, Jung developed his account of **archetypes** as the basic and universal formative processes that structure mythologies. In functionalist approaches to **cultural anthropology**, myths are explained in terms of the needs they meet in the reproduction and stabilisation of society. Thus, by encoding group **norms**, a mythology serves to strengthen the cohesion and integrity of the society. In Durkheimian sociology, mythology may be seen to be expressive of the **collective conscience**, that is to say, the norms and beliefs into which individuals are socialised, and that serve as the cement that holds together both pre-industrial and industrial societies. Something akin to this understanding of myth, as that which binds and motivates a group, is found in *Reflections on Violence*, by the French Marxist theorist Georges Sorel (and first published in 1907). Sorel treats accounts of contemporary political and social events as potential myths (notably in the example of the general strike). Such myths are necessary to evoke sentiments that would serve to motivate mass political action. This echoes, in a revolutionary manner, Plato's conservative account of golden lies. In his **utopian** republic, individuals will be motivated to keep to their place in society, thanks to a mythology of metals in the soul. The dominant guardians have gold in their souls, while the warrior class has silver, and the artisans iron. The social and political relationship between groups is thereby expressed in a fictional account of natural differences.

In Lévi-Strauss's **structuralist** anthropology, inspired by Saussure's **semiology**, myths are treated as **sign** systems. While myth is still important as the medium through which the cultures reflect upon the tensions of social existence, for Lévi-Strauss, the appropriate way to analyse them is as a surface expression of an underlying deep structure (akin to Saussure's **langue**). On one level, his four volume *Mythologies* recounts in faithful detail a vast array of myths from anthropological literature. On another level, the study attempts to identify the rules that govern the transformation from one myth to another. The semiological approach to myth is taken up by Roland Barthes (1973), particularly as a tool to analyse a wide range of images and activities in contemporary culture.

Barthes' analysis works as follows. A sign is understood to have both denotative and connotative orders. It denotes by pointing or referring to something in the world. Thus, a photograph of a family denotes two adults (a mother and a father) and let us say two young children. As connotation, the sign expresses or alludes to certain, culturally specific, values. The precise values involved will depend both upon the culture within which the sign is produced and interpreted, and the way in which the sign is presented. Thus, our family photograph could be brilliantly lit, emphasising bright colours and a sunny day. The photograph would then connote the contentment and security associated with family life. Conversely, a bleak, black and white photograph might express the pressures of family life and the tensions between generations. Mythology builds upon this structure of denotation and connotation. As myth, the sign gives concrete and particular expression to abstract concepts, through which we make sense of a particular social experience. Thus, when we look at a photograph, it does not merely evoke values of which we are consciously aware, but also values or ideas that are so taken-for-granted that we remain unaware of our own attention to them. Our photographs of the family then evoke myths of family-life. These may be myths of the harmonious heterosexual family, and benefits of marriage to the social and moral order (for our colour photograph), and the myth of the decline of family life in the other. The photographs work as mythology precisely in so far as they immediately give support for the taken-for-granted and oversimplified beliefs. The belief leads to a certain understanding of the photograph, and the photograph reinforces the veracity of that belief. The mythical beliefs transform complex cultural processes into apparently natural, unchangeable and self-evident ones. (The association with Plato's noble lies, where the cultural becomes natural, is worth noting.) [AE]

naming and necessity Influential line of argument in logic and philosophical semantics which also has some large (though so far largely unheeded) implications for cultural and literary theory. According to earlier descriptivist theories much of our knowledge is acquired *not* at first hand (e.g., through perceptual acquaintance) but rather – less directly – through our being informed as to certain relevant facts, properties, defining attributes, criteria for picking out objects of a given kind, etc. Such descriptions may change over time with the advancement of scientific knowledge or as new information comes to hand. Thus 'gold' was once thought of as 'a yellow ductile metal soluble in *aqua regia*', whereas now it is scientifically defined as 'the metallic element with atomic number 79'. (This enables us to distinguish genuine samples of the kind from samples of 'fool's gold', or iron pyrites.) Then again: when we use the name 'Aristotle' we are referring to just that historical figure of whom it is known that he lived in Athens, was a pupil of Plato, authored certain texts, acted as tutor to Alexander the Great, and so forth. In short, knowledge by description is a major (arguably *the* major) source of what we commonly claim to know.

However some philosophers – Saul Kripke among them – take issue with the descriptivist theory since it appears to give rise to some strongly counter-intuitive or downright nonsensical conclusions. What if we discovered that Aristotle (the person who actually bore that name) *didn't* in fact live in Athens, study with Plato, teach Alexander, write (or dictate) all those famous philosophical works, etc.? What if a researcher came up with decisive evidence that someone else (not William Shakespeare – maybe Francis Bacon) was the author of 'Hamlet', the Sonnets, and the rest of 'Shakespeare's' Collected Works? On the descriptivist theory it seems that we should have to conclude: 'Aristotle was not Aristotle' or 'Shakespeare was not Shakespeare'. Or again: What if we had been altogether wrong about gold and it did not have *any* of the properties assigned to it now or in the past? Would we then have to say – absurdly – 'gold is not gold'?

In which case (Kripke argues) there is something amiss with the standard descriptivist theory. Rather we should think of reference as fixed through an act of inaugural 'baptism', that is, what once occurred when somebody pronounced: 'this is a sample of *gold*', or when Aristotle's parents proudly declared: 'we name this child Aristotle'. From then on the name passes down through a causal 'chain' of transmission whereby it always refers back to *that* sort of substance (gold) or *just that* particular person (Aristotle) across and despite any subsequent changes in our state of knowledge concerning them. In Aristotle's case the name applies to that historically existent individual whose life started out at the moment of conception.

Kripke derives some far-reaching philosophical conse-quences from this argument. Among them is his claim that there exist certain *a posteriori* necessary truths, truths (that is to say) which might not have held in some alternative 'possible world' – a world where Aristotle was never conceived or where gold had no place in the periodic table of elements – yet which none the less obtain as a matter of necessity in the world we actually inhabit. Also he thinks that it helps to resolve various longstanding issues in epistemology and philos-ophy of science, especially with regard to natural-kind terms and the status of causal explanations. Cultural theorists might do well to ponder this topic – and other debates in recent 'analytic' philosophy of language – before endorsing the standard post-structuralist/postmodernist line (dubiously credited to Saussure) that reality is 'constructed by language', or a product of various culture-relative signifying codes and conventions. [CN]

Further reading: Kripke 1980; McCulloch 1989.

narrative   The organisation of language into a structure which thereby conveys an account of events in a connected and ordered manner. Thus, narratives invoke the notion of sequence: 'This happened . . . then this . . .', etc. There are a variety of theories which explain narrative, for example, Gérard Genette's, which explicates narrative according to the **structuralist** paradigm and hence provides a scientific explanation of narrative form (the discipline of 'narratology'). On this conception, a narrative is composed of the structured relationships between such things as the events narrated, the historical sequence in which they happened, the temporal sequence presented within the narrative, the narrator's perspective and tone, the relationship between the narrator and their audience, and the activity of narration itself. Amongst thinkers associated with **postmodernism** and **post-structuralism**, Roland Barthes sought to initiate a break with the scientific model espoused by structuralism, and turned instead to an emphasis upon the role of the reader in the generation of **meaning**; while Jean-François Lyotard's discussion of the postmodern in *The Postmodern Condition* (1979) is characterised by the view that narrative forms have a plurality and heterogeneity which cannot be overcome by way of resorting to a **meta-narrative** (or 'grand-narrative'). Thus, what constitutes one narrative form is incommensurable with another. The postmodern, in turn, is conceived of by Lyotard as the state which embodies the demise of meta-narratives and their replacement with a multiplicity of finite narratives which spurn the pretention to universality. Equally, writers such as Homi Bhabha have alluded to the relationship between narrative and issues of **identity**, principally in connection with the areas of nationalism and **post–colonialism**. [PS]

Further reading: Barthes 1974; Genette 1980; Lyotard 1989; Ricoeur 1984–8.

nation–state   In its modern sense, a political **community** is differentiated from other such communities in virtue of its autonomy with regard to its legal codes and governmental structures, head of state, boundaries, systems of military defence, etc. A nation-state likewise has a number of symbolic features which serve to present its **identity** in unified terms: a flag, national anthem, a popular self-image, etc. It is worth noting that the nation-state is not synonymous with the possession of nationhood. In the nineteenth century, nationalistic struggles to achieve the political autonomy of a nation-state were mounted by nations which did not possess political autonomy (e.g. the Italian states, or the unification of the German states under the leadership of Prussia in 1872). Likewise, today there are nations which do not necessarily have an accompanying status of statehood (e.g. Wales and Scotland in the UK). From this it follows that what a nation-state is cannot be determined with reference to such notions as nationality, nor **ethnicity**, **culture**, or **language**. It is, rather, the political, social and economic modes of organisation which appear fundamental with regard to this matter: nation-states have political autonomy, different **norm**s and codes with regard to their systems of social relations, and a relatively independent economic identity. [PS]

Further reading: Tivey 1981.

nationalism   Nationalism presents itself not simply as a political phenomenon, but also as a matter of cultural **identity**. As such, any conception of the nation to which it refers must take account of ethnic, historic and linguistic criteria, as well as political notions such as legitimacy, bureaucracy and presence of definable borders. Nationalists make a number of

specific claims for the nation, which vary in relative significance according to the particular historical situation. A
primary argument is that the nation has a right to autonomy,
and that the people of the nation must be free to conduct
their own affairs. As a corollary to this autonomy, nationalists
presuppose (or demand) that the members of the nation share
a common identity, which may be defined according to political or cultural (ethnic, linguistic) criteria. This notion of
identity may be extended to create a sense of unity of purpose,
whereby the projects of individuals are subsumed within the
projects of the nation.

Nationalism thus defined is a modern phenomenon,
becoming prevalent towards the end of the eighteenth century.
Despite the existence of similar ideas in ancient times, the
development of nationalism is concomitant with the development of the modern state, primarily in Europe and North
America. The dates of the American Declaration of Independence (1776) and the French Revolution (1789) are frequently
cited as marking the beginning of nationalism. Its roots as an
intellectual movement are nonetheless vague; although steeped
in the **Enlightenment** tradition of Rousseau and Herder,
nationalism's appeal to an authentic existence based on a
return to a shared cultural heritage has much in common
with the themes prevalent within **Romanticism** and the
writings of Fichte and Hegel. Analytical study of nationalism
as a political force had to wait, however, until the latter
half of the nineteenth century, and it was not until the **post-
colonial** era that scholarly interest became widespread.

Given the disputed nature of the nation in political and
cultural theory, it is hardly surprising that a universally
accepted theory of nationalism remains elusive. In particular,
theorists remain divided over the relative importance of
nationalism's political and cultural dimensions. Ernest Gellner's
definition of nationalism as 'a political principle, which holds
that the political and the national unit should be congruent'
is an example of a position stressing the former aspect, whereas
so-called 'primordialists', exemplified by the anthropologist
Clifford Geertz, argue that nationalism stems from patterns

of social ordering deeply embedded in all ethnic psyches. By contrast, Eric Hobsbawm and Elie Kedourie have proposed that nationalism is an invention on the part of social elites which fails to address the arbitrary and contingent formation of nations, instead positing invented traditions which thence constitute a superficial cultural heritage. In addition, scholars are divided as to whether a distinction can be made between 'good' and 'bad' nationalism (patriotism and chauvinism). Despite disagreement concerning its nature, however, nationalism remains a potent **ideology** in contemporary society, and its popularity appears to have diminished little in the face of potential threats such as globalisation, mass communication and multi-national institutions. [CW]

Further reading: Gellner 1983.

nature   'Nature' has a number of meanings. The oldest meaning is as the essential character or quality of something (see Williams 1976: 219f.). If each individual thing has its own nature, then Nature is the essential quality of everything. Nature is the vital or motivating force behind the universe. More modestly, nature may be equated simply with the universe and all its contents (rather than the force behind it). More restricted still, it is the living world (of plants and animals). The most recent use of the concept 'nature' is to refer to that which is opposed to, prior to, or simply outside human **society** and **culture**. Human culture and society is artificial, having been produced, manufactured or transformed through human invention and industry. Nature may be the material that is subject to this process of transformation, but it is not properly part of human society, until it has been so transformed.

It is this last sense of nature that is most relevant to cultural studies. If nature is opposed to human society, then it can either be because nature is seen to be superior to society, or because it is inferior. In the mid-seventeenth century the English political philosopher Thomas Hobbes described the condition into which society could collapse, not least through civil war, as a **state of nature** (1981). Hobbes' state of nature is brutal and violent, and so the task of political philosophy is to describe the forms of government that will most effectively prevent the disintegration of society into nature. An alternative vision becomes clear, at the very end of the eighteenth century and beginning of the nineteenth, in the writings of the German philosophers Kant (1983) and Hegel (1948). Both of them offer accounts of human history, based on interpretations of the Book of Genesis, that begin with primitive humans (Adam and Eve, Noah and Abraham) having to be expelled from the security of nature, in order to be forced to develop their potential as human beings. Nature, be it the idyll of the Garden of Eden, or the nomadic Abraham merely following the wanderings of his flock of sheep, poses no challenge to humans, and therefore no stimulus to the development of human self-understanding and reason.

The dominant view of nature in science and political philosophy in the seventeenth century European **Enlightenment** is of nature as superior to society. It is a source of order and reason (which was displayed, not least, by Newtonian physics). Politically, the appeal to nature and natural order served as a challenge and criticism of contemporary society. Nature promised an alternative to the seemingly arbitrary and even corrupt conventions that governed absolutist and **feudal** society. Thus, for example, the English philosopher John Locke appealed to the idea of a state of nature, but as a relatively benign condition existing prior to the formation of society (1980). In this state of nature, human beings enjoyed extensive freedoms (or natural rights). Such freedoms could easily be undermined or removed by the violent and selfish actions of others, so society (in the form of government or the state) emerged as people banded together to protect each other. It was therefore the task of any rational and acceptable form of government to protect the natural freedoms of its **citizens**. Feudal government notably failed to do this.

In the **Romanticism** of the late eighteenth and nineteenth centuries, this sense of a superior nature is modified. Society is now to learn from nature, and to renew itself through that study (rather than to be overthrown by an appeal to nature). The emphasis that the **Enlightenment** places on reason, and the rational order that it found in nature, is displaced by a concern with the diversity and fecundity of the organic. Nature becomes a source of spiritual values and emotion. It stands for that which is good and innocent. It is the world of the noble savage. This use is important, because it continues today, not least in the language used in advertising. It is the claim that the wheat from which your breakfast cereal is made is 'natural'. Strictly the wheat is a product of human culture (or more precisely, **agriculture**). It is the product of hundreds of years of selective breeding. (Natural wheat would be a fairly unpalatable Ethiopian grass.) Closely associated nuances of meaning are found today in the use of 'organic'.

This final twist of meaning in 'nature' is perhaps the use that is most central to cultural studies, for it reveals much about the working of **ideology**. Ideology may be understood as sets of ideas and concepts that shape our understanding of the world, and crucially shape and distort that understanding so that we do not challenge or question existing **power** relations. Nature plays a crucial role in ideology, for if social and cultural relations and events are perceived to be natural, then they will not be challenged. They will not appear to be the product of human agency and the exercise of political power, and to challenge them will appear no more rational or sensible than challenging the law of gravity or the fact that it is raining. The Hungarian philosopher Georg Lukács used the phrase 'second nature' to encapsulate this experience of society (1978). That which is the product of human action and invention (our society and culture) and thus that which should be full of meaning and the indications of human intention, actually confronts us as something that is as alien and as meaningless as first nature – real nature. The German Marxist philosopher T.W. Adorno summarised the challenge that this ideological inversion of nature and culture posed for a politically informed study of culture: 'What cannot be changed in nature may be left to look after itself. When it can be changed, it is up to us to change it' (Wiggerhaus 1994: 90).

That is to say that the task of cultural theory may be to see through second nature, and so change what appears to be unchangeable. [AE]

New Criticism The most significant influences on New Criticism were the scrupulous text-oriented literary interpretations of I.A. Richards. But the movement called New Criticism consisted chiefly of the expatriate poet T.S. Eliot and three writers from the American south: John Crowe Ransom, Allen Tate and Robert Penn Warren. It is largely a North American phenomenon even though it has significant parallels with the work of the British critics F.R. Leavis and William Empson. Through its emphasis on questions of literary form, New Criticism expressed a poet's interest in the possibilities of language. This entailed an aesthetic theory that moved the interest of criticism away from the author's life towards a detailed engagement with the language of literature and thus marked a decisive shift away from philology, source-hunting and literary biography to textual analysis. Although its emphasis on close reading was admirably suited to the classroom and still remains the starting point of most theoretically inspired interpretations, the intellectual premises of New Criticism were so firmly ingrained in a narrow conservative agrarian ideology that it became the target of fierce attacks.

New Criticism's insistent focus on the text was the result of understanding the work of art as a timeless and self-contained artefact. Although its interest in the materiality of the text also touched upon questions concerning text production, the institutionalised practice of applying New Critical methodology disconnected literature from its social context, so that, by and large, it became equated with an exclusive interest in the words on the page. This emphasis was testified by the publications of its chief representatives: most notably Cleanth Brooks's and Robert Penn Warren's series of textbooks, among them *Understanding Poetry* (1938) and Brooks's *The Well Wrought Urn* (1949). Other representatives are

Monroe Beardsley and R.P. Blackmur. Although the emphasis on form had started out as a means of introducing questions concerning the economic requirements for the production of art, it was appropriated as a bourgeois aesthetic in which the high valuation of rhetorical complexity displaced the need for political commitment. In the theory propounded by W.K. Wimsatt, the text was defined as being 'iconic': literary language figured as an end in itself and literature was taken to describe a world which differed from all historically perceived reality because it was thought to express a universally true perception of what it meant to be human (*The Verbal Icon* (1958)). This was as much as to say that literature represents profound human problems which are independent of both author and historical context, and it is in the appeal to this fundamental sense of humanity that the critic can understand and explicate the full meaning of a work of art.

The emphasis on close reading is the result of a critical theory which focused on the workings of language rather than on the psychology of the author. At its best, however, it combined an investigation of linguistic structures with a more open-minded interest in the psychology and sociology of language production. Although his work stands apart from New Criticism, William Empson had considerable influence on the movement. Two of his books, *Seven Types of Ambiguity* (1930), written at a time when New Criticism was about to take off as a critical practice, and the later *The Structure of Complex Words* (1951), combine close attention to textual-semantic details with a discussion of culturally salient ideas. But it has to be noted that Empson always incorporated contextual considerations into his interpretations and his work on ambiguity was careful not to posit an ultimate reconciliation through notions of 'paradox, irony', etc.

Recent approaches to art, especially those taking a **deconstructionist** line, also engage in minute textual analysis and concentrate on contradictory moments of the text. The chief difference is that New Criticism treated literature as an object that would reveal the complexities of life through its self-referential emphasis on rhetorical complexities (such as paradox, oxymoron, ambiguity, tension, irony). Poetry, especially, was taken as the highest cultural achievement because its rhetorical patterns were believed to express the possibility of reconciling contradictions, by analogy with the firmly defined system of beliefs held by western society and Christian religion. The subsequent objections to it voiced by those who struggled for the recognition of gender and racial rights showed that even though New Critical readings may have been immensely sensitive to the contradictory semantic potential of the texts, their ultimate conclusions were politically unacceptable. This is because the method adopted by the New Critics typically reduced the meaning of a text to a singular and all-inclusive statement about the individual's existence as a member of western (patriarchal and bourgeois) society. In contrast to this, a deconstructionist critical practice, especially if it engages in the politically motivated Marxist, feminist or postcolonial criticism, highlights plural interpretations of a text as instances where the meaning of central concepts, such as subjectivity or identity, are contested. Objections to New Criticism were not only raised on political grounds but also concerned its reductive understanding of language. For all its interest in rhetorical devices expressing contradiction, New Criticism adhered to the belief that it was possible to exert control over linguistic meaning and that paradoxical statements made in literature had the special virtue of awaiting a sufficiently sophisticated mind to explain and resolve them. [CK]

Further reading: Hosek and Parker 1985; Lentricchia 1980; Litz
et al. 1998.

norm   A norm is a **rule** that governs a pattern of social behaviour. Examples of norms include laws, moral principles and guidelines, customs, and the rules of etiquette, but also may express desirable values and goals. 'Norm' has two meanings, which in practice it is important to distinguish. On the one hand, a norm may encapsulate the usual behaviour within a society (and is thus a norm in the sense of being statistically normal behaviour). On the other hand, the norm is a pattern of behaviour that is desired or prescribed, whether or not actual behaviour complies with this ideal. Norms, especially in this latter sense, will be accompanied by positive and negative sanctions – that is to say respectively, rewards for conforming and punishments for breaking norms. The nature of the sanction will vary, from mild approval and a hard stare to, for example, large financial rewards and lengthy prison sentences, depending upon the sort of norm involved.

The idea that individual human beings learn the norms of their society through early upbringing (or **socialisation**), helps to explain how individuals become competent social agents, who by and large conform with the expectations of their culture. The early sociology of Durkheim emphasised the costs of a loss of norms (which he termed **anomie**). Without the guidance of norms, a person's life loses direction and becomes meaningless. However, a danger with this approach (which is seen particularly in **functionalist sociology**) is that it tends to assume that norms exist independently of any particular social event (and that there is no ambiguity as to which norms apply here and now), and that there is a general consensus in society about its norms. **Symbolic interactionism**, precisely because it focuses upon the construction of society through **interaction** between competent social agents, argues that norms may be better understood as the subject of negotiation. Agreement upon the relevant norms will be entwined with the activity needed to make sense of the sort of social event to which one is party. Marxist sociologists, conversely, have questioned whether norms can be understood as the site of a self-evident consensus. It is suggested rather, that the imposition and acceptance of a norm must be analysed in terms of the power structures within society (and thus as part of **ideology**). [AE]

objectivity True knowledge that is, or should be, value-neutral. Thus, objective knowledge is knowledge of how things really are, as opposed to how they appear to be. In the natural sciences (e.g. physics) objectivity is an indispensible notion (with regard to the application of theories and, above all, their verification by experiment). Objectivity presupposes that there is a real, external world which is independent of our knowledge of it, and that it is possible to describe this world accurately. On this view of science, scientific methodology aspires to provide the rules whereby reality can be known (a variant of this can be found in **positivism**). Philosophers like Nietzsche have criticised this notion. For Nietzsche, there is no knowledge which is not interested knowledge, i.e. which does not have an interest in, and therefore does not presuppose some value with regard to, its subject-matter. Likewise, Foucault has taken a similar line. The implication of this attitude is that the aspiration to value objectivity above all else in knowledge is itself generated historically and culturally. (See also **experiment**, **self**, **epistemology**.) [PS]

Oedipus Complex A key term in **psychoanalysis**, used to theorise the transition of the child (at approximately 3 to 5 years) from a dyadic relationship with the mother, to a triadic relationship that includes the father as a figure of authority. The failure to move through this transition correctly is an important source of psychopathology in the adult. The term is derived, by Freud, from the Greek myth, in which Oedipus kills his father and marries his mother. Freud, in part on a supposed recollection of his own childhood experience, argues that initially the child is in love with his mother and jealous of his father. (In the early theorisation of the complex, the child was presumed to be male.) The account of the Oedipus complex is complemented by Freud's account of the childhood theory of sexuality. The child assumes that all babies are born with penises. The absence of the penis in the women is interpreted as punishment inflicted by the jealous father. The male child therefore breaks from his relationship with his mother, under the perceived threat of castration. The female child, conversely, displaces her wish for a penis by the desire for a baby. [AE]

Further reading: Freud 1910, 1924, 1979.

oligarchy   Government by the few. The term can be traced back to Aristotle, who classified government into three types: monarchy, or rule by the one; aristocracy, or rule by the few; democracy, or rule by the many. Thinkers associated with the Aristotelean tradition (e.g. Niccolò Machiavelli (1469–1527) and James Harrington (1611–1677)) have advocated a mixed form of government, i.e. one in which each of these models was combined in a system of checks and balances in order to prevent the degeneration of these into tyranny, oligarchy, or anarchy. Oligarchy thus signifies a degenerate form of government, in which the few who administer power have succumbed to corruption and no longer serve the overall good of society but rather their own personal interests. [PS]

ontology   (i) Part of **metaphysics** which engages in the study of the nature of existence in general, *not* with the existence of particular entities. Thus, an ontological enquiry, such as that engaged in by Martin Heidegger in *Being and Time*, is concerned with 'the question of Being', by which he means the conditions of possibility for the existence of any particular entity. (ii) Any set of assumptions about the fundamental nature of existence which are presupposed within a theory. For example, the thought of classical **liberalism**, it has been argued, contains a particular conception of individual subjectivity which conceives of it as comprising a particular set of properties which make it what it is (this is sometimes termed an 'ontology of the **subject**'). [PS]

Further reading: Grossmann 1992; McCulloch 1995; Sadler 1996; Sprigge 1984.

organic analogy Comparison of society to a biological organism, as part of an explanation for the stability and cohesion of society, and as the basis of a methodology for social science. If an animal or plant is constituted from a number of separate organs, each with a specialist function that is necessary to continued life or 'homoeostasis' of the whole, then society is similarly constituted from a number of **institutions** and **roles**, each with specialist functions. Explanation, not merely of society as a whole, but of any element within that society, may be made in terms of the function that the part plays in the maintenance of the whole (see **functionalism**). While having extraordinary, if deceptive, explanatory power, the organic analogy places undue emphasis on social cohesion, and is thus ill equipped to deal with social conflict and social change. [AE]

organic solidarity Term in Durkheim's sociology, explaining the cohesion of modern industrial societies. A complex division of labour entails that each member of a society is a specialist, unable to provide for his or her needs without co-operation and exchange with others. Society therefore coheres because individuals do not have the resources to secede from it. [AE]

Orientalism   See **Other**.

Other   A concept that can be traced back to the work of Hegel, and to be found in a variety of approaches to **epistemology**, questions of cultural **identity** and **psychoanalysis**. Amongst others, a treatment of this notion is in the writings of Lacan, in Sartrean **existentialism**, Derridean **deconstruction**, and Edward Said's analysis of the colonial European study of Oriental cultures, *Orientalism* (inspired in part by the thought of Michel Foucault). The term, not surprisingly, is highly ambiguous. In the context of theories of culture, perhaps the most prominent contemporary use of this notion has been made by Said. In these terms, the Other may be designated as a form of cultural projection of concepts. This projection constructs the identities of cultural **subjects** through a relationship of power in which the Other is the subjugated element. In claiming knowledge about 'orientals' what Orientalism did was construct them as its own (European) Other. Through describing purportedly 'oriental' characteristics (irrational, uncivilised, etc.) Orientalism provided a definition not of the real 'oriental' identity, but of European identity in terms of the oppositions which structured its account. Hence, 'irrational' Other presupposes (and is also presupposed by) 'rational' **self**. The construction of the Other in Orientalist **discourse**, then, is a matter of asserting self-identity, and the issue of the European account of the Oriental Other is thereby rendered a question of **power**. [PS]

Further reading: Said 1978a.

P

paradigm   (i) In semiotics, a paradigm is the range of meaningful units from which a message may be composed. The letters of an alphabet, for example, are the paradigm from which words can be composed. (Thus, A, a, B, and b, are part of the paradigm of the Roman alphabet, while ¥ and $ are not.) Within a paradigm, units become meaningful in so far as they are distinguishable from each other and are potentially interchangeable. (See also **syntagm**.)

(ii) Term in the **philosophy of science**. As explained by Thomas Kuhn in *The Structure of Scientific Revolutions* (1962), paradigms are working theories or 'world views' which, within the domains of various scientific fields, facilitate the activity of study and research. For Kuhn, a paradigm may be considered as a conceptual 'achievement' (as exemplified by key works in the history of science, such as Newton's *Principia*, or Lyell's *Principles of Geology*) which lays down the guiding principles within a particular scientific discipline for the future interrogation and investigation of phenomena. It is thus a working model which allows scientists to engage in the activity of actual scientific practice. The achievement which marks the birth of a paradigm has two central features: (1) it 'attract[s] an enduring group of adherents away from competing modes of scientific activity'; and (2) the model is itself not complete but 'sufficiently open-ended to, leave all sorts of problems for the redefined group of practitioners to solve' (Kuhn 1962: 10).

A paradigm is thus a general theory which has succeeded in its struggle against other competing theories, but which has nevertheless not exhausted all the possible facts with which it has to deal. Once a paradigm is established, both the field it covers and its practitioners are more firmly defined, and future problems in need of investigation clearly stipulated. In such cases 'normal science' is in progress. A paradigm reaches a crisis point when the phenomena encountered within the discipline it defines become difficult to fit into it and become sufficiently important or numerous that they cannot be ignored: 'Failure of existing rules is a prelude to a search for now ones' (Kuhn 1962: 68). This crisis leads to a break-down of the theory, which nevertheless continues to operate until a new, more adequate one arrives to explain anomolous phenomena (1962: 77). The replacement of one paradigm by another in the wake of such crises constitutes a shift 'in the scientific community's conception of legitimate problems and standards' (1962: 108).

Most significantly, according to Kuhn, such paradigm shifts are not to be understood in terms of a cumulative process in which the same problems are thereby further refined and developed as objects of study (a view put forward by philosopher of science Karl Popper). A change of paradigm involves a substantive alteration with regard to the issues which are held to be of importance within a discipline. A new paradigm gains acceptance because it is more able to account for anomolous phenomena and, importantly, because it gains a significant number of adherents. Hence, such changes (or revolutions) are not to be understood as marking out a moment of **progress** in the history of a particular discipline which is to be understood in purely objective terms. Rather, these changes are to be taken as manifestations of a sociological nature. In this sense, science itself is rendered a cultural practice whose subject-matter and guiding problems are determined by forces which exist within the community of scientific interpreters themselves, rather than according to any objective standard of reference to an external world set apart from problems of interpretation. [PS]

Further reading: Kuhn 1970.

parole   In Saussure's linguistics, 'parole' refers to actual language or to the potentially infinite instances of language use (such as written and spoken sentences, poems and reports). Parole is contrasted to the underlying structure of the language, or **langue**. [AE]

participant observation   Participant observation is an **empirical** research methodology in the social sciences, that involves the researcher studying a community, or cultural activity of which he or she is a part (typically if only for the length of the study). Such an approach has the advantage over more controlled and experimental approaches in terms of the richness of qualitative detail that it can yield. A number of problems are well documented. First, the presence of an observer may distort normal social action within the group (so that the group ends up doing what it thinks the researcher wants it to do). Second, the **role** that the researcher occupies in the group is important. An inappropriate role can isolate the reseacher from important actors or decision-makers within the group, so giving a distorted view of how the group works. Participant observation is, in any case, frequently criticised for lacking **objectivity**, and being too vulnerable to the **value** assumptions that the observer imposes, unwittingly, on his or her observations. Conversely, a well chosen role can facilitate the task of observation. In a study of a Welsh rural community, Ronald Frankenburg (1957) was able to take on the role of 'stranger'. This at once allowed him access to communal activities (so much that he became secretary of the football club), without compromising his independence. Importantly, Frankenburg argues that this role existed prior to his entering the community, and so did not disrupt its structure. (See also **ethnography**.) [AE]

Further reading: Spradley 1980.

patriarchy   The term 'patriarchy' literally means the 'rule of the father'. It has been adopted by the majority of **feminist**

theorists to refer to the way in which societies are structured through male domination over, and oppression of, women. Patriarchy therefore refers to the ways in which material and symbolic resources (including income, wealth and power) are unequally distributed between men and women, through such social **institutions** as the family, sexuality, the state, the economy, culture and language. While there is no single analysis of the workings of patriarchy, debate over its nature and historical development has been important in the development and differentiation of schools of feminist thought. A number of key issues can be identified in the theorising of patriarchy. The relationship of male domination to biology was an early source of contention. While patriarchal structures may be found in all known human societies, the reduction of patriarchy to biological invariants, such as the roles of women and men in child-birth and nurturing, suggests that patriarchy is an essential and unchangeable **natural** relationship. Feminism tends, rather, to argue that patriarchy is, at least, the cultural interpretation of those natural relationships, if not itself wholly cultural. Psychological, and especially **psychoanalytic** theories, may associate patriarchy in the early socialisation of the child (and especially the break of the child from the mother at the **Oedipal** stage). Feminist responses to Lacanian psychoanalysis, from for example Kristeva and Cixous, are significant in seeing dominant culture, language and reason (Lacan's 'symbolic') as inherently patriarchal. They therefore seek to recover a pre-patriarchal stage, expressed in an *écriture feminine*, through which women can articulate themselves to themselves outside the distortions of male language. The relationship of patriarchy to other forms of oppression, such as **class** and **race** receives diverse theorisation. Questions include that of the primacy or otherwise of patriarchy over other forms of domination, and the way in which different forms of domination may interact and re-enforce each other. Thus, socialist feminists have typically sought to link patriarchy to class exploitation (Barrett 1980). The importance of race and **ethnicity** has indicated that a potential flaw in an all-encompassing theory of patriarchy is that it remains indifferent to divisions between women. The exploitation and domination of all women is not alike, and women cannot therefore be theorised as a single, homogeneous group. [AE]

Further reading: Mies 1986; Spivak 1987; Walby 1990.

phenomenology　Phenomenology refers to a cluster of approaches to philosophical and sociological enquiry, and to the study of art, deriving from the work of the German philosopher, Edmund Husserl (1859–1938). The diversity of approaches that have been described as phenomenology, not least in Husserl's own work (which continually changed and developed over his career), means that a precise and all-encompassing definition of phenomenology is not easily given. However, something of the flavour of Husserl's enterprise can be suggested, along with some indication of the reaction of his followers, who include Martin Heidegger, Maurice Merleau-Ponty, Jean-Paul Sartre and Alfred Schutz.

Phenomenology, as its name suggests, is concerned to describe basic human experience (and hence, a concern with phenomena, a word that is derived from the Greek for 'appearance'). The point of this is to explore that which is presupposed by the natural sciences and all other claims to knowledge, and which therefore makes those knowledge claims possible. Phenomenology attempts to describe how the world must appear to the naïve observer, stripped of all presuppositions and culturally imposed expectations. This is captured in the slogan that phenomenology returns to the 'things themselves' (*Zu den Sachen* (Husserl 1962: 74f.)). Phenomenological enquiry therefore proceeds through the method of 'bracketing'. Bracketing involves a suspension of belief. The scientist, for example, in observing a colour, observes it in terms of the assumption that it is light waves at a given frequency. Yet this assumption is not available to the untutored observer. It can therefore play no part in the phenomenologist's description. More radically, Husserl suspends what he calls the 'natural attitude'. In everyday experience, we take for granted certain assumptions about our experience, not least that there is a real object out there that is being experienced, and that we are unified egos that have that experience. These assumptions are again not given in experience. Crucially, Husserl is not arguing that the real world does not exist. Rather, bracketing draws our attention to the assumptions we (must) make in order to experience the real world at all.

This is clarified by recognising the centrality of another of Husserl's claims. He argues that all consciousness is intentional. This means that we are always conscious of something (and never just conscious). Thus, I see an oasis, I touch a desk, and I long for a pay-rise. Note that the objects of which we are conscious need not exist. (So the pay-rise may never be granted, and the oasis might be a mirage.) Husserl's point is that the account of experience cannot be made in terms of its causation by the material object. Rather, the object exists as it does (e.g. a real oasis or as mirage) because of the meaningful relationship that the observer has to the object. The object, for Husserl, fulfils the expectations of the observer, and in encountering an object, we will have a host of expectations that structure our relationship towards it. In Roman Ingarden's **aesthetics**, that draws on Husserl, the literary work is treated as a purely intentional object (1973). Concerned with describing genuinely aesthetic attitudes to the work of art, he rejects any identification of the work of art with its material substrate. The work is ascribing an enduring identity, independently of its multiple interpretations. The proper object of appreciation is therefore the content of the art work, in which the reader 'concretises' the work in imaginatively reconstructing what the author has left indeterminate.

Husserl's followers typically challenge his idealism. His phenomenology concentrates on the experience of a largely disembodied observer. In contrast, Heidegger (and following him, Sartre) begin from the experience of an embodied agent who is practically engaged with the problems of the real, material and contingent world. Thus, for example, Husserl strives to discover the 'meaning' of experience as necessary and universal essences. In contrast, for Heidegger, such meaning develops historically as we pursue practical problems in the world. The meaning of a 'hammer', to use a favourite Heideggerean example, depends upon the use that human beings make of hammers. The meanings of experience are not then universals to be discovered through phenomenological descriptions, but rather are ascribed to the world by human beings, in the pursuit of diverse goals. As Heidegger rather elegantly puts this: 'The wood is a forest of timber, the mountain a quarry of rock; the river is water-power, the wind is "wind in the sails" ' (1962: 40–1). Similarly, Merleau-Ponty sees meaning as being ascribed through the body, so that belief in the body cannot be bracketed (1962: 147)

In the social sciences, a phenomenological **sociology** has been developed from the work of Alfred Schutz (1899–1959). Again, Schutz (1962) rejects the idealism of Husserl's own programme, in order to describe human experience as it occurs within an inter-subjectively constituted social world (or **life-world**). The 'natural attitude' becomes for Schutz the taken-for-granted assumptions that competent social actors make about the social world and the people they encounter within it. Such actors take for granted the existence of other human beings, and assume a 'reciprocity of perspectives'. The social actor therefore has a 'stock-of-knowledge-at-hand' (in the form of a sets of skills, assumptions and 'typifications' – being the labels and concepts through which they orientate their actions to each other) that allow them, not merely to recognise and respond to social reality, but actively, if unwittingly, to construct it. [AE]

Further reading: Bell 1990; Schutz and Luckmann 1974.

philosophy of language A phrase which refers to those approaches to philosophy resulting from the 'linguistic turn' which dates from the early part of this century. The common tenet of these approaches is an acceptance that an understanding of language through its analysis is crucial to all areas of philosophical and theoretical study. The prime areas of concern are the function language plays in constructing:

(i) the philosophical and theoretical problems relating to the **discourses** of religion, morality, ethics, art, literature, politics, science, mathematics and even philosophy; (ii) our conception of ourselves, our social and material realities, and our relationship to those realities.

The influence of the linguistic turn is apparent in a number of schools of philosophical thought. Within **analytic philosophy** the historical emphasis has been on mapping language onto the world as accurately as possible. Attempts to accomplish this have focused on a rigorous analysis of the logical structures 'hidden' in ordinary language. The basic assumption of this school of philosophy has been that the prime use of language is to communicate facts about the world. However, in recent times, this assumption has come into question (see **reference** and **analytic philosophy**).

The complementary movement to analytic philosophy is 'ordinary-language philosophy'. Again the focus is, as the name suggests, upon ordinary language. However, rather than trying to expose its deep logical and syntactical structures, this group of philosophers has tended to concentrate upon how language is used in actual social contexts of utterance. As a result, contra analytic philosophy, there was a move away from the assumption that language has a single, primary function over to the idea that language has many functions, e.g. promising, commanding and interrogating (Austin 1955). The analysis of these various uses of language would, it was thought, yield a better understanding of the problems with which philosophy concerns itself.

In the **philosophy of science**, a study and understanding of language, at least as it is used to formulate theories, is seen as crucial to understanding how we come to know the natural world. The 'logical **positivists**' (see also **meaning**), for example, thought it important to tie language as closely as possible to the experimental methods employed by scientists to make truth claims about the world; thus, it was hoped, allowing language to mirror the world ever more accurately. Thomas S. Kuhn (1970), on the other hand, considered language as playing a crucial role in our very conception of the natural world. The radical implication of Kuhn's position is that language, rather than mirroring the world, actually constructs it.

Supporters of **structuralism** have tended to view a language, e.g. Welsh, as a rather homogeneous affair. Careful study of a language, on this account, would eventually reveal the meta-system of spoken and written **signs** which underlies the multifarious social discourses of a particular society. The ultimate goal of such study is a better understanding of the customs and practices of the particular culture under scrutiny.

The advocates of **post-structuralism** and **postmodernism** have rejected the notion of an underlying 'meta-system'. They view a language and its corresponding society as composed of a number of discourses, each operating in virtual independence of its other social counterparts. This view wholly undermines the possibility of reaching an overall understanding of particular cultures as hoped for by the structuralists. In addition, post-structuralists and postmodernists have tended to view language as having far less stability and far more influence upon the construction of social structures and the individuals of which they comprise than the structuralists.

Deconstruction is regarded by its supporters more as a technique than a school of thought. Although they share many of their assumptions about language with post-structuralism, not all post-structuralists are reciprocal in their support of deconstruction (see Said 1978). The technique has been used by its main protagonist, Jacques Derrida, as a more – or often less – serious weapon for exposing as merely social constructions what other philosophers and theorists take as the foundations of knowledge.

The **Frankfurt School**, particularly Habermas, see an analysis of language as providing the hope of overcoming the pessimism which Adorno and Horkheimer see as resulting from the moral outrages of the Second World War. In their *Dialectic of Enlightenment* (1944), they map out the process whereby the **Enlightenment** project undermines its potential for human emancipation. The conclusion they reach leaves little hope for positive socio-political change. Seeking a 'cure' for this pessimism, Habermas, partly inspired by the work of the later Ludwig Wittgenstein (1953) and partly by the work of Karl-Otto Apel (1976), turns to an analysis of language. What he tries to demonstrate is that the very possibility of language implies the existence of a deep reciprocity between speakers. It is this reciprocity, he thinks, which can form the basis of new emancipatory socio-political projects. The net result is Habermas's 'theory of communicative action' (1984 and 1987). [SH]

philosophy of science   One way to understand the philosophy of science is to think of it as divided up into three areas of concern: the **epistemology** of science; the **metaphysics** of science; and the social role and function of science.

The epistemologist of science asks questions like: 'Are scientific theories true?' and 'How do scientific theories relate to the world?'. The metaphysician of science investigates questions connected with the puzzling features of the world as described by science. For example, do the 'laws of nature' actually exist in the universe, or are they just a convenient way for us to think about the world? The philosophy of science also considers the function of science within society in conjunction with questions relating to the responsibilities of individual scientists.

It is sometimes difficult to distinguish clearly between issues of metaphysics and those of epistemology in scientific debates. A clearly metaphysical issue is one that arises out of a peculiarity of quantum physics. The theory of quantum physics seems to tell us that 'objects' such as photons can display both particle-like and wave-like properties. The 'fact' that such phenomena behave in this fashion prompts the question 'What are such objects really like?'. This sort of question falls within the bound of metaphysics. However, questions relating to how we come to learn about the world through theories like quantum mechanics are issues of epistemology.

It is probably easier to understand epistemological issues in science by looking at its subject matter. A crude and still

popular traditional view of science is that, by a process of
the experimental testing of theories, science produces an ever
more accurate picture of the world (see **induction**). Thus,
slowly but surely, through the efforts of individual scientists,
we come to know our world better. This model suggests a
view of scientific progress as a rather piecemeal affair, with
the scientist building steadily upon the work of those great
figures that have gone before. For this model of science to
hold true requires that we have a certain view of the world
and our relationship to it. The view that is suggested has
become known more generally as '**realism**'. This view rests
on two theses:

(i) The independence thesis: that a physical world exists and
is independent of our awareness of it.
(ii) The knowledge thesis: that we can come to know this
world as it 'really' is.

The basic epistemological issue here is that if the world is
independent of our direct awareness of it, then our knowledge
of it is mediated in some way. In the context of science, the
mediums of reference to the world are our various scientific
theories. However, if our access to the world is through
the theories we have about it, then how can we be sure
that the theories we have represent the world as it really is? If
we only reach the world through a particular theory, then how
can we confirm whether this theory is a correct representation
of the world or not? If our theories are what we use to
represent the world to ourselves, then we cannot ever 'step
outside' all of our theories to check to see if the body of theory
we depend upon to give us knowledge of the world is or is
not correct. This is because we have no access to a theory
independent point of view. Any view that suggests that we
do not have some sort of objective access to the world is
generally labelled 'anti-realist'.

Interconnected issues that arise in the epistemology of
science are those of progress and methodology. As a result
of the traditional view outlined above, science is seen as generating, piecemeal fashion, an increasingly accurate picture of

the world. Progress here is defined in terms of scientists improving their theories so that they represent the true structure of the world 'better'. However, if our theories are not ever improving 'pictures' of the real nature of our external reality, then what are they? If it turns out that they are merely one way amongst many of looking at the world, then if you change the theory you also change your picture of the world (see entry for **paradigm**). There is no direct implication here that the new picture we get of the world is 'better' than the old one – it is just different. Thus, the whole notion of 'scientific progress' seems to evaporate.

Crucial to the knowledge-yielding capacity of science is its methodology, i.e. the methods and procedures which science employs in its fact gathering and theory testing. Indeed, it is the methodology of science that is taken as one of its defining characteristics. Many philosophers of science take this methodology as marking science off from other disciplines such as metaphysics. Strong supporters of this view were the logical positivists (see entry for **positivism**). Perhaps the major debate within the philosophy of science is what the methodology of science amounts to or whether, in fact, it has a single, unifying methodology. This debate has been ongoing throughout the history of the philosophy of science. It started with the inductivists. The founder of falsificationism, Karl Popper, took up the problems associated with inductivism. Popper, in turn, was criticised by supporters of the Duhem–Quine hypothesis (see **holism** and **meaning**). Philosophers, such as Kuhn and Paul Feyerabend, challenged still further the traditional view of science by developing the work of Duhem and Quine.

When we focus upon the social role and function of science, different issues arise. Almost all scientists seem to accept the thesis that science is morally autonomous, i.e. that it is basically value free *vis-à-vis* its judgements. In other words, when scientists make decisions regarding experiments or theories, the methods they use contain only 'scientific' criteria, thereby setting moral considerations aside as irrelevant to the choices they make within science. However, such a thesis, even if it were true, is clearly about the theory building aspects of science. It takes no account of the consequences of scientific discoveries. For example, should scientists have considered the environmental effects of the large-scale use of atomic power? Moral questions also arise in connection with the experimental methods employed by certain scientists, e.g. with regard to the permissibility of using animals in painful scientific tests.

A connected issue is whether or not social trends and pressures affect science. Should we view scientists as independent and impartial or are they, like many of the rest of us, affected by financial and political considerations? For example, it seems reasonable to suppose that a scientist working for a particular company will be guided in his or her research by the business needs of that organisation. Again, it is not unrealistic to suggest that a scientist's judgement may be influenced *vis-à-vis* the direction of his or her research by a change of government, particularly if the continuance of his or her work depends upon state research funding. If this is so, then this seems to qualify, at least to some extent, the popular view of scientists as driven solely by a passion to expand the frontiers of human knowledge. [SH]

Further reading: Chalmers 1982, 1990; Feyerabend 1975; Gillies 1993; Kolakowski 1972, 1990; Popper 1959, 1963.

photography The belief that the camera never lies is, perhaps, one of the most flagrant examples of the working of **ideology** that can be imagined. The belief assumes that if the image recorded by the camera is dependent upon natural, optical processes, then what the photograph represents will be what is really out there in the world. The photograph is important to cultural studies, precisely because cultural studies attempts to expose such confusions of the natural and the artificial. In many respects, the work of Roland Barthes on photography is at the core of this approach (1973, 1981). Barthes identifies what he calls 'the photographic paradox' as the coexistence of two messages within a single photograph.

One message concerns what the photograph denotes. This is the neutral referent of the photograph, the object or person of which it is a photograph. The second message is the **myth** that is invested in this image. It is the way in which the object is represented, and invokes in the spectator, often unwittingly, a series of taken-for-granted assumptions about the social and political world. Precisely because this invocation is unremarked, the photograph serves only to reinforce prejudices. Barthes's famous illustration of this is of a cover of *Paris-Match*. 'On the cover, a young Negro in a French uniform is saluting, with eyes uplifted, probably fixed on the fold of the tricolour'. As myth, it signifies to the viewer, 'that France is a great empire, that all her sons, without colour discrimination, faithfully serve under her flag, and that there is no better answer to the detractors of an alleged colonialism than the zeal shown by this Negro in serving his so-called oppressors' (Barthes 1973: 125–6).

A more positive view of the photograph was suggested by Walter Benjamin in the 1930s, in his analysis of the work of art in the age of mechanical reproduction (1970b). Mechanically reproduced art, including photography and cinema, is seen to challenge concepts from orthodox aesthetics that could be of use to **fascism** (such as originality, genius and authenticity). The photography carries with it no 'aura' of being the original and authentic work of art. The audience is thus brought closer to the work, and is engaged politically, rather than being kept at a distance by the **rituals** that surround the viewing of hand-produced originals. Yet mechanical reproduction also changes the nature of the art work, and Benjamin makes a series of richly insightful and stimulating comments on the work of specific photographers. Thus, the photographs of the early twentieth-century French photographer Eugène Atget are 'like scenes of crime. . . . It is photographed for the purpose of establishing evidence' (Benjamin 1970b: 228). The photograph thus draws our attention to the otherwise taken-for-granted details of everyday life, just as Freud's analysis of parapraxis ('Freudian slips') drew our attention to the accidents, and suddenly imbued them with great significance.

Thus, Benjamin compares the painter to a magician or shaman, healing through the ritual of the laying on of hands. The photographer or cameraman is a surgeon, cutting into the patient (1970b: 235). [AE]

Further reading: Bolton 1989; Newhall 1982; Sontag 1973.

pluralism As the promotion of heterogeneity over homo-geneity, difference over sameness, or the dispersal of power over its centralisation, pluralism has informed social theory in appropriately multiple ways. It can take the form of an empirical or metaphysical claim (that reality, culture, truth, values, or practices simply are irrevocably plural in nature) or a normative agenda (positing diversification, devolution and openness as values), but mostly the two will be interlinked.

A concern for the tolerance of difference (in beliefs and social practices) has motivated liberal thinking from Milton and Locke, through Kant and Mill, and down to Berlin and Rawls – whether based on scepticism about the superiority of any single conception of the good life (and thus about the state's right to enforce one), or on a conception of the autonomous individual capable of choosing his or her own ends and taking responsibility for his or her actions. Various aporias and dilemmas have emerged: is it possible, desirable, or responsible for a state to remain neutral between competing ideals? Does one grant freedom of speech to those who would deny it for others? Does liberal (representative) democracy really allow for the articulation and pursuit of the full diversity of citizens' inclinations? How does liberalism account, or cater, for the possibility that ideas of the good stem from (rather than exist prior to) particular historical forms of social organisation? And so on. Significantly, contemporary pluralist thinking emerges strongly in the work of those **communi-tarian** thinkers (such as Charles Taylor and Michael Walzer) and in the discourse ethics of Jürgen Habermas, both of which reject the atomistic individualism of traditional liberalism in favour of some account of the intrinsically *social* nature of subjectivity.

281

A spin-off in political science is the form of pluralism (prominent since the 1950s) associated with a largely American tradition of 'polyarchic' democracy theory, represented notably by Talcott Parsons and Robert Dahl, linking western democratic practice to a wide dispersal of power and authority through a range of relatively autonomous forums and institutions. This is one way to counteract the potential tyranny of the state: ensure that rival interest groups and other factions have a definite checking and balancing role in the political process. As with classical liberalism before it, this position has been rejected, by Marxists among others, as a straightforward apologia for the systematic inequalities of liberal capitalist societies: a smokescreen to obscure the typical concentration of power in the hands of an ultimately unaccountable elite.

Wittgenstein's recasting of philosophy in terms of an exploration of the forms of life revealed and enacted in our everyday language practice preceded a much wider insistence on the incommensurability of different language games, ways of thinking and discourses, culminating in post-structuralism's scepticism towards all foundationalisms, claimed transcendences of socio-historical context and 'metanarrative' accounts of history, rationality and truth. Lyotard's work, in particular, has refused any attempt to reduce the multiplicity of 'phrase-regimens' and discursive 'genres' to any single, self-authenticating account (be this in historiography, science, or theories of political justice) – and finds the instrumentalist, cognitive genre typified in **Enlightenment**-generation discourse to wield an unfounded, exclusionary, 'terroristic' social influence. His pluralism finds its ethical articulation in a call to 'bear witness' to those discursive practices to which modernity has denied a voice.

Similarly, a pluralistic impetus underlies the 'post-Marxist' re-orientation of socialist theory by those, like Laclau and Mouffe, who wish to drop its allegedly **essentialist**, foundationalist and positivistic aspects in favour of a scrupulously anti-reductive 'radical democracy' rooted in the contingent, fluid, but constitutive nature of political identities. The 'politics of difference' that arise from talk around the postmodernist holy trinity of race, class and gender typifies the present affirmation of cultural pluralism. Does this mean cultural relativism, and a transition from a hesitancy to endorse a single worldview to a more problematic (and arguably self-refuting) 'anything goes' approach that would treat all such views as being strictly on a par? One aspect of pluralism since classical liberalism has been a tendency to slide from a liberating scepticism or fallibilism to an outright refusal to judge between different views and practices. [GC]

Further reading: Dahl 1956; Laclau and Mouffe 1985; Lyotard 1988; Walzer 1985; Young 1990.

political economy   The economic analysis of government. A good example of this form of study is Adam Smith's *Wealth of Nations*, a work generally hailed as the first of its kind. Smith offered an account of society in terms of socio-economic forces, and analysed economic relationships between **individual**s in terms of their implications for the role of government. In turn, Smith's analysis presents itself as a study of the general tendencies of social development which have marked out history. Thus, he examines the origins of modern **civil society** in terms of its evolution through succeeding stages, and accounts for that development in terms of its economic, psychological and power-related features. For example, Smith contended that the actions of a particular individual inspired by greed (namely, the pursuit of personal wealth through activity in the market-place) will have other actual social effects, namely, the production of a greater level of overall wealth in society. This, Smith says, is the operation of the 'invisible hand', which operates at psychological and economic levels to promote the conditions of wealth. Smith provided an account of the mechanisms of competition and the conditions which determine the value of commodities. He advocated a view of government which had a limited range of social duties (the provision for, and administration of, law and order; provision for defence; and the responsibility to build essential public utilities), since its main aim was to facilitate the mechanisms of the free-market.

From Smith's work it is plain that political economy can be seen to aim at a descriptive analysis of social forces. Political economy (not only Smith's, but also the work of others, such as Ricardo) was adopted by Karl Marx, who used it in the development of his theories. In the 1960s and 1970s many of the basic premises of political economy (e.g. the notion of **subjectivity** presupposed within it, its status as empirical science) were subject to criticism by thinkers such as Louis Althusser. [PS]

Further reading: McLellan 1975; Smith 1986.

Pop Art Intentionally provocative term, merging 'high' art with 'popular' culture. The most famous products of pop art are probably Roy Lichtenstein's famous 'Whaam!' (1963), and the various images reproduced by Andy Warhol, such as the screen-prints of Marilyn Monroe.

There are numerous strands of pop art, which may be differentiated on the basis of the ways in which the artists use the images which they find in popular culture. Some artists, such as David Hockney, were most interested in it as a source of new formal inspiration, and many of his canvases are essays on form rather than thematic works. On the other hand, most pop art contains, simply by virtue of its foregrounding of images from advertising and so on, some element of critique. It was American artists interested in collage who made the most obviously politicised use of pop art.

While both the formal and political implications of pop art are considerable, the style also points – quite intentionally – to a philosophical problem. Based as it is on reproduction, to what extent can this be taken before it ceases to be significant? Warhol's tins of soup are obviously fakes, and this is important for their interpretation, at both a formal and a thematic level. Many products of pop art do not reveal their fabricatedness too clearly, however, which has led certain critics of a **postmodernist** persuasion to argue that exact formal reproduction may in fact constitute the most radical critique of all. (See **simulacrum**.) [RC]

Further reading: Livingstone 1991.

popular culture A simple definition of the term 'popular culture', as the **culture** that appeals to, or that is most comprehensible by, the general public, may conceal a number of complexities and nuances of its use within **cultural studies**. The term is frequently used either to identify a form of culture that is opposed to another form, or as a synonym or complement to that other form. The precise meaning of 'popular culture' will therefore vary, for example, as it is related to folk culture, mass culture or high culture. In addition, popular culture may refer either to individual artefacts (often treated as **texts**) such as a popular song or a television programme, or to a group's **lifestyle** (and thus to the pattern of artefacts, practices and understandings that serve to establish the group's distinctive identity).

Theories of mass culture (that were dominant in American and European **sociology** in the 1930s and 1940s) tended to situate popular culture in relation to industrial production, and in opposition to folk culture. While folk culture was seen as a spontaneous production of the people, mass society theories focused on those forms of popular culture that were subject to industrial means of production and distribution (such as **cinema**, radio and **popular music**) and theorised them as being imposed on the people. The approach therefore tended to assume that the audience were passive consumers of the goods foist upon them. The message and purpose of these goods were interpreted within the context of a more or less sophisticated theory of **ideology**, so that the mass of the people were seen to be manipulated through the new **mass media**. Perhaps the most sophisticated version of this approach is found in the **Frankfurt School**'s concept of the **culture industry**.

With the development of the sociology of the mass media and of cultural studies from the 1950s onwards, not least with the work of Hoggart and the **Birmingham Centre for Contemporary Cultural Studies**, the consumers of popular culture came to be seen as increasingly active, and thus the process by which the message of popular culture is communicated, to be increasingly complex. The activity of the people can be identified at two levels. On the first, the people are identified as the producers of popular culture (so that popular culture becomes the folk culture of an industrial society). On the second, more sophisticated level, the people are the interpreters of this culture. Thus, using for example a theory of **hegemony**, the propagation of mass culture cannot be seen as simply inflicting a message on the audience, despite the use of industrial production and distribution techniques. Rather, the audience will interpret, negotiate and appropriate the cultural artefacts or texts to its own uses, and make sense of them within its own environment and life experience. Precisely in so far as more sophisticated (and especially semiological and structuralist) approaches to communication emphasised the fact that the interpretation of a message can never be self-evident, the audience came to be credited with greater interpretative skills, and thus with the ability to resist an interpretation of the culture that is simply in the interests of the dominant class. The analysis of women's magazines, for example, may at once recognise the systems of **codes** and other mechanisms that integrate the reader into a particular ideological construction of femininity (and thus into particular patterns of commodity consumption), but also the space that the magazine opens up in which the reader can enjoy and indulge in this construction and yet see through it as a fiction. Thus, popular culture may be understood in terms of ideological struggles, and as a central element in any cultural politics.

Popular cultural artefacts serve to articulate the differentiation of society in terms of gender, age or race, and to constitute the self-understanding of those groups. Popular music for example has a key role in articulating the gender, class and ethnic identities of teenagers (and indeed in constituting the 'teenager' as a distinctive age group). However, precisely because much popular culture continues to depend upon the resources of industrial **capitalism** for its production and distribution, a tension remains in the selection of popular cultural products between the interests of capitalism (even if these are the purely commercial interests of profit maximisation) and the cultural and political interests of the consumers.

Fiske, for example, distinguishes between the financial and the cultural economies within which cultural artefacts circulate. While the former is concerned with the generation of **exchange-value**, and thus with the accumulation of wealth and the incorporation of the consumer into the dominant economic order, the latter is concerned with the production of meanings and pleasures by, and for, the audience. Precisely because the production of meanings within the cultural economy is not as readily controlled as is the production of wealth, the audience, as producer of meanings, is credited with considerable power to resist the financial forces of incorporation. Popular culture is therefore seen by Fiske as a key site of resistance to capitalism. [AE]

Further reading: Fiske 1989; Hall *et al.* 1992; Storey 1996, 1997; Strianti 1995; Waites *et al.* 1989.

popular music   The study of popular music has followed a trajectory that is familiar in many areas of cultural studies, from a dismissive and elitist mass society theory to a concern with popular music as a creative expression and **articulation** of personal and group **identity**. The mass society approach, predominant from the 1930s, assumes that popular music, as the product of the music industry, is a highly standardised **commodity**. The differences between popular songs are seen to be largely superficial, depending on the mere rearrangement of familiar elements within a rigid formula. The consumer of this music is largely passive (with the **consumption** of music, as a leisure time activity, being a mere corollary to the work process, through which the labourer is renewed and prepared for the next day's work). Popular music (especially in its emphasis on the authoritarian power of rhythm) therefore 'adjusts' the listener to his or her existence in contemporary capitalism (see Adorno 1994). Crucially, a dichotomy is set up between popular music on the one hand, and some more authentic and aesthetically and politically valid music on the other. Popular music is seen to be manufactured and thus imposed upon an artificially constructed and maintained collective (the 'mass').

The authentic music expresses the real interests of the people, be this high art music (for Adorno), **jazz** (for Hall and Whannel (1964)), or folk (for Rosselson (1979)). The presence of such a **binary opposition** is highly persistent.

A political economy of popular music (associated with the political economy of the **mass media**) emerged in the 1960s and 1970s (see Golding and Murdock 1991). To a degree, it reproduced the assumptions of mass society theory, in that it examined the economic mechanisms that determined the access that the public has to musical products. Commercial control of recording studios, record manufacturers and even record store chains, was seen to radically restrict the music that was made available on the **market**. The cultural studies approach to popular music can be seen as a reaction to this, not least in so far as it argues that consumption is an activity, and an activity through which the consumer can resist industry. Thus, Hall and Whannel (1964) argue that popular music, and its associated commodities (such as magazines, concerts, posters and films), are selected in order to explore and establish a sense of **identity**. Commercial popular music therefore provides the teenager with resources ('guiding fictions') that are valuable in dealing with the difficulties of emotional and sexual transition. The teenager does not therefore simply buy what the record industry provides. Indeed, only 10 per cent of all records released actually make a profit for the industry (suggesting large-scale rejection of what is offered).

This approach was developed within the study of **subcultures** (Hall and Jefferson 1976). The emphasis here rests upon the use of popular music in a subordinate or minority groups resistance to the values and attitudes of a 'parent' culture. A specific form of popular music will be chosen as one of the elements that reflects a set of central values with which the subcultural group identifies. The choice is not then made arbitrarily or casually. The music is meaningful. Willis's analysis of the culture of bikers illustrates this (1978). Classic 1950s rock music is significant, for as a historically unified corpus of music, it is readily opposed to the contemporary popular music, and thus the biker is separated from the consumer of pop music. Classic rock'n'roll (for example by Elvis Presley and Buddy Holly) is expressive of masculine values. Finally, the driving rhythms are expressive of a life of movement (and thus the music provides an imaginary sound-track to bike-riding itself). This approach to subcultures and music is developed to an extreme, by Hebdige's (1979) explicit use of **semiotics**, in the analysis of **punk** and its precursors.

If the cultural studies approach to popular music culminates in a semiotics of subcultures, it may still be criticised for placing undue emphasis on the exotic resistance of these subcultures, as opposed to the more mundane consumption of music that is typical of much **youth culture** (so that a heavy hint of the authentic/manufactured music distinction remains). The ethnographic approach to music making and consumption explores this background. Ruth Finnegan's study of Milton Keynes (in England) reveals a rich and diverse world of music making (1989). Knowledgeable amateur musicians, valuing individual expression and innovation, are part of a complex set of social relations, that draw together and serve to define local communities. Bands are not simply groups of musicians, but rather musicians supported by followers and helpers. They rely on the support of existing social **institutions** (such as schools and colleges, pubs and families) for resources such as practice and performance space, as well as instruments and equipment. Thus, the expression of an oppo-sition or rebel stance is mitigated by this integration into the community. However, as Frith (1992) observes, this is still a world structured by **gender** and **class**. Women are largely excluded from bands, or marginalised into traditional domestic roles in support of the bands. Further, popular music is not seen by Frith as a predominantly working-class activity. Middle-class youths are not simply involved, but because they typically have more access to the resources (of money and time) necessary to promote and develop their art, they are also more likely to turn their amateur music making into professional music making. [AE]

Further reading: Frith 1981.

positivism A theory of knowledge which contends that what should count as knowledge can only be validated through methods of observation which are derived from the example set by the physical sciences. Thus, positivists hold to the view that what counts as knowledge is solely a matter of sense-experience. The roots of positivism can be traced at least as far back as the writings of Auguste Comte (1798–1857), although the seventeenth-century philosopher Francis Bacon (who propounded an account of knowledge in his *Novum Organum* (1620) which stressed the importance of empirical observation) might also be cited in connection with this approach. In the twentieth century, a number of thinkers have espoused what has been termed 'logical positivism', an approach derived from the early work of Ludwig Wittgenstein, as well as those of Bertrand Russell and Gotlob Frege. A.J. Ayer's book *Language, Truth and Logic* is often seen as a key work in the articulation of the basic tenets of logical positivism. In this work he argued that all propositions could be characterised as either true, false, or meaningless. In other words, if a proposition does not assert something which can, in principle, be either validated or disproven by way of observation according to the standards of scientific verification then, it is held, that proposition is devoid of meaning. This attempt to clarify the meaning of propositions/sentences, in these terms represented an attempt at a kind of 'ground-clearing' within philosophy, in so far as it was contended that many sorts of question (e.g. those concerned with issues of religion or **metaphysics**) were in fact meaningless.

There have been numerous critics of positivism, including Thomas Kuhn, W. Quine, Karl Popper, and **Frankfurt School** thinker Max Horkheimer. Amongst other things, Horkheimer's attack on positivism argues that methods adapted from the sciences cannot be taken as the sole criterion for knowledge, since positivists ignore the fact that the social and cultural domain within which scientific investigation is undertaken represents a fundamental factor in the construction of knowledge. By reducing the meaning of the term 'knowledge' to being equivalent to 'method', Horkheimer says, positivists conceptualise knowledge according to the precepts of a socially determined instrumentalism (i.e. the view that knowledge is a matter of the appropriate means for a given end) which characterises the tendency in modern industrial culture towards an abandonment of critical reflection with regard to its own nature and constitution. [PS]

Further reading: Ayer 1959, 1967; Hanfling 1981; Horkheimer 1992.

post-colonialism A term generally used to indicate a range of global cultural developments which occurred in the aftermath of the Second World War. To this extent, it has both historical nuances and theoretical ones. On the one hand, 'post-colonialism' signifies something distinctive about this period as one in which the cultural, economic and social events which have constituted it mark the decline of European imperialism. On the other hand, theories of 'postcoloniality' concern themselves with a wide range of **metaphysical**, ethical, methodological and political concerns. Issues which are addressed from this perspective include the nature of cultural **identity**, **gender**, investigations into concepts of **nationality**, **race** and **ethnicity**, the constitution of **subjectivity** under conditions of imperialism and questions of **language** and **power**. One of the earliest writers who brought attention to such issues was Frantz Fanon (1925–61), who sought to articulate the oppressed consciousness of the colonised subject. He argued that imperialism initiated a process of 'internalisation' in which those subjected to it experienced economic, political and social inferiority not merely in 'external' terms, but in a manner that affected their sense of their own identity. Hence, material inferiority creates a sense of racial and cultural inferiority. In turn, Fanon attempted to show the role of language within this process. Colonisation, he argues, also took place through language: under French domination the Creole language is rendered 'inferior' to French, and the colonised subject is compelled to speak the tongue of his or her imperial rulers, thereby experiencing their subjugation in terms of their own linguistic abilities and identity (an experience, it might be added, not uncommon within the context of Europe itself, e.g. the colonial experiences of Irish and Welsh cultures under the dominion of English expansion since the sixteenth century).

In the wake of the work of such figures as Fanon, writers have raised questions about the applicability of definitions of culture and humanity (for instance, the question of nationhood) which have been offered within the context of western cultural domination (see, for example, Bhabha 1990), or have elucidated the cultural bias inherent in particular forms of European discourse (see Edward Said's writings on Orientalism). Likewise, notions, such as those of 'hybridity' and diaspora, have been developed in order to emphasise the notion of an implicit cultural diversity underlying the identities of so-called 'Third World' or post-colonial cultures (see, for example, the writings of Stuart Hall or Homi Bhabha). Within this context, theories of **discourse** and **narrative** have often been deployed as a means of articulating the distinctions between western and non-western culture, and in turn questioning its hierarchical superiority. Some of these theories have been derived from **Marxism** or the thinking of **postmodernism** and **post-structuralism** – although the anti-**realism** implicit in the work of thinkers associated with these last two movements has led to some criticism, for instance by Said, of its applicability to the experience of 'post-colonial' subjects (and, perhaps, one ought to mention the possible criticism that much of the thought inherent in postmodernism and post-structuralism has itself been produced within the western academy).

It is also worth noting that the use of 'post-colonialism' to define such theories, or indeed even an historical period, is controversial. This is not least because it is possible to argue that the word preserves within it the presupposition that western culture retains the predominance it attained during the past two or three hundred years as a consequence of colonial expansion. To be identified as 'post-colonial', in other words, involves a retention of the belief that colonialism continues to exert its influence through providing a definition of the identity of 'post-colonial' subjects and their cultures. Equally, whether the post-war period can be seen as really signifying a move away from colonial forms is questionable. The rise of colonial imperialism rooted in the political form of the European nation-state occurred in conjunction with capitalism in the modern era, and the predominance of this form has perhaps subsided. But the cultural and economic power of the west, it is arguable, retains its dominance in the form of those processes of globalisation which have been delineated by some critics as characteristic of developments within late capitalism (see the discussion of David Harvey's work in the **postmodernism** entry). [PS]

Further reading: Bhabha 1990, 1994; Fanon 1989; Said 1978a, 1993.

post–industrial society   The idea of a 'post-industrial state', grounded on an economy of small-scale, workshop-based craft production was first proposed in the late nineteenth century, by followers of the utopia socialist William Morris. However, in current usage, 'post-industrial society' was articulated, almost simultaneously in the early 1960s, by Daniel Bell (1973) and Alain Touraine (1968). The concept of 'post-industrial society' is intended to encapsulate the changes that have occurred within **capitalism** in the post-war period. The post-industrial society was presented as a new social form, as different from industrial capitalism as capitalism had been from **feudalism**. The central idea is that theoretical knowledge has now become the source of social change and policy formation. The society is highly educated, with significant levels of resources invested into the production of theoretical knowledge (in higher education and commercial research and development). The economy therefore shifts from the production of goods and raw materials, to the production of services. The dominant industries become those which are dependent upon theoretical knowledge (such as computing and aerospace). This is accompanied by a decline in the old working **class**, and the rise of 'white collar' (or non-manual) classes. New professional and technical classes (or a 'knowledge class') become dominant. The difference between Bell and Touraine's accounts rests largely upon the enthusiasm with which they embrace post-industrial society. For Bell it is a positive development, leading to greater social integration, and the reduction of political conflict. For Touraine, post-industrial society threatens to become a society dominated by a technocratic **elite**, who are insensitive to the humanist values of traditional university education. [AE]

Further reading: Kumar 1978.

postmodernism 'Post-modern, if it means anything,' Anthony Giddens argues, 'is best kept to refer to styles or movements within literature, painting, the plastic arts, and archtecture. It concerns aspects of *aesthetic reflection* upon the nature of modernity' (1990: 45). Giddens in fact also links it to Nietzsche and Heidegger, and an abandonment of the **Enlightenment** project of rational criticism. Postmoderns, though, Giddens continues, have nothing better to offer in the place of the ideals of the Enlightenment. Amongst other critical works which have dealt with postmodernism, David Harvey's *The Condition of Postmodernity* has sought to analyse it in socio-economic terms. Harvey argues that the post-modern can be taken to signify a decentralised, diversified stage in the development of the market place, in which the Fordist rationale of production concentrated in a single site (the factory) has been replaced by a form of manufacture which co-ordinates a diversity of sources (e.g. parts of one final product are made in more than one place and then shipped elsewhere for purposes of assembly) in search of greater flexibility of production. In turn, this has had the effect of producing workforces which are mobile and dispos-able in a way in which the earlier labour markets of **Fordism** were not. Thus, for Harvey postmodernism is in fact an extension of those social processes which Marx diagnosed as being characteristic of the logic of capitalist society. In effect, on this view, postmodernism (at least in its philosophical guise) may well be regarded as a form of apology for **capitalism**.

One thing, therefore, is certain about postmodernism: the uses of the word display such a diversity of meanings, that it defies simple definition. In architecture, for example, postmodernism has been taken to mean the overcoming of earlier, rigid conventions underlying modernist tastes (as exemplified by Le Corbusier's functionalism) in favour of a more eclectic, playful and non-functional aesthetic. The 'postmodern' novel, in contrast, could be described as embodying an experimentalism with narrative form, through which a rejuvenation of the established conventions of the form itself is sought (by way of a simultaneous retention and redeployment of those conventions in the name of an avant-gardism which harks back to modernism). Writers often associated with postmodernism include Jean Baudrillard, Jacques Derrida, Michel Foucault, and Luce Irigaray.

Perhaps the most coherent account of what constitutes postmodernism has been offered by the philosopher Jean François Lyotard in *The Postmodern Condition: A Report on Knowledge*, and most succinctly in the essay included at the end of that volume, 'Answering the Question: What is Postmodernism?'. In *The Postmodern Condition*, Lyotard provides an account of postmodernity which stresses the collapse of 'grand narratives' (e.g. that of **Marxism**), and their replacement with 'little narratives' in the wake of **technologies** which have transformed our notion of what constitutes knowledge. To that extent, the view offered in this text concentrates on the **epistemology** of postmodernity, i.e. the postmodern conceived of in terms of a crisis in our ability to provide an adequate, 'objective' account of reality.

In the essay 'Answering the Question: What is Postmodernism?', Lyotard offers an analysis of Kant's notion of the **sublime** (as presented in the *Critique of Judgment*) as a means of elucidating the postmodern. The sublime, Kant argues, is a feeling aroused in the spectator by the presentation to the intellect of something which defies conceptualisation. Likewise, Lyotard holds, the postmodern can be characterised as a mode of expression which seeks to put forward new ways of expressing the sublime feeling. In other words,

295

postmodernism is an **avant-garde** aesthetic discourse, which seeks to overcome the limitations of traditional conventions by searching for new strategies for the project of describing and interpreting experience. Significantly, Lyotard argues that the postmodern ought not to be understood in terms of an historical progression which signals a present departure from a past modernism. Rather, modernism is in fact characterised as a response to a set of concerns which are themselves already postmodern. According to Lyotard, modernism embodies a nostalgic yearning for a lost sense of unity, and constructs an aesthetics of fragmentation in the wake of this. Post-modernism, in contrast, begins with this lack of unity but, instead of lamenting it, celebrates it – a claim made most evident by Lyotard's comparison of the modernist 'fragment' (i.e. the art-work conceived of as a part of a greater, albeit unattainable, whole) with the postmodern 'essay' (taken in the sense of an essaying-forth, in the spirit of an experimentalism which disdains either to construct or lament totality – the characterisation of the latter bearing a strong resemblance to T.W. Adorno's analysis in his 'The Essay as Form').

More recently, Lyotard has moved away from his earlier exposition of postmodernism. On the one hand, he has sought to redefine it in terms of a 'rewriting' of the project of modernity (see the essays collected in *The Inhuman*). On the other hand, a work like *The Differend: Phrases in Dispute* at least hints that postmodernism may be considered in a rather less positive (and certainly more modest) light than that afforded it in *The Postmodern Condition*: 'an old man who scrounges in the garbage-heap of finality looking for leftovers . . . a goal for a certain humanity' (*The Differend*, section 182).

Italian philosopher Gianni Vattimo has also offered an account of the postmodern in his essay 'Nihilism and the Postmodern in Philosophy' in *The End of Modernity*. Contrary to Giddens' view, Vattimo specifically relates postmodernism to philosophy, rather than the arts. As with Giddens, two thinkers mark the opening of postmodernity: Nietzsche and Heidegger. Vattimo turns to Heidegger's notion of *Verwindung* as a means of explicating his position. The word *Verwindung* represents neither an *Überwindung* (i.e. a critical overcoming of **contradiction** through the use of reason), nor a Kantian *Verbindung*, which seeks to establish *a priori* modes of combination as a means of grounding transcendental critique in primary rules of understanding and principles of reason. A *Verwindung*, rather, is a 'twisting' of meaning which makes room for a form of relativistic criticism which disdains all pretensions to objectivity. This, then, allows for Vattimo to account for the 'post-' in postmodernism, for it does not presuppose the possibility of transcendental critique. Interestingly, it is Nietzsche, and not Heidegger, whom Vattimo regards as the first philosopher to talk in the terminology of *Verwindung*. Indeed, for Vattimo, postmodernity is born with Nietzsche's writing (*The End of Modernity*, 164). Turning to Nietzsche's book *Human, All-Too-Human*, Vattimo argues that this work defines modernity as a process of constant replacement, wherein the old (expressed through notions such as 'tradition') is abandoned in favour of the new, which in its turn decays and is replaced by ever newer forms. Within such a context, the modern can never be overcome, since each overcoming is merely another repetition of the fetish of the new. Having offered this diagnosis, Nietzsche's text refuses to envisage a way out of modernity by way of recourse to, for example, a Kantian transcendentalism. Rather, a Nietzschean account seeks to radicalise the modern through a dissolution of 'its own innate tendencies' (p. 166). This is achieved through the following chain of reasoning: (i) a criticism of mores (dominant forms of ethical behaviour) is undertaken by Nietzsche through a strategy of 'chemical reduction' (see *Human, All-Too-Human*, sections 1ff., where Nietzsche writes of constructing a 'chemistry of the moral and religious sensations'); which leads to (ii) the realisation that the ontological ground and methodological basis for this reduction (i.e. truth) is destined likewise to dissolve under such scrutiny; and (iii) that truth, in consequence, is rendered the product of historical contingency. As such, it is realised that truth (and consequently the language of truth) is both (a) subject to and (b) moulded by forces such as the need for survival, and rests on such notions as the untenable belief that reality can be known; this, in turn, leads to the conclusion that (iv) truth is rooted in the metaphorical function of language (language as a tool for coping with the world, not as a means of describing reality). Within this context, truth is dissolved and (most famously) God dies, slain by his own metaphysics (the Christian metaphysical demand for truth having turned on Christianity itself, finds it unable to live up to its own ideal). For Vattimo, this nihilistic conclusion offers a way out of modernity, and marks the birth of postmodernity, i.e. an interest in grounding knowledge in concepts of truth and Being is replaced by one which stresses the historical analysis of 'appearance' and the predominance of contingency in our forms of knowledge. It is worth noting that such an account leaves out many aspects of Nietzsche's thought which would not conform with Vattimo's view (e.g. his later diagnosis of modernity as a decadent form which must be 'overcome', and likewise his criticisms of modern 'nihilism' as a symptom of 'decadence' or cultural decline). [PS]

Further readings: Giddens 1990; Harvey 1989; Hassan 1987; Jenks 1991; Lyotard 1988, 1989, 1991; Vattimo 1988.

post-structuralism Movement of thought in various fields – literary criticism, cultural studies, political theory, sociology, ethnography, historiography, psychoanalysis – which grew out of (and to some extent reacted against) the earlier structuralist paradigm adopted by mainly French theorists in the 1950s and 1960s. **Structuralism** took its methodological bearings from the programme of theoretical linguistics devised some four decades earlier by Ferdinand de Saussure. This work was rediscovered – with considerable excitement – by structuralist thinkers who proceeded to apply his ideas to a range of social and cultural phenomena supposedly exhibiting a language-like (systemic) character, and hence amenable to description and analysis in terms deriving from Saussure's structural-synchronic approach. Thus, in each of the above-mentioned disciplines, the aim was to break with an existing (merely 'empirical' or case-by-case) treatment of the innumerable narratives, myths, rituals, social practices, ideologies, case-histories, cultural patterns of belief, etc., and to focus rather on the underlying structure – the depth-logic of signification – which promised to fulfil Saussure's great dream of a unified general **semiology**. Such would be the structuralist key to all mythologies, one that explained how such a massive (empirically unmanageable) range of cultural phenomena could be brought within the compass of a theory requiring only a handful of terms, concepts, distinctions and logical operators. Among them – most importantly – were Saussure's cardinal distinctions between **signifier** and **signified**, **langue** and **parole**, and the twofold (diachronic and synchronic) axes of linguistic-semiotic research. Beyond that, the main task was to press this analysis to a point where it left no room for such supposedly naïve ideas as that of the subject – the 'autonomous' subject of humanist discourse – as somehow existing outside or beyond the various structures (or 'subject-positions') that marked the very limits of language and thought at some specific cultural juncture.

Thus structuralist thinking most often went along with a strain of theoretical anti-humanism which defined itself squarely against such earlier 'subject-centred' movements of thought as **phenomenology** and **existentialism**. In this respect, and others, there is a clear continuity between structuralism and post-structuralism. Indeed, there has been much debate among theorists as to how we should construe the 'post-' prefix, whether in the strong sense ('superseding and displacing the structuralist paradigm') or simply as a matter of chronological sequence ('developing and extending the structuralist approach in certain new directions'). Post-structuralism also finds its chief theoretical inspiration in the programme of Saussurean linguistics, though it tends to play down – or reject outright – any notion that this might give a 'scientific' basis for the analysis of texts, semiotic systems, cultural codes, ideological structures, social practices, etc. That claim is now viewed as just a species of 'meta-linguistic' delusion, an example of the old (typically structuralist but also

Marxist) fallacy which holds that theory can somehow attain to a critical standpoint outside and above whatever it seeks to interpret or explain. On the contrary, post-structuralists argue: there is no way of drawing a firm methodological line between text and commentary, language and metalanguage, ideological belief-systems and those other (theoretical) modes of discourse that claim to unmask ideology as a product of false consciousness or – in the language of a structural Marxist like Louis Althusser – a form of 'imaginary' misrecognition. Such ideas took hold through the false belief that theory could achieve a decisive 'epistemological break' with the various kinds of naturalised 'commonsense' knowledge which passed themselves off as straightforwardly true but which in fact encoded the cultural values of a given (e.g. bourgeois-humanist) sociopolitical order. However, this position becomes untenable once it is realised that *all* subject-positions – that of the analyst included – are caught up in an endless process of displacement engendered by the instability of language, the 'arbitrary' relation between signifier and signified, and the imposssibility that meaning can ever be captured in a moment of pure, self-present utterer's intent.

Thus the 'post-' in 'post-structuralism' is perhaps best understood – by analogy with other such formations, among them 'postmodernism', 'post-**Marxism**', and more lately 'post-feminism' – as marking a widespread movement of retreat from earlier positions more directly aligned with the project of political emancipation and critique. However, post-structuralism does lay claim to its own kind of radical politics, one that envisages a 'subject-in-process' whose various shifting positions within language or discourse cannot be captured by any theory (structuralist, Marxist, feminist or whatever) premised on old-style 'enlightenment' ideas of knowledge and truth. Most influential here, at least among literary theorists, was the sequence of changing allegiances to be seen in the work of Roland Barthes, from his early high-structuralist phase (in texts such as *Mythologies* (1957) and 'The Structural Analysis of Narratives' (1977b)) to his late style of writing (e.g. *S/Z* (1970) and *The Pleasure of the Text* (1973)) where he renounces all claims to theoretical rigour, and instead draws freely and idio-syncratically on whatever sources come to hand – literature, linguistics, structuralism psychoanalysis, Marxism, a vast range of intertextual allusions – while treating them all with a con-summate deftness and irony which disclaims any kind of ortho-dox methodological commitment. In *Mythologies* Barthes had provided by far the most convincing application of a highly systematic (Saussure-derived) structuralist method to the analy-sis of various items of late-bougeois 'mythology', from adver-tising images to French culinary fashion, from 'The Romans on Film' to the myth of the jet pilot, and from 'the brain of Einstein' (a fetish-object created by the modern ideology of scientific genius) to the spectacle of boxing as a prime example of cultural artifice passing itself off as a natural sport-ing event. A decade later he reflected ruefully that this method could now be applied by anyone who had picked up the nec-essary analytic tools and learned to demythologise just about everything that came their way. So one had to move on, renounce that false idea of 'metalinguistic' analysis, and instead produce readings that would 'change the object itself' – the title of a later essay – by actually *re-writing* the myths con-cerned through a process of creative textual transformation. Otherwise there would always come a stage – repugnant to Barthes – when radical ideas began to settle down into a new orthodoxy, or when theories that had once seemed challeng-ing and subversive (like those of 'classical' structuralism) were at length recycled in a safely packaged academic form.

In Barthes's later writing one can see this diagosis applied to certain aspects of post-structuralism even though that movement had not yet acquired anything like its subsequent widespread following. Thus, for instance, it became a high point of post-structuralist principle (deriving from the psycho-analytic theories of Jacques Lacan) that the unconscious was 'structured like a language', that its workings were by very definition inaccessible to conscious thought, and that the human subject was irreparably split between a specular realm of false ('imaginary') ego-identification and a symbolic realm where its 'identity' consisted of nothing more than a series of shifting, discursively produced subject-positions. Then again, post-structuralists have been much influenced by Michel Foucault's sceptical genealogies of knowledge, his argument that 'truth' is always and everywhere a product of vested power-interests, so that different regimes of 'power-knowledge' give rise to various disciplinary techniques or modes of subjectively internalised surveillance and control. These ideas are presented as marking a break – a radical break – with the concepts and values of a humanist discourse which concealed its own will-to-power by fostering the illusion of autonomous freedom and choice.

So the claim is that post-structuralism affords a potentially liberating space, a space of 'plural', 'decentred', multiple or constantly destabilised subject-positions where identities can no longer be defined according to such old 'essentialist' notions as gender or class-affiliation. For some theorists, Ernesto Laclau and Chantal Mouffe among them, it points the way towards a politics – an avowedly 'post-Marxist' politics – that acknowledges the sheer range and variety of present-day social interests. On this view it is merely a form of 'metanarrative' delusion to suppose that any one privileged theory (like that of classical Marxism) could somehow speak the truth of history or rank those interests on a scale of priority with socio-economic or class factors as the single most important issue. Rather we should think – in post-structuralist terms – of subjects as 'dispersed' over a range of multiple positions, discourses, sites of struggle, etc., with nothing (least of all some grand 'totalizing' theory) that would justify their claim to speak on behalf of this or that oppressed class or interest-group. Still there is a problem when it comes to explaining how anyone could make a reasoned or principled choice in such matters if every such 'choice' were indeed just a product of the subject's particular mode of insertion into a range of pre-existing discourses.

Nor is this problem in any way resolved by the idea that subjects are non-self-identical, that subjectivity is always an ongoing process, or again – following Lacan – that there never comes a point where the ego escapes from the endless 'detours' of the signifier and at last achieves a wished-for state of 'imaginary' plenitude and presence. For this still works out as a determinist doctrine, a theory of the subject as constructed in (or by) language, whatever the desire of some post-structuralists to give it a vaguely utopian spin by extolling the 'freeplay' of the signifier or the possibility of subjects adopting as many positions – or 'performative' roles – as exist from one situation to the next. In Barthes' later work it is the very act of writing, exemplified in certain *avant-garde* literary texts, that is thought of as somehow accomplishing the break with oppressive (naturalised or realist) norms, and thus heralding a new dispensation where identity and gender are no longer fixed by the grim paternal law of bourgeois 'classical realism'. Such ideas have a certain heady appeal when compared with the bleak message conveyed by theorists such as Foucault and Lacan. Nevertheless, they are open to the same objection: that the subject remains (in Lacan's phrase) a mere 'plaything' of language or discourse, and that reality likewise becomes just an optional construct out of various signifying codes and conventions.

One result – as seen in post-structuralist approaches to historiography and the social sciences – is a blurring of the crucially important line between fictive discourse (novels, stories, imaginary scenarios of various kinds) and those other kinds of narrative that aim to give a truthful account of past or present events. That confusion of realms is carried yet further in the writing of postmodernist thinkers like Jean Baudrillard who argue – largely on the same premiss – that we now inhabit a world of ubiquitous mass-media simulation where the very idea of a reality 'behind appearances' (along with the notions of truth, critique, ideology, false consciousness and so forth) must be seen as belonging to a byegone age of naïve Enlightenment beliefs. This is all – as post-structuralists would happily concede – a very long way from Saussure's original programme for a structural linguistics based on strictly scientific principles. Whether or not their more radical claims stand up to careful scrutiny is still a topic of intense dispute among theorists of various persuasions. [CN]

Further reading: Attridge *et al.* 1987; Barthes 1975; Belsey 1980; Harari 1980; Harland 1987; Sturrock 1979; Young 1981.

power A term which has a variety of meanings. Most usually, power is taken to mean the exercise of force or control over individuals or particular social groups by other individuals or groups. Power, in this view, is something extrinsic to the constitution of both individuals and society. For example, the theory of the role of the state in the writings of **liberalism** normally conceives of legislative power in terms of limitations on the state's ability to use justifiable force with regard to the behaviour of individuals who fall under its jurisdiction. On such a view, it does not follow that the exercise of power is *a priori* coercive in nature, since power exercised within the limits of legality is taken to be justly exercised. On the other hand, liberals would regard any exercise of power which compels individuals to behave in ways that they would not freely choose as coercive.

Power and authority are not necessarily synonymous. Thus, for example, the seventeenth-century political philosopher James Harrington (an exponent of **civic humanism**) drew a distinction between *de facto* power (the possession of power as a matter of fact) and *de jure* authority (authority by right, i.e. by means of justification). Harrington notes that one may have the one without the other. Power without authority expresses for him the essential feature of the modern or 'Gothic' form of government, which corresponds with the *de facto* possession of power by a monarch, who is not answerable to those citizens who fall under his or her jurisdiction and thereby rules without the authority of their consent.

The writings of French philosopher Michel Foucault have often been taken as influential (principally amongst exponents of one form or other of **post-structuralism** or **postmodernism**, both of which Foucault has been identified with at one time or another) in their attempt to redefine what the term 'power' means. Foucault, following Nietzsche, seeks to redefine power in a way that is notably different from how it is conceived within more traditional theory. Thus, power, in Nietzsche's view (see especially *The Will to Power*, 1968: section 1067), does not so much express differences in the relationships that exist between individuals or groups as permeate the entirety of reality and thereby become its essence. Likewise, Foucault conceives of power as existing *not* as something that is exercised over individuals or groups, but as being constitutive of both the relations which exist between groups and hence equally of individual and group identity themselves. Important in Foucault's analysis is the claim that power is not only constitutive of social reality and of such social forms as **subjectivity**. He also claims that discourses of knowledge are in fact an expression of power relations and themselves embodiments of power (a view that goes back to English philosopher Thomas Hobbes, who saw knowledge as an expression of power, and indeed well beyond him – for example, the Ancient Greek figure Georgias, discussed in Plato's dialogue of the same name). On this view, power becomes so universal and immanent to social relations that it is difficult not to regard it as a metaphysical conception. [PS]

Further reading: Foucault 1980; Harrington 1992; Mill 1984; Nietzsche 1968b.

pragmatism A philosophical movement that exerted a profound influence upon American thought during the first part of the twentieth century. Principal thinkers associated with pragmatism include C.S. Peirce (1839–1914), William James (1842–1910), John Dewey (1859–1952), George Herbert Mead (1862–1931) and Clarence Irving Lewis (1883–1964). However, these thinkers do not share one basic doctrine on the basis of which they may all straightforwardly be classified as pragmatists. It is, rather, in virtue of a shared approach to philosophical problems that the term 'pragmatism' is best applied to each of them. Although an exclusively American movement, unsurprisingly (given the fact that its thinkers were schooled in European philosophy and literature) pragmatism owes much to British and continental European philosophy. Thus, pragmatists like Peirce devoted their attention to elucidating problems in the sphere of theory of knowledge that they had encountered in the work of Descartes or Kant. It is perhaps best to turn to Peirce's own account of pragmatism, given in the essay 'What Pragmatism Is', for a concise exposition of his notion of pragmatism:

> a *conception*, that is, the rational purport of a word or other expression, lies exclusively in its conceivable bearing upon the conduct of life [. . .] if one can define accurately all the conceivable experimental phenomena which the affirmation or denial of a concept could imply, one will have therein a complete definition of the concept, and *there is absolutely nothing more in it.*

In other words, in Peirce's view, pragmatism involves placing emphasis upon the concrete outcomes of our concepts as a means of determining their value as expressions of knowledge. Thus, according to Peirce in 'Definition and Description of Pragmatism', there is 'an inseparable connection between rational cognition and rational purpose'. Hence, Peirce outlined pragmatism as 'the doctrine that the whole "meaning" of a conception expresses itself in practical consequences, consequences either in the shape of conduct to be recommended, or in that of experiences to be expected, if the conception be true'. In turn, he argued for viewing enquiry as a process which proceeds from a state of doubt and is resolved in belief. According to Peirce, the best way of establishing belief is according to the dictates of scientific method.

William James is probably the most famous thinker associated with pragmatism. James was a friend of Peirce and therefore formulated his ideas in conjunction with the development of Peirce's thought, so it is not easy to separate the intellectual development of the two men. However, James's conception of pragmatism differs from that offered by Peirce in so far as whereas Peirce (who, as a realist, formulated pragmatism primarily as a theory of meaning) sought to ground meaning in the sphere of practical and concrete human action, James looked elsewhere. For James, in contrast, what is highlighted is his account of the role of concepts and ideas in human experience. Our beliefs, he claims, affect our actions in the world, and his pragmatism therefore concentrates upon the ways in which ideas and beliefs relate to our experiences. In turn, James is not committed to the realism that Peirce endorses, but instead embraces a kind of nominalism. More significantly, for James, pragmatism involves constructing a more general account of human thought and action (including psychology) of which a pragmatic theory of *meaning* is merely one part.

John Dewey's work represents another variant of the pragmatist theme. As with James, Dewey started out by developing a psychological approach. However, he later turned to a more behaviouristic and socially nuanced account of human action. In time, Dewey came to term his own brand of pragmatism 'instrumentalism'. Principal amongst his philosophical concerns was education, which Dewey came to regard as having supreme importance as the primary means for the transmission of knowledge and ideas within **society**. Society, for the mature Dewey, comes to be regarded as a kind of educational institution, which as the sphere in which human life is actually lived, is taken as the educative means to the end of living. In turn, Dewey developed a view which emphasised the links between human action and the social realm: action does not occur 'in' a social space, since the social is itself an essential aspect of human behaviour. Dewey's criticism of the Cartesian conception of subjectivity (i.e. mind–body dualism) clarifies his view of the social realm: the philosophical division between mind and body allows us to ignore the fact that the thinking individual is itself a part of the social structure in which thinking occurs. Dewey envisaged this relationship in terms of a 'circuit' (see his 'The Unit of Behaviour: The Reflex Arc Concept in Psychology' of 1896). Equally, he was also interested in developing an account of the relationship between knowledge and value, arguing that self-reflexive scientific enquiry, understood as an active selecting and therefore valuing of what it investigates, is a prime example of ethical action.

From the consideration of Peirce's and James's 'pragmatism' and Dewey's 'instrumentalism', it is evident that the primary question pragmatists ask with regard to knowledge is 'does it work?' Dewey's term is thus apposite: pragmatists are essentially instrumentalists when it comes to the issue of what counts as reliable knowledge.

Amongst contemporary thinkers Richard Rorty (1931–) has adopted a form of pragmatism which endorses an anti-**essentialism** with regard to questions of **rationality**, **cultural identity** and politics. This is coupled with an extolling of bourgeois **liberalism**. Rorty is perhaps more Jamesean than Peircean in his approach. For example, he has consistently criticised realism, which is a central component of Peirce's pragmatism. For instance, on one of Rorty's arguments, since we cannot escape from language our thinking must, it follows, relate only to language, i.e. there is no 'reality' independent of language to which we refer when we speak (in philosophical parlance, there are no 'matters of fact'). Those who believe that there is an 'outside' to language Rorty has deemed 'representationalists'; and it is against this position that he espouses his own 'antirepresentationalism':

> By dropping a representationalist account of knowledge, we pragmatists drop the appearance-reality distinction in favour of a distinction between beliefs that serve some purposes and beliefs that serve other purposes [. . .] We drop the notion of beliefs being made true by reality [. . .] (1998: 206).

Hence, on Rorty's view, since our language cannot be identified in terms of some mind-independent realm, it must be culturally situated, and our knowledge of the world depends upon the cultural **norms** at our disposal and our aims. In short, Rorty views himself as a 'pragmatist' in so far as he, too, advocates an instrumentalism. Rorty likewise advocates a **cultural relativism**. Aspects of his views have been criticised by, amongst others, another thinker with a pragmatist heritage, Hilary Putnam (1926–), who has claimed that Rorty's argument in support of his account of language is 'terrible'. As

Putnam remarks, what if it were instrumentally useful for us to believe in things like 'matters of fact'? If so, then Rorty's argument hardly goes very far towards mounting a serious objection to such notions. Although not following Rorty's line of thought, Putnam too, has sought to develop some of the ideas first outlined by his pragmatist predecessors (addressing, for instance, the importance of education to democratic forms of life in the wake of Dewey's writings). [PS]

Further reading: Gallie 1975; Mounce 1997; Putnam 1995; Rorty 1982, 1991, 1998; Thayer 1982.

praxis   Strictly, 'praxis' is German for 'practice' (and is derived from the Greek). Thus, its use in English, which is common, can verge on pretension. When used with theoretical precision, it refers to the precise meanings that the young Marx ascribes to 'practice'. Two key senses can be usefully identified. At its simplest, and most dramatic, praxis suggests revolutionary practice. As such, it is a fusion of theory and practice, and thus the point at which philosophers have ceased to interpret the world (Marx 1975: 423), and have developed a (materialist) account of the world that will allow the **proletariat** to understand their place in it, and thus transform it. In the second, more complex sense, praxis refers to the early Marx's account of human nature and human history. The core of human nature is presented as the ability to consciously transform the environment. Humans therefore live in a world that they have built, and that they continue to rebuild and change. It is through this practical engagement with the world (this praxis) that humanity can come to understand itself. However, in class society, humanity is alienated from what it produces and thus does not understand its essential nature. Labour is a burden, rather than fulfilment. [AE]

prejudice   1. An aggressive and negative attitude towards, for example, a particular social group. Thus, **racism** can be described as a form of prejudice, in so far as it is predisposed to judge a designated racial group as being inferior (cf. **stereo-type**). Other attitudes may be regarded as embodying prejudice. For instance, attitudes towards women. The issue of how prejudice functions, of its relationship both to systems of **representation** (whereby stereotypical images are disseminated through the **media**) and questions of **power**, have been raised.

2. A term employed within the **hermeneutic**s of H.G. Gadamer. According to Gadamer, 'prejudice' is a precondition of an act of interpretation, and consists of the presuppositions which any interpreter brings to bear as a necessary precondition of achieving an understanding of a text. [PS]

Further reading: Banton 1977; Fanon 1989; Hartmann and Husband 1974; Miles 1989; Said 1978.

production Production has its most basic use and meaning in the field of economics, where it refers to the transformation of natural resources or already manufactured items through their being combined with **labour** and **capital**. Production is therefore always the transformation of something that already exists. The concept has usefully been applied to culture, not least by Marxists, in order to indicate the link between the production of cultural artefacts or events and economic production: either in so far as cultural production is grounded in, and determined by, economic production; or in that cultural production imitates certain aspects of economic production. Such an approach poses an effective challenge to orthodox **aesthetics**, that tends to isolate the work of art from the social and economic circumstances in which it is created. Benjamin's essay on Brecht, 'The Author as Producer' (1937) neatly illustrates this challenge. [AE]

Further reading: Macherey 1978; Wolff 1981.

progress As contested a concept as its question-begging dictionary definition ('forward movement', or 'improvement over time') would suggest. The idea of progress has been in circulation for upwards of 2500 years (see Nisbet 1980), but gained its most sustained momentum during the **Enlightenment**. Whether as the rationalisation of the capacity of things in general to get better, or with a tighter focus, say on the expansion of scientific knowledge, progress became bound up with the steady emancipation of humankind from blinkered subservience, blind faith, and the pull of myth and mysticism. Thus Condorcet and Kant among others proclaimed progress as a trajectory of increasing reflexive self-awareness, on a cultural as well as individual level. Even so, Kant's writing on the topic makes seemingly incongruous reference to a 'hidden plan of nature' to bring about 'the sole state in which all of humanity's natural capacities can be developed'.

The tension has proved stubborn. Treated on the one hand as a matter of uninterruptible historical evolution, the idea of progress took strongest hold as the interventionary power of human agency began finally to displace the fatalistic acceptance of providence in the tenor of social thinking. How, then, to *quantify* progress? Its intimate relations with notions as ideologically charged as development, civilisation, and technological advancement have made it eminently deconstructible – not least in its most emphatic, Hegelian version in which (since the real is rational and the rational is real) philosophy sets itself the task of revealing the gradual triumph of human reason in all departments of cultured and social life. Marx, in subverting Hegel's abstract, sanguine diagnosis of the seamless unfolding of universal reason, invoked a materialist conception of progress as emancipation through the realisation of hitherto-suppressed human potentialities and control of our natural environment. 'The philosophers have only interpreted the world, in various ways', as he famously stated in the *Theses on Feuerbach*; 'the point is to change it'. But for all Marx's emphasis on active participation in history, and the integral role of classed-based schism and revolution, crucial to both schema is an objective linearity to the historical process. This is progress as teleology: as a more or less vital journey towards a given, universally redemptive, end.

311

As such, it is a prime example of what postmodern theorists deem a 'metanarrative', their incredulity towards which accompanies the jettisoning of all ideas of Progress with a capital 'P'. This is usually on the basis of an appeal to recent history as flatly contradicting the very idea that general social improvement has, in any real sense, been afoot. Lyotard and Bauman, to name but two, have linked the atrocities and excesses of the twentieth century (for example, Auschwitz, the Gulag Archipelago, the nuclear build-up) to the overweening hubris of the Enlightenment's prediction of an emancipatory triumph of reason and virtue. Like Adorno and Horkheimer before them (though without their residual Marxist affinities), they trace the fruition of 'instrumental' reason exemplified in recent barbarities back to modernity's fetishizing of universal reason and the concurrent banishment of the irrational, illusory or retrograde. Thus scientific or technological advance does not by itself a good society make; and indeed the valorisation of science as supreme source of knowledge makes more likely the regimentation, normalisation and silencing of those not party to the expert culture – hardly 'progress' in the modern definition.

Whether this disposes of, or rather asks anew, the question of the nature of progress is another matter. Does the naïveté or danger of conceiving progress as structurally guaranteed bury too those alternative accounts which would put it down to collective human agency? Can we really look at the history of science or medicine and deny that substantive advances have taken place? Is the end of slavery just a culturally determined and administered value? 'We have stopped believing in progress', remarked Borges; 'What progress that is!' It's a pregnant contradiction. Hedgy and unfashionable as progress-talk has become, it is hard to see how normative social theory – whether at the *fin* of a given *siecle* or not – can get along without it. Nor has its theoretical beleaguering served fully to extinguish its obviously cultural and rhetorical import. [GC]

Further reading: Adorno and Horkheimer 1972; Bauman 1989; Kant 1970, 1971; Lyotard 1989; Nisbet, 1980.

proletariat The term 'proletariat' has been popularised through its use in Marxist theory, where it refers to the subordinate class within **capitalism**. The proletariat is composed of that proportion of the urban population who own only their own ability to **labour**. They are therefore compelled to sell this labour power in order to be able to purchase all other goods that are required for their continued existence. Less formally, the term is frequently used as a synonym for working **class**. Strictly, the working class, composed of those who are occupied in any form of manual labour, are only a portion of the proletariat, for few if any of the (non-manual) middle class owns enough productive property or **capital** to generate enough income to do away with the necessity of working for a living. [AE]

Further reading: McCarthy 1978; Perkins 1993.

propaganda Propaganda is the conscious attempt to control or change the attitudes and behaviour of a group, through manipulation of communication (either in the provision of information, or the use of imagery). Qualter (1962; 1985) identifies several properties of propaganda: it is deliberate, and aims to influence an audience; it attempts to affect behaviour by modifying attitudes (rather than through the threat of violence or offer of reward); it is essentially elitist, with a small group attempting to influence the behaviour of the many; it uses all forms of symbol (including verbal language, music and visual images). Given this definition, it is surprisingly hard to analyse, not least in terms of separating propaganda from **ideology**, and propaganda from the usual course of news reporting or political debate in the **liberal** democracies. Ideologies are belief systems that are in the interests of a dominant **class**, and are propagated throughout society. However, while the content of much school education may fruitfully be analysed as ideology (and is indeed deliberately designed to influence the behaviour and attitudes of pupils), it does not seem appropriate or fruitful to call it propaganda. Further, propaganda is not unproblematically untrue. While it may falsify facts, it may also simply be selective with facts, and present those facts in an emotive manner. To deem propaganda untrue is to minimise the degree to which the 'truth' is itself negotiated and contested in everyday life. What is one person's truth is an other's lie. Hence, while truth is frequently judged to be the first casualty of war, as propaganda and selective reporting take over, it is worth considering the degree to which news reporting in peace time is (and has to be) highly selective. The news cannot report everything that happens without discrimination. An analysis of propaganda is therefore posed with the problem of distinguishing legitimate selectivity with illegitimate selectivity, or at least, with explaining the particular circumstances that make the illegitimate selection propaganda, and not ideology. [AE]

Further reading: Foulkes 1983.

property 1. The possession of private goods. Land, wealth, even ideas can be property (e.g. patents, copyrights). Property is an area of central interest in the writings of many political philosophers. Both John Locke and Jean-Jacques Rousseau equated the private ownership of property with the development of **civil society** – albeit with very different conclusions (for a discussion of Locke's account of the basis of property ownership see **liberalism**; see also **state of nature**) – while **Marxism** advocates the dissolution of the private ownership of goods and their redistribution on the basis of need. What is clear from the work of these thinkers is that both the possession of property and the issue of what rights (i) ground and (ii) accompany property ownership, have important implications for the way in which the social and political domains may be understood.

If there is an important political idea which has been linked with property ownership it is that of *interest*. Locke draws our attention to this matter when, in the second of his *Treatises of Government*, he holds that the primary possession of each and every individual is his or her own body. If each of us is the legitimate possessor of their own body then, in turn, each individual has an interest which is related to their physical well being, and rights also devolve from this. Equally, for Locke, since the investment of labour involves an extension of the characteristic of self-possession associated with the body, labour thereby gives what is associated with it that same characteristic: a person can pick an apple or plough a piece of untended ground and, so long as nobody else already owns them, these become theirs by virtue of the investment of labour involved. Equally, legislative authority is in turn devolved by Locke from the right to own property, for the protection of property is regarded by Locke as the principal function of legitimate government.

It is possible to read Locke's argument as an implicit and *post facto* justification for the development of mercantile capitalism. Hence, if private property is held to be a legitimate form of ownership and, in turn, the role of government is primarily to protect individuals from being deprived of their property, as Locke argues, then it is private rather than public interest which is foregrounded in rank of social importance. Political freedom can be defined in the wake of such a commitment: on such a view, freedom always means 'freedom from . . .'. In other words, 'freedom' is taken to mean the freedom to pursue one's self interest with minimal hindrance from the activities of others, including the state. By contrast, a Rousseauean or Marxian reading of property would hold that its possession is the product of interests, but not, contrary to Locke, *a priori* legitimate interests. Thus, Rousseau, in his *Discourse on Inequality*, held that the invention of private property is a central component in the corruption of humanity, in so far as with property comes the unequal distribution of goods and, in turn, the domination of personal greed over virtue. For Marx, the private and unequal distribution of goods in society is one of the defining characteristics of the capitalist mode of production, and this form of production functions through the exploitation of a majority of the population at the hands of a property-owning minority. Indeed, from this perspective, one might say that the advocacy of the possession of private property is *the* defining feature of **capitalism**, for unless this right is granted legitimacy the capitalist **mode of production** is impossible. In contrast to the view advocated by liberal thinkers, a Marxian approach would tend to regard the private possession of goods as something which inhibits the freedom of others (understood as 'freedom to . . .').

In modern technological societies, the issue of property ownership has come to take on a more complex aspect with the advent of technologies of reproduction. For example, in the recorded music industry the increased public availability of convenient carriers for the transfer of music between formats (recording from the company manufactured compact disc to the privately owned recordable compact disc or to digital audio tape, for instance) has highlighted a problem with regard to the ownership of copyright on recordings. Legally, of course, the question of who owns a copyright (i.e. the legal owner of a recorded product) is not usually a problematic one. One might be tempted, however, to turn to the fact that copyright is being constantly infringed and claim that this will, in the long run, problematise what we mean when we talk about the ownership of such goods. Whether such a claim is justifiable is, though, another matter. Even if **technology** affects the practicalities of enforcing copyright on recordings, ideas or even designs, it is an open question as to whether the notion of property implicit within copyright is likely to be challenged seriously by such practices. Likewise, even if this does prove to be the case, it does not follow that 'property' in its more general sense will thereby be subject to some form of redefinition. It is, perhaps, more germane to recall that the issues surrounding property ownership identified by thinkers such as Locke, Rousseau and Marx (e.g. questions of the right to ownership as it relates to the concept of the 'individual', or of the social relationship between the distribution of goods and issues of political freedom and power) still remain central to our conception of it and its cultural ramifications. For example, when Locke's argument concerning the justifiable acquisition of untended land through the investment of labour is applied to geographical areas outside Europe, such as 'the wild woods and uncultivated waste of America left to nature' (second *Treatise*, section 37), it is worth noting that such a theory amounts to a justification for the appropriation of land occupied by other cultures.

2. feature or characteristic (cf. **essentialism**.) [PS]

Further reading: Locke 1988; Marx 1976; Rousseau (1984).

psychoanalysis Psychoanalysis is both a method of scientific investigation and a discipline that is concerned with the role of the unconscious in the mental life of the subject. It is primarily based on the interpretation of the analysand's free associations within the context of the **transference** in the analytic situation. Freud introduced the term 'psychoanalysis' as an analogy to the process of chemical analysis in a laboratory. Like a chemist, the analyst is engaged in the act of deconstructing the patient's symptom into its component parts.

> The patient's symptoms . . . are of a highly composite kind . . . we trace the symptoms back to the instinctual impulses which motivate them . . . which are present in his symptoms and of which he has hitherto been unaware – just as a chemist isolates the fundamental substance, the chemical 'element', out of the salt in which it had been combined with other elements and in which it was unrecognisable.

Psychoanalysis takes under its purview all the productions of the unconscious like dreams, parapraxes, etc. According to Freud, all the formations of the unconscious are characterised by a similar set of mechanisms (condensation, displacement, dramatisation and secondary revision). Hence, its results are not restricted to the so-called 'neurotic' subject but comprise the 'normative' as well. Since these mechanisms can be simplified along the lines of the primary linguistic topes viz., metaphor and metonymy, Jacques Lacan, following the lead of the linguist Roman Jakobson, understands the unconscious to be structured like a language.

It is difficult to date the exact origins of psychoanalysis as Sigmund Freud, its founder, was fond of finding an endless number of precursors starting with his nineteenth-century contemporaries, Arthur Schopenhauer and Friedrich Nietzsche, to the ancients like Plato. However, most histories of psychoanalysis begin with Freud's early work in collaboration with the Viennese physician, Josef Breuer. Freud's association with Breuer was prompted by the case of Bertha Pappenheim (better known under the pseudonym, 'Anna O'). The results of the psychoanalytic investigations in this and other cases were published as *Studies in hysteria* in 1895. Hysteria was defined as the product of a psychic trauma that had been repressed by the patient. The treatment was an attempt to get the patient to remember the trauma in order to abstract the cathexis which was attached to the causative event. The association between Freud and Breuer did not last long as they disagreed on the role of sexuality in the aetiology of hysteria.

Freud, unlike Breuer, believed that the trauma had a strong propensity to be of a sexual nature. Though there have been several attempts to revise the definition of hysteria in the subsequent history of psychoanalysis, it continues, at least in the Lacanian interpretation of psychoanalysis, to be the central problematic of the Freudian field. The term hysteria however is used less often in psychiatric and psychoanalytic circles in the United States, where it has been sub-divided into a host of mental disorders characteristic of women. Though it was Freud's insistence on the sexual aetiology of the neuroses that lead to charges of 'pansexualism', the dialectical opposition between Eros and Thanatos must not be overlooked. It may well be true that the real scandal of psychoanalysis is not sexuality but death, and that the former has functioned as a Trojan horse in popular perception. For Lacan, the end of analysis must mark 'death's death'. The subject must come to terms with the structural inevitability of symbolic castration: the fact that symbolic systems tear the subject away from the historical possibility of plenitude is a price which the subject must pay in order to distance itself from the trap of psychosis.

There has also been considerable debate within the psychoanalytic movement on whether psychotics can be 'reached' by the analytic method given their resistance to the transference. Subsequently, psychoanalysis has concerned itself mainly with the neuroses and not psychosis though there have been sporadic attempts to develop a theory of the latter. The most ambitious of these efforts has emerged from the work of French theorists influenced by psychoanalysists like Gilles Deleuze and Félix Guattari. Disagreements in psychoanalytic models generally emerge around the role of the **Oedipus Complex** and infantile sexuality in the constitution of the subject. Psychoanalysts tend to over-emphasise the Oedipal moment while schizoanalysts de-emphasise it radically. It should be possible to write the entire history of psychoanalysis around the changing fortunes of the term 'Oedipus'. [SKS]

Further reading: Deleuze and Guattari 1984, 1988; Ellenberger 1970; Freud 1966; Goux 1993; Grunbaum 1984; Henri 1993; Laplanche 1988; Lebovici and Widlocher 1990; Mehlman 1972; Meltzer 1987.

punk Punk was an approach to **pop music** and a youth **subculture** that emphatically came to public attention, at least in the UK, in the summer of 1976 (not least when the interviewer Bill Grundy encouraged the punk bank the Sex Pistols to utter extremely rude words during a live, teatime, regional news programme). As music, punk represented a return to basics, in reaction to the pretensions, and predominantly middle-class appeal, of such 'pomp rock' bands as Pink Floyd and Yes. In the heady days of 1976, musicianship was not at a premium. Guitars were bought from Woolworth's, and a working knowledge of three chords was generally considered to be sufficient. Legends of singers being three songs ahead of the rest of the band proliferated. As a subculture, punk responded to growing youth unemployment throughout the 1970s. Culturally, it drew on diverse influences, including the dress associated with 1960s mods, Rastafarianism, New York rock, and even glam rock. Hebdige analyses this style as tying together disparate fragments of culture, without any attempt to generate a new and coherent meaning out of those elements (1979). Its meaning, paradoxically, lay in the refusal and subversion of meaning. The safety-pin became emblematic of this style, and its attitude may usefully be summed up in the Sex Pistols' line: 'I don't know what I want but I know how to get it'. (A darker side is expressed in the anthem, 'Looking through Gary Gilmore's Eyes'. Gary Gilmore was a prisoner on death row, who requested execution.) Sadly, punk was rapidly codified and incorporated into mainstream culture. By the end of 1976, the fashion designer Zandra Rhodes was appropriating elements of punk dress, and declaring that it was 'chic to shock'. However, its influence on popular and high culture was still extensive (found, to take a single and arbitrary example, in Derek Jarman's film making). [AE]

Further reading: Hebdige 1979; Laing 1985.

queer theory   Since the early 1970s, there has been a steady and significant development in the study of gay, lesbian and bisexual experience. While the term 'queer theory' may usefully be taken to embrace that body of research, it cannot be characterised by any simple methodological or disciplinary unities. Queer theory refers a range of work occurring, for example, in history (David 1997), literary criticism (Sedgwick 1994, 1997), sociology, philosophy (Butler 1990, 1992), art history, musicology (Brett, Thomas and Wood 1994) and cultural studies (Doty 1993; Morton 1997), that seeks to place the question of sexuality as the centre of concern, and as the key category through which other social, political and cultural phenomena are to be understood. Queer theory may therefore be seen to explore the processes through which sexual identity is, and has been, constituted in contemporary and past societies. Sexuality is thus to be presented as a meaningful activity or achievement that is continually undergoing negotiation and dissemination, rather than as a mere natural (let alone medical) fact (see LeVay 1996). Such meaningful constitution of identity will entail study of both the active embracing and articulation of alternative experiences and lifestyles, and their repression, marginalisation and suppression. Crucial to any queer history will be the recovery of the otherwise concealed and denied presence of gay and lesbian protagonists and activities. While queer theory is inevitably to be linked to the propagation and defence of the politics of gay and lesbian groups in the face of repression and homophobia, the ramifications of its research spill out into fundamental questions about the political nature and even coherence of the supposedly normal and dominant categories of heterosexuality (Richardson 1996). [AE]

Further reading: Abelove, Barale and Halperin 1993; Weeks 1989.

R

race/racism   A mode of classification of human beings which distinguishes between them on the basis of physical properties (e.g. skin colour, facial features) which purportedly derive from genetic inheritance. The key problem with this mode of classification is that the processes of selection regarding what ought to count as 'racial' and therefore 'natural' (i.e. non-cultural) differences are themselves inextricably linked to the existence of cultural **norms** concerning what defines a 'difference' as peculiarly 'racial'. The criteria of differentiation between what are designated as 'races' may, it follows, be established as a result of other factors that have a predominantly social dimension and are related to, for instance, socially determined questions of **power** and **representation**. This particular point has been made by writers such as Edward Said. In his book *Orientalism* (1978) Said argues that the concept of the 'oriental' (taken in the sense of both a **subject** and a culture) as outlined in the European discipline of **'Orientalism'** in fact represents a projection of European concepts and values on to the 'oriental' subject. Thus, purportedly 'objective' descriptions of the oriental can be read as expressions of the European imperialist desire to conceptualise and thereby control the identity of the colonised subject. Equally, when the oriental is discussed in negative terms (for example, by attributing the characteristic of 'irrationality') this, too, can be interpreted as a projection of

323

western fears rather than as an accurate description of the
oriental subject's 'racial' and 'cultural' attributes.

The belief that physical differences in turn validate the attribution of additional characteristics which are not simply
physical but denote the existence of, for example, a determinate set of abilities, propensities or forms of behaviour, is
associated with the attitude of racism. The reader will scarcely
need reminding that the twentieth century has seen some of
the most powerful and disturbing expressions of racist sentiment, and indeed of the catastrophic outcome of this
sentiment in the form of German National Socialism.
Although it may not always be too difficult to describe racist
attitudes, how one accounts for racist phenomena such as
anti-Semitism is a difficult question. Doubtless, it is possible
to point to a wide number of intellectual domains (including
even the physical sciences) and claim that racism has at various
times found expression within them (the German philosopher Hegel springs to mind in such a context, with his
ill-informed comments on the African continent, which is
portrayed as an 'undeveloped' stage in the dialectic of Absolute
Spirit). To this extent, too, the discipline of 'Orientalism'
criticised by Said can with validity be regarded as a manifestation of racism. Yet Nazi ideology seems to have been far
too ad hoc an affair to have required comprehensive grounding
in intellectual respectability, although its anti-Semitism may
have gained support from Hitler's certain practitioners of
genetics. As Erie Hobsbawm has observed:

> Hitler's racism was [. . .] a late nineteenth-century post-
> Darwinian farrago claiming (and alas, in Germany often
> receiving) the support of the new science of genetics,
> or more precisely of that branch of applied genetics
> ('eugenics') which dreamed of creating a human super-
> race by selective breeding and the elimination of the
> unfit.
>
> (Hobsbawm 1995: 118)

So, although Hitler's racism was itself supported by some practitioners of eugenics (and thereby laid some ill-founded claim

324

to 'scientific' respectability), the origins and intellectual justification for this racism were an altogether thinner affair. More basic to this manifestation of racism was, Hobsbawm argues, the mass xenophobia which the late nineteenth century bequeathed to the twentieth (to which one might add the influence of a romantic and nostalgic conservatism). Thus, the culture of Nazi racism was, like the movement itself, a mass phenomenon, and pays ample testimony to the dangers which may be inherent in manipulative mass cultural forms

Whatever the causes of racism, it is clear that racists subordinate purportedly 'significant' physical or normative (i.e. behavioural) differences to the presupposition that the possession of one particular set of characteristics does not merely signify a physical difference but also an inherent difference of **identity**, nature and 'intrinsic value' (cf. **stereotype**). Racism thereby draws a hierarchical distinction between races, opening a gulf between them and setting one racially designated group over and above another on a scale of moral worth, intelligence or importance. A racist **ideology**, therefore, is constructed on the basis of hierarchical distinctions drawn between different groups. From the point of view of such ideologies, race is taken to be a more fundamental basis for the social differentiation between individuals and groups than, for example, that of **class**. Racism thus embodies the attitude of a rigid and naturalised conception concerning the nature of individuals and groups (see Miles 1989). Whether or not racism should therefore be defined solely in terms of ideologically constructed attitudes, or additionally in terms of the norms and practices of a given society is a matter of some debate. In this connection, a number of commentators on racism have pointed to the role of representation in contemporary society, e.g. the construction of racial identity through the presentation, for instance in the media, of stereotypical images of different cultural groups (a factor which, once more, raises the question of the links between racism and mass culture in the modern world).

The significance of racism is not necessarily limited to active discrimination against people, whether through the institutions, ideologies, or norms and practices of a given society. The sense of **self** that those subjected to racism may have, may likewise be affected. In the context of European colonialism, for instance, the construction of racial **identity** and its consequences have been studied not only by Said, but also by Frantz Fanon whose book *Black Skin, White Masks* (1952) considered the damaging influence of colonialism on the self-image of colonial subjects. [PS]

Further reading: Banton 1977; Fanon 1989; Hartmann and Husband 1974; Hobsbawm, 1995; Miles 1989; Said 1978.

rationalisation   Rationalisation is a term most readily associated with the German sociologist Max Weber. While rationalisation has numerous meanings in Weber's writings, it is centrally used to account for the rise to global dominance of **capitalism**. Capitalist society is seen to be uniquely rational, not merely in its economic and technical organisation, but also in science, law, religion, art and government. Rationalisation, in each case, consists of the refinement of instrumental rationality. That is to say, that each social **institution** is rational because it is structured according to rules that determine the most efficient means for achieving any given end, independently of any inhibition from traditional or conventional practices, or the personalities or **values** of any of the social agents involved. Weber's analysis of **bureaucracy**, as the most rational form for the exercise of power, manifests the darker side of rationality, as bureaucracy is seen to become an 'iron cage' that stifles individual liberty and democratic accountability. Weber's account of rationality, in so far as it comes to confront human agents as an external and constraining force, has much in common with Marx's analysis of **alienation**. The work of the Hungarian Marxist Lukács, as well as that of the **Frankfurt School**, explore the inter-relationships of Marxist and Weberian sociology precisely at this point. [AE]

Further reading: Brubaker 1984.

rationality   A word which usually signifies the possession of reason. The notion of rationality is a central theme in the western cultural tradition, and has been used by way of cultural self-definition and in order to define the **identity** of others. How rationality has been conceived of, what it consists in, and the main problems that the analysis of it entails, have formed the basis for much discussion of the nature of the **self**, **society** and **culture** within the western tradition.

In the thought of seventeenth-century philosopher René Descartes (*Meditations on First Philosophy* (1641)), rationality is an attribute of human minds and is shown in the form of self-evident truths, like the law of non-contradiction (the principle which states that a thing cannot both exist and not exist at one and the same time). Descartes' rationalism held, in common with the work of a wide variety of 'rationalist' approaches (e.g. Plato (*c.* 428–348 BC), Spinoza (1632–77), Leibnitz (1646–1716)), that it is possible through the use of reason to obtain knowledge of the nature of existence, and that there is a systematic relationship between existence and our knowledge. Thus, rationality, on this conception, pertains to objectivity, and is possessed independently of contingent factors, such as those to do with history or the constitution of society. On this view, rationality is a *universal* and *non-cultural* phenomenon.

One criticism of this view was inaugurated by the empiricists, who placed an emphasis upon the role of experience in grounding human subjectivity and knowledge. David Hume (1711–76) even went so far as to argue, notoriously, that 'Reason is, and ought only to be, the slave of the passions' (*Treatise of Human Nature*, III (iii): 3). For Hume, the self was not primarily rational, and human knowledge resided not in rational principles, but in the force of 'custom or habit'. In other words, reason is not transcendent, but is culturally located and linked to human desires and dispositions. In response to this view, Immanuel Kant (1724–1804) sought to present a critique of the nature and limits of rationality through an interrogation of the structures which must be in place in order for knowledge to be possible. Kant formulated the theory of the 'transcendental subject' which, rather than signifying an empirical subject, is an attempt to indicate the fundamental features of subjectivity which must be present in order for experience to be possible. On this view, subjectivity is, in essence, composed of a set of rules which we must follow if we are to have knowledge of the world, and these rules form the basis of our rationality. This conception of subjectivity is thus **normative**; but it is also a rational one in so far as it delineates the scope and boundaries of scientific and rational enquiry.

For Friedrich Nietzsche (1844–1900), Kant's criticisms of metaphysics were extended insufficiently far, and demanded to be expanded into the realms of subjectivity and reason themselves. On a popularly disseminated 'Nietzschean' reading, rationality is, in reality, an instrument which does not define humanity as such, but is a product of needs and drives which allowed humans to survive, or it is related to **power**. In other words, reason can be read as the production of a particular species of animal, and also in terms of its role in the cultural construction of concepts like 'truth' and 'reality'. The twentieth century has seen the development of criticisms which follow Nietzsche's injunction (in a poem which concludes the volume *Human, All-Too-Human* (1878)) to 'bring reason to its senses' by subjecting it to an extensive criticism. Criticisms of rationality and subjectivity have been forthcoming from a variety of perspectives, e.g. from the **Frankfurt School** theorists such as Adorno and Horkheimer, who argue that modern rationality has, through the influence of both the **Enlightenment** and as a consequence of the increasing **rationalisation** of modern societies, taken on the form of a primarily instrumental function, and thereby neglects its proper cultural role of critical reflection. Likewise, various criticisms have been offered by figures associated with **post-structuralism** and **communitarianism**, which replace dehistoricised conceptions of subjectivity and rationality with more historically aware, or linguistically-based, conceptions (e.g. by Foucault, although his analysis is not without its own problems, and Lyotard – see also **self**). In contrast to the latter thinkers' full-blown criticisms of the rational subject, Jürgen Habermas has sought in recent years to develop a theory of rationality which takes into account the normative and linguistic aspects of social interaction between agents. Habermas draws upon the work of both **analytical philosophy** (Austin's conception of speech-act theory) and the later Wittgenstein, to formulate a conception of rationality which argues for its being understood in terms of the material and historical factors underlying its development, and yet preserves a space for critical and rational discourse in the shape of 'communicative action'. This notion can be contrasted with that of instrumental rationality. The latter involves only the calculation of means to attain given ends (thus, in the sciences, a rationality based upon calculation is used as a means of problem-solving), whereas communicative action depends upon binding 'consensual norms' which serve to underpin interaction between social agents. On Habermas's conception, this realm of action constitutes a fundamental component in cultural life: it is the sphere in which questions about the validity of our norms and value-systems can be raised, and is therefore concerned with a non-instrumental form of rationality and justification. [PS]

Further reading: Descartes 1968; Habermas 1984; Hume 1990; Nietzsche 1986; Skirbekk 1993.

realism   (i) In literature and **aesthetics**, the term realism refers to those styles of artistic representation that are supposed to work through some resemblance or verisimilitude between the art work and what it represents. Thus, a painting by Vermeer or a novel by Walter Scott seem to offer a depiction or a description of events that resembles how those events would have been experienced in real life. In contrast, an **Expressionist** painting by Munch offers at best a distorted image of reality. In Marxist literary criticism and aesthetics, realism has been placed in opposition to **modernism**, with a significant debate occurring as to which is the most politically progressive. On the one hand, Georg Lukács has defended realism (for example in the work of Balzac) as serving to express the social totality, which is to say the social, economic and political forces that work beneath the surface of seemingly contingent social events. On the other hand, theorists within the **Frankfurt School** criticised realism for its failure to reflect upon the conventions that governed the production of the artistic image (so that rather than expressing society as it reality was, realism merely reproduced a naturalised and **ideological** account of society) (see Bloch *et al.* 1977).

Certain non-Marxist philosophers, and most notably Nelson Goodman (1976), have questioned the distinction between realist and non-realist works. By picking up on a number of problems in explaining exactly in what the resemblance between the art work and reality consists (for example, by pointing out that one painting resembles another painting far more closely than either resemble their subject-matter, yet one painting is rarely a representation of another painting), Goodman suggests that realism is in fact governed by conventions for interpretation, and thus is highly artificial. We are confused into thinking that the relationship between a realist painting and its subject-matter is immediate or natural, simply because we have learnt these interpretative conventions so well and so early in our development.

(ii) In philosophy in general, realism is the doctrine that certain things exist, independently of any human observer or of any description of them that may be offered. As Danto has pointed out, philosophy emerges only in those rare **cultures** where the question, 'Is it real?' can sensibly be asked of objects (such as tables) that self-evidently do exist. In effect, philosophy (and it may be noted, for Danto, art as well) presupposes a culture in which the 'real' world can be set against something that is not real (such as an image, appearance, illusion, representation, sensory impression, or concept) (Danto 1981: 78–80). Thus, I might for example doubt the reality of the table, if I were to argue that I had no direct evidence for its existence, only the sensory data I have of seeing, smelling and touching it. Thus, if I was of a mind,

I might argue that only these sensory data are real, and not tables.

In the **philosophy of science**, more precisely, realism has come to refer to an account of science that, again, presupposes that the objects of scientific enquiry exist independently of the process of enquiry itself, and then argues that science progresses by building theoretical models of those objects of enquiry. While the object of enquiry may itself be unobservable (as, for example in the case of atoms or molecules), the model will allow predictions of observable events to be made. The model can be revised, so that it becomes an ever more accurate representation of reality, in the light of experimental evidence. [AE]

Further reading: Bhaskar 1975; Chalmers 1982; Harré 1970.

reference   The term 'reference' is generally used to indicate the relationship which linguistic terms have with an extra-linguistic reality. In its most traditional and most straightforward sense it indicates the relationship between a name and its object or referent. Thus, on this model, a name is taken as 'standing for' the object it refers to in a language (see the discussion of 'nomenclaturism' in **meaning**). 'Reference' is a primary concern of those working within the tradition of **analytic philosophy**.

This view, in its most modern guise, is reflected in the 'causal theory of reference', the seminal theorist of which is Saul Kripke (1980). On this view, once a proper name or kind name comes to stand for an object in a language it retains its referential power regardless of how it is used or misused by individual speakers. It is via this supposed referential stability that supporters of this theory hope to avoid the more radical implications for the physical and social sciences of semantic **holism** (see also **meaning**). However, it is far from certain that such stability can be guaranteed by the theory granted that the referential use of kind names and proper names seems to depend unavoidably upon the intentional capacities of individual language users (Evans 1973).

The alternative view of reference is the 'description theory of reference'. This theory has its roots in the work of Frege (1892) and his seminal 'sense determines reference' thesis. On this view a proper name or kind name is a short-hand term for one or a number of definite descriptions which come to be associated with it. Accordingly, we can only refer to an object if we can, first, describe it in some way. If we accept this view, we appear to be defining the properties of one part of language, i.e. proper names and kind names, in terms of another part of language, i.e. definite descriptions. Thus, in effect, we have introduced a linguistic wedge between language and the world. Bertrand Russell (1905, 1910) held to a qualified acceptance of this theory, although, ultimately, he thought it needed to be backed up by a form of 'logical atomism'. Peter Strawson (1966) supports a somewhat stronger version of the theory.

Accepting the implication of the description theory, i.e. that we can only refer to an object via some definite description or other, effectively accepts that we can only reach the world *through* language. Again, if we admit that we need descriptions to speak about or think about the world, then it seems that how we think about or speak about the world and the 'objects' of which it is comprised depends on the meanings available to us within a particular language. The fear of the theory's critics is that from here it is but a short step to an acceptance of full-blown semantic holism (see Devitt and Sterelny 1987). [SH]

reflexivity   Reflexivity is the property of referring to oneself. Thus, a reflexive cultural theory will take into account its own position and construction as a cultural artefact. [AE]

Further reading: Elders 1974.

reification   Reification is literally the transformation of something **subjective** or human into an inanimate object. In social and cultural theory it therefore refers, most generally, to the process by which human society (that is ultimately the product of largely conscious and intentional human actions) comes to confront its members as an external, seemingly **natural** and constraining force. In a more precise or technical sense, the theory of reification (or *Verdinglichung* in the original German) was developed by Georg Lukács (1923) from Marx's theory of **commodity fetishism**. Marx analysed the process in **capitalism** by which relationships between human beings (i.e. the meeting of humans in commercial exchange in the **market**), take on the appearance of relationships between things (such that the relationships between humans come to be governed by properties – **exchange-values** – that appear to be inherent to the **commodities** exchanged). For Lukács, this inversion is manifest in all social relations (and not merely in the economy), as in an increasingly **rationalised** and **bureaucratic** society, that which is qualitative, unique and subjective in human relationships is lost, as they are governed according to the purely quantitative concerns of the bureaucrat and the manager. (See also **Frankfurt School**.) [AE]

Further reading: G. Rose 1978; Thomason 1982.

relations of production In **Marxism**, the relations of production are the social relations that exist between the **class** of producers and the class of owners within an economy. In Marxist theory, all societies are characterised in terms of conflict between two major classes. The subordinate class is the class that actually produces goods and services, through the exercise of its **labour** power. The dominant class owns and controls the resources that are used in the production process (the **means of production**), and as such are able to control the production process and the fate of the product. Different modes of production, or historical epochs, are characterised by distinct relations of production and levels of technology (or **forces of production**). The relations of production are inherently static, and social revolution occurs when the productive potential inherent in developing forces of production can no longer be contained or fully exploited within the existing relations of production. (See **mode of production**.) [AE]

relative autonomy   The notion that the social forms or structures which operate within a **culture** are *neither* wholly determined by *nor* wholly independent of the cultural whole (a notion which is well illustrated by Louis Althusser's conception of **ideological state apparatus**es). [PS]

religion   Many attempts have been made to define religion from the points of view of a number of different disciplines: psychologists have characterised it as a projection of human desires (or even as a kind of neurosis), while political thinkers have understood it to be a means of social control which preys upon instinctive human fears. Anthropological definitions, by contrast, attempt to describe religion on its own terms – to understand it from within.

Emile Durkheim argued that the cardinal distinction between the sacred and the profane lies at the heart of all religious experience. It is, he claimed, 'the most profound distinction ever made by the human mind'. On this basis, he defined religion as 'a unified system of beliefs and practices relative to sacred things, that is to say, things set apart and forbidden'.

In more recent times, Durkheim's notion of the sacred has come to be viewed as inadequate on the grounds that it cannot be defined by scientific criteria. Alternative definitions have tended to be more descriptive, avoiding the use of privileged terms like 'sacred' and 'profane'. Clifford Geertz, for example, has proposed the following definition: 'a religion is: (i) a system of symbols which acts to (ii) establish powerful, pervasive, and long-lasting moods and motivations in men by (iii) formulating conceptions of a general order of existence and (iv) clothing these conceptions with such an aura of factuality that (v) the moods and motivations seem uniquely realistic.'

The problem of definition attested to by the bewildering array of claims and counter-claims aimed at uncovering the essence of religion, is a reflection of the sheer scope and diversity of its formulations, both temporal and geographical. As Ninian Smart has said: '. . . we are not confronted in fact by some monolithic object, namely religion. We are confronted by *religions*. And each religion has its own style, its own inner dynamic, its own special meanings, its uniqueness'. In order to reflect this diversity, and to attempt to do justice to the multi-faceted nature of each and every example, Smart proposes a kind of anatomy of religion rather than a definition: 'a religion is . . . a six-dimensional organism, typically containing doctrines, myths, ethical teachings, rituals, and social institutions, and animated by religious experiences of various kinds' (Smart 1971: 31).

Another problem associated with the issue of definition is that it is difficult to be clear about the nature of a phenomenon whose origins are obscure. There is evidence to suggest that Neanderthals practised ritual burial of their dead, which may indicate that they believed in an invisible realm or some kind of an afterlife. But it is open to question whether such beliefs can be termed 'religious'. Smart points out that where life is bound up in cultural practices associated with an all-embracing belief-system, people are not free to opt in or out of 'religion'. There is, in such circumstances, no secular life by contrast with which religious life can be defined.

The development of religion is also contested. Those who have propagated evolutionary theories (Rudolf Otto, for example), have construed the history of religion as a process by which primeval polytheisms have been refined. Sometimes such refinements result in monotheism, sometimes in more highly developed versions of polytheism. E.B. Tylor, influenced by Darwinian theory, contended that all religion has its roots in animism. According to his developmental narrative, belief in the existence of the human soul led to the inference that natural objects also have souls. Gradually, natural phenomena came to be perceived as working together, and a controlling influence was inferred: a single deity emerged from the primaeval dispersion. Wilhelm Schmidt, on the other hand, claims that the most primitive form of religion

335

was monotheistic, and that, subsequently, it was overlaid with animistic and spiritistic elements.

Some approaches to the subject characterise religious phenomena as purely human constructs. On this account, religious beliefs grow out of the need to explain human existence, to answer its problems, and to account for its sufferings. Raymond Firth writes: 'Everywhere belief in religion arises from attempts to save man or console him from the consequences of his own and other people's impulses, desires, fears and actions.'

This **humanistic** view is the result of the decline of Christianity in western cultures after more than a thousand years of dominance. That is to say: in order for religion to be defined 'from the outside', its grip had first to be loosened sufficiently to make such a perspective possible. It was, above all, the rise of science in the West in the seventeenth century that opened a way beyond religious thought. Human life and natural phenomena came to be explained in a radically different ways. The mysterious cosmos, controlled by capricious, and in some cases malign, entities, was supplanted by a rational universe which operates according to fixed laws, and which can be grasped by human reason. Once this leap was made, religious explanations began to appear obsolete.

A post-mythological paradigm is evident in the philosophies of seventeenth-century Rationalism as well as in scientific study. In the eighteenth century, Immanuel Kant attempted to redefine the role of religion in the new age of enlightened thought. It should be confined, he contended, 'within the limits of reason alone'. In Kant's view, morality does not require religion, but the former inevitably produces the latter. Human capacities are inadequate to ensure that moral goodness leads to happiness, so it is necessary to postulate the existence of an omnipotent, moral Being who can act as the cosmic guarantor of the benefit of behaving according to the dictates of reason.

Nineteenth-century thinkers like Auguste Comte and Ludwig Feuerbach sought to take the Kantian critique of religion even further by removing God altogether. They argued for a 'religion of humanity'. 'The divine being', Feuerbach asserted, 'is nothing else than the human being.' Karl Marx, acknowledging the humanist argument, pressed for the abandonment of the idea of a 'religion' of humanity, in favour of a policy of action aimed at overthrowing the social order which religion had produced. He described religion as: 'man's self-consciousness and self-awareness . . . the sigh of the oppressed creature . . . the opium of the people.'

Alongside the rise of Reason and the concomitant decline of religion in western thought, a stream of sceptical (and in some cases irrationalist) thought has persisted. Kant's contemporary, J.G. Hamann, pointed out the strains and contradictions inherent in the **Enlightenment** valuation of Reason. He had a marked influence on the work of the Danish philosopher Soren Kierkegaard, and on the strain of German Romanticism which produced Friedrich Nietzsche's anti-Kantianism. Today, the so-called '**postmodern**' thought which draws on the work of writers like Michel Foucault, Jean-François Lyotard and Jean Baudrillard, owes much to this intellectual lineage. The suspicion aimed by such thinkers at the categories and concepts of the Kantian tradition has given rise to a rethinking of religious possibilities. It has produced an anti-humanism, which, while it has not reasserted pre-humanist, religious values, has, according to Philippa Berry, 'dissolved the clear-cut distinction between secular and religious thinking which Kant and the Kantian tradition had carefully secured.' [KM/GH]

Further reading: Durkheim 1975, 1976; Geertz 1976; Smart 1960, 1972, 1973; Schmidt 1935.

repetition   Repetition, along with the **drive**, the **unconscious** and the **transference** are, according to Jacques Lacan, the four fundamental concepts of **psychoanalysis**. Since the term 'repetition' bears a similarity to the **deconstructive** concept of iteration, it is necessary to distinguish between the two. Iteration, according to Jacques Derrida, governs the conditions of possibility for the use of the linguistic **sign**. It is because the sign can be repeated, iterated, on more than one occasion that it is recognisable. In other words, there is no such thing as a *hapax legomenon* at the level of the symbolic. Though Derrida's theory of iteration is correct, it must not be conflated with repetition. There is something in repetition that is in excess of the cognitive necessity or the linguistic function of iteration. It is this element that psychoanalysis seeks to isolate. As John Forrester points out, repetition in psychoanalysis is akin to a Kantian category, it is a principle of interpretation, and is not reducible to an empirical or clinical generalisation.

What does the **subject** repeat? And why does the subject repeat? What the subject repeats is the **symptom**; the subject repeats the symptom because of an unconscious compulsion to do so. Here the term 'symptom' can be understood in two senses. The symptom is either an act that the subject feels compelled to perform or is inhibited from performing. Again, the symptom is the libidinal matrix from which the subject acts: it indexes the sexual life of the subject. In the former, the repetitive aspect of the symptom takes on the function of a **ritual**: it displaces the anxiety that assails the subject and prevents anxiety from breaking into the subject's consciousness unexpectedly. It becomes a form of existential punctuation. Repetition therefore becomes an attempt at mastering anxiety and can be subsumed under the aegis of the pleasure principle.

However, it is repetition that is beyond the pleasure principle which really interested Freud. Here what the subject repeats is the trauma *per se*. Freud defined a trauma as a situation where the subject is overwhelmed by stimuli. This necessitates repetition since the subject seeks to master the stimuli retroactively. But in this attempt at retroactive mastery, Freud detected a 'daemonic' force whose function was in excess of being an existential shock absorber. Repetition, by taking on an excessive character, became a rehearsal for death. It was the mechanism that would return the organism to its material origins, so that it could die in its own fashion. [SKS]

Further reading: Derrida 1982; Fink 1995, Forrester 1990, Freud 1984, Lacan 1979, Laplanche and Pontalis 1973.

representation   1. On some theories, a function of **language** (i.e. representation conceived of as (a) the representation of thoughts in language, (b) the linguistic representation of the world of empirical experience). 2. In social terms, representation has (a) a political meaning (in the sense of meaning the representation, through institutional bodies or pressure groups, of the interests of political **subjects** – a notion inextricably linked with modern, **liberal** conceptions of the democratic process), and (b) a more nuanced meaning, which has linked the practices and **norms** of representing and which may, for example, be used in the **mass media**, in order to present images of particular social groups. In sense 2b, representation does not necessarily signify the representing of the interests of the group or individual represented. A group can be represented in a manner which might be conceived of as **stereotyping** them. Thus, in this context, 'representation' may be characterised as misrepresentation: as the 'presentation' or construction of **identity**. Such constructions of identity may be closely allied to questions of **ideology** and **power**, and to the forms of **discourse** implicated in the procedures whereby such images are created. Thus, the construction of concepts relating to issues of **gender**, **race** or **sexuality** are questions of representation. Sense 2b is, in many ways, a matter related to senses 2a and 1b. In terms of the representation of political subjects (2a), the constitution of modes of representation may have an important role to play within the political process, in so far as such issues as those concerned with the construction of discourses surrounding matters of race or **ethnicity** can also be conceptualised as being political issues. Likewise, the view that language may have a role in constructing 'reality', rather than simply reflecting it (1b), is an important one in this connection; for, if we were to be convinced that language does not merely 'mirror' the world of experience but constructs it, the same must go for its role in the world of social experience. The question of the role of representation can also be raised in the context of discourses of knowledge (cf. Edward Said's account of **Orientalism**). [PS]

Further reading: Haldane and Wright 1993.

reproduction   see **cultural reproduction**

rhetoric   The art of persuasion. Rhetoric is the putting to work of language in order to influence other people, either in terms of their future actions or their beliefs. 'Rhetoric' also signified the formal study of persuasion. In the medieval period this was a branch of academic learning, akin in status to the study of grammar, mathematics or logic. In the Renaissance, rhetoric was regarded as a practical field of study for those interested in politics and law (handbooks of rhetoric included in Erasmus's *De copia* (1521)). A new interest in rhetoric has been developed in the post-war period by figures associated with **post-structuralism**, such as Paul de Man (1919–83). De Man, who developed a form of **deconstruction**, analysed linguistic tropes and their functions, paying particular attention to rhetorical language in critical and philosophical texts. [PS]

Further reading: de Man 1989, 1979.

rites de passage   The term 'rites de passage' comes from **cultural anthropology**, and refers to those public ceremonies or **rituals** that mark the transition from one stage of life to another. The rites de passage tends to presuppose the complete submission of the individual to the collective, and thus the exact execution of the requirements of the ritual. A typical example would be the ceremonies associated with the transition from childhood to adulthood. While such ceremonies are readily associated with pre-industrial societies, they continue to play a significant part in contemporary society, for example, in the forms of baptisms, the High School prom, graduation ceremonies and funerals. [AE]

ritual   A ritual is a formal action, following set and repeatable patterns, that is expressive of communal **values**, meanings and beliefs. The original use of ritual would suggest that the ritual entailed some link with sacred, supernatural or magical worlds. Indeed, Durkheim argued that the distinction between the 'sacred' and the 'profane' is fundamental to ritual, which entails crossing the usual boundary between the two. For Durkheim, the sacred is expressive of the community within which individuals live. Ritual therefore serves the function of integrating the individual more closely into the social whole. Taking this theme further, ritual may also be seen as a response to threats to the community. Ritual activity intensifies in the face of social change or during other periods of social instability. Within cultural studies, these notions of ritual have been used, more or less precisely or **metaphorically**, to explore the ways in which secular groups (and especially **subcultures** or **ethnic** groups) define and articulate their identity, and resist external pressures in contemporary **capitalism** (hence, for example, the title of Hall and Jefferson's collection, *Resistance through Rituals* (1976)). [AE]

role   At its simplest, 'role' is a useful **metaphor** for the social activities that members of **society** undertake in their day to day life. Thus, being a 'daughter', 'student', 'fan', 'party-goer' are all roles (and indeed roles that one person could take on, either sequentially or in combination).

Behind this metaphor lie at least two diverse theoretical approaches. In functionalist **sociology**, a role is seen as a more or less precisely prescribed set of behavioural expectations, that effectively define the role. The role is thus circumscribed by a set of **norms**, rules and **values**, that determine how the individual in that role is to behave. Failure to behave appropriately will be punished through some form of negative sanction. Thus, the role of 'teacher' would be understood in terms of the rules that govern the technical skills and stocks of technical knowledge that the teacher must possess, along with the moral rules that govern his or her relationship to pupils and to colleagues, and the aspiration to certain values (such as a belief in the value of teaching as a profession). **Socialisation** (the process of learning to be a social and cultural being) is thus understood as the preparation of individuals to take on certain roles.

341

In contrast, roles within **symbolic interactionist** approaches are seen as more fluid, and in need of achievement and negotiation. This approach is grounded in the work of George Herbert Mead (1934), who argued that we come to understand and fulfil our own roles only by imaginatively taking the roles of others. A role, and thus in part our own **self**-understanding or self-identity, is composed in response to, or in anticipation of, the actions of others. The teacher's role does not then exist in isolation. It is constructed (or 'made' in Mead's terminology) only in relation to the expected behaviour of pupils, and in responding to their actual reactions, and each teacher may work this role out in his or her own way. Roles are continually modified through **interaction**. Mead thus defines a role as a sequence of gestures that highlight and refer to an individual's actions and dispositions. The concept of role thus indicates how we read, and give **meaning** to, each other's actions or gestures (and indeed think about the meaning of our own actions), in order to anticipate and respond to the future actions of others.

Two important associated concepts are 'role conflict' and 'role distance'. Role conflict occurs either when an individual finds that two of the roles that he or she performs make incompatible demands, or when two groups have different, and again incompatible, expectations of one's role. Thus, an off-duty friendship may clash with the need to impose discipline while on-duty; or a trade union shop steward may find that managers and workers have radically different expectations as to what he or she can do. Role distance was coined by Goffman (1959), to refer to the degree to which performers of a role are detached from it, and in being aware that they are performing a role for a specific audience, can manipulate it to achieve some end. (See also **dramaturgical model**.) [AE]

Further reading: Biddle 1979.

Romanticism The Romantic period in European culture runs from approximately 1780–1850. While Romantic works of art are generally readily identifiable as such (for example in the painting of Turner and Delacroix, the poetry of Wordsworth and Byron, and the music of Wagner), the precise formulation of what Romantic artists and thinkers have in common is elusive. Romanticism is perhaps best seen as a cluster of attitudes and themes, rather than as a single coherent doctrine. At its core is a reaction to **Enlightenment** emphasis on reason and order, and thus as a reaction to classicism in the arts.

Originally 'romantic' referred merely to the romance languages, and hence to writing in the vernacular French, rather than Latin. In 1755, Dr Johnson defined 'Romantick' as 'resembling the tales or romances; wild . . . improbable; false . . .; fanciful; full of wild scenery'. This definition already begins to capture something of the cluster of Romantic concerns. The Romantic breaks free of classicism through a renewed appeal to emotion, and crucially to the darker emotions of fear and suffering. Thus, while the Enlightenment was interested in **nature** as a source of reason and order (exemplified by Newtonian mechanics), the Romantic found in it organic growth and diversity. For the Romantic, the natural and the supernatural are entwined, giving nature an emotional and spiritual force that is alien to Enlightenment thinking. In addition, Romanticism marked a renewed interest in medieval and even pagan culture. The Romantic therefore turned to the gothic (culminating in the revival of Gothic architecture), and where classicism had looked to Greek and Roman mythology, Romanticism looked to European mythology and folk culture (for example in the German Nibelungenlied, or the Finnish Kalevala). Above all, Romanticism celebrates the exceptional individual.

Writing towards the end of the eighteenth and beginning of the nineteenth century, Friedrich and August Wilhelm von Schlegel are key figures in the development of Romanticism. Both emphasise the fluid and fragmentary nature of the Romantic work of art. For Friedrich, romantic poetry is always in a state of becoming, and thus never achieves the perfection or harmonious coherence to which classical art aspires. For August, the romantic is encapsulated in the

343

problem of interpretation, and the ultimate incomprehensibility of the work of art. His doctrine of Romantic **irony** stresses the paradoxical nature of the poem, so that no objective or definitive meaning can ever be derived from it. In drama, Shakespeare is celebrated for his ironic detachment from his characters. He is thus able to portray contradictory positions, through the opposition of characters, without resolving the drama in favour of one viewpoint.

In philosophy, the emergence of Romanticism may be associated with the work of Jean-Jacques Rousseau, both in his criticism of the corrupting effect of contemporary civilisation on humanity, in the emotional and sentimental tone of his novel, *Julie, ou la Nouvelle Héloïse*, and in the self-exploration of the *Confessions*. As Rousseau turns to the image of a state of nature, prior to civilisation, in order to recover an image of a noble and uncorrupted humanity, so the German philosopher Johann Gottfried Herder (1744–1803) turns to folk cultures and to non-European cultures, understanding them not as primitive precursors of European civilisation, but as having their own validity, and their own criteria of meaning and excellence. While Herder writes in reaction to the rationalism of Kant, Kant himself stands in a complex relationship to Romanticism. His ethics are dominated by reason, but his theory of knowledge and **aesthetics** explores the limits of knowledge and reason (constraining scientific enquiry in order to make 'room for faith'). However, it is Arthur Schopenhauer (1788–1860), himself reinterpreting Kant, who is the purest example of a Romantic philosopher. His pessimistic account of the world in terms of the continual strivings of the will, from which art provides one of the few sources of relief, was influential on the archetypal Romantic artist, Richard Wagner. [AE]

Further reading: Cranston 1994; Honour 1979; Le Huray and Day 1987; Lovejoy 1948; Praz 1970; Rosen and Zerner 1984; Simpson 1988; Wu 1994.

rule　A term which has gained an increasing importance in the sphere of the analysis of **language**, where it has sometimes come to be used in a manner which is akin in meaning to 'convention'. Rule-based views of language assert that it is by way of rules or conventions that meaning is constituted, not through, for example, the manner in which words **refer** to non-linguistic states of affairs. The work of the later Wittgenstein provided much of the impetus toward the analysis of rules in language in the post-war period (principally through the notion of 'language games'). One good example of a rule-based account of language is Jean-François Lyotard's *The Differend: Phrases in Dispute* (1983). On this conception, the rules which constitute any particular way of speaking make up a **genre** of discourse. A genre has a purpose, and the rules tell you what to do in order to achieve that purpose. One might draw the analogy between this notion and cooking: if one wishes to make a cake, then the genre of cooking contains within it the rules one needs to observe in order to attain this goal. It follows that rules are not of themselves obligatory – there is no rule which tells you that you ought to follow a particular rule – since they are dependent upon the existence of particular goals; nor do they tell you how to 'play well': one can follow the rules of chess and still play badly (although, if a man allows himself to be beaten at chess by his boss, one might be tempted to argue that he is playing another game with a different set of stakes). Conventions differ from rules at the level of social interaction when this term is taken as signifying a way of behaving in a particular context which is adopted by the members of a community as a **norm** (e.g. shaking hands when meeting; knocking on a door before going in a room; wearing a particular style of clothes in a particular context, e.g. a wedding). Taken in this sense, conventions also underlie the identities of particular genres (e.g. in literature the novel form stipulates a set of conventions which, at least in theory, all novels share in some manner or other, although the 'goal' of any individual novel is not stipulated by way of its conforming to the conventions which characterise the genre). [PS]

self A term which is linked to issues of **subjectivity** and **identity**, and which also has ramifications in a variety of discursive contexts (e.g. politics, **liberalism**, **individualism**, **epistemology**, ethics).

The notion of the self is invoked as soon as one asks a question like 'Who am I?'. At first glance, this might not seem very difficult to answer, and you might respond by just giving your name. But giving your name does not adequately answer the 'Who am I?' question if you also take it to mean 'What am I?'. In general, philosophers have held that asking who you are necessarily also involves considering *what* you are. Here is one possible answer to this question: 'I am a mind and a body. I think and I also move about in the world as a material being'. But answering in this way does not solve the problem, unless you are also able to say how such things as minds and bodies are related to one another. In turn, then, a consideration of the nature of the self usually entails a number of related questions; e.g. *how* is the mind connected to the body? (put another way: What is the relationship between mind and body?). Also, if one holds the view that each of us is a mind plus a body, another issue arises, namely, which came first?

A number of approaches to this issue are possible. Plato, in the *Phaedo* (*c.* 380 BC, cf. 63e ff.), argued that the soul (mind) and the body are distinct. Moreover, he held that the soul must have existed prior to the body. The essence of what each of us is resides in this contrast. The essential part of each of us (the mind/soul) never changes, because what is essential (and hence true) must by definition never change. In contrast, the realm of the material world changes. Here is Plato's argument, presented by Socrates in the *Phaedo*: (i) There are two sorts of existence: the seen (the physical world) and the unseen. (ii) The world of experience (the seen) is a realm of change, whereas the unseen is unchanging. (iii) We are made of two parts – body and soul. (iv) The body is akin to the seen, and therefore changing; and the soul is akin to the unseen, and therefore unchanging. (v) Of these two, the soul is akin to the divine (which is unchanging) – in short, we have an immortal soul. (vi) Therefore, the soul is indissoluble. From this, it follows that the self is the immortal part of each of us, and the body the mere vessel in which this essence is instantiated. Plato, following this chain of reasoning, held that what is essential about each of us endures after death (i.e. that the soul/mind is immortal).

Such a view can be contrasted with eighteenth-century philosopher David Hume's treatment of the matter in the *Treatise of Human Nature* (1739: cf. Book 1, part iv, section 6). According to Hume, whenever I speak of *myself* I always do so in the context of some particular thought or feeling. There is no self over and above thoughts and feelings which can be held to be independent of them. What 'I' am is a bundle of sensations; the self, therefore, is a product of a body's ability to have sensations, experiences, etc. Hence, on Hume's account, nothing about the self can be said to exist independently of such sensations: the self is mortal. Moreover, the self is therefore something *added* to experiences; it is a fiction or an illusion. Put another way, the self is not an entity independent of the sensations a body is capable of feeling, but is produced by them. Thus, for Hume the self is a kind of *interpretation* of these sensations.

These two accounts, whatever their respective shortcomings, offer contrasting ontological views about the nature of the self. In making some claim about the nature of the self

347

(i.e. what the self is), we are committed to some kind of ontology. This is the case even if, like Hume, we are tempted to deny that the self exists in any ontological sense: we are still making an ontological claim about the self on the basis of what we hold reality to be.

Important elements of Plato's view are by no means restricted to him. Many philosophical, religious and ethical attitudes and ideas contain within them the (albeit perhaps tacitly held) belief that mind and body are distinct from one another in kind. Likewise, with regard to knowledge, considered from both a philosophical point of view and from the vantage point of science, the question of the self is a significant one. This is because in talking of knowledge the question necessarily arises concerning who or what is it that has, or is the subject of, knowledge. For example, within the sciences some notion of what an enquirer is must be presupposed.

The seventeenth-century philosopher René Descartes, in reply to the writings of contemporary sceptics who questioned whether we can have any certain knowledge, attempted to show that there is at least one certain piece of knowledge we are in possession of. Descartes starts by claiming that he has been struck by the large number of false beliefs he has accepted since being a child. He resolves to 'demolish' all his beliefs as a prologue to constructing the foundations of knowledge (this approach is often known as the 'sceptical method', since it precedes from doubt). In order to do this, it is sufficient to bring into question all one's opinions, i.e. to show that they are *not certain*, rather than that they are false. However much one may doubt the veracity of one's beliefs, Descartes claims, one thing remains true: whatever happens I am still thinking: 'I must conclude that this proposition, *I am, I exist*, is necessarily true whenever it is put forward or conceived by me in my mind'. This is most famously expressed in the phrase 'I think, therefore I am' (*cogito, ergo sum*).

What is this 'I' that thinks? Descartes draws a distinction between (i) the mechanical structure of the human body and (ii) the activities which humans pursue: they walk about, eat, have perceptions through their senses, etc. These activities are, he claims, the actions of a soul or mind. The properties of a body are physical: it can be seen, touched, occupies a particular space, can be moved, etc. The 'power of self-movement', however, is not a property we can attribute to a body. In line with the precepts of the sceptical method, the body can be doubted. But the self that thinks, Descartes argued, cannot be doubted. Thus, Descartes holds that he is a mind, 'not that structure of limbs which is called a human body' (a view termed 'mind-body dualism'). In other words, this standpoint contends that what is essential about humans is that they are thinking things, and that the property denoted by the term 'mind' is essentially different from that denoted by the term 'body'. This forms the basis for his view of knowledge: certain (i.e. true) knowledge derives from the 'I think', the self conceived as a mental essence. Amongst those who have criticised this approach was Nietzsche, who, in *Beyond Good and Evil* (section 16) pointed out that there was no necessary connection between thinking and the self; that is, we cannot show with complete certainty that it is the self which is the agency behind the activity of thinking. For Nietzsche, in contrast, the self is always to be comprehended as being situated within particular contexts and, indeed, as the product of human **culture**, rather than an ontological category which grounds the basis of experience and therefore knowledge.

With the 'linguistic turn' in philosophy during the twentieth century (see **philosophy of language**) and also in the light of intellectual developments such as **psychoanalysis**, accounts have been offered of the self which address, for example, the question of its construction within the domain of language and **discourse**. For Jean-François Lyotard, for example, the notion of a self apart from language derives from an anthropocentric view of the nature of meaning which can be challenged. Selves, on this account, are not situated in a language-independent realm, nor are their attitudes, dispositions and intentions alone sufficient to secure an epistemological foundation for knowledge. Rather, such things as intentions, dispositions and interests are realised in and through language. Thus, Lyotard criticises Wittgenstein's conception of 'language games' as being too limited. For instance, in drawing an analogy between language games and the game of chess, Wittgenstein, says Lyotard, remains trapped within a view of meaning which privileges a self which is independent of language: he presupposes that a 'player' moves a piece in a chess game, yet remains apart from the game. Equally, Jacques Derrida has argued that the meaning of such things as propositions is not simply a matter of the intentions of a speaker. For Derrida, although 'meaning has its place' what is instrumental in the production of meaning are language and context. Also, the work of Michel Foucault has, following Nietzsche, also concentrated on reconceptualising the notion of the self in terms of the relations between discourses of power. [PS]

Further reading: Derrida 1988; Descartes 1986; Hernadi 1995; Lyotard 1988; Nietzsche 1968a, Plato 1975.

semiotics/semiology The terms 'semiotics' and 'semiology' alike refer to the theory of **signs**, and thus to the way in which a study of signs and systems of signs can explicate problems of **meaning** and communication. (While 'semiotics' was coined in the seventeenth-century by the English philosopher John Locke, and 'semiology' by the twentieth-century linguist Ferdinand de Saussure, the former term is perhaps used more frequently.) The study of signs can be broadly traced back to ancient Greece, for example in the medical study of symptoms as signs of disease. Similarly, modern semiotics may embrace everything that can act as a sign, and which can therefore generate and communicate meaning. Zoosemiotics, for example, is concerned with the natural processes that exist in animal communication. However, the importance of semiotics for cultural studies lies in the insight that it can provide into communication within human cultures, and thus with the artificial (as opposed to natural) processes that make possible human communication. It may not be an exaggeration to suggest that semiotics is the single most important set of theoretical tools that is available to cultural studies, precisely because of its power to recognise and analyse meaningful relationships in a vast range of human activities and products. Within cultural studies, semiotics may be applied, equally productively, to such diverse artefacts as literary texts, popular songs, photographs, advertisements, road signs, food and clothing. Crucially, semiotics therefore allows cultural studies to break from the evaluative approach of traditional literary criticism and **aesthetics**, for it does not seek to assess the worth of **texts**, but rather to understand the processes through which they become meaningful and how they are variously interpreted.

Language is the dominant model of a sign system for semiotics, and the linguistics of Saussure has had a major influence on the development of modern semiotics. At the core of Saussure's approach to language is the claim that language (and thus the words or signs within a language) do not merely correspond to a pre-existing (extra-linguistic) reality. Rather, language is seen as constituting the reality we experience. Thus, the word 'herb' does not point to some pre-existing segment of reality, for the distinction between, say, herbs, flowers and vegetables depends upon our possessing a language that allows us to recognise differences between these three types of plant. (We might readily imagine a language that did not make this distinction, and perhaps then imagine the difficulty we would have in explaining the difference to someone who did not speak English, even if we were fluent in this other language.) Saussure therefore argues that language, as a sign system, works, not through the simple relationship of its component signs to external objects, but rather through the relations of similarity and difference that exist between signs (and thus wholly within language). Part of the meaning of 'herb' is that it is not 'vegetable'. Similarly, to use a common example, the word 'man' in English means 'not-animal', 'not woman', and 'not boy'. This may be extended, to suggest that it has further associations, such as 'not vulnerable', 'not emotional'. The meaning of the word 'man' therefore depends upon the particular understanding of masculinity that is

351

current in language-users' culture. One more example will serve to develop this point, and particularly to emphasise the arbitrariness of semiotic structures. In western cultures 'white' is typically associated with positive emotions and events (hence a white wedding dress). White is therefore not black, for black is associated with negative emotions and events. In eastern cultures, while the opposition of white and black may be retained, the associations may be reversed. The white is therefore the colour associated with funerals.

The above examples may begin to indicate how semiotics moves from language, as the model of a sign system, to other forms of sign system. A person's choice of clothing, for example, is meaningful. A black dress is appropriate in certain social contexts, inappropriate in others, precisely because it communicates a message about the wearer (she is in mourning; is being formal; is being sexy). Just as there are conventions governing the meaning of a written or spoken word in a sentence, so there are conventional rules governing the meaning of a chosen item of clothing. Crucially these rules govern the choice of one item from a range of possibilities (a black dress, not a white or yellow or blue dress) (see **paradigm**), and the combination of the chosen items (see **syntagm**). Thus, one may differentiate between funeral wear, a suit for the office and a party dress, although all may be black, by recognising the combination of colour (as one sign) with style, hemline, material and so on (as other signs), just as a sentence or any other spoken or written **text** makes sense through the combination of words.

The examples of 'man' and 'black' used above indicate that signs typically have a range of meanings, some of which are fairly literal (man is not woman), while others are more allusive (man is not emotional). Thus, a distinction is made between the denotations of a sign, being its most literal and stable meanings, and the connotations, being the associations or more emotional, expressive and evaluative nuances of meaning that the sign evokes. In practice, no sign (with the possible exception of those used in mathematics and formal logic) is purely denotative. To choose to talk, say, of 'steeds' rather than 'horses' places a small but important twist upon what is said. Using the distinction between connotation and denotation, Roland Barthes builds upon Saussure's original conception of semiotics in order to argue that connotation should be understood as calling forth the value-system of the culture within which the sign is used and interpreted. Crucially, these culturally specific evaluations are linked to the distribution of power within the society (so that, for example, the association of masculinity – in the sign 'man' – with rationality, action, and strength is indicative of a patriarchal society). The fact that we take connotations for granted, confusing them with denotations and thereby accepting them as if they were natural or unchangeable, leads to what Barthes calls **myth**. The evaluative, and ultimately political, implications of signs are concealed, so that the reader may unwittingly absorb the dominant value-system as he or she responds to the text. Thus, in looking at an advertisement, the naïve reader will absorb evaluations of masculinity and femininity, simply through the way in which men and women are portrayed and related to each other, and other signs in the advertisement. (Fiske and Hartley have therefore argued that an understanding of semiotics and mythology, in Barthes's sense of the term, leads to a theory of **ideology**.)

For all the analytical power that semiotics offers to cultural studies, not least in the model of Barthes's work, the Saussurean approach to signs may be seen to have certain weaknesses. An early alternative to Saussurean semiotics was posed by the Russian theorist V.N. Voloshinov. Voloshinov sees Saussure's emphasis on the linguistic or sign system as giving a false objectivity to language. Voloshinov is concerned not with the ahistorical structure of language, but rather with the realisation of language and meaning in particular social situations. A sign may thereby be understood as a potential area of class struggle, for although all members of a society may share a common language, different classes will appropriate that language to different political uses. Signs thus have a 'social multiaccentuality', although this will be most explicit only in times of crisis and revolution.

353

A further criticism may be made through reflection on the great emphasis that Saussurean semiotics places on the role of language in structuring, and indeed creating, the world which we experience. This gives rise to the danger that semiotics collapses into a form of anti-realism, which is to say that it says too little about the restraints that the world external to languages and sign systems places upon us, and the way in which signs refer to that external, non-linguistic world. A number of approaches have been developed to deal with this problem, not least through elaborating some notion of **reference**. However, the work of the American philosopher Charles S. Peirce, has received attention, precisely because his semiotics is, from the first, more sensitive to the problem of the relationship of the sign to an extra-linguistic object.

Peirce's theory of signs involves a three-part scheme. What Pierce terms the 'sign' is related to an 'interpretant', via an 'object'. A simple example (borrowed from Hookway) best illustrates this. If I see bark stripped from a tree, then this may be a sign that deer are around. The stripped bark is the sign, the real deer that did the stripping are the object, and my idea of a deer is the interpretant. The interpretant is thus the mental response of the reader to the original sign. Crucially, Peirce goes on to argue that signs generate chains of interpretants, which is to suggest that a sign is not self-evidently or transparently meaningful. Each reader will generate his or her own interpretation of the sign. The reader is therefore always separated from the real object by the sign and its interpretation. However, as the chain of interpretants progresses, Peirce argues (at least for certain types of sign, such as those used in communication within the community of scientists) that interpretants (and thus the reader's understanding) gradually become more adequate to the object. In effect, the object, outside language, may then be seen to exert pressure on signs and sign systems. Thus, while different cultures may classify the realm of plants differently, a practical engagement and study of plants will, for Peirce, eventually lead the botanist and the cook to distinguish herb from vegetable, and rosemary from carrot.

Peirce's semiotics offers one further, useful set of concepts, in so far as he distinguishes three types of sign. Symbols are signs that are only conventionally related to the objects to which they refer. Thus, the word 'dog' has nothing physically or otherwise in common with real dogs. A flag may signify a nation, but need be nothing more than an abstract design. Indices, conversely, have some causal or existential link to the object. Thus, the stripped bark is an index, because it is caused by the deer. Smoke is an index of fire. Finally icons share certain properties with their object. A map is thus iconic, as are representational paintings and photographs. [AE]

Further reading: Barthes 1967b, 1973; Eco 1976; Fiske and Hartley 1978; Hookway 1985; Innis 1986; Peirce 1986; Saussure 1983; Voloshinov 1973.

serialism   Serialism is a compositional technique in modernist music invented around 1923 by Schoenberg. In the tonal music we are most used to (at least in western cultures), typically only eight notes of the twelve notes of the scale are used, and certain notes will sound more important than others (e.g. by being the note upon which we expect the music to finish). In atonality, all twelve notes are used, and the security of many expected musical landmarks is lost. In serialism, the twelve notes of the chromatic scale are arranged in a certain order or series. This is intended to guarantee that no note should sound more important than any other. Apart from certain manipulations – inversion and retrograde, i.e. playing the series upside down and backwards – the notes must always remain in that order throughout the piece. Many composers (notably Milton Babbitt and Boulez) felt that Schoenberg's approach, while revolutionary, was too narrowly focused on pitch, and turned to total serialism, so that serial rows were used to organise not just the notes, but also rhythm and volume There are two criticisms to which Schoenberg's serialism seems immediately open. The first is that it is not thoroughgoing enough to avoid tonal centres, which often emerge in Schoenberg's own music. The second is that tonality is very effectively erased by serialism, but that some sense of tonal centre is essential to the tension and resolution which is said to characterise so much of the aesthetic response to music. While serialism has been used most in art music, it is also found in **jazz** and rock (for example, in some Deep Purple). [RC/AE]

Further reading: Adorno 1973a; Forte 1973.

sexuality 'Sexuality' is probably the most misunderstood concept in Freudian **psychoanalysis**. It is commonly conflated with the term 'genital'. For Freud, sexuality functions as a superordinate term: the genital is merely one of the aspects of sexuality. The pansexualist criticism of psychoanalysis is based on the idea that Freud reduces everything to sexuality (i.e. the genital). In his *Three Essays on the Theory of Sexuality* (1905), Freud widens the ambit of sexuality to include infantile sexuality, polymorphous perversity, the function of symptoms (which represent the sexual life of the subject), and the sheer diversity and deviations that pertain to object choice. Sexuality cannot be reduced to instinctual behaviour since the relationship between the **drive** and the object is arbitrary. Sexuality does not merely frame the phenomenology of the neurotic **symptom** but helps the psychoanalyst to understand its aetiology as well. It was Freud's insistence on the sexual aetiology of the neuroses that led to a parting of ways between him and his early followers, Alfred Adler and Carl Gustav Jung.

Sexuality in psychoanalysis is described through a developmental model where the infant progresses through different stages: the oral, the anal, the genital and the phallic. Contingent disturbances in any of these levels will determine the distributions of libido that structure the subject's life. Neuroses were initially understood as regressions to one of these levels of libidinal fixation. The regression is made necessary by the subject's inability to respond to the demands of 'reality'. Sexuality is understood to manifest itself from the time of early infancy. The premature demands of the sexual drive are repressed in the so-called Oedipal phase and the child switches from an *Imaginary* identification with the mother to a *Symbolic* identification with the father. This is followed by a period of latency. At puberty, sexuality once again makes its exorbitant demands on the subject thereby leading to the revival of modes of behaviour that constitute the libidinal matrix of childhood.

In subjects who fail to make a proper Oedipal crossover from the mother to the father, sexual impressions of early childhood take on a traumatic aspect during puberty resulting in the return of the repressed. This leads to the production of neurotic symptoms, which constitute the sexual life of the subject. The typology of neuroses can also be classified along a model of stages. For example: in terms of fixation, hysteria is to orality what obsessionality is to anality. Lacan, however, called this model of biological stages into question without doing away with it completely. In the Lacanian model, though the infant must travel through these stages, there is nothing specifically biological about it. It is the fear of castration that mediates the subject's relation to any of these 'stages'. Castration has a specifically symbolic dimension in Lacan. Symbolic castration is the radical disjunction between the subject and its object of desire, such that no object can exhaust the restlessness of the drive. The Oedipal drama is the symbolic realm where the subject is first alienated in its desire. Subsequently, the sexual drive can only seek an object in a complex imitation or distortion of the lost object. Sexuality therefore cannot be reduced to instinctual behaviour, instead it takes on a dialectical relationship with the absent, the forbidden, and finally, the impossible. [SKS]

Further reading: Freud 1977, 1979; Laplanche and Pontalis 1973.

sign   A sign may be understood as anything that stands for, refers to, or represents something else. A sign is analysed into two elements. A **signifier** is the material form the sign takes, such as a written word ('rose'), an object (the stem and flower of a rose), a trade mark, photographic images, scents, colours and so on. A **signified** is the abstract concept to which the signifier points (so that a rose or the image of a rose may signify the idea of love more adequately than the word 'love', giving you, as a sign, what Barthes has called a '"passionified" rose'). Signs may be understood as the most important units that carry and produce **meaning** in any act of communication. Signs are meaningful due to their position within a conventional and culturally specific set of rules (or **codes**) that govern their use and appropriateness. (See also **semiotics**.) [AE]

Further reading: Silverman 1983.

signifier/signified   In **semiotics**, a **sign** is analysed in terms of two constitutive components: the signifier and the signified. The signifier is the physical form taken by the sign, such as a spoken or written word ('remembrance'), an object (a herb, the drawing of a herb), and so on. The signifier is distinct from any particular utterance, use or presentation of it. Thus, a dozen people with diverse accents and intonations of voice may all say 'remembrance' in their own way, and yet we will recognise the signifier that is common to each of these utterances. The signified is the concept to which the sign refers (and thus, in these examples, the idea of remembrance). Crucially, the signified is not to be understood as a particular object or event in the real world. So the word 'remembrance' no more signifies a particular act of remembrance than the word 'herb' refers to any particular herb. Similarly, a photograph of the herb rosemary, for example in a botany book, signifies what might be called 'rosemary-ness', and not the particular plant that the photographer used for a model.

It must also be noted that a signifier may have many signifieds, and a signified may have many signifiers. Thus, the word 'remembrance', the herb rosemary, or an artificial poppy, as signifiers, may all have the abstract concept of remembrance as their signified. Similarly, the word 'rosemary' might well signify different concepts if used within a poem than if used in a cookery or botany book. The relationship between signifier and signified is thus recognised as largely arbitrary, and dependent on the cultural conventions that govern a particular sign system. [AE]

Further reading: Barthes 1967b.

simulacrum   Conventionally, a simulacrum is a copy of a copy in Plato's **ontology**. A copy is inferior to the ideal form of which it is a copy, while the simulacrum is further still from the form, and is therefore inferior to the straight copy. In particular, a drawing of an object, since it is a copy of the thing, which itself is simply a copy of the form, is undesirable because it contains less inherent truth about the form than the object itself.

In the wake of Nietzsche, some philosophers associated with the more extreme kinds of **postmodernism** have tended to stress the importance of the simulacrum. This is probably associated with their general aesthetic disposition. Jean Baudrillard has given particular importance to the simulacrum, while Gilles Deleuze and Jean-François Lyotard also took this approach, especially in their earlier works. The general consensus is that the simulacrum is not simply a copy of the copy: it somehow avoids contact with the ideal form. Given that the order of forms represents, for Plato, the rational ordering of the universe, the simulacrum comes to stand for that which is incommensurable with conceptual reason. [RC]

Further reading: Deleuze 1990.

social contract   A social contract theory envisages the drawing up of a contract between free individuals with a view to establishing the basic political, civil or moral principles of a community. A contract theory therefore aims to legitimise these principles by invoking the notion of consent. Through consent the contract lays claim to a form of authority which is derived from the agreement of those who undertake to be bound by it. A variety of philosophers have dealt with this notion: Hobbes, Locke and Rousseau all propounded social contract theories, while thinkers such as Hume, Hegel and

Marx have provided criticisms of this approach. (See also **liberalism**.) [PS]

Further reading: Boucher and Kelly 1994.

Social Darwinism   An appropriation of the evolutionary principles outlined in Charles Darwin's *Origin of Species* (1859), Social Darwinism was first propounded by Herbert Spencer (1820–1903). Spencer's theories in fact pre-date the publication of Darwin's own text; he first drew on contemporary science as a means of justifying his hypotheses, and later used Darwin's work in order to validate the authority of his own. Spencer's project aimed to integrate different disciplines (e.g. the then developing discipline of **sociology**, and the methods and theories of the physical sciences) within an evolutionary account of human **society**. Thus, whereas Darwin's model of evolution is concerned with physical fact (the realm of nature), Spencer's conception of evolution may be characterised by way of its claim to be a science of society.

Spencer holds that the evolutionary process is one in which there is a spontaneous 'change from incoherent homogeneity (i.e. unity) to a coherent hetereogeneity (i.e. diversity), accompanying the dissipation of motion and integration of matter' (*Structure, Function and Evolution*, 1971: 92). From this premise he constructs a depoliticised model of society which is both naturalised and ahistorical: left alone, society will regulate itself according to the principle of the 'survival of the fittest', which is driven by this movement towards increasing coherence and diversity. His view is highly conservative in its implications: hierarchical stability is considered by Spencer to be essential to the 'coherence' (i.e. stability) of **social structure**. Hence, any outbreak of social disorder which threatens hierarchy is conceived of as a negative force, akin to illness in the human body. Both are disorganising regressions and obstruct the evolutionary process by causing heterogeneity *without* coherence. Defining the production of disease in the human body, Spencer comments on how, in successive stages, 'lines of organisation, once so precise disappear' and parallels this description with social disorder, which is a 'loosing of those ties by which citizens are bound up into distinct classes and subclasses' (1971: 94). The 'survival of the fittest' is thereby taken as being fought out in the form of an economic and social struggle for existence, and the only justifiable attitude to matters of social organisation is one which lets the forces of progressive evolution take their course. Spencer held his view to be the most 'scientific' of philosophical theses because it could, he thought, be tested empirically. The theory attracted a number of adherents associated with **fascism**, most notably Nazi leader Adolph Hitler.

Leaving the question of the history of authoritarianism to one side, there are, of course, a number of objections to Spencer's evolutionary theory. For instance, although the 'survival of the fittest' principle may apply to nature, it is not clear that it is applicable in the same way, if at all, to the sphere of human **culture**. Also, recent empirical work in paleanteology has suggested that natural forms do not necessarily develop from states of relative 'simplicity' and homogeneity to states of 'complexity' and heterogeneous diversity. (See Stephen J. Gould's account of the enormous diversity of forms of life found in the Burgess Shale – a deposit of sedimentary rock around 530 million years old. Gould argues that, on this evidence, evolutionary history cannot be thought of as a straightforward progression towards increasing diversity and hetereogeneity, since the forms of animal design existing today represent a reduction of the number of designs found in the *older* Burgess Shale. Interestingly, Gould holds that seeking to explain why certain forms survived and others became extinct only in terms of which had 'better' body-designs will not work, since it is not always possible to see what perceptible advantages one Burgess form may have had over another. He argues that chance may play a key role in the process of evolution: run the clock of history again from the same starting point and it might turn out differently – i.e. there might have been no humans.) [PS]

Further reading: Appleman 1970; Gould 1991; Lacquer 1988; Spencer 1971.

social fact   In Durkheim's **sociology**, especially, a social fact is a social phenomenon that has a coercive effect upon the individual. Thus, although social facts may originally be the product of human action, they have developed an autonomy from their human authors, and now confront humans as something external to them, They have an objectivity akin to that of natural objects and physical laws. For Durkheim (1982), the goal of sociology is to study these facts. [AE]

socialisation   Socialisation is the process by which the individual learns to be a member of a particular society and **culture**, and thus to be a genuinely social and cultural being. The individual internalises his or her culture. While this process is of fundamental importance to understanding how cultures work, and particularly how they **reproduce** themselves over generations, the precise nature of socialisation has been theorised in widely different ways, and continues to be at the heart of an number of key debates over the nature of human being and human society.

In the **functionalist** tradition in **sociology** and **cultural anthropology**, socialisation adapts the individual to perform the social **roles** that will be expected of him or her. The newborn human was largely presupposed to be a blank slate (or tabula rasa), onto which society could inscribe almost any characteristics. These characteristics would include fundamental beliefs about the natural, social, and indeed supernatural worlds, along with an associated cosmology; **values** and preferences, be these aesthetic, culinary or moral (what else could explain Icelanders' ability to eat rotten shark?); the moral **norms** of which he or she would approve and by which he or she would abide and judge others; and his or her patterns of behaviour (including, most significantly, those patterns associated with **gender**). Thus, an individual's personality or **self** could be seen as a product of the particular society into which he or she was born.

Functionalism focused heavily upon the 'primary' socialisation that occurs in the family. As such, socialisation tended to be theorised as a process that was largely completed in the early years of childhood, and could be completed more or less well. If socialisation failed, the consequence would be that the individual would be ill-adapted to his or her society. This would lead to criminality or some other form of **deviance**, in that the individual would be unable to abide by the norms and goals valued within his or her society. This view was challenged, famously, by Denis Wrong (1980), as the 'over-socialised' view of human being. The view of socialisation thus changes, most notably in the **symbolic interactionist** tradition, to recognise that the individual is not simply a passive recipient of the process, and further that the process is not necessarily ever concluded. This tradition draws on the work of George Herbert Mead and Alfred Schutz. Mead (1934), for example, distinguishes between the 'I', as the unselfconscious subject that responds to the actions and attitudes of others, and the 'Me', as our self-understanding of ourselves as an object. Socialisation works, most significantly, through the 'Me', in so far as the individual actively assumes an organised set of attitudes from others, and thus comes to recognise him- or herself in terms of socially constructed concepts. This approach to socialisation recognises the space that individuals have to negotiate and challenges the values and beliefs with which they are confronted, in a struggle to make sense of the situations within which they find themselves, and thus in a struggle to understand and interpret their own self-identity.

Socialisation need not then be understood as a finite process, for the negotiation and struggle to find **meaning** in new and unpredictable situations, that is inherent in it, will continue throughout the individual's life. Socialisation in the family is followed, reinforced and challenged by the formal education of school; contact with equals and contemporaries; the **mass media**; participation in **subcultures**; and work. If socialisation is a continuing process, then it cannot easily be seen as successful or unsuccessful. The symbolic interactionist approach to socialisation may suggest that the apparent failure of socialisation may be the failure of the external culture to meet the needs of the individual, rather than that of the individual to meet the needs or expectations of society. Paradoxically, Willis (1977) has shown how the active resistance of underprivileged school boys to socialisation from school, leads to their socialisation into unskilled labour.

At the basis of the analysis of socialisation are complex, and possibly irresolvable questions concerning the relationship between **nature** and culture, and thus exactly how much an individual absorbs from his or her society (and thus the degree of malleability in human nature), and how much is innate or biologically determined. [AE]

Further reading: Berger 1963.

socialism　A political creed whose origins are normally traced back to the mid-nineteenth century. There have been many types of socialist (e.g. utopian socialists, Fabian socialists, Guild socialists) but they share in common an adherence to particular principles with regard to how human **society** should be organised. In contrast to **liberalism**, which advocates the primacy of the individual's liberty and rights, socialists have traditionally placed emphasis upon the importance of equality as a political principle. This is, in turn, expressed in terms of the importance of economic relationships within society. Socialists are particularly opposed to the **individualism** of liberal capitalist society, holding that a desirable form of social order (which would be based upon mutuality, co-operation and shared public ownership of the means of production) is not possible as long as human relationships are dominated by the self-interested and antagonistic principles which underlie **civil society**. In contrast to liberals, therefore, socialists see justice as a matter of how society is ordered with regard to the distribution of goods within it, not in terms of the guardianship of freedoms which enable individuals to pursue their own purposes. Socialism thus has much in common with communism with regard to its holding that the most desirable form of social organisation embodies principles of egalitarianism. However, whereas advocates of communism traditionally adhere to a theoretical perspective derived from Marx's claim that his analysis of the development of capitalist societies pertains to a scientific status, which in turn holds that proletarian revolution is the inevitable outcome of class antagonisms, socialism has tended to be more pragmatic and less confrontational in its approach. Socialists have, for example, emphasised the importance of democratic procedures within the political process.

Socialism like communism can be defined as an internationalism. This tendency can be traced back to the organisation (by Marx) of the First Socialist International in London in 1864, although the spirit of unity embodied by this event gave way to fragmentation into opposed groups (socialists, communists, anarchists) by the time of the Second International, nearly a quarter of a century later. The international aspect of socialism can be seen in its adherence to values associated with **humanism**, for instance, the notion of a universal conception of value with regard to such things as the establishment of supranational mutuality, shared norms of justice and human rights between different nations. [PS]

Further reading: Berki 1975; Crozier 1987; Forman 1973.

social mobility   Social mobility refers to the movement of individuals between hierarchical social groups, most typically between **classes**. Study of social mobility is an important complement to studies of **social stratification**, because a hierarchical society may not be considered undesirable if there is free movement between the different levels of the hierarchy. Such free movement would suggest that the ruling class or **elite** may not be a closed and self-serving group, and similarly, a person born in the lower strata of society is not condemned to a life of relative powerlessness and low income. However, Marxist approaches to social mobility have long suggested that the ruling class will recruit the most able members of the lower classes into its ranks in order to prevent them becoming effective agents of revolution. [AE]

Further reading: Heath 1981.

365

social stratification   The differentiation of society into separate groupings becomes social stratification when these groupings can be seen as forming a hierarchy. Traditionally, in **sociology**, three major types of strata have been recognised. In a caste system, different strata are characterised in terms of ethnic purity, with no movement between castes (so that a person lives his or her entire life within the caste into which he or she is born). In an estate system, typical of **feudal** societies, again there is little or no mobility between strata. The estates are defined through land ownership (on the part of the dominant stratum) and bondage. In industrial societies, stratification is in terms of **class**, with classes understood as economically defined. Class hierarchies formally allow for **social mobility** (although the actual amount of mobility and thus the real opportunities to leave the class of one's birth, may be restricted through unequal access to economic and cultural resources, such as education). Disputes continue, firstly over the relevant criteria for defining class. In the Marxist tradition, two major classes are identified and distinguished in terms of ownership and control of the **means of production**. (In **Marxism**, estates and castes are subsumed within the concept and theory of class, being understood as different forms that class and exploitation take in different historical epochs.) In other sociological traditions, defining class in terms of occupation allows for a more subtle and comprehensive account of social stratification. However, it is not clear that other hierarchies, such as power, material reward and **status** necessarily map onto class hierarchies in any simple manner. (Thus, as Max Weber noted, the *nouveaux riches* may have the income and wealth typical of the highest class, yet they will not have the status or respect that traditionally attends old money.) Further, a predominantly economic analysis of social stratification can fail to recognise the significance of other hierarchical social groupings, such as **gender** and **ethnicity**. [AE]

Further reading: Scott 1996.

social structure   While social structure is one of the most widely used of concepts in sociology and social theory, and indicates some regular and stable patterning of social action and social **institutions**, its precise meaning is not easily determined. While 'structure' itself may be defined as the organising relationships between parts in a whole, and in social structure the whole is **society** (albeit that 'society' is by no means an unproblematic term), the parts or elements of the whole may be variously understood. In the organic analogy, whereby society is compared to an organism, the elements are institutions which perform functions, necessary to the survival and stability of the whole. Thus, in **functionalism**, social structure may be understood as a set of relationships between institutions. Conversely, the elements may be understood as **roles**, or as variously defined (or self-defining) groups within the society. The validity of the concept may however be challenged. While critical theorists, such as the first generation members of the **Frankfurt School**, tend to adopt the concept very much in the sense in which it is used in functionalism, they do not treat it as a value neutral description of society. That society is structured, and that these structures can confront the individual as natural forces, constraining and determining their action, is taken to be indicative of a **reified** and thus false society. Conversely, the existence of social structures is denied altogether by certain micro-social theories, such as **ethnomethodology**. This is to reject the idea of any social entity existing independently, or prior to, individuals' mundane competence to produce that entity (through common acknowledgement of each others' skills and practices) in social **interaction**. Thus, while particular interactions may be structured, in the sense of being ordered and meaningful events, this order is produced, spontaneously and co-operatively by the agents involved, and is not determined by some independent mechanism. [AE]

Further reading: Crothers 1996; Merton 1968.

society   In its modern sense, an arrangement of **institutions**, modes of relationship, forms of organisation, **norms**, etc. constituting an interrelated whole within which a group of humans live. That said, there is no simple definition which will fit all theories with equal ease. How one understands the term usually depends upon how one conceives of the distinction between the **individual** and society. Traditional **liberalism** (e.g. Locke, Mill, Rawls) conceives of society as a collection of free agents whose properties and characteristics are constituted independently of the modes of relationship which operate within any particular context. Thus, society is not coterminous with the individual, and the institutions which go to ground social relations are independent of the individual's **identity**. **Communitarian** critics have argued against the liberal view, asserting that there is a necessary link between being a social entity and any conception of the **self** we might have. Marxists traditionally view society in terms of the history of economic and institutional relationships (the economic base-structure and ideological superstructure) which have exerted a determinant effect on **class** interests and differences, and would likewise oppose the liberal conception.

Writers associated with **fascism** also attacked the view that individuals could be contrasted with society. On the fascist model, the assertion of a fundamental division between individual and society embodies a 'mechanistic' attitude, which is opposed to the unity of collectivity and tradition which underlies the organic whole that makes up human relationships. Equally, **conservatives** (e.g. Edmund Burke) have often discussed society in terms of the organic unity of its traditions and, in contrast to the liberal conception of it as an aggregate of individuals, have used this to argue that the life of society must be preserved by way of safe-guarding these traditions.

Within **sociology** (the science which studies society) a similar contrast is detectable. Thus, functionalism shares in common with the conservative viewpoint an adherence to the organic model; while the Weberian and **interactionist** approaches tend to view society in terms of the abilities of individuals to make sense of their social environment and react to it in an independent way. [PS]

Further reading: Frisby and Sayer 1985; Welford 1967.

sociobiology   While the term sociobiology was in use in the 1940s, it came to popular attention as the title of Edward O. Wilson's synthesis of recent work in population biology, ecology and the study of invertebrate and vertebrate animal behaviour, *Sociobiology: The New Synthesis* (1975). The book (and its proposed discipline) caused a public sensation because Wilson extended methods for studying animal behaviour, that had been developed in the biological sciences, to the study of human beings. Sociobiology is controversial, precisely because it offers an approach to the study of **culture** that is radically at odds with a number of basic assumptions made in such social sciences as **sociology** and **cultural anthropology**.

Sociobiology had its real origins in a paper, by W.D. Hamilton (1964), that offered an evolutionary explanation of self-sacrificial behaviour in animals. The problem for evolutionary biology was this. An individual member of a species should be striving to pass its particular genes on to the next generation. To do this, it must reproduce. Yet there are plentiful cases of individual animals sacrificing themselves, prior to reproduction, in order to allow other members of the species to survive and reproduce. This self-sacrifice, if a genetically determined trait, should die out (precisely because it is not being passed on). Hamilton accounted for the survival and spread of genes that determine such altruistic behaviour by recognising the importance of kinship. The animal that sacrifices itself will be close kin with the animal it saves. If they are close kin, they will share many genes, including the genes for altruism. The altruistic animal is then, after all, protecting it own genes, or at least the sort of genes that have made it the animal it is. (This insight has led most famously to Richard Dawkins's (1976) account of the 'selfish gene', and thus the proposal that individual animals are merely the bearers and instruments of their genes. As an aside, this is an interesting bit of anti-**humanism** – or is if applied to human beings – and as such is not so different, at least in form, to the anti-humanism of Lacan's **structuralist psychoanalysis** – where human subjects are determined by the structures of language – or Althusser's structuralist **Marxism** – where subjects are bearers of ideological and economic structures.)

This new approach to evolutionary explanation was widely applied in biology, for example to problems of how animals choose mates, optimise their chances of reproductive success, or develop successful strategies in foraging for food. The problem as far as human beings go is that it appears to reduce some of the most noble and valued characteristics of human life, morality and altruism, to a matter of genetics and evolutionary survival, at the expense of free human choice. Nature appears to be completely dominant over nurture (or **socialisation**). The possibility that human nature could be transformed, over history, through the development and change of **culture** is seemingly denied or side-lined. In practice, few if any sociobiologists would actually deny the influence of culture over human life (even if particular analyses frequently seem to be insensitive to the cultural and historical construction of **gender** and **sexuality**, for example). What sociobiology does is to pose important, and at times uncomfortable, questions about the biological heritage of human beings, or the relationship between the biological (or genetic) and the cultural and artificial in human life.

What is perhaps most disturbing about sociobiology, or at least sociobiology at its least sensitive and most territorial, is its assumption that sociology (cultural anthropology and presumably cultural studies) can be reduced to (or replaced by) biology. Sociobiology appears to be informed by a crude **philosophy of science** that assumes that the only way to account for any phenomenon (be it natural or social) is through explanatory models that are associated with the natural sciences. The alternative methodologies of the social and cultural sciences, not least in so far as they focus on problems of **meaning**, interpretation and **ideology**, are ignored, misunderstood or ridiculed. If this crude understanding of the nature of science and scientific inquiry is dealt with, cultural studies might find that questions of importance for human society can be stimulated by the study of ants. [AE]

Further reading: Wilson 1994.

sociology   Sociology is the study of **society**. (The word is derived from the Latin for companion (*socius*) and the Greek *logos*, for study or reason, and was coined by the French **positivist** philosopher, August Comte, around 1830.) In practice, this simple definition is rather uninformative, first because there are clearly other **disciplines** that study part of the whole of society (for example, economics, history, geography, political science), so that the precise meaning of 'society' is left unclear, and second because it says nothing about the manner of this study. The history of sociology may, in consequence, be seen as an extended debate over precisely these issues: What is society? and, How is it to be studied?

It is usual to cite Karl Marx (1818–83), Emile Durkheim (1858–1917) and Max Weber (1864–1920) as the three founders of sociology (with Georg Simmel (1858–1918) sometimes being included, depending upon current fashion). Indeed, it is fair to say that most of the approaches and problems in contemporary sociology can be traced back to some problem raised by these founders. From Durkheim, there arises a tradition of sociology that grounds itself as a science (closely modelled on the natural sciences of either physics or biology), and understands society as a form of objective reality. Society is seen as having a reality over and above that of the individuals from whom it is composed. A sociological explanation cannot then be broken down into an explanation grounded in the psychology of individual human beings. Rather, a genuinely sociological explanation will appeal to regularities and laws that exist uniquely at the level of society, and of which ordinary members of society need not even be aware. (Durkheim's own spectacular illustration of this phenomenon concerns suicide. While suicide is a uniquely personal and isolated act, the annual number of suicides occurring within a given society are more or less constant. This suggests that the individual decision is actually influenced by overarching social forces.) Durkheim's approach to sociology led to **functionalism**, the approach that was dominant in America until the 1960s. Functionalism drew on the analogy of society to an organism (see **organic analogy**), to argue that the key feature of any society was its ability to maintain its stability and form over many generations (akin to the homeostasis of organisms). The various parts or **institutions** within a society were therefore explained in terms of the contribution that they made to that continued stability. All social institutions therefore have specific functions.

In contrast to Durkheim, who very much saw himself as a sociologist, Weber's intellectual affiliations are broader (encompassing law, history and economics). His approach to sociology can, however, be characterised by a central concern with the development (and technical superiority) of western European civilisation particularly in terms of its **rationality**. He is less concerned with universal laws of social organisation than with the specific conditions that led to the rise of **capitalism** in western Europe, and not elsewhere. His work is thus a good deal more historically sensitive than Durkheim's. Further, Weber's approach to sociology as a discipline owes less to the natural sciences, and more to the methods of historical interpretation (or **hermeneutics**). Weber is concerned to empathise with social actors, and grounds explanations in the motivations and meanings that they ascribe to particular situations, and the way in which they then respond. In effect, while functionalist approaches to sociology tend to reduce the individual actor to a mere tool of the **social structure**, and thus a creature that needs little skill or awareness, for it meekly acts as society tells it to, Weber presents individuals as having social competence. This approach is taken up in the work of **interactionists**, such as Alfred Schutz (who is also influenced by Husserl's **phenomenology**), and the **symbolic interactionists**. These schools of sociology placed great emphasis on the ability of individuals, acting with and in response to other individuals, to construct and make sense of the social world about them. Society is not then seen as some special form of objective reality that simply constrains individuals (as it is by Durkheim and the functionalists), but rather is presented as a product of **intersubjective** action. (This approach is pursued to its theoretical extreme in **ethnomethodology**.) While phenomenological and interactionist schools of sociology had flourished at least since the 1930s (for example, in the Chicago School), they came to the fore of sociological work only in the 1960s, displacing functionalism.

Marxism has, in certain respects, a marginal role in the history of sociology. Its initial influence was possibly most strongly felt as the form of sociological explanation to which Weber reacted. Thus, Weber's own approach to the explanation of the origin of capitalism (that placed a central emphasis on the role of cultural and especially religious factors as stimulants to social change) challenged Marx's materialist account. Similarly, Weber developed a many-layered account of **social stratification**, in contrast to Marx's exclusive emphasis on **class**. Despite, or perhaps because of, this tension, the core developments of Marxism in western Europe in the first half of this century came about through a fusion of Marx and Weber, for example in the work of Georg Lukács and in the **Frankfurt School**. A Marxist sociology entered the mainstream of sociological debate, at least in the English speaking world, in the 1960s and 1970s, not least through the assimilation of the French structuralist Althusser and the recovery of the work of the Italian Marxist Gramsci.

Sociology in the 1970s, and at least in the British case, sociology as the intellectual context from which a significant part of cultural studies developed, was a rich source of conceptual and theoretical tools for the analysis of social and also cultural life. The rise of forms of interactionism and phenomenology had shifted sociology away from large-scale social structures, to allow an emphasis on the competence of ordinary human beings, and thus the importance of everyday life. The re-emergence of Marxism (along with the rise of **feminism**) complemented this focus, by providing new tools to analyse power relations (the lack of which had always been a weakness of interactionism), and **culture**. The theorisation of **ideology** and **hegemony** by Althusser and Gramsci opened up a new awareness of the way in which culture is the outcome and site of negotiation between conflicting social groupings.

The difficulty of generating a single, coherent approach to sociology, that can encompass the insights of macro-sociologists (such as the functionalists and Marxists), along with those of the micro-sociologists (the phenomenologists and interactionists), continues to be a central concern of sociological theory. The work of Jürgen Habermas (on the relationship of society as an objectified system, to the everyday experience of the **life-world**), and the work Anthony Giddens developed on **structuration**, represent important attempts to respond to this problem. (See also: **agency/structure**.) [AE]

Further reading: Bilton *et al.* 1996; Bocock *et al.* 1980; Elias 1970; Giddens 1997.

sociology of knowledge and culture   Sociological approaches to knowledge, science and art have posed fundamental challenges to orthodox understandings of the nature and **value** of these activities and their products. Scientific knowledge, for example, would aspire to be valid independently of the particular society or culture in which it was produced. While such knowledge may be refutable (which is to say that it may well be revised or improved upon in the future), the assumption would be that such improvement would come about through better observation or accumulation of information from the external world. The value of scientific knowledge would therefore depend upon the degree to which it corresponds to how an external and independent world really is. Similarly, orthodox **aesthetics**, at least since Kant's *Critique of Judgement* was published at the end of the eighteenth century, tends to presuppose that the value of a work of art lies in the degree to which it expresses or possesses some ahistorical aesthetic value. Equally, the art work is understood as the product of genius, and genius transcends the restrictions of its age. The value, and indeed **production**, of works of art is therefore indifferent to the social conditions of the audience or artist. **Sociology** challenges these assumptions, by suggesting that knowledge and cultural artefacts are fundamentally conditioned by the societies within which they are produced.

While the concept of the 'sociology of knowledge' was coined by the German philosopher Max Scheler in the 1920s (1980), elements of a sociology of knowledge were already present in the work of Karl Marx and Emile Durkheim. Marx's analysis of society according to the **metaphor** of the **base and superstructure** (where the base is the economic activity in society and the superstructure is composed of legal and cultural forms) suggested that different economic formations could lead to different cultures, not least in so far as these cultures were involved in the **class** struggle as forms of **ideology**. Durkheim (1976) (along with the **cultural anthropologist** Marcel Mauss (1966)), through the study of the social organisation and classificatory systems of small-scale pre-industrial societies, argued, perhaps even more radically, that the very way in which we perceive reality (down to our experience of time and space) was conditioned by our social experience. Thus, where Kant, in his theory of knowledge, had argued that our experience of time and space depend on the way in which the universal human mind structures experience, Durkheim argues that the human mind is itself socially structured, and thus people from different cultures will experience the world differently (or more radically, that they will live in different worlds). For the Marxist Lukács, the experience of time and space that Kant takes to be fundamental and universal is in fact a product of life in **capitalism**, with its **division of labour** and the spatial and temporal disciplines of the factory.

Karl Mannheim (1960) developed Marx's account of ideology into a sociology of knowledge. He extended Marx's concern with a purely economic base, in order to suggest that different groups in society will experience the world differently, and will therefore accept different claims as knowledge. Mannheim's approach appears to open the way to a cultural **relativism**, such that there is no knowledge that can be deemed true, independently of the social standpoint in which it is produced and used. The relativistic implications of the sociology of knowledge were boosted by the influence of Thomas Kuhn's **philosophy of science** on sociology (1970).

Kuhn argued that scientific inquiry depended not simply, or even primarily, on independent observation of an external world, but rather upon a **paradigm** or set of assumptions (about the nature of that world, and about the nature of science and scientific knowledge) that would structure any experience of the world. It is a small step from the theory of paradigms, to the argument that paradigms themselves depend upon wider social and cultural conditions. Thus, it may be observed that Newton's conception of absolute time and space depended, not upon observation, but upon prior theological and cosmological beliefs. (More concretely, Newton apparently observed only five colours in the spectrum. Being influenced by alchemy and the magical significance of numbers, he added two extra colours to get to the magical seven.) At its extreme, the sociology of science may therefore advocate that science constructs the physical world, rather than responds to an independent world.

If science falls to the sociological assault with such apparent ease, art is an even softer target. The production and consumption of art can readily be placed within a political and economic context. Thus, prior to the rise of a **market** for the arts, most noticeably in seventeenth and eighteenth century Europe, much that is now regarded as art had a clear and unproblematic social function. (Music, for example, could serve to structure the ritual movements of a religious service, or maintain co-ordination within a group of workers. The visual arts, more indirectly, might serve as ostentatious displays of the wealth and power of their patrons.) With the rise of a middle-class market in art, art comes to appear as something that is useless. It does not have the instrumental utility of other **commodities**. The contemporary development of **aesthetics** has therefore been interpreted as a response to this problem. The attribution of aesthetic value serves, on the one hand, to justify the consumption of something that is otherwise useless, and on the other hand, promotes the economic value of the art work (see Bourdieu 1984). More subtly, and in line with the sociology of knowledge, the work of art may be seen to articulate the values and worldview of particular social groups.

(Thus, the **Frankfurt School** theorist Lowenthal approaches literature as an expression of class ideologies and strives to account for 'the extent to which particular social structures find expression in individual literary works and what function these works perform in society' (1989: 44). His analysis of Knut Hamson's novels, for example, places them in relation to an authoritarian cult of nature (1978).)

While the extreme positions in the sociology of knowledge and culture may reduce the value of both knowledge and art to mere functions or effects of some social or political base, the more complex approaches attempt to incorporate socio-logical insight into the more traditional concerns of interpre-tation and criticism. Thus, art historians such as Tim Clark (1973) and Baxandall (1980) (following on a tradition of inter-pretation that runs back, at least, to the work of the Warburg Institute in the 1930s), or musicologists such as Treitler (1989) and Tomlinson (1984) have drawn significantly on sociologi-cal approaches to enrich the reading of art. Perhaps pre-eminently, within the Frankfurt School, T.W. Adorno's aesthetic theory (1984) and theory of knowledge (1967) revolve about the recognition of the **dialectical** tension between the autonomy of art and science on one hand, and their status as '**social facts**' (and thus the legitimate subject-matter of sociological analysis) on the other. [AE]

Further reading: Meja and Stehr 1990; Wolff 1981.

speech act A speech act is an action which is performed *when* a word is uttered. Speech act theory is derived from the work of British philosopher J.L. Austin (1911–60), and has been taken up subsequently by philosophers, linguists, literary theorists and even psychologists. Austin distinguishes between different classes of words which perform different functions. Thus, he holds that the activity of uttering words is a complex matter which can in turn be analysed in terms of the indi-vidual functions of various types of word. Austin's analysis concentrates on everyday language, which is used in as direct and literal a manner as possible.

In outlining his theory, Austin was resisting the view of **language** (put forward by, for example, exponents of **positivism**) which held that all meaningful sentences or propositions which declare something are descriptions of states of affairs ('constatives') and hence either true or false. Austin's point is that some parts of language express meanings which may be neither true nor false. These Austin terms 'performative utterances'. Performatives are those utterances with which people do things like make promises, warn others, make declarations, etc. (e.g. 'I promise I will give you the money', 'Look out!', 'I name this ship . . .'). Performatives do not pertain to truth conditions, but are conventional (i.e. they are either appropriate or inappropriate). However, Austin does not rest content with the constative/performative distinction. Instead he complicates the distinction by attempting to show that there is a sense in which constatives can pertain to a performative status, and *vice versa*. On this model, *all* utterances are susceptible to being described as speech acts in so far as any fact-stating utterance can be re-phrased in the form 'I hereby assert that . . .' (i.e. all language use can be viewed as speech acts).

John Searle has developed Austin's theories by attempting to stipulate the particular rules specific to different forms of speech act. On this view, a promise can be characterised as necessarily involving some form or other of future action; additionally, it must be about something that the person promising would not do in any case, and must involve consideration of the intentions of the promiser, who is undertaking to be bound by that promise. Prominent amongst those who have been influenced by speech act theory is German philosopher and critical theorist Jürgen Habermas, who has turned to the notion of performativity as a means of elucidating his theory of 'communicative action'. The notion of speech acts is significant not least because it offers an approach to issues concerning **meaning** which can be contrasted with those theories that draw upon the heritage of **structuralism** (i.e. **post–structuralism**). This may explain its appeal to Habermas who, against thinkers such as Lyotard, has used the notion of perfomativity to argue that a normative model of communal consensus is fundamental to both the functioning, and the reproduction, of the conditions necessary for human existence. [PS]

Further reading: Austin 1975; Searle 1969.

state of nature   A conception deployed by a number of political philosophers of different persuasions (e.g. Thomas Hobbes, John Locke, Jean-Jacques Rousseau). In brief, a state of nature theory envisages the human individual in a state of existence outside the constraints of civil society or civilisation. In Hobbes's *Leviathan* (1651) the state of nature is famously described in violent terms, a form of life devoid of the rule of law and entailing the 'war of all against all'. In this state, individuals have absolute freedom to pursue their own ends, but unfortunately so do others. Without the rule of law, it follows, the individual has no rights of protection beyond their own physical capabilities to defend themselves. Hobbes uses this view as a means of arguing that it is reasonable to trade-off individual freedom in return for the protection afforded by an absolute monarch (the leviathan of the book's title) through the establishment of a **social contract**. Equally, for Locke and Rousseau the state of nature is one which prefigures the bonds of civil society. On the Lockean view, individuals in the state of nature possess rights which are God-given (namely, the right to self-protection, the possession of their own bodies, and the right to own the products of their labour). With the growth of property ownership, Locke argues, individuals seek to protect their interests through the formulation of a social contract which grants legal protection to these rights – although, contrary to Hobbes, he is clear about the fact that, on his view, individuals do not as a consequence divest themselves of all their rights. Interestingly, Locke claims that a state of nature still exists in the relationships which exist between absolute monarchs or nation-states. Rousseau in constructing a state of nature narrative in his *Discourse on Inequality* (1754) was more interested in deploying an heuristic device (he writes at the beginning of the work of his interest being in humans as they are now) with the aim of laying bare the social injustices of contemporary civilisation. His account envisages the emergence of humans from the state of nature into a state of tribal social organisation (that of the 'noble savage') and the subsequent development of an unjust and corrupt **civil society** which ensues from the institution of property. A more recent exponent of the state of nature theory is Robert Nozick (see **liberterianism**); whilst a variant of it is offered by John Rawls's use of the notion of the 'original position' to ground his conception of justice (see **liberalism**). [PS]

Further reading: Hobbes 1994; Locke 1988; Rousseau 1984.

status   Social status refers to the prestige and honour publicly ascribed to particular positions and occupations within society. The possibility of identifying a hierarchy of status groups within society, that would strictly be independent of **class** hierarchies, was recognised by Max Weber (1946c, 1946d). The classic example is that of priests and other religious professionals in contemporary society, whose status is disproportionate to their income or political power (although it may be indicative of their influence on the formation of public opinion). Status groups may be expected to have distinctive **lifestyles**, including patterns of behaviour, belief systems, and patterns of preference and **consumption**. For Weber a caste system was representative of a hierarchy of status groups, not of classes. Crucially, social status is to be understood as the prestige that is ascribed to the social position, which need not necessarily correspond to an individual member's self-perception. [AE]

Further reading: Turner 1988; Weber 1978.

stereotype   A stereotype is an oversimplified and usually value-laden view of the attitudes, behaviour and expectations of a group or individual. Such views, which may be deeply embedded in **sexist**, **racist** or otherwise **prejudiced cultures**, are typically highly resistant to change, and play a significant role in shaping the attitudes of members of the culture to others. Within cultural studies, the role of stereotypes is possibly most marked in the products of the **mass media** (including the portrayal of women and ethnic minorities in drama and **comedy**, and in the shaping and construction of news coverage), although they are also significant in education, work and sport (in channelling individuals into activities deemed appropriate to their stereotyped group). [AE]

Further reading: Macrae *et al.* 1996; Oakes *et al.* 1994.

stigma   A stigma is a culturally recognised attribute that is used to differentiate and discredit a person. The stigma may be physical (a bodily deformity), behavioural (for example, a sexual preference), or social (in the sense of membership of a group). The identification of the stigma is used to reduce the person from a complex whole, to a single, tainted and discounted trait, upon which all social **interaction** with the person will be based. (See also **stereotype**.) [AE]

Further reading: Goffman 1963; Page 1984.

structuralism   A methodological approach which has been employed in a wide range of fields (e.g. the social sciences, anthropology, literary criticism). It is generally accepted that structuralism can be traced back to Ferdinand de Saussure's book *Course in General Linguistics* (1916), although the term itself was coined by Russian structuralist theorist Roman Jakobson. In his work Saussure attempted to construct a scientific account of the process of **signification** which he termed **semiotics** – the **science** of **signs**. On Saussure's view, all **language** (the definition of which includes forms of **communication** other than simply spoken language) can be analysed as a structural system of relations. Saussure held that **meaning** is determined by this relation, rather than by the referential function of the signs in language. A sign is thus held to have meaning because of its relationship to the other words, not because it refers to a particular object. In turn, Saussure argued for the view that language could be described in terms of one fundamental distinction: that between **langue** and **parole**. Langue constitutes the fundamental structural element of language (the network of meanings which must be in place at any given time if a speaker is to be able to speak), parole the actual use of these elements as they are actualised within any individual utterance.

An important notion within structuralism is that of **binary opposition**, which in effect contends that meaning is determined by the oppositional relationship which inheres between different signs (good–bad, light–dark, etc.) and exerts a fundamental determining force on the construction of meaning. This, on Jakobson's view, at least, has been taken to constitute the fundamental structure of any language. This notion has led to the development of a number of critical approaches – for instance, that of structuralist literary criticism, which has sought to use the notion of opposition as a means of scientifically decoding the organisation of meanings which are to be found in literary **texts**. Thus, there is an explicit commitment to the view that an objective, universal account of meaning can be used in order to uncover the particular meanings hidden within texts. Likewise, the structuralism of anthropologist Claude Lévi-Strauss concentrates on seeking to elucidate the universal structures which operate in human **society** and **culture**, while Louis Althusser's structural-**Marxism** sought to rearticulate the ideas of Marx within a structuralist framework (most notably in his account of the nature of **ideology**).

Structuralism can therefore be described as an attempt to elucidate the objective conditions which constitute all linguistic and social relations. As such, it put forward a claim to be regarded as an objective science. The emphasis on structure has often led exponents of structuralism to take a critical stance towards **empiricism** and **humanism**. This is basically due to the structuralist presupposition that meaning is a matter of nothing more than the causal relationships which pertain within a given structure. Thus, such questions as those pertaining to matters of human agency, individual or shared interests, **community**, etc., have generally been either ignored by structuralists or explained within the confines of the structural–causal framework of analysis.

A number of criticisms of the structuralist approach are possible. Thus, in the wake of structuralism itself, an attack on the purported **objectivity** of its methods of analysis was made by such writers as philosopher Jacques Derrida (see, for example, his essay 'Force and Signification' in *Writing and Difference* (1967)), or literary theorist Roland Barthes (both of whom came to be associated with **post-structuralism**). Such criticisms began by casting doubt on the notion that there is a fixed and universal structure of linguistic or social relations. Other criticisms, however, can be made. For instance, the relationship between structure and **agency** as it is articulated within the confines of structuralist analysis could be accused of embodying a reductive approach to questions concerning how subjectivity is constituted. Likewise, structuralism has difficulty accommodating the fact of change: if meaning is determined by rigid structures, then how history is possible is a question which falls outside the domain of a structuralist mode of analysis. For if these structures themselves are subject to change then either (i) the process of change must be an immanent feature of any such structure – which implies that the very notion of 'structure' is itself a problematic one, or (ii) change itself is external to structure, and hence structure is not decisive with regard to the constitution of social relations or meanings but is itself subject to some other causal factors that are different in kind. Also, the 'meaning is use' thesis advocated by the later Wittgenstein (admittedly a thesis which has its own problems) might be opposed to the view that meaning is a structural matter, for what constitutes 'use' need not necessarily be defined in terms of the structural metaphor. Likewise, the notion of binary opposition is highly problematic: it is not clear, for instance, that it makes much sense to assert that the meaning of a sentence like 'This is a closed door' is the binary opposite of the sentence 'This is an open door'. [PS]

Further reading: Clarke 1981; Culler 1975; Derrida 1978; Harland 1987; Jameson 1972; Kurzweil 1980; Lévi-Strauss 1968a, 1977; Pettit 1975; Saussure 1983; Sturrock 1979.

structuration Structuration is a concept and theory, developed by the British social theorist Anthony Giddens, that is offered as an explanation of the relationship between individual human agency and the stable and patterned properties of society as a whole. On the one hand, orthodox social theories such as **functionalism** or **structuralism** tended exclusively to emphasise the organised nature of society, so that society was presented as existing independently of the agents who composed it (and indeed, as a force that constrained and determined their actions, much as natural forces do). On the other hand, another strand of social theory (including **symbolic interactionism** and **hermeneutics**) emphasised the skills of social agents in creating and managing the social world in which they lived. Giddens recognises a partial truth in both extremes, for society is patterned, so that the isolated and self-interested actions of its individual members take on the appearance of having been planned or co-ordinated. Annual social statistics, for example, show remarkable stability for the occurrence of many everyday events and activities. Furthermore, precisely because this stability and order is outside the control of individual agents, society does appear to constrain and control them. However, agents are highly competent, with a vast stock of knowledge and range of skills that allow them to make sense of complex and often unique situations, and to manage their relationships with others.

Giddens therefore talks of the 'duality of structure'. **Social structure**, which is to say, the organised and enduring character of social life, is dual in that it is at once external to the society's members, and internal (constituting the agent as a competent member of society). As Giddens rather cryptically puts it, 'the structural properties of social systems are both medium and outcome of the practices they recursively organise' (1984: 25). The social structure exists primarily as the competence that the society's members have to organise their own social life. Social structure is thus a set of rules and resources available to the competent agent. It exists in agents' memories. The crucial point that Giddens makes, though, is that agents do not have to be consciously aware of this. A great deal of their competence is non-discursive, which is to say that agents would not be able to give a verbal account of what they know. They do, however, know how to 'go on' in a given situation. They have 'practical consciousness'. In practice, the social structure is then realised as something external to the agents. The consequences of the agents' actions in a particular situation are likely to go beyond anything that is simply intended by them. Giddens draws on geography as well as sociology to analyse the external stability of social structures as **institutional** relations that are articulated across time and space. It is important to the agent that social structure does confront him or her as something external. Giddens' concept of 'ontological security' captures this. Competent social agents are confident that the social and natural worlds (and indeed their own **self**-identity in relation to those worlds) is stable and secure. The world is made a matter of routine. Anything that disrupts this expectation of the routine is highly disturbing (and a feature exploited in Goffman's analysis of embarrassment, and in the 'breaching experiments' carried out by **ethnomethodologists**).

In summary, Giddens presents social life (and centrally the **reproduction** of society) as a circle. Agents interact with others. Their taken-for-granted social competence allows them to make sense of the situation, and to carry on within it, according to routine practices. Agents thereby create (and sustain) the very conditions that make their social action possible. Their knowledge of society and social competence is thereby regenerated (along with society) by the very success with which they conduct the interaction, or repair difficulties encountered within it. (See also **agency and structure**.) [AE]

Further reading: Cohen 1989; Giddens 1984; Held and Thompson 1990.

style 'Style' has many meanings, or nuances of meaning. Consider the association of style with fashion, or with a style of dress (whether it is a stylish style or not); or style in the performance of music, so that one may perform with style or just in a style that is distinguishable from other styles. These examples suggest a value-laden use of 'style', in which it refers to some preferred **aesthetic value**, and a more neutral sense, in which it suggests a meaningful combination of elements (be these the components of dress, of musical performance, of literary writing, or whatever). In the neutral sense of style, the choice of elements and the rules by which they can be combined may be analysed as **semiotic codes**. As such, styles may be understood as expressive of the values and **identity** of social groups. (See also **subculture**.) [AE]

subculture The concept of a 'subculture', at its simplest, refers to the **values**, beliefs, **attitudes** and **life-style** of a minority (or 'sub-') group within society. The **culture** of this group will diverge from, although be related to, that of the dominant group. Although now associated in large part with the cultures of young people (mods and rockers, skinheads, **punks**), it may also be applied to **ethnic**, **gender** and **sexual** groups. The concept was in fact developed largely through work in the **sociology** of **deviance** (referring, for example, to the culture of 'delinquents', criminals or drug-users). An early explanation of the behaviour of working-class delinquents, saw it as youths over-conforming to the working-class values of their parents (such as toughness and masculinity, cunning as against gullibility, risk-taking), and that in over-conforming, they come to violate the dominant norms of middle-class culture (Miller 1958).

The concept of 'subculture' is important, precisely because it allows recognition of the diversity of cultures within a society. While the older concept of **youth culture** tended to assume a single, homogeneous, culture amongst young people, the subcultural approach stresses the fragmentation of that culture, especially along class lines. As with the concept of '**counterculture**', 'subculture' tends to presuppose some form of resistance to the dominant culture. However, 'counterculture' increasingly comes to refer to groups that are able to provide an intellectual justification and account of their position. Subcultures articulate their opposition principally through exploiting the **significance** of **styles** of dress and patterns of behaviour (or **rituals**). (**Semiotic** approaches, decoding the dress and behaviour of subcultures, have therefore been highly influential. The skinhead's dress of braces, cropped hair and Doc Martins makes sense as a comment upon an imagined industrial past, and as an attempt to come to terms with powerlessness in the face of a predominantly middle-class culture, in which the skinhead has neither the financial nor the cultural resources to participate.) The subculture may therefore be seen to negotiate a cultural space, in which the contradictory demands of the dominant parent culture can be worked through, or resisted, and in which the group can express and develop its own **identity**. The subcultural approach can therefore be characterised by its sympathy with the position of the subculture, suggesting that subcultures are an important source of cultural variation and diversity – as opposed to the implicit or explicit condemnation of subcultural activity that accompanied earlier studies of deviance.

The sixties mods offer a neat illustration of a subculture and its analysis. Mods may be characterised by their concern with fashion and **consumption**, and a hedonist life-style. Typically, the mod was employed in low grade, non-manual (clerical) work. The mod is thus very much part of his or her time, responding to the increased consumerism of the 1960s, and the shift in economy from traditional manual and manufacturing work, to non-manual, service industry. Indeed, the mod takes consumerism to its limits. Unlike so many other subcultures, the mod is disturbing, not because he or she shuns the 'parent' culture's demands for smart dress, but because he or she is just too smart. The problem faced by the mod is that employment (that is traditionally associated with a work ethic of self-denial and self-discipline) is at once necessary, in order to pay for a hedonistic life-style, and yet at odds with the life-style (for self-discipline is the opposite of hedonism). The mod therefore conforms to the paradoxical demands of consumerism and work, through the use of amphetamines.

Certain criticisms have been made against the subcultural approach as it has developed within cultural studies. It has been seen to be overly selective in the subcultures it has studied. Crucially, much of its work has focused on masculine activities, at the exclusion of either female participation in the subculture, or more importantly, the recognition of distinctive female subcultures. Similarly, it may be argued that it has been excessively concerned with working-class subcultures, leading to a romanticising of the subculture as a source of resistance (and politically progressive values). Further, an over-emphasis on subcultures may serve to distort the picture that cultural studies has of youth as a whole. The concept of youth culture remains important. An emphasis on subcultures may serve to highlight the spectacular at the cost of ignoring the more mundane forms that are of concern to the majority of young people. This majority may be more appropriately seen as belonging to youth culture (or cultures), not to a resisting subculture. A crude opposition between conformist youth (or even 'pop') culture and a radical subculture is itself inappropriate, as it fails to recognise the degree to which the two merge. (See also **punk**.) [AE]

Further reading: Clarke 1982; Hall and Jefferson 1976; Hebdige 1979; McRobbie 1991, 1994; Mungham and Pearson 1976; Willis 1990.

subject/ivity   A term whose origins can be traced as far back as the philosophy of seventeenth-century thinker Descartes. Descartes sought to refute the arguments of contemporary sceptics, who claimed that nothing could be known for certain. Against this view, he propounded the famous dictum 'I think, therefore I am' as an instance of the one certain piece of knowledge any thinking being must have even if it is engaged in doubting everything else. The subject, therefore, is that which thinks and, in thinking, possesses certain essential properties which serve to define it. Likewise, the term 'transcendental subject' is used by Kant in his philosophy to signify the structural precondition of all thinking (cf. *Critique of Pure Reason*, 'Transcendental Deduction' B). The transcendental subject is the 'I think' which, Kant argues, must accompany all my representations when I am in the process of thinking. It is this which makes all the thoughts I have mine. The transcendental subject is not an empirical (i.e. material) entity, but a necessary metaphysical precondition of my having any thoughts at all. In this sense, the subject is the source of self-consciousness. The word is also associated with Lacan's version of **psychoanalysis** (where the subject is contrasted with the 'ego'). Additionally, it has been discussed and criticised by advocates of **structuralism** (e.g. Althusser, who holds that the subject is a product of **ideology**) and **post-structuralism** (e.g. Foucault, who argues that the subject is an effect of relations of **power** – an argument derived from Nietzsche). Both approaches share in common the view that subjectivity (i.e. the property of being a subject) is constituted by social forces and relationships; in other words, that all conceptions of subjectivity are dependent upon political, social and cultural factors. Likewise, thinkers such as Lyotard have argued that subjectivity cannot be taken as something which is independent of forms of **language**; rather, subjectivity is constituted both within and by ways of speaking. Thus, from a Lyotardean standpoint, the notion of 'language games' propounded by the later Wittgenstein, wherein he draws an analogy between language games and the game of chess, contains within it the anthropocentric presupposition that human agents are the source of meaning (i.e. that something external to the language game 'moves' the pieces in the game). Such criticisms can be contrasted with the perspective propounded by advocates of classical **liberalism**, who have in general opposed the notion of subjectivity to that of **society** or language. Equally important therefore is the notion of a 'political subject', i.e. of an entity which has a specified political status and a particular set of characteristics which exist either independently of or in virtue of (depending on your point of view) a given socio-political mode of organisation (cf. **citizenship**). (See also **individual, self**.) [PS]

Further reading: Block *et al.* 1997; Bowie 1990; Dallmayr 1981; Farrell 1994.

sublime　The meaning and significance of the sublime has been most famously considered by Kant in his *Critique of Judgement* (sections 18ff.). Put simply, the sublime moment of cognition is one in which an object is presented to the mind which, in turn, can only comprehend it in terms of an absolute magnitude which itself defies conceptualisation (e.g. the overwhelmingly large): 'That is sublime in comparison with which everything else is small' (ibid., section 25). As such, the sublime moment is one which involves the aesthetic rather than cognitive/empirical capacities of the human mind: it embodies a feeling. Within the Kantian model there are two modes of representing an object as sublime: the dynamical and the mathematical. The mathematical relates to the notion of largeness or magnitude, in that the mathematically sublime involves the presentation of something of such sheer magnitude (such as huge objects) that our understanding is unable to provide a concept capable of containing it. The dynamical sublime, on the other hand, involves the presentation of such magnitudes in terms of force or might (exemplified by the fearful might of nature, e.g. volcanoes, storms, hurricanes), which again cannot be contained within a concept. The sublime is ultimately a consequence of the demands of our rationality, in so far as reason demands that any object presented to the mind through the imagination (which structures our empirical intuitions of the world around us) be presented as a totality. The imagination itself, however, is incapable of doing this since it is tied to the empirical world of nature, and no empirical presentation of the feeling of absolute magnitude involved in the sublime is possible within this domain, i.e. it is impossible on the empirical level to present an object of absolute largeness, since the empirical world itself can only be understood in terms of relationships of relative, not absolute, magnitude. For Kant, therefore, the sublime moment, and resultant feeling which arises from it, resides not in the actual object which inspires it, but in the human mind: 'It is a magnitude that is equal only to itself. It follows that the sublime must not be sought in things of nature, but must be sought solely in our ideas' (ibid.). The sublime, therefore, involves the presentation of an idea which can have no empirical referent. Rather, the sublime object is the object of an idea (the idea of absolute magnitude).

For Kant, this chain of reasoning leads to two conclusions. First, when we consider ourselves as 'natural beings', the sublime moment allows us to 'recognize our physical impotence' (ibid., section 28), i.e. it demonstrates finitude of human existence when understood in the context of the sheer and fearful might of nature. On the other hand, however, since the sublime feeling does not reside in nature, but only in the human mind, it allows us at the same time to consider ourselves as being to some extent independent of nature, and thereby demonstrates our superiority over it: 'This keeps the humanity of our person from being degraded, even though a human being would have to succumb to that dominance [of nature]' (ibid.). The sublime feeling thus functions as a means of elevating the human imagination in such a way that the displeasure which accompanies it (viz. the feeling of impotence in the face of nature) is off-set by the fact that it also causes a feeling of pleasure, in that 'this very judgement . . . is [itself] in harmony with rational ideas' (ibid., section 27). Reason is thus identified by Kant with the absolute measure of what is great – the sublime. Moreover, since the attainment of rationality is the prerequisite of the attainment of freedom, and such freedom makes us cultured and moral beings, the Kantian account of the sublime is linked to his account of the nature and purpose of culture.

More recently, Kant's analysis of the sublime has been taken up, by thinkers such as Jean-François Lyotard, as a means of explicating **postmodernism**. [PS]

Further reading: Kant 1987; Lyotard 1994.

superstructure   See **base and superstructure**

surplus-value   'Surplus-value' is a key term in Marx's economics, and particularly in his explanation of exploitation. In any historical epoch (or **mode of production**) the dominant **class** will extract surplus value from the subordinate, labourer class. In pre-capitalist societies, this is done explicitly (thus for example, the slave works directly for his or her master, with no reward other than his or her subsistence; in **feudalism**, a portion of the serf's product is directly appropriated by the lord). The position in **capitalism** is more subtle. According to the labour theory of **value**, the price of a commodity depends upon the amount of labour-time that has gone into its production. Ideally, the money that the labourer receives for the expenditure of his or her labour-time should be equivalent to the value of the product he or she has produced. So, if you have worked for 5 hours and have produced, say, 10 yards of linen, and if 10 yards of linen has the same **exchange-value** (which is to say, sells at the same price) as 5 loaves of bread, your wages should be enough to purchase 5 loaves of bread. Marx argues that the capitalist system is such that the labourer's wage will typically be less than the value of his or her product. The difference is the surplus-value, which the capitalist appropriates for him or herself. Thus, the worker is working part of the day for him-or herself, and part of the day for the capitalist. Crucially, workers will not typically recognise this exploitation, for as far as they are concerned, the wages they receive will be the 'fair' wages, as determined by a free labour market.

A more precise analysis of surplus-value recognises that the capitalist is required to buy certain resources before production can take place. On the one hand, machines, buildings and raw materials are required (which Marx terms constant capital). On the other hand, labour power, or variable capital, must be bought. Marx argues that the value of the constant capital is simply transmitted into the finished product. (Thus, if the capitalist buys linen for coat manufacture, the value of that linen must be included in the value of the finished coats.) As such, the surplus-value cannot be extracted from constant capital. This nice technicality leads Marx to prophesy the eventual collapse of the capitalist system, because as technology gets more powerful, the proportion of constant capital to variable capital will increase. If the capitalist can only extract surplus-value from variable capital, and that is an ever reducing proportion of his or her total capital expenditure, the capitalist can only continue to maintain the profitability (that is to say, maintain the level of surplus-value) of the capitalist enterprise by reducing payments to labour (so impoverishing the **proletariat**). Much of the most interesting work in twentieth-century **Marxism** has focused on the problem of how late capitalism has avoided this fate. [AE]

Further reading: Mandel 1972; Marx 1976.

Surrealism   Surrealism may be regarded as a radical socio-artistic movement. The Surrealists' concern with art and literature was motivated by a desire to transform everyday life, by revealing the marvellous, 'objective chance' that lay behind the apparent order of reality. In the 1930s, the group tried to align itself with the French Communist Party, unsuccessfully.

The term 'surréaliste' was first used in 1917, by Guillaume Apollinaire to describe his play *Les Mamelles de Tiresias*. It was adopted in 1922 by a group of poets, including André Breton, Louis Aragon and Paul Eluard, associated with the magazine *Littérature*. Breton became the leader of the Surrealists, with the group becoming one of the most tightly organised movements in modern art. Surrealism derived much from Dada, but drew more heavily on Freud's work on the **unconscious** and especially on dreams. Isidore Ducasse's description of the beautiful as 'the chance encounter of a sewing machine and an umbrella on an operating table' (made in 1866, in *Les Chants de Maldoror*), encapsulated much that is typical of Surrealism.

Three strands of Surrealist work may be noted. First, a stress on 'pure psychic automatism' to access 'real processes of thought' (made by Breton in his *Manifesto*), leads to genuine automatic imagery, akin to the automatic writing of mediums. Second, the concern with dreams leads to the imagery of Dali and Magritte, where a hallucinatory dream space is created, not least through a painting style that exploits a realist's attention to precise detail. Third, the juxtaposition of unrelated objects is exploited by the use of montage and collage. Surrealism therefore serves to disrupt the extreme intellectual control and formalism that characterised many other forms of modernist art.

Surrealism was influential well beyond its French origins, as the nationalities of key Surrealist artists such as Magritte (Belgian), Miró and Dali (Spanish), and Max Ernst (German) suggest. Many other artists passed through Surrealist phases. The presence of émigré Surrealists in America during the Second World War was one of the formative conditions for the rise of **Abstract Expressionism**. Its influence on **comedy** (the Goons, and Monty Python for example), and sixties **pop music** and **pop art**, indicates a continuing influence. [AE]

Further reading: Gascoyne 1970; Lynton 1980; Spector 1997.

symbol   A word with a variety of meanings. Symbols pervade human life, and are used in a wide range of specialised **discourses**, as well as in everyday living. Usually, the word 'symbol' is taken as referring to a **sign** or action of some kind which is used to communicate a **meaning** to somebody in virtue of a shared set of **norms** or conventions. A symbol therefore communicates a meaning because it stands for something else, although there is no necessary connection between it and what it stands for (hence its use and meaning are both matters of convention; a conception which **Peirce** uses in his **semiotics**). In **analytic philosophy** 'symbolic logic' involves the substitution of symbols for terms which occur in natural language ('~' means 'not'; '·' means 'or', etc.) as a means of analysing the structure of arguments. In Freudean **psychoanalysis**, symbols are taken to stand in place of some object which has been repressed (in this sense, symbols usually have some (often metaphorical) relation to their referents; although Freud – a smoker – stated that there are times when a cigar is simply a cigar, from the psychoanalytic point of view the latter could be taken as a metaphor for the phallus when it occurs in a patient's dreams). In Peirce's **semiotics**, a symbol is a kind of sign which bears no relation or resemblance to what it stands for. A symbol can also have historic significance and a multitude of resonances of meaning linked to this (e.g. in European **culture**, the sign of the cross can be a potent symbol not only for Christian faith, but also for the institutions, **identity**, traditions and **values** associated with that culture). [PS]

symbolic interactionism   Within **sociology**, symbolic **interactionism** is a theoretical framework that focuses upon the relationships between human **agents** (and as such, upon 'micro' social phenomena, rather than the large scale or 'macro' concern with social structure, found in **Marxism** or **functionalism**). Crucially, it is concerned with the way in which competent social agents construct and make sense of the social world which they inhabit. Such explanations are typically grounded in the detailed recording of everyday life, through **participant observation** or non-participant observation. Symbolic interactionism was developed at the University of Chicago, in the early part of this century, not least under the influence of the pragmatist philosopher G.H. Mead. The term itself was coined by Herbert Blumer in 1937, although symbolic interactionism became a widely accepted approach only in the late 1960s and 1970s.

Mead (1934) argued that the **self**, or our personal identity and self-consciousness, does not exist independently of our social relationships with others. It is produced and continually modified through our actions with respect to others, their responses and our anticipation of those responses (and hence, through our social interaction). Mead compares the **communication** between humans with that between non-human animals. In communication between non-human animals, one animal responds to the patterns of behaviour (or gestures) of another, by modifying its own gestures. What, for Mead, is distinctive about human communication is that the human does not simply respond to a gesture, but to the relationship between the gesture and the object or event that stimulated or motivated that gesture. Above all, the human does so from the standpoint of the original actor. In effect, the human attempts to understand why the other is acting so. The gesture becomes symbolic, and thus meaningful, precisely in so far as one person empathises with the position, **role** and attitudes of the other. Humans can therefore imagine the effect that a gesture will have upon others through an internal conversation between the 'I' (or spontaneous side of the self) and the 'me' (crudely, the self as seen by others). The human self is therefore constituted and continually reconstituted by internalising the 'generalised other', i.e. the typical attitudes and perspectives of the group.

Blumer, simplifying Mead's philosophy, presented symbolic interactionism as a programme for sociological research, by focusing on the manner in which social agents negotiate the meaning of the particular social situations in which they are involved. Functionalists, for example, tend to assume that social roles and norms exist prior to the individual (having objectivity as **social facts** that constrain and determine social behaviour). A competent social agent simply has the ability to apply the appropriate rules (or to adopt the appropriate role) in a given situation. In contrast, the interactionist stresses the work that social agents must do – not in recognising the already existing meaning and significance of a situation – but in creating a shared understanding of a situation, and thus a common approval of the roles and norms that are adopted. Society is not therefore objective, existing independently of the social agents, but is constructed and maintained by agents through interaction.

In the 1960s, Erving Goffman's work developed a form of symbolic interactionism with particular reference to face-to-face interaction. He explored the fragility and fluidity of such interactions. Analysis of such phenomena as embarrassment pointed to moments when social interaction breaks down (with one or more of the participants being exposed as incompetent). A significant part of social life may then be seen to revolve about the avoidance, or fending off, of charges of being incompetent (so that, echoing Mead's interior conversation, it is important for the competent social actor to mark their isolation as atypical moments of incompetence, for example through swearing at oneself). Goffman further suggests (again echoing Mead, albeit in a more extreme form) that our 'selves' are constructed, uniquely, in each distinct social interaction. Our attitudes and patterns of behaviour are shaped according to the people around us (and thus in Goffman's (1959) now classic example, the waiter's attitudes before a customer are fundamentally different to those before colleagues in the kitchen).

Despite its important insights into **socialisation** and **deviance** (and especially **labelling theory**), symbolic interactionism has been criticised for its failure to take full account of power relations. [AE]

Further reading: Becker 1963; Berger and Luckmann 1961; Blumer 1969; Denzin 1992; Goffman 1959.

symptom It is the term 'symptom' that best encapsulates the origins of **psychoanalysis** in Freud's medical practice. While other terms like 'patient' and 'neurosis' have given way to neologisms like 'analysand', 'disorder', etc., the concept of the symptom continues to be as relevant as ever before. It is the inconvenience caused by the symptom – especially when it takes on a pathological cast as in conversion hysteria or obsessive-compulsive neurosis – that prompts the analysand to seek psychoanalysis or one of the other modes of psychotherapy. In other words, the first interpretation of the symptom is made by the analysand themselves: it is he or she who generally decides to present himself or herself to an psychoanalyst rather than to a general practitioner.

The insistence of the medical subtext in the discourse of the symptom arises from the fact that the symptom, more often than not, is constituted as an interference in the vital functions of the subject. The classic psychoanalytic symptom must then be psychosexual impotence. For Freud, psychosexual impotence, which is caused by the shadows of **Oedipal** fixation, is the index of civilised love. Man, unlike the beasts, is restricted in terms of object choice – the modalities of this restriction are both structural (the incest taboo) and symptomatic (the historical particularities of the subject's sexual drive). Not only is the subject restricted in terms of object choice, the very choice of the object is made in a dialetical relation to the libidinal matrix of childhood, which is Oedipal. Hence the subject behaves almost as an automaton in his object choices. On encountering the master signifier of his desire (a tone of voice, a name, a turn of the neck or other such libidinised features), the subject repeats in transferential awe the fantasy scenarios of childhood. The tenor or the structure of this repetition is the symptom. Even outside the sexual relation, the symptom constitutes the sexual life of the subject. It is emblematic of the idea that substitutes can be libidinised – hence the primordial object of love is always already lost.

Like the drive, the symptom too has four features or axes: the imaginary, the symbolic, the real and the *sinthome*. The imaginary aspect of the symptom is manifest as a compromise, as a condensation of conflicting demands in the unconscious. The symbolic elements of the symptom are those which constitute its **hermeneutic** demand for meaning and recognition: the analysand does not merely wish to be loved for his virtues, he or she demands more particularly to be loved for his or her idiosyncratic traits, than for his or her symptoms. The real of the symptom constitutes its *jouissance*. *Jouissance* is not *plaisir*: it is not an object of fun but one of suffering. However, since the analysand has a propensity to domesticate the symptom, a quanta of pleasure is generated out of this suffering. Even when a symptom is inflicted on the subject via a trauma or an organic affliction, the real of the symptom is only too ready to hijack it for its own satisfaction. Finally, the *sinthome*, a Lacanian neologism, which unites the symptom with its underlying phantasy, is that which gives the analysand his sense of identity. The trajectory of a Lacanian analysis must prepare the analysand to 'traverse the phantasy' beyond his symptom. The analysand must be prepared to pose the symptomatic insistence of his suffering as the fundamental question of his existence. It is when the subject of analysis can assume his or her 'subjective destitution', in a radical renunciation of narcissism that the analysis can come to an end. The symptom, then, is Lacan's answer to the question: 'Why is there something when there could be nothing?' [SKS]

Further reading: Breuer and Freud 1974; Freud 1977, 1979; Zizek 1989, 1992.

synchronic/diachronic The distinction between the synchronic and diachronic was used by Saussure in developing his linguistics, and has become fundamental to much work in **structuralism**. To take a synchronic approach to a phenomenon is to approach it at a single moment in history, or as something existing outside history. The diachronic is therefore concerned with the historical or temporal aspects of a phenomenon. Saussure's structural linguistics examines language as an unchanging structure, in contrast to the approach of nineteenth-century linguistics, that was concerned with the historical origin and development of language. [AE]

syntagm In **semiotics**, a combination of signs, from a **paradigm**, that constitutes a meaningful whole. A set of rules or **codes** will determine the correct and thus meaningful way in which potentially meaningful units can be combined, in order to form a syntagm. For example, considered as a syntagm, a European road sign is a combination of one of a small set of coloured, geometric shapes (such as a red triangle; a blue circle), with one of a set of silhouettes or more abstract shapes (an arrow; the silhouette of a motor car). [AE]

syntax The rules which stipulate the ways of ordering words into sentences and propositions within a language. The syntax patterns of a language in effect state how individual words relate to one another. The observation of syntactical rules thereby allows for the construction of 'well-formed' sentences, although from the basic rules which determine the syntactical structure of any language an effectively infinite number of combinations of words is possible. The fact that children are able to construct new sentences on the basis of encountering different combinations of words led linguist Noam Chomsky to argue that all humans possess a common grammatical capacity which transcends social and cultural differences. [PS]

Further reading: Chomsky 1957.

systems theory   Various forms of systems theory have been used in analyses of **society** throughout the twentieth century, with **functionalism** being perhaps the longest lasting and most influential variant. In general, a system may be understood as a collection of interrelated parts. The system is divided from an external environment by a boundary. The environment is more complex than the system. The system is thus characterised by the degree of order it manifests, not least in so far as it excludes certain relationships between its parts and enforces others. (For example, a meaningful sentence is a relatively simple affair, its meaning being determined by the rules of its language. The sounds of traffic, other people, bird song, rain and so on around me, when I utter that sentence, are far more complex and indeed seemingly chaotic.) A system maintains this boundary between itself and its external environment, both maintaining an internal order and also drawing the resources necessary for its survival and reproduction from the external environment. (Thus, an animal organism can be understood as a system. Its skin is a boundary between it and the external world. It must be able to draw sustenance from that world, and maintain itself as a vital organism. At its death, the boundary collapses, and the organism decays into its environment.) It may be argued that any system must satisfy a set of abstract conditions in order to remain stable and vital. These include adaptation to the external environment, internal integration, and the motivation to realise the goals of the system as a whole.

Society may be treated as a system at a number of different levels. For example, the **interaction** between two people can be understood as a system. That interaction will have a purpose. The system, strictly, co-ordinates not the people, but their actions. Other people and other irrelevant events and actions will be excluded from it. It will be conducted according to various rules that give it coherence and integrity. Thus, for example, a market is a system that co-ordinates together the actions, not merely of two, but potentially of many people. In systems theory the market is not understood as a meaningful exchange between people (so the systems theorist is not interested in social background or motivations of those involved in the market) but only in the co-ordination of the actions of buying and selling. Society as a higher level, for example that of a nation-state, or country, may similarly be understood as a system. The systems theorist therefore responds to a particular aspect of contemporary societies: the way in which they confront their members as having a power to constrain and control them. (The point is, not simply that a market can be viewed as a system, theoretically blanking out our subjective experience of it, but that markets are increasingly becoming pure systems. The argument would be that markets, like **bureaucracies**, increasingly only recognise the ability of agents to buy or sell. Money alone matters in co-ordinating our actions together. The market thus takes on the force of an objective law, so that we are thus obliged to obey it, whether we like it or not, and in addition, despite the fact that we may realise that the market is really just one more set of cultural conventions.) It has then been argued that **modern** societies may be characterised by this high level of systematisation: social actions are increasingly co-ordinated by sets of rules and conventions that fall outside of the understanding (or even experience) of society's members. For some, such as Niklaus Luhmann (who has done much to revive systems theory in the social sciences), this is a good thing, for it removes a burden of responsibility from the individual.

For others, such as Jürgen Habermas, it can pose a threat, in removing society from the control of the people who constitute it (1984 and 1987). [AE]

Further reading: Habermas 1984, 1987; Luhmann 1982; Parsons 1951.

Taylorism The scientific management movement, that developed in the early twentieth century in association with the writings of F.W. Taylor (1964), sought to bring rational administration to the workplace. Scientific management seeks to increase the efficiency of industrialised mass **production**. Taylor proposed three principles for the reorganisation of work: (i) an extreme **division of labour** reducing tasks to the simplest possible actions (and if possible to a single repeated operation), and as such reducing the skills required of manual **labour**; (ii) managers (rather than foremen or skilled workers) would have complete control of the workplace, which in turn serves to validate management as a skill distinct from mere ownership; (iii) time-and-motion studies would be used to control costs and the efficiency of movement within the workplace.

Taylorism is a key component of **Fordism**, which is the term coined by the Italian Marxist Gramsci to refer to the writings of the industrialist Henry Ford. Fordism, however, combines scientific management with an extreme mechanisation of the production process. Ford, in addition, advocated high wages, that at once rewarded the workforce for submission to the disciplines of the scientifically managed workplace, and (if the policy were adopted by all producers) would facilitate the market for mass produced products. The **proletariat** are thereby incorporated into **capitalism**, in that they come to benefit, to some degree, from its advance.

In the late 1970s, the inapplicability of Taylorism to the new knowledge based technologies (such as computing and micro-electronics) was partially responsible for a crisis in Fordism, leading to the prospect of a 'post-Fordism', where production would be grounded in the return of craft specialisation and greater flexibility and responsibility amongst the workforce. [AE]

technology The word 'technology' is derived from the Ancient Greek word '*tekhne*', meaning either 'art' or 'craft'. In modern parlance, however, the meaning of 'technology' has tended to take on the instrumental aspect implied by the word 'craft'. The use of the word 'technology' can in turn be divided into two separate but linked domains. First, 'technology' concerns that web of human practices within which the manipulation of (raw) materials is undertaken with a view to giving them a functional and useful form. In this sense, technology is primarily a matter of technique, and its employment presupposes some notion of purpose or design with regard to the manner in which materials are subsequently used. Second, the end product of such a process of manipulation is also called 'technology'. Thus, when we refer to a 'piece of technology', such as a computer or an aircraft, we are not referring to the manipulation of materials which gave rise to them, but in each case to something which, by its very nature, is deemed different in kind to other types of object that we might encounter in the world (e.g. rocks and stones, plants, animals etc.). 'Technology', therefore, refers both to a web of human practices and to the products of those practices.

In the late modem era, it might, with some good cause, be argued that the burgeoning of particular forms of technology has been a significant element in the social and political transformations which mark out the history of the industrial and post-industrial periods. Thus, with the rise of industrial forms of production in Britain dating from the late eighteenth century there were accompanying changes in the distribution and concentration of population (an increased concentration in urban centres) and the concentration and distribution of wealth (a burgeoning capitalist **class**). Equally, there were accompanying developments in the political constitutions of representative bodies (e.g., by the end of the nineteenth century, there was an increasingly widening political franchise who elected members of parliament). Without attempting to fill in the historical picture, it is clear what the possible links between technological developments and such social and political developments might be. First, the development of industrial technology increases the viability of producing more goods at cheaper prices, since such technology brings with it the possibility of mass production. In economic terms, this implies an increased turnover both at the levels of production and consumption: speaking from the vantage point of the mercantile capitalist, the more items of a product you can make efficiently (i.e. cheaply) the cheaper you can sell it, and the cheaper you can sell it the more you can sell. In turn, the efficient mass production of goods requires the concentration of **labour** forces in restricted areas, and this is achieved through offering more financial enumeration for labour than can be obtained in what can subsequently be deemed 'rural' (i.e. non-industrialised) areas. Such movement and concentration of population, it is clear, will have important social effects, in so far as some of the social relations which predominated in rural social forms will no longer apply. Hence, there may be increased fluidity of labour and job opportunity; likewise, there is the possibility that new social antagonisms will develop (e.g., between those who own systems of production and those who work for them) and, following the account offered by **Marxism**, individuals will develop self-consciousness through the development of class divisions resulting from the **division of labour** that mass production institutes. These social ramifications can have knock-on effects, in that the development of wealth among the mercantile class is probably going to be accompanied by an increased desire to see that wealth realised in terms of concrete political **power**. Likewise, one might expect those who work for the capitalists to want to see an expression of their interests in political terms.

Alongside the approach represented by, for instance, Marx's analysis of social relations, the kind of understanding of the significance of technology implicit in the above approach is also present in the work of thinkers associated with more recent intellectual developments that are often classified under the rubric of **postmodernism.** One such example is Jean-François Lyotard's *The Postmodern Condition* (1979). In this book, Lyotard puts forward the view that technology has a determining influence on forms of knowledge. In other words, Lyotard is claiming that the social and cultural effects of technology are not limited to such matters as the socio-historical development of classes with defined interests which spring from the predominance of the economic relation to industrial technological forms. Rather, according to Lyotard, the ways in which we think about, categorise and valorise experience are also subject to change at the hands of technological forces. In short, the question concerning what knowledge is (cf. **epistemology**), on Lyotard's account, an issue which must itself be transformed by the advent of modern technology. This is because technology comes to serve as the primary criterion for evaluating what counts as knowledge within contemporary culture. Technology, in this sense, transforms knowledge to the extent 'that anything in the constituted body of knowledge that is not translatable in this way will be abandoned [. . .] the direction of new research will be dictated by the possibility of its eventual results being translatable into computer language' (1979: p. 4). Thus, on Lyotard's view the postmodern era is one which bears witness to the '**hegemony** of computers', for it is this hegemony which serves to dictate what counts as knowledge by imposing the criterion of 'translatability' upon those propositions which make claims about reality. One outcome of this is that the primacy of human subjectivity is displaced by the machinic tendencies of modern technology. This displacement, in turn, renders the thinking subject a secondary phenomenon with regard to knowledge, simply because subjectivity can no longer be taken as the foundational principle which underlies what counts as knowledge. Speaking from the point of view of an inwardly oriented conception of subjectivity (as exemplified by, for example, the Cartesian *cognito* – cf. **self**), knowledge, under the conditions dictated by technology, becomes externalised. Knowledge, transformed in this way, becomes linked to market **exchange-value** and the play of exterior forces. What is noteworthy in Lyotard's account is the claim that material forces (in the shape of technology) have the capability to transform not merely social **norms** and relations, but can alter radically the ways in which we think about ourselves and our abilities. How 'radical' an insight this is may well be a point of some debate. For example, if one understands 'knowledge' to be best defined in terms of justification (i.e. as 'justifiable belief'), then what has been transformed through the technological process Lyotard alludes to is not necessarily something delineated by the proper name 'Knowledge', but rather the criteria and practices which serve to define what justification is. In other words, even if we might accept that what counts as knowledge must now be judged in terms of its suitability for translation into technological terms, this does not necessarily entitle us to the further claim that knowledge 'itself' has been thereby transformed, since the definition of knowledge as 'justifiable belief' has not changed, only the criteria which constitutes justification.

As with Lyotard, aspects of Jean Baudrillard's conception of the postmodern are articulated in the wake of technological developments. Thus, on Baudrillard's argument, technology is again regarded as something capable of transforming our conceptions of experience and knowledge. On Baudrillard's view, the power of technology to influence our understanding of the significance of events through processes of **representation** is highlighted. Most famously (or notoriously, depending on where your sympathies lie in this context) Baudrillard claimed that the Gulf War was a staged spectacle enacted through the technology of the **mass media** which, in 'reality', never happened. In other words, the issue of what constitutes an 'event' is taken by Baudrillard to be a matter which is now determined by the representational function of technology. His views, understandably, have been met with a variety of responses.

Whatever their merits as forms of possible explanation of socio-historical events, such accounts as those mentioned above do not, however, necessarily take us any further towards clear understanding of what technology is. Equally, if we do not understand what technology is, then it might be somewhat problematic to claim that we can construct a persuasive account of its social or cultural significance. One possible approach to this problem has been offered by the German philosopher Martin Heidegger. In his 1953 essay 'The Question Concerning Technology' (Heidegger 1996), he attempts to show that a purely instrumental understanding of technology is a reductive one: it is reductive because if we discuss technology only in instrumental terms we miss out of our account what technology presupposes, and thereby something essential concerning what technology is. Thus, Heidegger claims, if we do not account for technology in terms of what is presupposed by it, then we ignore its 'essence'. Equally, Heidegger is careful to show that 'the essence of technology is by no means anything technological' (1996: 311). In other words, what is presupposed by technology (namely what is essential to it in order for it to be what it is) cannot be accounted for in technological terms. The contemporary view of technology, in contrast, is regarded by Heidegger as being both 'instrumental' and 'anthropological'. In short, this means that technology is generally taken to be a means to an end, and this implies that the desires and purposes of humans constitute an exhaustive definition of it. Such a view is, according to Heidegger, correct as far as it goes. But this view does not go far enough, for it presupposes that we can define notions like 'means' and 'ends' in an unproblematic manner. '[W]herever instrumentality reigns there reigns causality' (1996: 313), and therefore if we do not provide an acceptable account of *causality*, then we cannot be said to have engaged with the question of what technology is in sufficient depth.

On Heidegger's account, causality can be best elucidated in terms of its 'fourfold' nature: (1) The matter out of which a thing is made; (2) The form which is imposed on the material; (3) The purpose of the thing; (4) That which brings about this transformation (the agent). Heidegger claims that it is essential to see the relationship between each of these four elements as an immanent one. In other words, the agent (4) does not stand 'outside' of, or independently of, 1–3. Rather, each of these is a mode of 'bringing-forth', i.e. a process in which what is hidden in the world is made manifest. Moreover, 'bringing-forth' is itself 'grounded in revealing' (1996: 318), and revealing involves uncovering and thereby showing how things are. 'Technology is [. . .] no mere means. Technology is a way of revealing. If we give heed to this, then another whole realm for the essence of technology will open itself to us. It is the realm of revealing, i.e., of truth' (1996: 318). Above all, it is in its capacity as a *mode* of revealing, *not* as a mere 'manufacturing', that technology is a 'bringing-forth'. The 'bringing-forth' involved in modem technology is a 'challenging' which 'sets upon' nature so as to impose order upon it with the aim of achieving 'the maximum yield at the minimum expense' (1996: 321). Nature, in short, is conceptualised as a mere resource by modern technology, a storehouse of energy. But even this is 'no mere human doing' (1996: 324). In the same way as a mountain range is formed and folded by forces which are not to be confused with the range itself, so humans are propelled into this 'challenging' by what Heidegger calls '*Gestell*' (enframing). 'Enframing means the gathering together of the setting-upon that sets upon man' (1996: 325). In modern technology, humans are themselves 'set-upon' and thereby engage with the world in a manner which cannot be accounted for in purely anthropological terms. Although the process of enframing which occurs as technology takes place within the sphere of human action, enframing does not 'happen exclusively *in* man, or definitively *through* man' (1996: 329). This is because humans are themselves set upon by the conditions of their existence and hence challenged into responding to these conditions through the enframing which underlies technology. Thus, the essence of technology is revealed in the process of enframing, and enframing itself is shown to be a mode of engaging with, and thus revealing, the conditions of existence. This mode of engagement 'starts man upon the way of that revealing through which the actual everywhere [. . .]

409

becomes standing reserve [i.e. a resource]' (1996: 329). In this sense, there is a determinacy with regard to how humans encounter the conditions of their existence, once the enframing which constitutes the essence of technology has set them upon the course of revealing which technology embodies. This process, which underlies all modes of revealing, Heidegger calls 'destining' (*Geschick*). Humans exist within the domain of destining, but are never compelled by it, since destining is itself the 'free space' within which human action is rendered possible. As such, it is 'the realm of freedom' (1996: 330). Technology, in turn, is thus always already situated within the domain of freedom. Given this last point, it cannot make sense to talk of our being 'compelled' by technology, either in the sense of 'a stultified compulsion to push on blindly' with it 'or, what comes to the same, to rebel helplessly against it and curse it as the work of the devil' (1996: 330).

On Heidegger's view, then, we cannot take a stand either 'for' or 'against' technology. However, the danger presented by technology lies in the fact that it may come to subvert all other possible modes of revealing in its pursuit of ordering the world (i.e. mastery over it). In turn, such mastery would reduce both humanity and all other entities to the status of a mere resource for technological goals. Nevertheless, the technological mode of enframing can never entirely subvert the very conditions which gave rise to its historical development, and for Heidegger this means that a space must remain within which articulate different modes of thinking that can engage with the world. For Heidegger this means, above all, formulating a poetic form of dialogue with which to engage with Being – a theme which pervades much of his work.

Of other accounts of technology, thinkers associated with the **Frankfurt School** have alluded to the relationship between the rise of technology and the development of modem forms of rationality. Significant amongst these is Max Horkheimer's conception of 'instrumental rationality' and his accompanying criticisms of **positivism**. According to Horkheimer, modernity can be characterised in terms of a modulation towards a conception of reason which highlights its purposive/

instrumental aspect. In short, by 'reason' what is meant in modern culture is a form of thinking which gives priority to the attainment of a given purpose or end, rather than any process of critical reflection upon a broader range of issues which fall outside the purview of the 'means and ends' rationality of instrumental reason. Instrumentalism is thus a form of thinking which takes purposes as 'givens' which are then to be acted upon, rather than a reflective and critical engagement with the question as to whether particular purposes are justifiable. In philosophy, Horkheimer argues, this has led to the development of 'positivism', which seeks to emulate the methodology of science. Positivism, in seeking to emulate science, Horkheimer claims, merely becomes a passive and uncritical voice with regard to questions of knowledge, since it is content to leave the arbitration of what counts as justification to the hegemony of modern instrumental reason. [PS]

Further reading: Heidegger 1996; Horkheimer 1992; Lyotard 1989.

television The decisive developments in the technology of modern television broadcasting, such as electronic scanning, were made in the 1920s, and the first experiments in public broadcasting occurred in the 1930s. In the post-war period, television rapidly developed its now central position as the dominant form of popular entertainment (displacing radio and **cinema** in the USA in the 1950s, and in Britain in the 1960s). The cultural, economic and sociological theorisation of television, however, did not come to maturity until the 1970s. Perhaps, more accurately, it could be suggested that the theorisation of television as a distinctive medium, separate from more general theories of the **mass media**, did not occur until the 1970s. At this time, key studies of television were published by Williams (1974), Hall (1973) and the Glasgow University Media Group (1976).

A concern with television may be seen as an extension of Raymond Williams's earlier and continuing work on cultural transformation and democratic forms of communication. The dominant approach in Marxist analyses of the mass media had been to treat them as instruments of **ideology**, not least in terms of the threat that they were seen to pose to any politically emancipatory cultural practice. While sharing these concerns, Williams develops one of the more subtle versions of Marxist cultural theory. This may be seen in the three elements of his analysis of television. First, he is concerned to relate television as a cultural phenomenon to an account of the material conditions of society. Rejecting any simple **base-superstructure** model, according to which the development of a technology determines the cultural superstructure, he identifies the social preconditions of the growth of television in what he terms 'mobile privatism'. Television technology could only be commercially exploited by being adapted for consumption within the home. This privatism was to some extent (and especially within the UK), balanced by the dominance of public service broadcasting, and thus the state control of television. Crucially, Williams recognises in the public aspect of television (not least in its possible responses to an Amercian dominated global television culture), the potential for increasingly local and democratic forms of communication. Williams's second concern is with the structure of the experience and content of television. Programmes are ordered in a sequential flow, as opposed to a sequence of discrete units. This structure may be seen to lead the audience into passivity, as the programmes make only a superficial and transcient impression, during periods of relaxation. Finally, Williams begins to question the dominant models of audience research. These are seen to entail a crude examination of the isolated effects that television was supposed to have on its audience (e.g. in causing violence), and thereby ignoring the complex institutional structures within which television is produced and consumed.

Stuart Hall, similarly, questions the assumption that there is any simple causal model that can account for the impact that television has upon its audience. Hall is concerned with the (ideological) message that television is supposed to communicate. By recognising the complexity of the processes of production (or encoding) and interpretation (or decoding) of a message, Hall argues that the makers of television programmes cannot determine the sense that the audience will make of them. The message will be encoded in the context of a set of cultural preconceptions and taken-for-granted knowledge, **relations of production** and technologies (that will influence, for example, the way material from the everyday world is selected and transformed for transmission). These frameworks may or may not correspond to those of the audience. Audiences may therefore be understood as responding within one of three broad categories. The 'dominant-**hegemonic** position' entails decoding the message (for example of a news or current affairs programme) within the same, ideological framework as it was encoded. A 'negotiated position' entails a partial (and contradictory) reinterpretation of the message in the light of the immediate experience of the viewer. Finally, an 'oppositional position' entails that the viewer sees through the dominant framework, for example, recognising an appeal to national interest as a promotion of **class** interest. Morley's (1980) analysis of the news and current affairs programme *Nationwide*, provided an empirical test of the utility of this typology, as well as allowing further exploration of the relationship between positions of interpretation and other social variables, such as class, education and age.

The Glasgow University Media Group published a series of **empirical** and **semiotic** analyses of British television news. Extensive analysis of videotaped programmes indicated a systematic ideological bias. Thus, for example, the coverage of industrial action was demonstrated to distort the actual level and nature of industrial action occurring in the country. The level of television coverage, for industry as a whole, or for specific industries, did not correspond to the nature or number of strikes occurring. The newsworthiness of strike action was, rather, determined by the perceived inconvenience that the strike would have on the public. Further, coverage and commentary would presuppose the interests of capitalism and the middle classes (from which the producers of these programmes are disproportionately recruited). While this research has come in for subsequent criticism, as to its theoretical

413

presuppositions and methodology, it may be seen to have influenced, not just subsequent research, but also news broadcasting practices, at least in the UK.

While the work of Hall, and to a lesser extent the Glasgow Group, opened up issues of the analysis of television as **text**, they focused on news coverage. Subsequent analysts broadened the range of programmes under consideration (including soap opera and sitcoms). Further, while media sponsored research typically focused on the number and type of viewers for particular programmes (for advertising purposes), sociological and cultural studies research examines the diversity of ways in which television programmes were interpreted and used. Ang (1985) examined the consumption of the soap opera *Dallas*. The programme is understood as 'emotional realism', in that while the situations portrayed will not correspond to the life experience of the audience, the emotions expressed will. She emphasises the diverse pleasures that are gained from consuming *Dallas*, including, for example, an 'escapism' that makes the boundaries of reality and fiction fluid (so that the pleasure may lie in accepting *Dallas* as part of the drabness of everyday life, rather than a simple flight from it). Other feminist theorists have developed on this work through appeal to **psychoanalytic** theory, and thus further questions of the relationship between television consumption and the construction of gendered identity. Taking television as typical of **popular culture**, Fiske (1987 and 1989) again focuses on the pleasure of consumption, and identifies a necessary separation between the programme as a commercial product and its interpretation (and thus cultural production) by 'the people'. The 'people' embraces diverse sets of allegiances, so that the programme will be variously interpreted and used in ways that are not proscribed by the makers. The consumption of popular culture therefore amounts to an irreverent and pleasurable opposition to the dominant power bloc. (A counter to this conclusion may be found in Eagleton (1991). While critical of approaches that overemphasise the ideological content of television programmes, he argues that television has an ideological effect in the political passivity that privatised television consumption engenders.)

The work of Baudrillard has been central to the development of **postmodernist** theories of television. At the core of Baudrillard's approach (the theories of hyperreality and simulations) is an attempt to undermine the opposition between reality and fiction. The current level of media technology is seen to be such that it does not reproduce a pre-existing reality, but rather produces the real. The world that we experience is produced through the interplay of various media (television, cinema, video, **popular music**, and so on), in so far as simulations now have real consequences. Thus, Baudrillard (1991) could notoriously claim that the Gulf War did not take place. Behind this rhetorical flourish is a claim that the Gulf War was conducted, not simply under the gaze of television cameras, but rather that it was conducted for those cameras. The war becomes a spectacle (manifest most clearly in guided missiles carrying cameras), albeit a spectacle that will leave death and destruction in its wake. The very nature of war is thus seen to be changed by television. [AE]

Further reading: Morley 1992; Stevenson 1995.

text The concept of a 'text', particularly within **semiotics**, is a meaningful structure, understood as being composed of **signs**. The meaning of a text is determined by rules (or **codes**) governing the choice and combination of those signs. The rules that govern this meaningful combination of signs will be conventional, so that any reader of the text will require certain skills or competencies in order to interpret (or decode) the text. Readers from different social and cultural backgrounds, who have different socially acquired skills and expectations, may therefore read the same text in very different ways.

A text typically has a material existence, but is not necessarily simply a written message (such as a sentence, memo, report or novel). Thus a photograph, a song, an advertisement (combining photographic or other visual signs with written signs), a video or a costume may all be understood as texts. [AE]

theology   In western cultures theology has been dominated by Christian approaches to the doctrine of God since Roman times. Broadly speaking, this view characterises God as an all-powerful, all-knowing Being, who created the universe, and who made himself known to humankind in the person of Jesus of Nazareth. Jesus is worshipped as God the Son, along with the other persons of the divine trinity: God the Father and God the Holy Spirit. These are not thought of as three co-equal gods, but as one Divine essence manifest in three persons.

While it serves as a basic description, the above overview is somewhat misleading. Christian theology has never been a monolithic system of dogmatic assertions to which all believers subscribe. Within the New Testament itself there is evidence that a number of different approaches divided the primitive Church. By the second century, certain long-standing theological tendencies associated with Gnosticism had developed into sects like that which grew up around Marcion. He expressed the view (shared by many thinkers ever since – including the nineteenth-century philosopher J.S. Mill) that the God of the Old Testament is not the God of whom Jesus spoke as a loving Father.

Other conflicts centred on ways of interpreting the Bible. Some, like Origen (*c.* 185–254), favoured allegorical interpretations, while others, like Tertullian (*c.* 155–222), stressed what they saw as the literal truth of biblical texts. This was still a major issue for Martin Luther and the theologians of the Reformation in the sixteenth century. Many other theological conflicts arose during the Reformation period, including that between those who asserted that the Pope and the bishops wielded a legitimate, God-given right to decide on doctrinal matters, and those who appealed to the Bible as the highest authority. The same era also saw the emergence of unitarianism: the denial of the divine trinity in the assertion that God is one person.

In the wake of the Renaissance and Reformation in Europe, the study of the Bible took a critical turn. Richard Simon's *Histoire critique due Vieux Testament* (1678) began the process of textual criticism of the Bible which resulted in the gradual dismantling of its authority. As this process quickened and deepened during the eighteenth century, a liberal theology grew up which jettisoned all things supernatural and judged religious matters by the criteria of an elevated Reason.

One development which pre-dates the Reformation is of particular importance in contemporary theological thought. Early in the fourteenth century, the mystical writer Johannes 'Meister' Eckhart developed a negative theology which drew on the writings of a fifth- or sixth-century Syrian monk called Dionysius the Areioagute (or Pseudo-Dionysius). Dionysius had argued that God is beyond the grasp of the human intellect, and that, consequently, human language is inadequate to express anything wholly true about the divine nature. Negative theology thus describes God only in terms of what 'he' is not: 'a not-God, a not-spirit, a not-Person, a not-image . . .' (Eckhart).

The suspicion with regard to language and conceptuality evident in the works of Eckhart, John Ruysbroeck, and other mystical theologians of the period, has found an echo in a strain of contemporary philosophical thought to draw its inspiration from Friedrich Nietzsche (1844–1900) and Martin Heidegger (1889–1976). In *The Trespass of the Sign*, Kevin Hart explores the relationship between negative theology and contemporary continental philosophy, concluding that the former is a species of deconstructive thought which has strong affinities with the work of Jacques Derrida.

Nietzsche's work has had a profound influence on twentieth-century theology, not only because he questioned the philosophical presuppositions upon which the Christian theological tradition depended, but also because he (famously) announced God's death. This conclusion was premised upon the fact that science had offered new, non-theological explanations of many natural phenomena. God was no longer required and religious belief appeared to be in terminal decline. In response to this, theologians such as Paul van Buren and Thomas Altizer in America, and Don Cupitt in Britain, have propounded a 'theology' of the death of God – a paradoxical Christian atheism.

Chief among the God-obscuring scientific advances of the nineteenth century was Charles Darwin's theory of evolution by natural selection. *The Origin of the Species* (1859) divided Christian opinion, provoking the rise of fundamentalism on the one hand, and, on the other, influencing more liberal thinkers to produce new accounts of the relationship between Creator and creation.

Profoundly influenced by Darwin, the work of the twentieth-century Catholic mystic Teilhard de Chardin (1881–1955) has had a significant impact upon the work of subsequent Christian theologians. 'Evolution,' he claimed, 'is a light illuminating all facts, a curve that all lines must follow.' For Teilhard, the world is unfinished, and is progressing towards its 'Omega point' – the moment at which God will be fully manifest in humanity and in nature. The so-called 'process theology' of Schubert Ogden, John Cobb *et al.* owes much to this kind of approach, as do recent developments in Creation spirituality.

Among proponents of the latter trend, Matthew Fox has had the highest profile. His book *Original Blessing* (1983), its title implicitly rejecting the traditional Christian notion of 'original sin', seeks to shift Christian theology away from its emphasis on a primeval 'fall' and the need for redemption, towards a celebration of Creation as the central theme of worship. Ecological consciousness, New Age thinking, Celtic Christianity, negative theology and various forms of non-Christian mysticism all combine in Fox's work. What Fox thinks of as the 'creation-centred tradition' is also broadly feminist in character. It rejects both the male image of God as Father and the patriarchal structure of Church tradition.

Feminist theology has grown up alongside political and cultural movements towards the equalisation of female/male roles in society. Since the production of Elizabeth Cady Stanton's *The Woman's Bible*, in the last few years of the nineteenth century, the masculine construction and male domination of Christianity have come under ever-intensifying scrutiny. Today there is a substantial (and increasing) body of work, covering all areas of theological concern from a variety of feminist perspectives. In her introduction to *Feminist Theology: A Reader* (1990), Ann Loades writes:

> feminist theologians are particularly concerned with the way [religious] traditions work, the symbolism they use, the characteristics of roles within them, the way the traditions reflect social assumptions and shape and reshape those assumptions, and especially the gender-related way in which we talk about God.

Taken together, the 'death of God', ecological consciousness, feminist reinterpretations and the cross-fertilisation of different faith traditions, are elements of a major shift in attitudes to the study of divinity. It is probably not an exaggeration to speak of the combined effect of these changes as the dawn of a new era in theology. [KM/GH]

Further reading: Altizer 1968, 1977; Cobb 1977; Cupitt 1988; Fox 1983; Loades 1990; Ogden 1979, 1996; Stanton 1990.

transference Transference in the Freudian model is the displacement of affect from a **signifier** to which it rightfully belongs to one to which it does not. Freud first used this term in his *The Interpretation of Dreams* (1900) to call attention to the mobility of affect as a mechanism of semantic distortion in the dream work. Later on, having established a common grammar in all the formations of the **unconscious** (the dream, the joke, the slip, the symptom), he used the term to subsume the set of affects that an analysand experiences in analysis. These effects which take the psychoanalyst as their object are repetitions of primordial responses to **Oedipal** signifiers. It is in fact the transference that is often cited as proof of the sexual nature of the unconscious. The lay person understands this phenomenon to involve falling in love with the analyst. Not all transferences however are positive. Both in clinical and extramural settings, excessive affect aimed at what Lacan terms the 'subject presumed to know' is transferential. They can take both positive and negative forms. In fact, there is no transference that does not, at least to some measure, oscillate between the two. (On the other hand, the psychoanalyst's affective response to the analysand is termed the counter-transference.)

Lacan has defined the transference as the disclosure of the reality of the unconscious, which, after Freud, he too understands to be sexual. For Lacan, transference is the love aimed at knowledge; hence, its structural requirement – the presence of a 'subject presumed to know'. Lacan's definition of the transference can be understood as a decentring of the concept. It is no more restricted to the clinic but becomes a cultural phenomenon of interest in politics, pedagogy, entertainment, etc. What then is the difference between a clinical and a non-clinical notion of the transference? Both Freud and Lacan seem to believe that in moderate doses, an extramural transference can energise the subject in its endeavours. The clinical transference, however, is an interruption of the speech of the analysand. The analysand falls in love with the analyst in order to prevent the process of free association. In other words, instead of remembering the details of his or her trauma, the neurotic prefers to repeat the trauma under the aegis of the transference. Again, transferential love must be distinguished from the popular conception of love. Lacan was fond of asking why it is that neurotics are so susceptible to transference while they are incapable of love. The answer may well be that while the transference is a structural response, love is an individuated one – the neurotic lacks individuation. The end of analysis depends on the liquidation of the transference. In other words, the analysand must be able to get on with the tasks of everyday life without idealising a particular set of actors as uniquely equipped to sanction the authenticity of his acts. It is this which prepares the analysand to be an analyst in his turn. [SKS]

Further reading: Breuer and Freud 1974; Freud 1991a; Gueguen 1995; Klotz 1995; Lacan 1977; Laplanche and Pontalis 1973.

unconscious   Though the concept of the unconscious predates
Freud, it was through **psychoanalysis** that it took on a radical
dimension. In Freud's metapsychology, the unconscious is
defined as that which comes between perception and consciousness. It is the realm of the primary process (as opposed to
the secondary process of consciousness that is characterised by
a greater 'binding' of affects). It is marked by a fluidity of
cathexes, of displacements, condensations, symbolism and the
substitution of external reality by the subjective Real. It lacks a
sense of time or the substitution of external reality by the subjective Real. It also lacks logical contradictions. Opposing tendencies can coexist within it. It partakes of the infantile but is
not reducible to it. In Freud's early topographical model, the
unconscious is opposed to the preconscious and the conscious.
The unconscious becomes less important in the later structural
model where the psyche is divided into the id, the ego and the
superego, Freud argues that the better part of all these agencies
may well be unconscious. The concept is necessitated by the
fact that there are gaps in the analysand's memory which have
a traumatic significance. Moreover, Freud argues, these gaps in
the mental life must be understood as belonging to some one
other than the subject. It is this notion which Lacan takes up in
his formula: 'the unconscious is the discourse of the Other'.

   The term 'unconscious' must be rigorously differentiated
from the notion of 'repression'. Though the repressed is the

prototype of the unconscious, it is the latter which has a wider compass. All that is repressed is unconscious but not all that is unconscious is repressed. Though a final cleavage between the conscious and unconscious does not appear until puberty, the unconscious must be presupposed in the infant to explain the act of repression. Repression is not characteristic of neurotics, as the popular depiction of someone as 'repressed' would imply. The 'neurotic' is merely the subject in whom repression has failed. All subjects must undergo primary repression during the **Oedipal** phase. For Lacan, the fall of this first signifier from the chain of signification is a structural necessity. The Lacanians refer to this as a **signifier en plus**. Secondary repression is a derivative of primary repression: it distorts the expression of those signifiers that bear a traumatic link to the complex ideas associated with primary repression. It is always the signifier that is repressed and not the affect. Affects can only be displaced in relation to the logic of the signifier. The formations of the unconscious can therefore be understood as an interplay between those elements which offer themselves to interpretation (desire) and those which resist it (phantasy). Hence (contrary to **postmodernist** misinterpretations) the Lacanian analyst, Jacques-Alain Miller, has argued that the unconscious is not reducible to the **metonymy** of desire. The unconscous is structured *both* like a language and unlike a language. For Lacan, ultimately, the unconscious is not just an-*other* scene, which requires an alternate ontology. It is instead *pre*-ontological: it is more fundamentally, on overlooking (*un bevue*), the order of the unrealised. [SKS]

Further reading: Freud 1991a; Klein 1992/93; Lacan 1977a, 1995; Laplanche and Pontalis 1973; Miller 1988.

underclass 'Underclass' is a term often used vaguely, and that is intermittently in fashion and social and political thought, which refers to a structured group at the bottom of the **class** hierarchy in **capitalist** societies. The presence of a 'new working class' in the North American cities was proposed by

S.M. Miller (1965). This class was composed of ethnic minorities (including Puerto Ricans, Mexicans and African Americans), who were employed in low income service occupations, without union representation, and who suffered long periods of unemployment (and could thus be compared to the more affluent and secure, and predominantly white 'old working class'). Further theorisation of this concept would include women alongside ethnic minorities as typical members of the underclass. [AE]

urbanism Urbanism or urbanisation is the growth in the proportion of the population of a country who are living in towns and cities, and the social and cultural effects of this predominantly urban life. Urbanisation is caused either by the migration of people from the countryside to the town, or by the fact that the birth rate of the urban population is higher than its death rate. Urbanisation is a historically recent phenomenon. For example, in the United Kingdom, in 1800 approximately 24 per cent of the population lived in urban centres. By 1900, this figure was 77 per cent. However, with the growth of suburbs, and changes in the structure of towns and cities due to the decline of manufacturing industry, the rate of urbanisation typically tends to slow and even decline.

Two broad, if inevitably overlapping, approaches to the problem of urban life can be identified. On the one hand, there is the description and characterisation of what is distinctive about urban existence. On the other hand, there are attempts to explain this way of life. The first approach is perhaps the more relevant to **cultural studies**. In the nineteenth century, the city had already become a central theme of novelists such as Dickens and Balzac, and poets such as Baudelaire. Within cultural and social theory will be found, in the early years of the twentieth century, the work of Georg Simmel, Walter Benjamin, the Chicago School, and a host of contemporary writers offering **modernist, postmodernist** and **feminist** approaches. For Simmel (1950), life in the metropolis is characterised by a relative increase in mental stimulation. Rural existence, or life in a small community, is more emotional and stable, yet lacking in personal freedom. The over-stimulation of metropolitan life, however, paradoxically threatens the individual in his or her search for **identity**. The excess of stimuli, and threat of others leads to reserve, or a blasé attitude, expressed in a perpetual search of novelty and eccentricity. Benjamin's analysis of nineteenth century Paris (1973a) offers a dazzling range of fragmentary readings of the city, the most famous of which is the image of the *flâneur* (and which is not dissimilar to Simmel's characterisation of urban humanity). The *flâneur* strolls anonymously about the city (like Edgar Alan Poe's 'The Man of the Crowd' (1982)), consuming it in a succession of transient impressions.

Louis Wirth (1938), following in the tradition of the Chicago School of urban sociology, summarises the urban experience in terms of the loss of personal relationships, and thus of a greater instrumentality in our dealings with others. He explains this way of life by appealing to features of the urban environment itself: the size, density and heterogeneity of the population. Subsequent approaches within urban sociology question the assumption that there is a single distinctive urban experience. H.J. Gans, for example, recognises the impersonality, anonymity and superficiality of urban relationships that are formed under conditions of transience and heterogeneity, but argues that such conditions apply to only a portion of the urban population, and need to be understood in terms of sociological factors, such as **class** and employment opportunities (1968). The city therefore comes to be seen more as the context within which other social and political forces are played out. Thus, Marshall Berman explores the relationships between cities, modern art and modernisation (1983). In contemporary geography Harvey (1989) and Castells (1989), working within **Marxist** frameworks, analyse the role of **capitalism** and the state in the structure and development of the city. Advocates of postmodernism, conversely, find in the city of the late twentieth century its transformation as a centre for consumption and spectacle. Las Vegas replaces Paris as the archetypal urban experience. Wilson's (1991) feminist approach questions the masculine bias in much work on the city, analysing the city, not merely as a place of threat and danger to women, but also as a positive site. (See also **architecture**.) [AE]

Further reading: Leach 1997; Pahl 1968; Saunders 1981; Soja 1989.

uses and gratifications   The uses and gratifications approach to the analysis of **mass media**, and especially the relationship between the mass media and its audience, begins from the assumption that individual members of that audience will have their own needs which they expect to be met by viewing or listening to the media programme. Such needs may be various, but might include escapism, 'company', or a means of constructing and understanding one's **identity** (through the recognition or comparison of personal **values** with those represented in the media). The approach, which emerged in the 1940s, was important in challenging the excessively passive view of media **consumption**, associated with **mass society** theories. [AE]

use-value   The concept of use-value is fundamental to Marxist economics. For Marx, it refers to the usefulness of a thing, and as such is grounded in the inherent and natural properties of the thing. Bread has use-value because it satisfies our hunger. Use-value thus indicates something that is qualitatively distinctive about the thing, in terms of the particular purpose it serves. Marx contrasts the use-value of **commodities** with their **exchange-value**. [AE]

Further reading: Cunningham-Wood 1988.

utilitarianism   An approach to questions of ethics which argues that an action can be evaluated in terms of its moral worth by calculating its effects or consequences. The view is associated with thinkers such as Jeremy Bentham (1748–1832) and J.S. Mill (1806–73). Utilitarianism is generally associated

425

with the maxim which advocates 'the greatest happiness of the greatest number', or principle of Utility, as providing the basis for understanding the worth of an action. This states that, faced with a moral dilemma, one should act in such a way as to maximise the greatest happiness of the greatest possible number of people who would be affected by that action ('happiness' in this context signifies the presence of pleasure and absence of pain; while 'unhappiness' would mean the presence of pain and dimunition of pleasure). In the twentieth century, utilitarians have come to be divided into two kinds: (i) 'act utilitarians', who argue that individual actions should be judged according to the principle of Utility, and (ii) 'rule utilitarians', who hold that different actions can be subdivided into different types, and that each action can be brought under a rule which applies to all such instances of that type.

There are a number of criticisms of the utilitarian theory. First, how is it possible to assess exhaustively the consequences of any action? Second, although the 'greatest number' may benefit from an act, what about those in a minority who suffer as a result of it? Third, utilitarians presuppose that 'happiness' is something quantifiable; but there is no way of showing what, exactly, 'happiness' or 'pleasure' is, nor, therefore, that there is any universally applicable definition of the term. Fourth, it is not clear that the meaning of social and cultural life can be reduced to the pursuit of happiness or pleasure, as the utilitarians must, at least implicitly, hold (a point made by Nietzsche, when he noted, somewhat dryly, that only the 'English' (i.e. utilitarians) strive after happiness, not humanity).

Aspects of utilitarian theory embody a view of cultural **identity** implicit in **liberalism**. For example, it presupposes that agents are the authors of their own destinies, and are basically self-interested beings (in so far as they all seek to maximise their pleasures, and that such maximisation is good). [PS]

Further reading: Glover 1990; Mill 1985; Plamenatz 1958; Scarre 1996; Sen and Williams 1982; Singer 1993.

utopia/nism   The word 'utopia' means 'nowhere'. The common use of the term as meaning 'unrealistic', 'fanciful' or 'illusory' is derived from Sir Thomas Moore's book *Utopia* (1516), which offers a description of an ideal and imaginary state. Utopianism is the belief that it is possible to establish a **society** which is not merely 'better' than present society, but a perfect one. Utopian texts thus seek to provide a vision of future possible worlds in which the conflicts and injustices which dominate contemporary societies are overcome. The attempt to describe such a society and the principles which underlie it can be traced as far back as the Ancient Greek philosopher Plato. His *Republic* seeks to justify the view that the rule of philosopher-kings (who are envisaged as being rational beings endowed with true knowledge who, in turn therefore, possess knowledge of the good) will lead to the perfect social order. On Plato's account, the highest form of cultural life is envisaged as being realisable through the elucidation of a model of human nature which reflects the order of objective reality and reason. Other works in this **genre** include Francis Bacon's *New Atlantis* (1624) and William Morris's *News from Nowhere* (1890).

Civic humanist thinker James Harrington's *The Commonwealth of Oceana* (1656) also provides a good example of the utopian genre and the uses to which it may be put (although it is disputable as to whether the substance of Harrington's thought could be called 'utopian'). Harrington uses an 'imaginary' state, *Oceana*, as a means of outlining the basic structure which, he argues, a society should adopt with regard both to establishing legitimate political authority and the conditions necessary to a fulfilling civic life. The interest of *Oceana* lies in its combination of utopian elements, political theory and **allegory**. The city of *Oceana* is an allegorical discourse on the historical developments which led up to the English Revolution and the establishment of the British Commonwealth under Oliver Cromwell, and Harrington's text presents in utopian form what he considers to be the best constitution of government that the Commonwealth might adopt.

Some forms of **Marxist** and **socialist** thought could be described as containing utopian elements (e.g. Bakunin) –

although Marx himself contrasted his 'scientific' analysis of economic and social relations with the work of earlier 'utopian' socialists. In the twentieth century the utopian genre seems to have given way to **narrative** forms which envisage more disturbing possible futures, e.g. Aldous Huxley's *Brave New World* (1931) or George Orwell's *1984* (1948). Likewise, the conception of harmonious social order underlying utopian thought has been questioned by, amongst others, advocates of **postmodernism**. [PS]

Further reading: Davis 1981; Kelly 1982; Kumar 1991.

utterance   For V.N. Voloshinov, the utterance is the basic unit of the 'concrete reality of **language**' (1973: 93). It is to be distinguished from concepts such as 'linguistic form' which, unlike it, are derived through abstraction from the reality of language, but which certain theorists, including Saussure, nevertheless have a tendency to imply correspond to that reality (see Voloshinov 1973: 71, 79, 82, 98). Although Voloshinov sometimes uses the term 'speech act' as a synonym for 'utterance', his writings make clear that his concept covers all forms of language-use and thus is applicable to, say, written **texts** or thought as well as to the spoken word.

According to Voloshinov, the utterance is dialogic and social. In outlining the former characteristic he advances some of the better-known (although by no means the only) ideas on the concept of dialogism to be offered from within the Bakhtin Circle of intellectuals to which he belonged (see Morson and Emerson 1990; Hirschkop 1986; Morson 1986). These include the theory that each utterance is an element in an ongoing dialogue – or a 'moment' in a 'continuous process of verbal communication' – and that, consequently, each responds to a previous utterance or utterances and, also, is shaped by the utterer's anticipation of potential responses and objections to what she might utter (Voloshinov 1973: 95, and see pp. 72–3).

Voloshinov's thought on the social nature of the utterance may be summarised by saying that, for him, it is socially situated, oriented and determined. In *Marxism and the Philosophy of Language*, the account of the social character of the utterance overlaps with that of its dialogic character. A major component of it is the theory of the addressivity of the utterance. The utterance is always oriented towards an addressee. The addressee need not be a person in the presence of the utterer. Nor, Voloshinov intimates, need it be an actual person. Rather, an addressee may be presupposed in the form of a 'representative' of a particular social group (1973: 85). Voloshinov (1973: 86) theorises the utterance as determined equally by, and as a 'product of the reciprocal relationship between' addresser and addressee, and thereby implies that it may be thought of as socially or co-authored.

Further reflections on the utterance are contained in Voloshinov's essay 'Discourse in Life and Discourse in Poetry'. There, he puts forward the theory that, in addition to a verbalised component, an unverbalised context, assumed by utterer and 'receiver', is a part of the utterance (Clark and Holquist 1984: 204). He posits (1988: 11) three elements which may comprise the context of the utterance in everyday life: the common spatio-temporal situation of the interlocutors involved; their shared knowledge and understanding of the situation; and their shared evaluation of it. He indicates that the assumed context of an utterance contributes to its sense, and, in a comparison of the everyday utterance with the aesthetic verbal utterance, theorises that the latter cannot be as dependent for its sense as the former upon its unverbalised context.

He holds, additionally, that in the everyday utterance aspects of the 'social essence' of all utterances are relatively manifest. Intonation in the everyday utterance, in particular, is of significance in this respect. It discloses, through its expression of communal values, the connectedness of utterances with their surrounding social milieus. It also reveals the existence of relation of 'social interaction' (1988: 17) not only between utterer, or author, and 'listener' but also, through its direction of social values at, and related tendency to personify, the object of the utterance, between utterer and the topic or 'hero' of the utterance.

429

Theories of the utterance similar to those offered by Voloshinov are forwarded by Mikhail Bakhtin (1986) although, unlike Voloshinov (1973: 97), Bakhtin does not understand himself as contributing to a Marxist philosophy of language. In Bakhtin's writings, moreover, there is greater emphasis on the conventional distinction between utterance and sentence, with the former being portrayed as, *inter alia*, the employment of the sentence or sentences in speech communication. A similar distinction is present in the work of Jürgen Habermas (1979), where the utterance is theorised as the object of universal pragmatics, a discipline which Habermas contrasts with linguistics which is concerned with the abstract sentence. [RW]

Further reading: Bakhtin 1986; Clark and Holquist 1984; Hirschkop 1986; Morson 1986; Morson and Emerson 1990; Voloshinov 1988.

value   To value something may be defined as ascribing worth to it, and thus placing it within some hierarchy. Three core areas of value are of relevance to cultural theory: the **aesthetic**; the moral; and the economic.

Aesthetic value includes the worth of cultural goods and activities. Orthodox aesthetics is, in part, concerned with the principles that ground the ascription of value to particular works of art. While aesthetics may not itself be concerned with valuing particular works of art (which is more properly the task of art criticism), the attention that it gives to art, and especially the cultural products consumed by the dominant **classes** within society (not least, European society since the eighteenth century) presupposes that they are valuable objects and activities, and that there is such a thing as aesthetic value. At the end of the eighteenth century, Kant's *Critique of Judgement* (1987) is significant for proposing and defending a distinction between the pleasure that is derived from beauty (and thus art) and the mere sensuous enjoyment of useful, non-art objects (such as food). The autonomy and distinctiveness of aesthetic value has been increasingly challenged. On the one hand, politically, links have been drawn between art and **ideology**. The aesthetically valued art of the dominant class is explained by reference to the role it plays in legitimating and propagating the political and moral values of the dominant class. On the other hand, aesthetic value

431

may be linked to economic value. It may be argued that the prime purpose of aesthetics is not to ascribe the ultimately illusionary aesthetic value to objects, but to give that which is otherwise of minimal use an economic value. Aesthetically valued objects can be traded at high prices (Bourdieu 1984)

The development of **sociology** as a discipline may be seen to centre on the empirical study of values, not least in Emile Durkheim's conception of 'moral facts' (1982). The integration and stability of a society is seen to depend upon the internalisation of the consensual values of the society (encapsulated in Durkheim's concept of the '**conscience collective**'), through the process of **socialisation**. **Functionalism**, as the dominant American approach to sociology up to the 1960s, presupposed a consensus on moral values as a precondition of a stable society. This presupposition was increasingly challenged by the sociology of **deviance**, with the recognition of a wide-range of alternative **subcultures**, with markedly divergent value systems, within a single society. Similarly, the re-emergence of **Marxism** as a significant force within sociology in the 1960s, led to an increased recognition that consensual values were themselves the products of political and above all **ideological** and **hegemonic** practices, as conflicting groups sought to defend, promote and negotiate conflicting values systems. The work of Michel Foucault (1971), on punishment (1977) and sexuality (1981)) served to restore to sociology Nietzschean perspectives on the power struggles that underpin value systems, and in which values are inculcated.

The question of economic value centres upon explanations of the value and price ascribed to **commodities**. Marxism is characterised by an appeal to the **labour theory of value**, whereby the **exchange-value** of a good depends upon the amount of labour-time that has gone into its production. Orthodox economics, in contrast, explains value (or price) through appeal to the interaction of supply and demand in the market. [AE]

Further reading: Hechter *et al.* 1993; Squires 1993.

value-freedom   A view advocated by sociologist Max Weber, which states that those involved in scientific enquiry (e.g. in analyses within the discipline of **sociology**) should avoid making **value**-judgments with regard to the individuals, communities or institutions that they study. (See also **objectivity**.) [PS]

W

worldview From the German 'Weltanschauung'. A short-hand term signifying the common body of beliefs shared by a group of speakers about the world and their relationship to it. There is a close interrelationship between this notion and that of 'language-game' (see **meaning**), **discourse** or **paradigm**. Thus, it is one's place within a language-game, discourse or paradigm which supplies one with the beliefs and assumptions necessary to construct one's worldview. It therefore follows from this close interrelationship that, given a change of language-game, discourse or paradigm, there will be a corresponding change of worldview (see also **cultural relativism**). [SH]

Y

youth culture   The idea of a youth culture emerges in sociology in the 1950s and 1960s, in recognition of the fact that the **culture** of young people, especially in their teens or early twenties, is distinctive to that of their parents. Youth will have different **values**, **attitudes** and patterns of behaviour to those current in the dominant culture. Youth cultures are seen to emerge under certain conditions. First, youth must form a sufficiently large cohort. Second, rapid social change may disrupt young people's integration into the adult world, through, for example, changes in industry removing the traditional occupations or simply causing unemployment. Finally, an increasing **pluralism** in society will provide a stimulus to new ideas and **life-styles**. The idea of a youth culture, however, came under criticism for assuming that youth culture is largely homogeneous. It was particularly challenged by theories of youth **subcultures**, that recognise the fragmentation of youth culture according to class, gender and ethnic divisions. A swing back in favour of theories of youth culture may now be perceived, as subcultural accounts are seen to place too much emphasis upon exotic or marginal aspects of the everyday life of young people. (See also **counterculture**.) [AE]

Further reading: Clarke 1982; Frith 1984; Gillis 1974; McRobbie 1991.

BIBLIOGRAPHY

Abelove, H., Barale, M.A. and Halperin, D.M. (eds) (1993) *The Lesbian and Gay Studies Reader*, New York, Routledge.

Abercrombie, N., Hill, S. and Turner, B.S. (1980) *The Dominant Ideology Thesis*, London, Allen & Unwin

Adorno, T.W. (1967) (*1955*) *Prisms*, London, Spearman.

Adorno, T.W. (1973a) (*1948*) *The Philosophy of Modern Music*, London, Sheed & Ward.

Adorno, T.W. (1973b) (*1966*) *Negative Dialectics*, London, Routledge & Kegan Paul.

Adorno, T.W. (1978a) (*1951*) *Minima Moralia: Reflections from Damaged Life*, London, New Left Books.

Adorno, T.W. (1978b) (*1938*) 'On the Fetish Character in Music and the Regression of Listening', in A. Arato and E. Gebhardt (eds), *The Essential Frankfurt School Reader*, Oxford, Blackwell.

Adorno, T.W. (1982) (*1956*) *Against Epistemology*, tr. Willis Domingo, Oxford, Blackwell.

Adorno, T.W. (1984) (*1970*) *Aesthetic Theory*, London, Routledge & Kegan Paul.

Adorno, T.W. (1991a) *The Culture Industry: Selected Essays on Mass Culture*, ed. J.M. Bernstein, London, Routledge.

Adorno, T.W. (1991b) (*1957–1963*) *Notes to Literature*, volume 1, New York, Columbia University Press.

Adorno, T.W. (1992a) (*1965–1974*) *Notes to Literature*, volume 2, New York, Columbia University Press.

Adorno, T.W. (1992b) (*1963*) *Quasi una fantasia: Essays on Modern Music*, London, Verso.

Adorno, T.W. (1994) (*1941*) 'On Popular Music', in J. Storey (ed.), *Cultural Theory and Popular Culture: A Reader*, London, Edward Arnold.

436

Adorno, T.W., Frenkel-Brunswik, E., Levinson, D.J. and Sanford, R.N. (1950) *The Authoritarian Personality*, New York, Harper.

Adorno T.W. and Horkheimer, M. (1973) (*1944*) *Dialectic of Enlightenment*, tr. John Cummings, London, Allen Lane.

Aggleton, P. (1987) *Deviance*, London, Routledge.

Allport, G. (1980) *The Nature of Prejudice*, Reading, MA, Addison-Wesley.

Althusser, L. (1969) (*1959*) *For Marx*, tr. Ben Brewster, London, New Left Books.

Althusser, L. (1971) *Lenin and Philosophy and Other Essays*, London, New Left Books.

Althusser, L. and Balibar, E. (1970) *Reading Capital*, London, New Left Books.

Altizer, T. (1968) *Radical Theology and the Death of God*, Harmondsworth, Penguin.

Altizer, T. (1977) *The Self-Embodiment of God*, New York, Harper and Row.

Amin, A. (ed.) (1995) *Post-Fordism: A Reader*, Oxford, Blackwell.

Anderson, P. (1979) *Lineages of the Absolutist State*, London, Verso.

Ang, I. (1985) *Watching 'Dallas': Soap Opera and the Melodramatic Imagination*, London, Methuen.

Ansell-Pearson, K. (1991) *Nietzsche contra Rousseau: A Study of Nietzsche's Moral and Political Thought*, Cambridge, Cambridge University Press.

Apel, K.-O. (1976) 'The Transcendental Conception of Language Communication and the Idea of a First Philosophy', in H. Parret (ed.) *The History of Linguistic Thought and Contemporary Linguistics*, Berlin and New York, DeGruyter.

Apel, K.-O. (1981) *Charles S. Peirce: From Pragmatism to Pragmaticism*, tr. John Michael Krois, Amherst, University of Massachusetts Press.

Appleman, P. (ed.) (1970) *Darwin*, London, W.W. Norton and Co.

Arato A. and Gebhardt, E. (eds) (1978) *The Essential Frankfurt School Reader*, Oxford, Blackwell.

Arnold, M. (1993) *Culture and Anarchy and other Writings*, ed. Stefan Collini, Cambridge, Cambridge University Press.

Atkinson, J.M. and Heritage, J. (eds) (1984) *Structures of Social Action: Studies in Conversation Analysis*, Cambridge, Cambridge University Press.

Attali, J. (1985) *Noise: The Political Economy of Music*, Manchester, Manchester University Press.

Attridge, D., Bennington, G. and Young, R. (eds) (1987) *Post-Structuralism and the Question of History*, Cambridge, Cambridge University Press.

437

Bibliography

Austin, J.L. (1975) (*1955*) *How to Do Things With Words*, second edn, Oxford, Oxford University Press.

Avineri, S. and De-Shalit, A. (eds) (1992) *Communitarianism and Individualism*, Oxford, Oxford University Press.

Ayer, A.J. (1967) (*1946*) *Language, Truth and Logic*, second edn, London, Victor Gollancz.

Ayer, A.J. (ed.) (1959) *Logical Positivism*, London, Allen & Unwin; Glencoe, IL, Free Press.

Bachelard, G. (1964) (*1938*) *The Psychoanalysis of Fire*, London, Routledge & Kegan Paul.

Bachelard, G. (1969) (*1957*) *The Poetics of Space*, Boston, Beacon Press.

Badcock, C.R. (1975) *Lévi-Strauss: Structuralism and Sociological Theory*, London, Hutchinson.

Bakhtin, M. (1981) *The Dialogic Imagination: Four Essays by M.M. Bakhtin*, ed. M. Holquist, tr. Caryl Emerson and Michael Holquist, Austin, TX, University of Texas Press.

Bakhtin, M. (1984) *Rabelais and His World*, tr. Hélène Iswolsky, Bloomington, Indiana University Press.

Bakhtin, M. (1986) *Speech Genres and Other Late Essays*, ed. C. Emerson and M. Holquist, tr. Vern McGee, Austin, TX, University of Texas Press.

Balibar, E. (1970) 'The Basic Concepts of Historical Materialism', in L. Althusser and E. Balibar, *Reading Capital*, London, New Left Books.

Banton, M. (1977) *The Idea of Race*, London, Tavistock Publications.

Barker, M. (1989) *Comics: Ideology, Power and the Critics*, Manchester, Manchester University Press.

Barrett, M. (1980) *Women's Oppression Today: Problems in Marxist Feminist Analysis*, London, New Left Books.

Barrett, M. (1991) *The Politics of Truth: From Marx to Foucault*, Cambridge, Polity Press.

Barry, N.P. (1986) *On Classical Liberalism and Libertarianism*, Basingstoke, Macmillan.

Barry, N.P. (1989) *An Introduction to Modern Political Theory*, second edn, Basingstoke, Macmillan.

Barthes, R. (1967a) (*1953*) *Writing Degree Zero*, New York, Hill and Wang.

Barthes, R. (1967b) (*1964*) *Elements of Semiology*, New York, Hill and Wang.

Barthes, R. (1973) (*1957*) *Mythologies*, St Albans, Paladin.

Barthes, R. (1974) (*1970*) *S/Z*, New York, Hill and Wang.

Barthes, R. (1975) (*1973*) *The Pleasure of the Text*, New York, Hill and Wang.

Barthes, R. (1977a) *Image, Music, Text*, tr. Stephen Heath, London, Fontana.

Barthes, R. (1977b) 'Introduction to the Structural Analysis of Narratives', in *Image, Music, Text*, London, Fontana.

Barthes, R. (1977c) 'The Death of the Author', in *Image, Music, Text*, London, Fontana.

Barthes, R. (1977d) 'From Work to Text', in *Image, Music, Text*, London, Fontana.

Barthes, R. (1977e) (*1975*) *Barthes, R. by Barthes, R.*, New York, Hill and Wang.

Barthes, R. (1978) (*1977*) *A Lover's Discourse: Fragments*, New York, Hill and Wang.

Barthes, R. (1981) (*1980*) *Camera Lucida: Reflections on Photography*, New York, Hill and Wang.

Barthes, R. (1987) (*1966*) *Criticism and Truth*, Minneapolis, University of Minnesota Press.

Baudrillard, J. (1983) *Simulations*, tr. Paul Foss, Paul Patton and Philip Beitchman, New York, Semiotext(e).

Baudrillard, J. (1988) *Selected Writings*, ed. Mark Poster, Cambridge, Polity Press.

Baudrillard, J. (1990a) *Revenge of the Crystal: Selected Writings on the Modern Object and its Destiny, 1968–1983*, London, Pluto Press.

Baudrillard, J. (1990b) 'Mass Media Culture', in *Revenge of the Crystal: Selected Writings on the Modern Object and its Destiny, 1968–1983*, London, Pluto Press.

Baudrillard, J. (1990c) *Fatal Strategies*, London, Pluto Press.

Baudrillard, J. (1991) 'The Reality Gulf', *Guardian*, 11 January.

Baudrillard, J. (1993) *Symbolic Exchange and Death*, London, Sage.

Bauman, Z. (1989) *Modernity and the Holocaust*, Cambridge, Polity Press.

Baxandall, M. (1980) *The Limewood Sculptors of Renaissance Germany*, New Haven, CT, Yale University Press.

Bazin, A. (1967) *What is Cinema?*, Berkeley, CA, University of California Press.

Becker, H. (1961) *Boys in White: Student Culture in Medical School*, Chicago, University of Chicago Press.

Becker, H. (1963) *Outsiders: Studies in the Sociology of Deviance*, New York, Free Press.

Becker, H. (1982) *Art Worlds*, Berkeley, CA, University of California Press.

Becker, H., Geer, B. and Hughes, E.C. (1968) *Making the Grade: The Academic Side of College Life*, New York, Wiley.

Beetham, D. (1996) *Bureaucracy*, second edn, Buckingham, Open University Press.

Behr, S., Fanning, D. and Jarman, D. (eds) (1993) *Expressionism Reassessed*, Manchester, Manchester University Press.

Bell, D. (1960) *The End of Ideology*, Glencoe, IL, Free Press.

Bell, D. (1973) *The Coming of Post-Industrial Society: A Venture in Social Forecasting*, New York, Basic Books.

Bell, D. (1976) *The Cultural Contradictions of Capitalism*, London, Heinemann.

Bell, D. (1990) *Husserl*, London, Routledge.

Bell, D. (1993) *Communitarianism and its Critics*, Oxford, Clarendon Press.

Bell, M. (1988) *F.R. Leavis*, London, Routledge.

Belsey, C. (1980) *Critical Practice*, London, Methuen.

Bendix, R. (1960) *Max Weber: An Intellectual Portrait*, Garden City, NY, Doubleday.

Benedict, R. (1935) *Patterns of Culture*, London, Routledge & Kegan Paul.

Benedict, R. (1989) *Chrysanthemum and the Sword*, New York, Houghton Mifflin.

Benjamin, W. (1970a) *Illuminations*, ed. H. Arendt, London, Jonathan Cape.

Benjamin, W. (1970b) (*1936*) 'The Work of Art in the Age of Mechanical Reproduction', in *Illuminations*, London, Jonathan Cape.

Benjamin, W. (1970c) (*1940*) 'Theses on the Philosophy of History', in *Illuminations*, London, Jonathan Cape.

Benjamin, W. (1973a) *Charles Baudelaire: A Lyric Poet in the Era of High Capitalism*, London, New Left Books.

Benjamin, W. (1973b) *Understanding Brecht*, London, New Left Books.

Benjamin, W. (1977) (*1928*) *The Origin of German Tragic Drama*, tr. John Osborne, London, New Left Books.

Benjamin, W. (1978) (*1937*) 'Author as Producer', in A. Arato and E. Gebhardt (eds), *The Essential Frankfurt School Reader*, Oxford, Blackwell.

Benjamin, W. (1979) *One-Way Street and Other Writings*, London, New Left Books.

Bennett, J. (1966) *Kant's Analytic*, Cambridge, Cambridge University Press.

Bennett, J. (1974) *Kant's Dialectic*, London, Cambridge University Press.

Bennett, T., Martin, G., Mercer, C. and Woollacott, J. (eds) (1981) *Culture, Ideology and Social Process*, London, Batsford in association with the Open University Press.

Bennington, G. (1988) *Lyotard: Writing the Event*, New York, Columbia University Press.

Berger, J. (1972) *Ways of Seeing*, Harmondsworth, Penguin.

Berger, P.L. (1963) *Invitation to Sociology*, Harmondsworth, Penguin.

Berger, P.L. and Luckmann, T. (1961) *The Social Construction of Reality: A Treatise in the Sociology of Knowledge*, London, Allen Lane.

Berkeley, G. (1975) *Philosophical Works: Including the Works on Vision*, London, Dent.

Berki, R.N. (1975) *Socialism*, London, Dent.

Berlin, E.A. (1980) *Ragtime: A Musical and Cultural History*, London, University of California Press.

Berlin, I. (ed.) (1979) *The Age of Enlightenment*, Oxford, Oxford University Press.

Berliner, P.F. (1994) *Thinking in Jazz: The Infinite Art of Improvisation*, Chicago, University of Chicago Press.

Berman, M. (1983) *All This is Solid Melts into Air: The Experience of Modernity*, London, Verso.

Bernstein, B. (1977) *Class, Codes and Control*, volume 1, *Theoretical Studies Towards a Sociology of Language*, London, Routledge & Kegan Paul.

Bernstein, B. (1996) *Pedagogy, Symbolic Control and Identity: Theory, Research, Critique*, London, Taylor & Francis.

Bernstein, R.J. (1983) *Beyond Objectivism and Relativism: Science, Hermeneutics, and Praxis*, Oxford, Blackwell.

Bhaskar, R. (1975) *A Realist Theory of Science*, Hemel Hempstead, Harvester.

Biddle, B.J. (1979) *Role Theory: Expectations, Identities and Behaviours*, New York, Academic Press.

Bilton, T., Jones, P., Skinner, D., Stansworth, M. and Webster, A. (1996) *Introductory Sociology*, third edn, Basingstoke, Macmillan.

Biriotti, M. and Miller, N. (eds) (1993) *What is an Author?*, Manchester, Manchester University Press.

Black, M. (1979) 'More about Metaphor', in A. Ortony (ed.), *Metaphor and Thought*, Cambridge, Cambridge University Press.

Blauner, R. (1964) *Alienation and Freedom*, Chicago, University of Chicago Press.

Bloch, E. *et al.* (1977) *Aesthetics and Politics*, London, Verso.

Bloch, M. (1961) *Feudal Society: Social Classes and Political Organisation*, London, Routledge & Kegan Paul.

441

Block, N., Flanagan, O. and Guzeldere, G. (eds) (1997) *The Nature of Consciousness: Philosophical Debates*, Cambridge, MA, MIT Press.

Blumer, H. (1969) *Symbolic Interactionism: Perspective and Method*, Englewood Cliffs, NJ, Prentice-Hall.

Blumer, M. (1984) *The Chicago School of Sociology: Institutionalization, Diversity, and the Rise of Sociological Research*, Chicago, University of Chicago Press.

Bocock, R. (1986) *Hegemony*, London, Tavistock.

Bocock, R. (1993) *Consumption*, London, Routledge.

Bocock, R., Hamilton, P., Thompson, K. and Walton, A. (eds) (1980) *An Introduction to Sociology*, London, Fontana in association with the Open Press University.

Bogue, R. (1989) *Deleuze and Guattari*, London and New York, Routledge.

Bolton, R. (ed.) (1989) *The Contest of Meaning: Critical Histories of Photography*, Cambridge, MA, MIT Press.

Bottomore, T. (ed.) (1983) *A Dictionary of Marxist Thought*, Oxford, Blackwell.

Bottomore, T. (1985) *Theories of Modern Capitalism*, London, Routledge.

Bottomore, T. (1993) *Elites and Society*, second edn, London, Routledge.

Boucher, D. and Kelly, P. (eds) (1994) *The Social Contract from Hobbes to Rawls*, London, Routledge.

Boulez, P. (1968) (*1966*) *Notes of an Apprenticeship*, London, Faber.

Boulez, P. (1971) (*1963*) *Boulez on Music Today*, London, Faber.

Boulez, P. (1976) (*1975*) *Conversations with Célestin Deliège*, London, Eulenburg.

Boulez, P. (1986) (*1981*) *Orientations*, London, Faber.

Boundas, C.V and Olkowski, D. (eds) (1994) *Gilles Deleuze and the Theater of Philosophy*, New York, Routledge.

Bourdieu, P. (1973) 'Cultural Reproduction and Social Reproduction', in R. Brown (ed.), *Knowledge, Education and Cultural Change*, London, Tavistock.

Bourdieu, P. (1984) (*1979*) *Distinction: A Social Critique of the Judgement of Taste*, London, Routledge & Kegan Paul.

Bourdieu, P. (1993) *The Field of Cultural Production*, Cambridge, Polity Press.

Bowie, A. (1990) *Aesthetics and Subjectivity: From Kant to Nietzsche*, Manchester, Manchester University Press.

Boyer, R. and Durand, J.-P. (1997) *After Fordism*, tr. Sybil Hyacinth Mair, Basingstoke, Macmillan.

Bradbury, M. and McFarlane, J. (eds) (1976) *Modernism: 1890–1930*, Harmondsworth, Penguin.

442

Braudel, F. (1972) (*1949*) *The Mediterranean and the Mediterranean World in the Age of Philip II*, London, Collins.

Braudel, F. (1958) 'History and the Social Sciences', in *On History*, London, Weidenfeld & Nicolson.

Braverman, H. (1974) *Labour and Monopoly Capitalism: The Degradation of Work in the Twentieth Century*, New York, Monthly Review Press.

Brett, P., Thomas, G. and Wood, E. (eds) (1994) *Queering the Pitch: The New Gay and Lesbian Musicology*, New York, Routledge.

Breuer, J. and Freud, S. (1974) (*1895*) *Studies on Hysteria*, ed. A. Richards, tr. James Strachey, Harmondsworth, Pelican Books.

Bronner, S.E. and Kellner, D.M. (eds) (1989) *Critical Theory and Society: A Reader*, London, Routledge.

Brooks, C. (1938) *Understanding Poetry: An Anthology for College Students*, New York, Henry Holt.

Brooks, C. (1949) *The Well Wrought Urn: Studies in the Structure of Poetry*, London, Dennis Dobson.

Brubaker, R. (1984) *The Limits of Rationality: An Essay on the Social and Moral Thought of Max Weber*, London, Allen & Unwin.

Buck-Morss, S. (1991) *The Dialectics of Seeing: Walter Benjamin and the Arcades Project*, Cambridge, MA, MIT Press.

Bukofzer, M. (1939) 'Allegory in Baroque Music', *Journal of the Warburg Institute*, 3: 1–21.

Bullough, E. (1957) *Aesthetics: Lectures and Essays*, Palo Alto, CA, Stanford University Press.

Bürger, P. (1984) *Theory of the Avant-Garde*, Minneapolis, University of Minnesota Press.

Burke, E. (1982) (*1790*) *Reflections on the Revolution in France*, Harmondsworth, Penguin.

Burke, J. and Moore, S. (1979) 'Reification and Commodity Fetishism Revisited', *Canadian Journal of Political and Social Theory*, 3(1): 71–86.

Burke, P. (1990) *The French Historical Revolution: The Annales School, 1929–1989*, Cambridge, Polity Press.

Burke, S. (1992) *The Death and Return of the Author: Criticism and Subjectivity in Barthes, Foucault and Derrida*, Edinburgh, Edinburgh University Press.

Burns, T. (1992) *Erving Goffman*, London, Routledge.

Butler, J. (1990) *Gender Trouble: Feminism and the Subversion of Identity*, London, Routledge.

Cage, J.M. (1966) *Silence*, Cambridge, MA, MIT Press.

Callinicos, A. (1976) *Althusser's Marxism*, London, Pluto Press.

Callinicos, A. (1983) *Marxism and Philosophy*, Oxford, Clarendon Press.

Bibliography

Camus, A. (1990) (*1942*) *The Myth of Sisyphus*, tr. Justin O'Brien, Harmondsworth, Penguin.

Carr, E.H. (1987) (*1961*) *What is History?*, Harmondsworth, Penguin.

Carver, T. (1975) 'Marx's Commodity Fetishism', *Inquiry*, 18(1): 39–63.

Carver, T. (ed.) (1991) *The Cambridge Companion to Marx*, Cambridge, Cambridge University Press.

Castells, M. (1989) *The Informational City*, Oxford, Blackwell.

Cavell, S. (1971) *The World Viewed: Reflections on the Ontology of Film*, New York, Viking.

Chadwick, R.F. and Cazeux, C. (eds) (1992) *Immanuel Kant: Critical Assessments*, London and New York, Routledge.

Chalmers, A.F. (1982) *What is This Thing Called Science?*, second edn, Milton Keynes, Open University Press.

Chalmers, A.F. (1990) *Science and its Fabrication*, Milton Keynes, Open University Press.

Chancy, D. (1996) *Lifestyles*, London, Routledge.

Chipp, H.B. (1968) *Theories of Modern Art: A Source Book by Artists and Critics*, Berkeley, University of California Press.

Chomsky, N. (1957) *Syntactic Structures*, The Hague, Mouton.

Chomsky, N. (1966) *Cartesian Linguistics*, New York, Harper & Row.

Chomsky, N. (1972) *Studies on Semantics and Generative Grammar*, The Hague, Mouton.

Chomsky, N. (1973) *For Reasons of State*, New York, Pantheon.

Chomsky, N. (1978) *Language and Politics*, Montreal, Black Rose Books.

Christie, R. and Jahoda, M. (eds) (1954) *Studies in the Scope and Method of 'The Authoritarian Personality'*, Glencoe, IL, Free Press.

Churchland, P. (1988) *Matter and Consciousness: A Contemporary Introduction to the Philosophy of Mind*, Cambridge, MA, MIT Press.

Churchland, P. (1995) *The Engine of Reason, the Seat of the Soul: A Philosophical Journey into the Brain*, Cambridge, MA, MIT Press.

Cixous, H. (1987) *The Newly Born Woman*, Manchester, Manchester University Press.

Cixous, H. (1981) (*1975*) 'The Laugh of the Medusa', in E. Marks and I. de Courtivron (eds), *New French Feminisms*, Brighton, Harvester.

Clark, K. and Holquist, M. (1984) *Mikhail Bakhtin*, Cambridge, MA, Belknap Press of Harvard University Press.

Clark, M. (1988) *Jacques Lacan: An Annotated Bibliography*, New York, Garland Publishers.

Clark, T.J. (1973) *The Absolute Bourgeois: Artists and Politics in France 1848–1851*, London, Thames & Hudson.

Clarke, G. (1982) *Defending Ski-Jumpers: A Critique of Theories of Youth Sub-Cultures*, Stencilled Paper 71, Centre for Contemporary Cultural Studies, Birmingham University.

Clarke, K. (1956) *The Nude*, New York, Pantheon.

Clarke, S. (1981) *The Foundations of Structuralism: A Critique of Lévi-Strauss and the Structuralist Movement*, Brighton, Harvester.

Clement, C. (1983) (*1981*) *The Lives and Legends of Jacques Lacan*, tr. Arthur Goldhammer, New York, Columbia University Press.

Cobb, J. (1977) *Process Theology: An Introductory Exposition*, Belfast, Christian Journals.

Cohen, G.A. (1978) *Karl Marx's Theory of History*, Oxford, Clarendon Press.

Cohen, I.J. (1989) *Structuration Theory: Anthony Giddens and the Constitution of Social Life*, London, Macmillan.

Cohen, P. (1980) 'Subcultural Conflict and Working-Class Community', in S. Hall, D. Hobson, A. Lowe and P. Willis (eds), *Culture, Media, Language*, London, Hutchinson.

Cohen, S. (1980) *Folk Devils and Moral Panics*, second edn, Oxford, Martin Robertson.

Collier, G. (1977) *Jazz*, Cambridge, Cambridge University Press.

Collini, S. (1988) *Arnold*, Oxford and New York, Oxford University Press.

Collins, R. (1975) *Conflict Sociology: Toward an Explanatory Science*, New York, Academic Press.

Connerton, P. (ed.) (1976) *Critical Sociology*, Harmondsworth, Penguin.

Cook, D. (1996) *The Culture Industry Revisited: Theodor W. Adorno on Mass Culture*, Lanham, MD, Rowman and Littlefield.

Cooper, D.E. (1986) *Metaphor*, Oxford, Blackwell.

Cooper, D.E. (1992) *A Companion to Aesthetics*, Oxford, Blackwell.

Cooper, D.E. (1997) *Aesthetics: The Classic Readings*, Oxford, Blackwell.

Cornforth, M. (1971) *Dialectical Materialism*, London, Lawrence & Wishart.

Corrigan, P. (1997) *The Sociology of Consumption*, London, Sage.

Coser, L.A. (1956) *The Functions of Social Conflict*, New York, Free Press.

Crane, T. (1995) *The Mechanical Mind: A Philosophical Introduction to Minds, Machines and Mental Representation*, London, Penguin.

Cranston, M. (1994) *The Romantic Movement*, Oxford, Blackwell.

Crothers, C. (1996) *Social Structure*, London, Routledge.

Crouch, D. and Ward, C. (1997) *The Allotment: Its Landscape and Culture*, Nottingham, Five Leaves.

Crozier, B. (1987) *Socialism: Dream and Reality*, London, Sherwood Press.

Culler, J. (1975) *Structuralist Poetics: Structuralism, Linguistics and the Study of Literature*, London, Routledge & Kegan Paul.

Culler, J. (1983) *Roland Barthes*, New York, Oxford University Press.

Culler, J. (1986) *Ferdinand de Saussure*, Ithaca, NY, Cornell University Press.

Cunningham-Wood, J. (ed.) (1988) *Karl Marx's Economics: Critical Assessments*, volume 2, *Marx's Capital*, London, Croom Helm.

Cupitt, D. (1979) *Explorations in Theology*, London, SCM Press.

Cupitt, D. (1988) *The New Christian Ethics*, London, SCM Press.

Curtis, W.J.R. (1992) *Le Corbusier: Ideas and Forms*, London, Phaidon Press.

Cutler, A., Hindess, B., Hirst, P.Q. and Hussain, A. (1977) *Marx's Capital and Capitalism Today*, Volume 1, London, Routledge & Kegan Paul.

Dahl, R.A. (1956) *A Preface to Democratic Theory*, Chicago, University of Chicago Press.

Dahrendorf, R. (1979) *Life Chances*, London, Weidenfeld & Nicolson.

Dallmayr, F.R. (1981) *Twilight of Subjectivity: Contributions to a Post-Individualist Theory of Politics*, Amherst, MA, University of Massachusetts Press.

Dancy, J. (1985) *An Introduction to Contemporary Epistemology*, Oxford, Blackwell.

Dancy, J. and Sosa, E. (1992) *A Companion to Epistemology*, Oxford, Blackwell.

Dant, T. (1996) 'Fetishism and the Social Value of Objects', *Sociological Review*, 44(3): 495–516.

Danto, A.C. (1964) 'The Artworld', *Journal of Philosophy*, 61: 571–84.

Danto, A.C. (1981) *The Transfiguration of the Commonplace*, Cambridge, MA, Harvard University Press.

David, H. (1997) *On Queer Street: A Social History of British Homosexuality 1895–1995*, London, HarperCollins.

Davidson, D. (1984a) (*1977*) *Inquiries into Truth and Interpretation*, Oxford, Clarendon Press.

Davidson, D. (1984b) (*1973*) 'Radical Interpretation', in *Inquiries into Truth and Interpretation*, Oxford, Clarendon Press.

Davidson, D. (1984c) 'Belief as the Basis of Meaning', in *Inquiries into Truth and Interpretation*, Oxford, Clarendon Press.

Davidson, D. (1991) 'Truth and Meaning', in *Inquiries into Truth and Interpretation*, Oxford, Clarendon Press.

Davidson, D. (1993) 'A Coherence Theory of Truth and Knowledge', in E. Lepore (ed.), *Truth and Interpretation*, Oxford, Blackwell, pp. 307–19.

Davies, T. (1997) *Humanism*, London and New York, Routledge.

Davis, J.C. (1981) *Utopia and the Ideal Society: A Study of English Utopian Writing, 1516–1700*, Cambridge, Cambridge University Press.

Dawkins, R. (1976) *The Selfish Gene*, Oxford, Oxford University Press.

Day, G. (1996) *Re-reading Leavis: Culture and Literary Criticism*, Basingstoke, Macmillan.

De Certeau, M. (1984) *The Practice of Everyday Life*, Berkeley, University of California Press.

Deleuze, G. (1983) (*1962*) *Nietzsche and Philosophy*, tr. Hugh Tomlinson, London, Athlone Press.

Deleuze, G. (1990a) (*1969*) *The Logic of Sense*, tr. Mark Lester with Charles Stivale, London, Athlone Press.

Deleuze, G. (1990b) 'The Simulacrum and Ancient Philosophy', in *The Logic of Sense*, London, Athlone Press.

Deleuze, G. (1991) *Cinema*, 2 volumes, Minneapolis, University of Minnesota Press.

Deleuze, G. and Guattari, F. (1977) (*1972*) *Anti-Oedipus: Capitalism and Schizophrenia*, tr. Robert Hurley, Mark Seem and Helen R. Lane, New York, Viking Press.

Deleuze, G. and Guattari, F. (1987) (*1980*) *A Thousand Plateaus: Capitalism and Schizophrenia*, tr. Brian Massumi, Minneapolis, University of Minnesota Press.

De Man, P. (1979) *Allegories of Reading: Figural Language in Rousseau, Nietzsche, Rilke, and Proust*, New Haven, CT, Yale University Press.

De Man, P. (1989) *Blindness and Insight: Essays on the Rhetoric of Contemporary Criticism*, London, Routledge.

Denzin, N.K. (1992) *Symbolic Interactionism and Cultural Studies*, Oxford, Blackwell.

Derrida, J. (1973) '*Speech and Phenomena*' *and Other Essays on Husserl's Theory of Signs*, tr. David B. Allison, Evanston, IL, Northwestern University Press.

Derrida, J. (1976) (*1967*) *Of Grammatology*, tr. G. Spivak, Baltimore, Johns Hopkins University Press.

Derrida, J. (1978) (*1967*) *Writing and Difference*, tr. Alan Bass, London, Routledge & Kegan Paul.

Derrida, J. (1979) *Spurs: Nietzsche's Styles*, tr. Barbara Harlow, Chicago, University of Chicago Press.

Derrida, J. (1981) *Dissemination*, tr. Barbara Johnson, Chicago, University of Chicago Press.

Derrida, J. (1982) *Margins of Philosophy*, tr. Alan Bass, Chicago, University of Chicago Press.

Derrida, J. (1987) *The Truth in Painting*, Chicago, University of Chicago Press.

Derrida, J. (1988a) *The Ear of the Other: Otobiography, Transference, Translation Texts and Discussions with Jacques Derrida*, ed. C. McDonald, tr. Peggy Kamuf, Lincoln and London, University of Nebraska Press.

Derrida, J. (1988b) *Limited Inc.*, Evanston, IL, Northwestern University Press.

Derrida, J. (1992) *Given Time. I. Counterfeit Money*, tr. Peggy Kamuf, Chicago and London, University of Chicago Press.

Derrida, J. (1994) *Specters of Marx: The State of Debt, the Work of Mourning, and the New International*, tr. Peggy Kamuf, New York and London, Routledge.

Derrida, J. (1996) *Archive Fever: A Freudian Impression*, tr. Eric Prenowitz, Chicago and London, University of Chicago Press.

Descartes, R. (1968) (*1637 and 1641*) *Discourse on Method and the Mediations*, Harmondsworth, Penguin.

Descartes, R. (1986) (*1641*) *Meditations on First Philosophy*, tr. J. Cottingham, Cambridge, Cambridge University Press.

Devitt, M. and Sterelny, K. (1987) *Language and Reality*, Oxford, Blackwell.

Dews, P. (1988) 'Nietzsche and the Critique of *Ursprungsphilosophie*', in D.F. Krell and D. Wood (eds), *Exceedingly Nietzsche*, London, Routledge.

Dickie, G. (1974) *Art and the Aesthetic: An Institutional Analysis*, Ithaca, NY, Cornell University Press.

Dickie, G. (1984) *The Art Circle: A Theory of Art*, New York, Havens.

Diprose, R. (1994) *The Bodies of Women: Ethics, Embodiment and Sexual Difference*, London, Routledge.

Doty, A. (ed.) (1997) *Making Things Perfectly Queer: Interpreting Mass Culture*, Minneapolis, University of Minnesota Press.

Douglas, M. (1973) *Natural Symbols: Explorations in Cosmology*, Harmondsworth, Penguin.

Downes D. and Rock, P. (1982) *Understanding Deviance*, Oxford, Clarendon Press.

Draper, H. (1987) *The 'Dictatorship of the Proletariat' from Marx to Lenin*, New York, Monthly Review Press.

Dreyfus, H. and Hall, H. (eds) (1992) *Heidegger: A Critical Reader*, Oxford, Blackwell.

Du Gay, P., Hall, S., Janes, L., Mackay, H. and Negus, K. (1997) *Doing Cultural Studies: The Story of the Sony Walkman*, London, Sage.

Dube, W.D. (ed.) (1997) *German Expressionism: Art and Society 1909–1923*, London, Thames & Hudson.

Duhem, P. (1962) *The Aim and Structure of Physical Theory*, tr. Philip P. Wiener, New York, Atheneum.

Dummett, M. (1973) *Frege: Philosophy of Language*, London, Duckworth.

Durkheim, E. (1952) (*1897*) *Suicide: A Study in Sociology*, tr. John A. Spaulding and George Simpson, London, Routledge & Kegan Paul.

Durkheim, E. (1975) *Emile Durkheim on Religion*, ed. W.S.F. Pickering, London, Routledge & Kegan Paul.

Durkheim, E. (1976) (*1912*) *The Elementary Forms of the Religious Life: A Study in Religious Sociology*, London, Allen & Unwin.

Durkheim, E. (1982) (*1895*) *The Rules of Sociological Method*, London, Macmillan.

Durkheim, E. (1984) (*1893*) *The Division of Labour in Society*, tr. W.D. Halls, Basingstoke, Macmillan.

Durkheim, E. and Mauss, M. (1963) (*1903*) *Primitive Classification*, Chicago, University of Chicago Press.

Dyer, R. (1979) *Stars*, London, British Film Institute.

Dyer, R. (1985) 'Entertainment and Utopia', in B. Nichols (ed.), *Movies and Methods*, volume 2, Berkeley, Los Angeles and London, University of California Press.

Eagleton, T. (1983) *Literary Theory: An Introduction*, Oxford, Blackwell.

Eagleton, T. (1984) *The Function of Criticism*, London, Verso.

Eagleton, T. (ed.) (1989) *Raymond Williams: Critical Perspectives*, Cambridge, Polity Press.

Eagleton, T. (1991) *Ideology: An Introduction*, London, Verso.

Eagleton, T. (1999) *The Ideology of the Aesthetic*, Oxford, Blackwell.

Eatwell, R. (1996) *Fascism: A History*, London, Vintage.

Eco, U. (1976) *A Theory of Semiotics*, Bloomington, Indiana University Press.

Eco, U. (1986) *Faith in Fakes: Travels in Hyperreality*, London, Minerva.

Edgell, S. (1993) *Class*, London, Routledge.

Ehrenberg, J. (1992) *The Dictatorship of the Proletariat: Marxism's Theory of Socialist Democracy*, New York, Routledge.

Elders, F. (ed.) (1974) *Reflexive Water: Basic Concerns of Mankind*, London, Souvenir Press.

Eldridge, J. and Eldridge, L. (1994) *Raymonds Williams: Making Connections*, London, Routledge.

Elias, N. (1970) *What is Sociology?*, London, Hutchinson.

Ellenberger, H. (1970) *The Discovery of the Unconscious: The History and Evolution of Dynamic Psychiatry*, London, Allen Lane, The Penguin Press.

Empson, William, (1951) *The Structure of Complex Words*, London, Chatto & Windus.

Engels, F. (1947) (*1876–8*) *Anti-Dühring*, Moscow, Progress Publishers.

Engels, F. (1973) (*1873–83*) *Dialectics of Nature*, tr. C. Dutt, New York, International Publishers.

Erikson, E. (1968) *Identity: Youth and Crisis*, London, Faber & Faber.

Esslin, M. (1980) *The Theatre of the Absurd*, third edn, Harmondsworth, Penguin.

Evans, G. (1973) 'The Causal Theory of Names', *Proceedings of the Aristotelian Society*, 47: 187–208.

Evans-Pritchard, E.E. (1951) *Kinship and Marriage Among the Nuer*, Oxford, Clarendon Press.

Falk, P. and Campbell, C. (eds) (1997) *The Shopping Experience*, London, Sage.

Fanon, F. (1989) (*1952*) *Black Skin, White Masks*, tr. Charles Lamm Markmann, New York, Grove Press.

Farrell, F.B. (1994) *Subjectivity, Realism, and Postmodernism: The Recovery of the World*, Cambridge; New York, Cambridge University Press.

Felstein, R., Fink, B. and Jaanus, M. (eds) (1995) *Reading Seminar XI: Lacan's Four Fundamental Concepts of Psychoanalysis*, Albany, SUNY Press.

Feyerabend, P. (1975) *Against Method*, London, Verso.

Fine, B. (1977) 'Labelling Theory: An Investigation into the Sociological Critique of Deviance', *Economy and Society*, 6(2): 166–93.

Fink, B. (1995) 'The real cause of repetition', in R. Feldstein, B. Fink and M. Jaanus (eds), *Reading Seminar XI: Lacan's Four Fundamental Concepts of Psychoanalysis*, Albany, SUNY Press.

Finnegan, R. (1989) *Hidden Musicians*, Cambridge, Cambridge University Press.

Fiske, J. (1987) *Television Culture*, London, Methuen.

Fiske, J. (1989) *Understanding Popular Culture*, Boston, MA, Unwin Hyman.

Fiske, J. and Hartley, J. (1978) *Reading Television*, London, Methuen.

Fleming, R. and Duckworth, W. (eds) (1989) *John Cage at Seventy-Five*, Lewisburg, PA, Bucknell University Press.

Fodor, J. and LePore, E. (1991) *Holism: A Shopper's Guide*, Oxford, Blackwell.

Fontana, B. (1993) *Hegemony and Power*, Minneapolis, University of Minnesota Press.

Forman, J.D. (1973) *Socialism: Its Theoretical Roots and Present Day Development*, New York, New Viewpoints.

Forrester, J. (1990) *The Seductions of Psychoanalysis: Freud, Lacan and Derrida*, Cambridge, Cambridge University Press.

Forte, A. (1973) *The Structure of Atonal Music*, New Haven, CT, Yale University Press.

Foster, G. (1960) *Culture and Conquest*, New York, Wener-Gren Foundation for Anthropological Research.

Foster, S. L. (ed.) (1996) *Corporealities: Dancing Knowledge, Culture and Power*, London, Routledge.

Foucault, M. (1970) (1966) *The Order of Things: An Archaeology of the Human Sciences*, London, Tavistock.

Foucault, M. (1971) (*1961*) *Madness and Civilization: A History of Insanity in the Age of Reason*, London, Tavistock.

Foucault, M. (1972) (*1969*) *The Archaeology of Knowledge*, tr. A.M. Sheridan Smith, New York, Pantheon Books.

Foucault, M. (1976) (*1963*) *The Birth of the Clinic*, London, Tavistock.

Foucault, M. (1977a) (*1975*) *Discipline and Punish: The Birth of the Prison*, Harmondsworth, Penguin.

Foucault, M. (1977b) 'Nietzsche, Genealogy, History', in D.F. Bouchard (ed.), *Language, Counter-Memory, Practice*, Oxford, Blackwell.

Foucault, M. (1980) *Power-Knowledge: Selected Interviews and Other Writings 1972–1977*, ed. Colin Gordon Hassocks, Harvester.

Foucault, M. (1981) (*1976*) *The History of Sexuality*, volume 1, *An Introduction*, Harmondsworth, Penguin.

Foulkes, A.P. (1983) *Literature and Propaganda*, London, Methuen.

Fox, M. (1983) *Original Blessing*, London, Bear/Mountain.

Frankenburg, R. (1957) *Village on the Border*, London, Cohen and West.

Frege, G. (1953) (*1884*) *The Foundations of Arithmetic*, second revised edn, tr. J.L. Austin, Oxford, Blackwell.

Frege, G. (1984) *Collected Papers on Mathematics, Logic and Philosophy*, ed. B. McGuinness, Oxford, Clarendon Press.

Frege, G. (1993) (*1892*) 'On Sense and Reference', in A.W. Moore (ed.), *Meaning and Reference*, tr. Max Black, Oxford, Blackwell.

Freud, S. (1908) 'On the Sexual Theories of Children', in *The Standard Edition of the Complete Psychological Works of Sigmund Freud*, Volume 9, tr. J. Strachey, London, Hogarth Press and Institute of Psychoanalysis.

Freud, S. (1910) 'A Special Type of Choice of Object Made by Men', in *The Standard Edition of the Complete Psychological Works of Sigmund Freud*, Volume 11, tr. J. Strachey, London, Hogarth Press and Institute of Psychoanalysis.

Freud, S. (1924) 'The Dissolution of the Oedipus Complex', in *The Standard Edition of the Complete Psychological Works of Sigmund Freud*,

Volume 19, tr. J. Strachey, London, Hogarth Press and Institute of Psychoanalysis.

Freud, S. (1955) 'Beyond the Pleasure Principle', in *The Standard Edition of the Complete Psychological Works of Sigmund Freud*, Volume 18, tr. J. Strachey, London, Hogarth Press.

Freud, S. (1966) *The Standard Edition of the Complete Psychological Works of Sigmund Freud,* ed J. Strachey, London, Hogarth Press.

Freud, S. (1977) (*1905*) *On Sexuality: Three Essays on the Theory of Sexuality and Other Works*, A. Richards (ed.), tr. James Strachey, London, Penguin.

Freud, S. (1979) (*1909*) 'My Views on the Part Played by Sexuality in the Aetiology of the Neuroses', in *On Psychopathology*, ed., A. Richards tr. James Strachey, Harmondsworth, Pelican Books.

Freud, S. (1984) (1920) 'Beyond the Pleasure Principle', in *On Metapsychology*, A. Richards (ed.), tr. A. Strachey, London, Penguin.

Freud, S. (1991a) (*1900*) *The Interpretation of Dreams*, ed. A. Richards, tr. James Strachey, London, Penguin.

Freud, S. (1991b) (*1915*) 'Instincts and their vicissitudes', in *On Metapsychology: The Theory of Psychoanalysis*, ed., A. Richards, tr. James Strachey, London, Penguin.

Fried, M. (1992) (*1965*) 'Three American Painters', in C. Harrison and P. Wood (eds) *Art in Theory 1900–1990: An Anthology of Changing Ideas*, Oxford, Blackwell.

Friedman, M. (1953) *Essays in Positive Economics*, Chicago, University of Chicago Press.

Frisby, D. (1988) *Fragments of Modernity*, Cambridge, Polity Press.

Frisby, D. (ed.) (1994) *Georg Simmel: Critical Assessments*, London, Routledge.

Frisby, D. and Sayer, D. (1985) *Society*, London, Tavistock Publications.

Frith, S. (1981) *Sound Effects*, New York, Pantheon.

Frith, S. (1984) *Sociology of Youth*, County of Lancashire, Causeway Books.

Frith, S. (1992) 'The Cultural Study of Popular Music', in L. Grossberg, C. Nelson and S. Frith (eds), *Performing Rites: On the Value of Popular Music*, Oxford, Oxford University Press.

Gabbard, K. (ed.) (1995) *Jazz Among the Discourses*, London, Duke University Press.

Gadamer, H.G. (1975) (*1962*) *Truth and Method*, tr. Garrett Barden and John Cumming, London, Sheed & Ward.

Gallie, W.B. (1975) *Peirce and Pragmatism*, Westport, CT, Greenwood Press.

Gans, H. J. (1968) 'Urbanism and Suburbanism as Ways of Life', in R. Pahl (ed.), *Readings in Urban Sociology*, Oxford, Pergamon.

Gardiner, M. (1992), *The Dialogics of Critique: M. M. Bakhtin and the Theory of Ideology*, London, Routledge.

Garfinkel, H. (1967) *Studies in Ethnomethodology*, Englewood Cliffs, NJ, Prentice-Hall.

Gascoyne, D. (1970) *A Short Survey of Surrealism*, London, Cass.

Gay, P. (1984) *The Bourgeois Experience: Victoria to Freud*, Volume 1, *Education of the Senses*, Oxford, Oxford University Press.

Gay, P. (1986) *The Bourgeois Experience: Victoria to Freud*, Volume 2, *The Tender Passion*, Oxford, Oxford University Press.

Gay, P. (1988a) *The Enlightenment: An Interpretation*, 2 Volumes, London, Weidenfeld and Nicolson.

Gay, P. (1988b) *Freud: A Life for Our Time*, London, Macmillan.

Geertz, C. (1973) *The Interpretation of Cultures*, New York, Basic Books.

Geertz, C. (1976) *The Religion of Java*, Chicago, University of Chicago Press.

Gelb, I.J. (1963) *The Study of Writing*, second edn, Chicago, University of Chicago Press.

Gellner, E. (1983) *Nations and Nationalism*, Oxford, Blackwell.

Genette, G. (1980) *Narrative Discourse: An Essay on Method*, Oxford, Blackwell.

Gettier, E.L. (1963) 'Is Justified True Belief Knowledge?', *Analysis*, Vol. 23.

Giddens, A. (1973) *The Class Structure of the Advanced Societies*, London, Hutchinson.

Giddens, A. (1977) *Studies in Social and Political Theory*, London, Hutchinson.

Giddens, A. (1978) *Durkheim*, London, Fontana.

Giddens, A. (1979) 'Agency, Structure', in *Central Problems in Social Theory*, London, Macmillan.

Giddens, A. (1984) *The Constitution of Society: Outline of the Theory of Structuration*, Cambridge, Polity Press.

Giddens, A. (1990) *The Consequences of Modernity*, Cambridge, Polity Press.

Giddens, A. (1991) *Modernity and Self-Identity*, Cambridge, Polity Press.

Giddens, A. (1997) *Sociology*, third edn, Cambridge, Polity Press.

Giddens, A. and Held, D. (eds) (1982) *Classes, Power and Conflict: Classical and Contemporary Debates*, Basingstoke, Macmillan.

Gillies, D. (1993) *Philosophy of Science in the Twentieth Century: Four Central Themes*, Oxford, Blackwell.

Gilligan, C. (1982) *In a Different Voice: Psychological Theory and Women's Development*, Cambridge, MA, Harvard University Press.

Gillis, J.R. (1974) *Youth and History*, New York, Academic Press.

Gilloch, G. (1996) *Myth and Metropolis: Walter Benjamin and the City*, Cambridge, Polity Press.

Giner, S. (1976) *Mass Society*, London, Martin Robertson.

Gjertsen, D. (1989) *Science and Philosophy: Past and Present*, Harmondsworth, Penguin.

Glasgow University Media Group (1976) *Bad News*, London, Routledge & Kegan Paul.

Glover, J. (1990a) *Causing Death and Saving Lives*, Harmondsworth, Penguin.

Glover, J. (ed.) (1990b) *Utilitarianism and its Critics*, New York and London, Macmillan.

Goffman, E. (1956) 'Embarrassment and Social Organization', *American Journal of Sociology*, 62: 264–71.

Goffman, E. (1959) *The Presentation of Self in Everyday Life*, Harmondsworth, Penguin.

Goffman, E. (1961) *Asylums: Essays on the Social Situation of Mental Patients and Other Inmates*, New York, Doubleday.

Goffman, E. (1963) *Stigma: Notes on the Management of Spoiled Identity*, New York, Prentice Hall.

Goffman, E. (1974) *Frame Analysis*, New York, Harper & Row.

Golding, P. and Murdock, G. (1991) 'Culture, Communications and Political Economy', in J. Curran and M. Gurevitch (eds), *Mass Media and Society*, London, Arnold.

Goldman, A. (1986) *Epistemology and Cognition*, Cambridge, MA, Harvard University Press.

Goodman, N. (1976) *Languages of Art*, second edn, Indianapolis, Hackett.

Goodman, N. (1978) *Ways of Worldmaking*, Indianapolis, Hackett.

Gorz, A. (ed.) (1973) *The Division of Labour: The Labour Process and Class Struggle in Modern Capitalism*, Hassocks, Harvester.

Gould, S.J. (1991) *Wonderful Life*, London, Penguin.

Goux, J.-J. (1993) *Oedipus, Philosopher*, tr. Catharine Porter, Stanford, CA, Stanford University Press.

Gove, W. (1980) *The Labelling of Deviance*, Beverly Hills, Sage.

Graham, G. (1997) *Philosophy of the Arts: An Introduction to Aesthetics*, London, Routledge.

Gramsci, A. (1971) (*1929–1935*) *Selections from Prison Notebooks*, London, Lawrence & Wishart.

Grant, R.W. (1987) *John Locke's Liberalism*, Chicago, University of Chicago Press.

Gray, J. (1990) *Liberalisms: Essays in Political Philosophy*, London, Routledge.

Gray, R.M. (1996) *Archetypal Explorations: Towards an Archetypal Sociology*, London, Routledge.

Grayling, A.C. (1988) *Wittgenstein*, Oxford, Oxford University Press.

Greenberg, C. (1992) (*1961*) 'Modernist Painting', in C. Harrison and P. Wood (eds), *Art in Theory 1900–1990: An Anthology of Changing Ideas*, Oxford, Blackwell.

Greenblatt, S. (1980) *The Forms of Power and the Power of Forms in the Renaissance*, Norman, University of Oaklahoma Press.

Grossberg, L., Cary, N. and Treichler, P.A. (eds) (1992) *Cultural Studies*, New York, Routledge.

Grossmann, R. (1992) *The Existence of the World: An Introduction to Ontology*, London, Routledge.

Grosz, E. (1989) *Sexual Subversions. Three French Feminists: Julia Kristeva, Luce Irigaray, Michèle Le Doeuff*, Sydney, Allen & Unwin.

Grosz, E. (1994) *Volatile Bodies: Toward a Corporeal Feminism*, Bloomington and Indianapolis, Indiana University Press.

Grunbaum, A. (1984) *The Foundations of Psychoanalysis: A Philosophical Critique*, Berkeley, University of California Press.

Gueguen, P.-G. (1995) 'Transference as Deception', in R. Feldstein *et al.* (eds), *Reading Seminar XI: Lacan's Four Fundamental Concepts of Psychoanalysis*, Albany, SUNY Press.

Habermas, J. (1970a) 'On Systematically Distorted Communication', *Inquiry*, 13: 205–18.

Habermas, J. (1970b) 'Towards a Theory of Communicative Competence', *Inquiry*, 13: 360–75.

Habermas, J. (1971) (*1968*) *Knowledge and Human Interests*, Boston, Beacon Press.

Habermas, J. (1976a) (*1971*) *Theory and Practice*, Boston, Beacon Press.

Habermas, J. (1976b) (*1973*) *Legitimation Crisis*, London, Heinemann.

Habermas, J. (1979) (*1976*) *Communication and the Evolution of Society*, Boston, Beacon Press.

Habermas, J. (1983) 'Modernity – An Incomplete Project', in H. Foster (ed.), *Postmodern Culture*, London, Pluto Press.

Habermas, J. (1984) (*1981*) *Reason and the Rationalisation of Society*, Volume 1 of *The Theory of Communicative Action*, Cambridge, Polity Press.

Habermas, J. (1987) (*1981*) *Lifeworld and System: A Critique of Functionalist Reason*, Volume 2 of *The Theory of Communicative Action*, Cambridge, Polity Press.

Habermas, J. (1988) (*1985*) *The Philosophical Discourse of Modernity*, Cambridge, MA, MIT Press.

Habermas, J. (1989a) (*1962*) *The Structural Transformation of the Public Sphere: An Inquiry into a Category of Bourgeois Society*, Cambridge, Polity Press.

Habermas, J. (1989b) (*1985*) *The New Conservatism: Cultural Criticism and the Historians' Debate*, Cambridge, MA, MIT Press.

Habermas, J. (1990) *Moral Consciousness and Communicative Action*, Cambridge MA, MIT Press.

Hahn, L.E. (ed.) (1990) *The Philosophy of Paul Ricoeur*, Oxford, Blackwell.

Haldane, J. and Wright, C. (eds) (1993) *Reality, Representation, and Projection*, New York, Oxford University Press.

Hall, S. (1973) 'Encoding and Decoding in Television Discourse', *CCCS* stencilled paper (see Hall (1980)).

Hall, S. (1975) 'Television as a Medium and Its Relation to Culture', *CCCS* stencilled paper, no. 34.

Hall, S. (1980) 'Encoding/Decoding', in S. Hall, D, Hobson, A. Lowe and P. Willis (eds), *Culture, Media, Language*, London, Hutchinson.

Hall, S. (1982) 'The Rediscovery of "Ideology": The Return of the "Repressed" in Media Studies', in M. Gurevitch, T. Bennett, J. Curran and J. Woollacott (eds), *Culture, Society and the Media*, London, Methuen.

Hall, S. (1985) 'The Toad in the Garden: Thatcherism amongst the Theorists', in C. Nelson and L. Grossberg (eds), *Marxism and the Interpretation of Culture*, Urbana, University of Illinois Press.

Hall, S. (1990) 'Cultural Identity and Diaspora', in J. Rutherford (ed.), *Identity, Community, Culture, Difference*, London, Lawrence and Wishart.

Hall, S. (1996) *Critical Dialogues in Cultural Studies*, London, Routledge.

Hall, S. and Jefferson, T. (eds) (1976) *Resistance Through Rituals: Youth Subcultures in Post-War Britain*, London, Hutchinson.

Hall, S. and Whannel, P. (1964) *The Popular Arts*, London, Hutchinson.

Hall, S., Critcher, C., Jefferson, T., Clarke, J. and Roberts, B. (eds) (1978) *Policing the Crisis: Mugging, the State and Law and Order*, London, Macmillan.

Hall, S., Hobson, D., Lowe, A. and Willis, P. (eds) (1992) *Culture, Media, Language: Working Papers in Cultural Studies, 1972–79*, London, Hutchinson.

Hamilton, P. (1996) *Historicism*, New York, Routledge.

Hamilton, P. and Turner, B.S. (eds) (1994) *Citizenship: Critical Concepts*, London, Routledge.

Hamilton, W.D. (1964) 'The Genetic Evolution of Social Behaviour', *Journal of Theoretical Biology*, 7: 1–52.

Hampton, J. (1997) *Political Philosophy*, Boulder, CO, Westview Press.

Hanfling, O. (ed.) (1981) *Essential Readings in Logical Positivism*, Oxford, Blackwell.

Haralambos, M. (1985) *Sociology: Themes and Perspectives*, second edn, London, Bell and Hyman.

Harari, J.V. (ed.) (1980) *Textual Strategies: Perspectives in Post-Structuralist Criticism*, London, Methuen.

Harker, D. (1985) *Fakesong: The Manufacture of British Folksong, 1700 to the Present Day*, Milton Keynes, Open University Press.

Harland, R. (1987) *Superstructuralism*, London, Methuen.

Harré, R. (1970) *The Principle of Scientific Thinking*, London, Macmillan.

Harrington, J. (1992) (*1656*) *Commonwealth of Oceana*, ed. J.G.A. Pocock, Cambridge, Cambridge University Press.

Harris, R. (1987) *Reading Saussure: A Critical Commentary on the Cours de Linguistique Générale*, London, Duckworth.

Harris, R. (1988) *Language, Saussure and Wittgenstein: How to Play Games with Words*, London, Routledge.

Harris, R. (1995) *Signs of Writing*, London, Routledge.

Harrison, C. (1991) *Essays on Art and Language*, Oxford, Blackwell.

Hartmann, P. and Husband, C. (1974) *Racism and the Mass Media*, London, Davis-Poynter.

Harvey, D. (1989) *The Condition of Postmodernity: An Enquiry into the Origins of Cultural Change*, Oxford, Blackwell.

Hassan, I. (1987) *The Postmodern Turn: Essays in Postmodern Theory and Culture*, Colombus, Ohio State University Press.

Hauser, A. (1962) *A Social History of Art*, volume 2, *Renaissance, Mannerism and Baroque*, London, Routledge & Kegan Paul.

Hayes, P. (1973) *Fascism*, London, Allen & Unwin.

Heath, A. (1981) *Social Mobility*, London, Fontana.

Hebdige, D. (1979) *Subculture: The Meaning of Style*, London, Methuen.

Hechter, M., Nedel, L. and Michael, R. (eds) (1993) *The Origin of Values*, New York, de Gruyter.

Hedges, I. (1983) *Language of Revolt: Dada and Surrealist Literature and Film*, Durham, NC, Duke University Press.

Hegel, G.W.F. (1931) (*1807*) *The Phenomenology of Mind*, tr. by J.B. Bailley, London, Allen & Unwin.

Hegel, G.W.F. (1942) (*1821*) *The Philosophy of Right*, tr. T.M. Knox, Oxford, Clarendon Press.

Hegel, G.W.F. (1948) *Early Theological Writings*, tr. by T.M. Knox, Chicago, University of Chicago Press.

Hegel, G.W.F. (1970) (*1817*) *Philosophy of Nature*, tr. A.V. Miller, Oxford, Clarendon Press.

Hegel, G.W.F. (1971) (*1817*) *Philosophy of Mind*, tr. W. Wallace and A.V. Miller, Oxford, Clarendon Press.

Hegel, G.W.F. (1975a) (*1817*) *Hegel's Logic*, tr. W. Wallace, Oxford, Clarendon Press.

Hegel, G.W.F. (1975b) *Hegel's Aesthetics*, 2 volumes, tr. T.M. Knox, Oxford, Clarendon Press.

Hegel, G.W.F. (1977) (*1807*) *The Phenomenology of Spirit*, tr. A.V. Miller, Oxford, Clarendon Press.

Hegel, G.W.F. (1988a) *Introduction to the Philosophy of History*, tr. L. Rauch, Indianapolis, Hackett.

Hegel, G.W.F. (1988b) (*1827*) *Lectures on the Philosophy of Religion*, Berkeley, University of California Press.

Hegel, G.W.F. (1991) (*1821*) *Elements of the Philosophy of Right*, tr. H.B. Nisbett, ed. Alan Wood, Cambridge, Cambridge University Press.

Heidegger, M. (1962) (*1927*) *Being and Time*, tr. John MacQuarrie and Edward Robinson, Oxford, Blackwell.

Heidegger, M. (1993) (*1951*) 'Building, Dwelling, Thinking', in D.F. Krell (ed.), *Basic Writings*, London, Routledge.

Heidegger, M. (1996) *Basic Writings: Martin Heidegger*, ed. David Farrell Krell, London, Routledge.

Held, D. (1980) *Introduction to Critical Theory: Horkheimer to Habermas*, London, Hutchinson.

Held, D. and Thompson, J. (eds) (1990) *Social Theory of Modern Societies: Anthony Giddens and his Critics*, Cambridge, Cambridge University Press.

Henri, M. (1993) (*1985*) *The Genealogy of Psychoanalysis*, tr. Douglas Brick, Stanford, CA, Stanford University Press.

Heritage, J. (1984) *Garfinkel and Ethnomethodology*, Cambridge, Polity Press.

Hernadi, P. (1995) *Cultural Transactions: Nature, Self, Society*, Ithaca and London, Cornell University Press.

Hilbert, R.A. and Collins, R. (1992) *The Classical Roots of Ethno-methodology: Durkheim, Weber and Garfinkel*, Chapel Hill, NC, University of North Carolina Press.

Hilferding, R. (1981) (*1910*) *Finance Capital: A Study of the Latest Phase of Capitalist Development*, London, Verso.

Hill, C. (1975) *The World Turned Upside Down: Radical Ideas During the English Revolution*, Harmondsworth, Penguin.

Hindess, B. and Hirst, P.Q. (1975) *Pre-Capitalist Modes of Production*, London, Routledge & Kegan Paul.

Hirsch, E.D. (1967) *Validity in Interpretation*, New Haven, CT, Yale University Press.

Hirschkop, K. (1986) 'A Response to the Forum on Mikhail Bakhtin', in G.S. Morson (ed.), *Bakhtin: Essays and Dialogues on His Work*, Chicago, University of Chicago Press.

Hitchcock, H.-R. and Johnson, P. (1966) *The International Style*, New York, W. W. Norton.

Hobbes, T. (1994) (*1651*) *Leviathan*, ed. R. Tuck, Cambridge, Cambridge University Press.

Hobsbawm, Eric (1995) *Age of Extremes*, London, Abacus.

Hodder, I. (1992) *Theory and Practice in Archaeology*, London, Routledge.

Hoggart, R. (1957) *Uses of Literacy*, London, Chatto & Windus.

Hoggart, R. (1988) *Life and Times*, 3 volumes, London, Chatto & Windus.

Holdcraft, D. (1991) *Saussure: Signs, System and Arbitrariness*, Cambridge, Cambridge University Press.

Hollingdale, R.J. (1973) *Nietzsche*, London, Routledge & Kegan Paul.

Hollis, M. and Lukes, S. (eds) (1982) *Rationality and Relativism*, Oxford, Blackwell.

Holquist, M. (1990) *Dialogism: Bakhtin and His World*, London, Routledge.

Holub, R.C. (1992) *Crossing Borders: Reception Theory, Poststructuralism, Deconstruction*, Madison, University of Wisconsin Press.

Honderich, T. (1993) *How Free Are You?: The Determinism Problem* Oxford, Oxford University Press.

Honour, H. (1979) *Romanticism*, London, Allen Lane.

Hookway, C. (1985) *Peirce*, London, Routledge & Kegan Paul.

Horkheimer, M. (1972a) (*1937*) 'Traditional and Critical Theory', in *Critical Theory: Selected Essays*, New York, Herder and Herder.

Horkheimer, M. (1972b) (*1941*) 'Art and Mass Culture', in *Critical Theory: Selected Essays*, New York, Herder and Herder.

Horkheimer, M. (1992) (*1947*) *Eclipse of Reason*, New York, Continuum.

Horkheimer, M. and Adorno, T.W. (1972) (*1947*) *Dialectic of Enlightenment*, London, Allen Lane.

Hosek, C. and Parker, P. (eds) (1985) *Lyric Poetry: Beyond New Criticism*, Ithaca, NY, Cornell University Press.

Hume, D. (1978) *Enquiries Concerning Human Understanding and Concerning the Principles of Morals*, Oxford, Clarendon Press.

Hume, D. (1985) (*1757*) 'Of the Standard of Taste', in *Essays: Moral, Political and Literary*, ed. E.F. Miller, Indianapolis, Liberty Press.

Hume, D. (1990) (*1739*) *A Treatise of Human Nature*, ed. P.H. Nidditch, Oxford, Clarendon Press.

Hunt, J.D. (1976) *The Figure in the Landscape: Poetry, Painting and Gardening during the Eighteenth Century*, Baltimore, Johns Hopkins University Press.

Hunt J.D. and Willis, P. (eds) (1988) *The Genius of the Place: The English Landscape Garden 1620–1820*, Cambridge, MA, MIT Press.

Husserl, E. (1954) (*1938*) *The Crisis of European Sciences and Transcendental Phenomenology*, Evanston, IL, Northwestern University Press.

Husserl, E. (1962) (*1913*) *Ideas*, New York, Collier.

Hylton, P. (1990) *Russell, Idealism, and the Emergence of Analytic Philosophy*, Oxford, Clarendon Press.

Ingarden, R. (1973) *The Literary Work of Art*, Evanston, IL, Northwestern University Press.

Inglis, F. (1993) *Cultural Studies*, Oxford, Blackwell.

Ingold, T. (ed.) (1996) *Key Debates in Anthropology*, London, Routledge.

Innis, H.A. (1950) *Empire and Communications*, Oxford, Oxford University Press.

Innis, H.A. (1951) *The Bias of Communication*, Toronto, Toronto University Press.

Innis, R.E. (ed.) (1986) *Semiotics: An Introductory Reader*, London, Hutchinson.

Inwood, M. (1992) *A Hegel Dictionary*, Oxford, Blackwell.

Irigaray, L. (1985a) (*1974*) *Speculum of the Other Woman*, Ithaca, NY, Cornell University Press.

Irigaray, L. (1985b) (*1977*) *This Sex Which is Not One*, Ithaca, NY, Cornell University Press.

Irigaray, L (1986) *Divine Women*, Sydney, Local Consumption.

Irigaray, L. (1991) (*1980*) *Marine Lover of Friedrich Nietzsche*, New York, Columbia University Press.

Irigaray, L. (1992) (*1990*) *Culture of Difference*, New York, Routledge.

Irigaray, L. (1993a) (*1984*) *An Ethics of Sexual Difference*, Ithaca, Cornell University Press.

Irigaray, L. (1993b) (*1990*) *Je, tu, nous. Towards a Culture of Difference*, London, Routledge.

Jaanus, M. (1995) 'The *démontage* of the drive', in R. Feldstein, B. Fink and M. Jaanus (eds), *Reading Seminar XI: Lacan's Four Fundamental Concepts of Psychoanalysis*, Albany, SUNY Press.

Jakobson, R. (1971–85) *Selected Writings*, Volumes 1–6, The Hague and Berlin, Mouton.

Jakobson, R. (1987) 'Linguistics and Poetics', in *Language and Literature*, ed. K. Pomorska and S. Rudy, Cambridge MA, Harvard University Press.

Jakobson, R. (1990) *On Language*, Cambridge, MA, Harvard University Press.

James, A., Hockey, J.L. and Dawson, A.H. (eds) (1997) *After Writing Culture: Epistemology and Praxis in Contemporary Anthopology*, London: Routledge.

Jameson, F. (1971) *Marxism and Form*, Princeton, NJ, Princeton University Press.

Jameson, F. (1972) *The Prison-House of Language: A Critical Account of Structuralism and Russian Formalism*, Princeton, NJ, Princeton University Press.

Jameson, F. (1991) *Postmodernism, or, The Cultural Logic of Late Capitalism*, London, Verso.

Jay, M. (1973) *The Dialectical Imagination*, Boston, Little, Brown and Company.

Jay, M. (1984) *Adorno*, London, Fontana.

Jenger, J. (1996) *Le Corbusier: Architect of a New Age*, London, Thames & Hudson.

Jenks, C. (1991) *The Language of Postmodern Architecture*, sixth edn, London, Academy Editions.

Jenks, C. (1993a) *Culture*, London, Routledge.

Jenks, C. (ed.) (1993b) *Cultural Reproduction*, London, Routledge.

Joas, H. (1996) *The Creativity of Action*, Cambridge, Polity Press.

Johnson, B. (1980) *The Critical Difference: Essays in the Contemporary Rhetoric of Reading*, Baltimore, Johns Hopkins University Press.

Johnson, L. (1979) *The Cultural Critics: From Matthew Arnold to Raymond Williams*, London, Boston and Henley, Routledge & Kegan Paul.

Jones, E. (1964) *The Life and Work of Sigmund Freud*, London, Penguin.

Jones, L. (Baraka, A.) (1965) *Blues People: Negro Music in White America,* London, MacGibbon and Lee.

Jost, E. (1981) *Free Jazz*, New York, Da Capo Press.

Jung, C.G. (1959) *The Collected Works of C. G. Jung*, volume 9I, *Archetypes and the Collective Unconscious*, London, Routledge & Kegan Paul.

Jung, C.G. (1993) (*1917*) *Psychology of the Unconscious: A Study of the Transformations and Symbolism of the Libido*, London, Routledge.

Kant, I. (1964) (*1781*) *Critique of Pure Reason*, tr. Norman Kemp Smith, London, Macmillan.

Kant, I (1970) *Political Writings*, ed. H. Reiss, Cambridge, Cambridge University Press.

Kant, I. (1976) (*1788*) *Critique of Practical Reason, and Other Writings in Moral Philosophy*; tr. and ed. Lewis White Beck, New York, Garland.

Kant, I. (1983) (*1786*) 'Speculative Beginning of Human History', in *Perpectual Peace and Other Essays*, tr. T. Humphrey, Indianapolis, Hackett.

Kant, I. (1987) (*1790*) *The Critique of Judgement*, tr. W.S. Pluhar, Indianapolis, Hackett; (1952) Oxford, Oxford University Press.

Kaplan, E. Ann and Sprinker, M. (1993) *The Althusserian Legacy*, London, Verso.

Kaufmann, W. (1974) *Nietzsche: Philosopher, Psychologist, Antichrist*, Princeton, NJ, Princeton University Press.

Keane, J. (ed.) (1988) *Civil Society and the State: New European Perspectives*, London, Verso.

Kearney, R. and Rainwater, M. (eds) (1996) *The Continental Philosophy Reader*, London, Routledge.

Kelley, T.M. (1997) *Reinventing Allegory*, Cambridge, Cambridge University Press.

Kellner, D. (1989) *Jean Baudrillard: From Marxism to Postmodernism and Beyond*, Cambridge, Polity Press.

Kelly, A. (1982) *Mikhail Bakunin: A Study in the Psychology and Politics of Utopianism*, Oxford, Clarendon Press.

Kenny, A. (ed.) (1994) *The Wittgenstein Reader*, Oxford, Blackwell.

Kermode, F. (1975) *The Classic*, London, Faber & Faber.

Kierkegaard, S. (1966) (*1841*) *The Concept of Irony*, London, Collins.

Kim, J. and Sosa, E. (1994) *A Companion to Metaphysics*, Oxford, Blackwell.

Klein, R. (1992/3) 'Notes on the Foundations', *Journal of the Centre for Freudian Analysis and Research*, Winter.

Klotz, J.-P. (1995) 'The Passionate Dimensions of Difference', in R. Feldstein *et al.* (eds), *Reading Seminar XI: Lacan's Four Fundamental Concepts of Psychoanalysis*, Albany, SUNY Press.

Kolakowski, L. (1972) *Positivist Philosophy*, London, Penguin.

Kolakowski, L. (1978) *Main Currents of Marxism*, 3 volumes, Oxford, Oxford University Press.

Kolb, D. (1990) *Postmodern Sophistications: Philosophy, Architecture and Tradition*, Chicago, University of Chicago Press.

Korner, S. (1955) *Kant*, Harmondsworth, Penguin.

Kracauer, S. (1947) *From Caligari to Hitler*, Princeton, NJ, Princeton University Press.

Kracauer, S. (1960) *Theory of Film: The Redemption of Physical Reality*, London, Oxford University Press.

Krell, D.F. and Wood, D. (1988) *Exceedingly Nietzsche: Aspects of Contemporary Nietzschean Interpretation*, London, Routledge.

Kripke, S. (1980) *Naming and Necessity*, Oxford, Blackwell.

Kristeva, J. (1969) *Séméiotiké: Recherches pour une sémanalyse*, Paris, Seuil.

Kristeva, J. (1982) (*1980*) *Powers of Horror: An Essay on Abjection*, New York, Columbia University Press.

Kristeva, J. (1984) (*1974*) *Revolution in Poetic Language*, New York, Columbia University Press.

Kristeva, J. (1986a) 'Word, Dialogue and Novel', in T. Moi (ed.), *The Kristeva Reader*, Oxford, Blackwell.

Kristeva, J. (1986b) 'The System and the Speaking Subject', in T. Moi (ed.), *The Kristeva Reader*, Oxford, Blackwell.

Kristeva, J. (1987) (*1983*) *Tales of Love*, New York, Columbia University Press.

Kristeva, J. (1989) *Black Sun*, New York, Columbia University Press.

Kristeva, J. (1991) (*1988*) *Strangers to Ourselves*, New York, Columbia University Press.

Kuhn, T.S. (1970) (*1962*) *The Structure of Scientific Revolutions*, second edn, London and Chicago, The University of Chicago Press.

Kukathas, C. (1989) *Hayek and Modern Liberalism*, Oxford, Clarendon Press.

Kumar, K. (1978) *Prophecy and Progress*, Harmondsworth, Penguin.

Kumar, K. (1991) *Utopianism*, Milton Keynes, Open University Press.

Kurzweil, E. (1980) *The Age of Structuralism: Lévi-Strauss to Foucault*, New York, Columbia University Press.

Kymlicka, W. (1989) *Liberalism, Community and Culture*, Oxford, Clarendon Press.

Laclau, E. and Mouffe, C. (1985) *Hegemony and Socialist Strategy*, London, Verso.

Lacan, J. (1977a) (*1973*) *Four Fundamental Concepts of Psychoanalysis*, London, Hogarth.

Lacan, J. (1977b) (*1966*) *Écrits: A Selection*, tr. Alan Sheridan, ed. Jacques-Alain Miller, London, Routledge.

Lacan, J. (1979) 'Tuché and Automation', in *The Four Fundamental Concepts of Psychoanalysis*, ed. J.A. Miller, tr. A. Strachey, London, Penguin.

Ladurie, E. Le Roy (1980) (*1978*) *Montaillou: Cathars and Catholics in a French Village 1294–1324*, Harmondsworth, Penguin.

Laing, D. (1985) *One Chord Wonders: The Power and Meaning in Punk Rock*, Milton Keynes, Open University Press.

Bibliography

Langer, S.K. (1942) *Philosophy in a New Key: A Study of the Symbolism of Reason, Rite and Art*, Cambridge, MA, Harvard University Press.

Laplanche, J. and Pontalis, J.-B. (1973) 'Instinct (or drive)', in *The Language of Psychoanalysis*, tr. Donald Nicholson-Smith, London: Karnac Books and the Institute of Psychoanalysis, pp. 214–17.

Laplanche, J. and Pontalis, J.-B. (1988) (*1967*) *The Language of Psychoanalysis*, tr. Donald Nicholson-Smith, London, Karnac Books and the Institute of Psychoanalysis.

Laqueur, W. (ed.) (1988) *Fascism: A Reader's Guide*, London, Wildwood House.

Lareau, A. and Shultz, J. (eds) (1996) *Journeys through Ethnography: Realistic Accounts of Fieldwork*, Boulder, CO, Westview Press.

Larrain, J. (1979) *The Concept of Ideology*, London, Hutchinson.

Lasdun, S. (1991) *The English Park: Royal, Private and Public*, London, Deutsch.

Lash, S. and Urry, J. (1987) *The End of Organised Capitalism*, Cambridge, Polity.

de Laszlo, V.S. (ed.) (1992) *The Basic Writings of C.G. Jung*, London, Routledge.

Lavers, A. (1982) *Roland Barthes: Structuralism and After*, London, Methuen.

Lavie, S., and Swedenburg, T. (eds) (1996) *Displacement, Diaspora, and Geographies of Identity*, Durham, NC, Duke University Press.

Leach, E. (1970) *Lévi-Strauss*, London, Fontana.

Leach, E. (1982) *Social Anthropology*, Glasgow, Fontana.

Leach, N. (ed.) (1997) *Rethinking Architecture: A Reader in Cultural Theory*, London, Routledge.

Leavis, F.R. (1972) *Nor Shall My Sword: Discourses on Pluralism, Compassion and Social Hope*, London, Chatto & Windus.

Leavis, F.R. (1977) *The Living Principle: 'English' as a Discipline of Thought*, London, Chatto & Windus.

Leavis, F.R. (1979) (*1933*) *For Continuity*, London, Norwood Editions.

Leavis, F.R. (1986) *Valuation and Criticism and Other Essays*, ed. G. Singh, Cambridge, Cambridge University Press.

Leavis, F.R. and Thompson, D. (1933) *Culture and Environment*, London, Chatto & Windus.

Lebovici, S. and Widlocher, D. (eds) (1990) *Psychoanalysis in France*, New York, International Universities Press.

Lechte, J. (1990) *Julia Kristeva*, London, Routledge.

Le Corbusier (1954) (*1948*) *The Modulor: A Harmonious Measure to the Human Scale Universally Applicable to Architecture and Mechanics*, London, Faber & Faber.

Le Corbusier (1958) (*1955*) *Modulor II*, London, Faber & Faber.

Le Corbusier (1967) (*1933*) *The Radient City: Elements of a Doctrine of Urbanism to be used as the Basis of our Machine-Age Civilization*, London, Faber & Faber.

Le Corbusier (1987a) (*1923*) *Towards a New Architecture*, London, Architectural Press.

Le Corbusier (1987b) (*1924*) *The City of Tomorrow and Its Planning*, London, Architectural Press.

Lecourt, D. (1975) (*1969*) *Marxism and Epistemology: Bachelard, Canguilhem and Foucault*, London, New Left Books.

Le Doeuff, M. (1982) 'Utopias: Scholarly', *Social Research*, 49(2).

Le Doeuff, M. (1986) (*1980*) *The Philosophical Imaginary*, Stanford, Stanford University Press.

Le Doeuff, M. (1989) *Hipparchia's Choice: An Essay Concerning Women, Philosophy etc.*, Oxford, Blackwell.

Lee, D. (1992) *Competing Discourses: Perspective and Ideology in Language*, London, Longman.

Leech, K. (1973) *Youth-Quake: The Growth of a Counter-Culture Through Two Decades*, London, Sheldon Press.

Lefebvre, H. (1982) *The Sociology of Marx*, New York, Columbia University Press.

Le Huray, P. and Day, J. (eds) (1987) *Music and Aesthetics in the Eighteenth and Early-Nineteenth Centuries*, Cambridge, Cambridge University Press.

Leibniz, G.W. (1973) *Philosophical Writings*, London, Dent.

Lemert, E. (1951) *Social Psychology*, New York, McGraw-Hill.

Lenin, V.I. (1992) (*1917*) *The State and Revolution*, Harmondsworth, Penguin.

Lentricchia, F. (1980) *After the New Criticism*, London, Athlone Press.

Leupin, A. (ed.) (1991) *Lacan and the Human Sciences*, Lincoln and London, University of Nebraska Press.

LeVay, S. (1996) *Queer Science: The Use and Abuse of Research into Homosexuality*, Cambridge, MA, MIT Press.

Lévi-Strauss, C. (1966) (*1962*) *The Savage Mind*, London, Weidenfeld & Nicolson.

Lévi-Strauss, C. (1968a) (*1958*) *Structural Anthropology*, Harmondsworth, Penguin.

Lévi-Strauss, C. (1968b) 'The Structural Study of Myth', in *Structural Anthropology*, Harmondsworth, Penguin.

Lévi-Strauss, C. (1969) (*1949*) *The Elementary Structures of Kinship*, London, Eyre and Spottiswoode.

Lévi-Strauss, C. (1970) (*1964*) *The Raw and the Cooked: Introduction to a Science of Mythology*, Volume 1, London, Jonathan Cape.

Lévi-Strauss, C. (1973) (*1967*) *From Honey to Ashes: Introduction to a Science of Mythology*, Volume 2, London, Jonathan Cape.

Lévi-Strauss, C. (1975) (*1955*) *Tristes Tropiques*, New York, Atheneum.

Lévi-Strauss, C. (1977) (*1973*) *Structural Anthropology*, volume 2, Harmondsworth, Penguin.

Lévi-Strauss, C. (1978) (*1968*) *The Origin of Table Manners: Introduction to a Science of Mythology*, volume 3, London, Jonathan Cape.

Lévi-Strauss, C. (1981) (*1971*) *The Naked Man: Introduction to a Science of Mythology*, volume 4, London, Jonathan Cape.

Lewis, H. (1990) *Dada Turns Red: The Politics of Surrealism*, Edinburgh, Edinburgh University Press.

Lipietz, A. (1987) *Mirages and Miracles: The Crises of Global Fordism*, London, Verso.

Lipton, P. (1991) *Inference to the Best Explanation*, London, Routledge.

Litz, W.A., Menand, L. and Rainey, L. (forthcoming) *The Cambridge History of Literary Criticism*, volume 7, *Modernism and New Criticism*, Cambridge, Cambridge University Press.

Livingstone, M. (ed.) (1991) *Pop Art*, London, Royal Academy of the Arts.

Llewelyn, J. (1985) *Beyond Metaphysics? The Hermeneutic Circle in Contemporary Continental Philosophy*, New Jersey, Humanities Press.

Lloyd, A.L. (1967) *Folk Song in England*, London, Lawrence & Wishart.

Loades, A. (1990) *Feminist Theology: A Reader*, London, SPCK.

Locke, J. (1975) (*1690*) *An Essay Concerning Human Understanding*, Oxford, Clarendon Press.

Locke, J. (1980) (*1690*) *Second Treatise of Government*, ed. C.B. Macpherson, Indianapolis, Hackett.

Locke, J. (1988) (*1690*) *Two Treatises of Government*, ed. P. Laslett, Cambridge, Cambridge University Press.

Lodge, D. (ed.) (1972) *20th Century Literary Criticism: A Reader*, London, Longman.

Lodge, D. (1990) *After Bakhtin: Essays on Fiction and Criticism*, London, Routledge.

Loos, A. (1966) (*1908*) 'Ornament and Crime', in L. Münz and G. Künstler, *Adolf Loos: Pioneer of Modern Architecture*, London, Thames & Hudson.

Lovejoy, O.A. (1948) *Essays in the History of Ideas*, Baltimore, Johns Hopkins University Press.

Lowenthal, L. (1978) (*1937*) 'Knut Hamsun', in A. Arato and E. Gebhardt (eds) *The Essential Frankfurt School Reader*, Oxford, Blackwell.

Lowenthal, L. (1989) (*1932*) 'On Sociology of Literature', in S.E. Bronner and D.M Kellner (eds), *Critical Theory and Society: A Reader*, London, Routledge.

Lucie-Smith, E. (1995) *Artoday*, London, Phaidon.

Luhmann, N. (1982) *The Differentiation of Society*, New York, Columbia University Press.

Lukács, G. (1963) (*1958*) *The Meaning of Contemporary Realism*, London, Merlin Press.

Lukács, G. (1971) (*1923*) *History and Class Consciousness: Studies in Marxist Dialectics*, tr. R. Livingstone, London, Merlin Press.

Lukács, G. (1978) (*1916*) *The Theory of the Novel*, London, Merlin Press.

Lukács, G. (1983) (*1937*) *The Historical Novel*, Lincoln and London, University of Nebraska Press.

Lukes, S. (1969) 'Alienation and anomie', in P. Laslett and W.G. Runciman (eds), *Philosophy, Politics and Society*, Oxford, Blackwell.

Lukes, S. (1973a) *Emile Durkheim*, London, Allen Lane.

Lukes, S. (1973b) *Individualism*, Oxford, Blackwell.

Lunn, E. (1982) *Marxism and Modernism: An Historical Study of Lukács, Brecht, Benjamin and Adorno*, Berkeley, University of California Press.

Lynon, H. (1980) *The Story of Modern Art*, London, Phaidon.

Lyons J. (1977) *Chomsky*, London, Fontana.

Lyotard, J.-F. (1988) (*1983*) *The Differend: Phrases in Dispute*, tr. Georges Van Den Abeele, Manchester, Manchester University Press.

Lyotard, J.-F. (1989) (*1979*) *The Postmodern Condition: A Report on Knowledge*, tr. Goeff Bennington, Manchester, Manchester University Press.

Lyotard, J.-F. (1991) *The Inhuman: Reflections on Time*, tr. Geoffrey Bennington and Rachel Bowlby, Cambridge, Polity Press.

Lyotard, J.-F. (1993) *Political Writings*, tr. Bill Readings and Kevin Paul Geiman, London, UCL Press.

Lyotard, J.-F. (1994) *Lessons on the Analytic of the Sublime: Kant's Critique of Judgment, [sections] 23–29*, tr. Elizabeth Rottenberg, Stanford, CA, Stanford University Press.

Macherey, P. (1978) (*1966*) *A Theory of Literary Production*, London, Routledge.

Macherey, P. (1995) *The Object of Literature*, Cambridge, Cambridge University Press.

Machiavelli, N. (1983) (*1531*) *The Discourses*, ed. B. Crick, tr. Leslie J. Walker with revisions by Brian Richardson, Harmondsworth, Penguin.

MacIntyre, A. (1981) *After Virtue*, London, Duckworth.

MacIntyre, A. (1988) *Whose Justice? Which Rationality?*, London, Duckworth.

MacPherson, C.B. (1962) *The Political Theory of Possessive Individualism: Hobbes to Locke*, Oxford, Oxford University Press.

Macrae, C.N., Stanger, C. and Hewstone, M. (eds) (1996) *Stereotypes and Stereotyping*, London, Guilford Press.

Magnus, B. and Higgins, K.M. (eds) (1996) *The Cambridge Companion to Nietzsche*, Cambridge, Cambridge University Press.

Malinowski, B. (1922) *Argonauts of the Western Pacific*, London, Routledge & Kegan Paul.

Mandel, E. (1972) *Marxist Economic Theory*, London, Merlin.

Mannheim, K. (1960) (*1929*) *Ideology and Utopia: An Introduction to the Sociology of Knowledge*, London, Routledge & Kegan Paul.

Mannheim, K. (1972) (*1924*) 'Historicism', in *Essays on the Sociology of Knowledge*, tr. Paul Kecskemeti, London, Routledge & Kegan Paul.

Marcuse, H. (1972) *An Essay on Liberation*, Harmondsworth, Penguin.

Margolis, J. (1991) *The Truth About Relativism*, Oxford, Blackwell.

Marini, M. (1992) *Jacques Lacan: The French Context*, tr. Anne Tomiche, New Brunswick, NJ, Rutgers University Press.

Marshall, T.H. (1950) *Citizenship and Social Class, and Other Essays*, Cambridge, Cambridge University Press.

Marx, K. (1968) (*1852*) 'The Eighteenth Brumaire of Louis Bonaparte', in *Karl Marx and Frederick Engels: Selected Works*, London, Lawrence & Wishart.

Marx, K. (1971) (*1859*) *A Contribution to the Critique of Political Economy*, London, Lawrence & Wishart.

Marx, K. (1973) (*1857–8*) *Grundrisse*, Harmondsworth, Penguin.

Marx, K. (1975) *Early Writings*, tr. R. Livingstone and G. Benton, introduction by L. Colletti, Harmondsworth, Penguin.

Marx, K. (1976) (*1867*) *Capital: A Critique of Political Economy*, volume 1, tr. B. Fowkes, Harmondsworth, Penguin.

Marx K. and Engels, F. (1970) (*1845–6*) *The German Ideology*, London, Lawrence & Wishart.

Marx, K. and Engels, F. (1985) (*1848*) *The Communist Manifesto*, Harmondsworth, Penguin.

Mauss, M. (1966) (*1925*) *The Gift: Forms and Functions of Exchange in Archaic Societies*, London, Routledge & Kegan Paul.

Maynard, P. and Feagin, S. (eds) (1997) *Aesthetics: An Oxford Reader*, Oxford, Oxford University Press.

McCarthy, T. (1978) *Marx and the Proletariat: A Study in Social Theory*, Westport, Greenwood Press.

McCarthy, Thomas, (1978) *The Critical Theory of Jürgen Habermas*, London, Hutchinson.

McCloud, S. (1993) *Understanding Comics*, Northampton, MA, Tundra Publishing.

McCulloch, G. (1989) *The Game of the Name: Introducing Logic, Language and Mind*, Oxford, Clarendon Press.

McCulloch, G. (1995) *The Mind and its World*, London, Routledge.

McLellan, D. (1973) *Karl Marx: His Life and Works*, New York, Harper & Row.

McLellan, D. (1975) *Karl Marx*, New York, Viking.

McLuhan, M. (1994) *Understanding Media: The Extension of Man*, London, Routledge.

McQuail, D. (1994) *Mass Communication Theory: An Introduction*, third edn, London, Sage.

McRobbie, A. (1981) 'Settling Accounts with Subcultures: A Feminist Critique', in T. Bennett, G. Martin, C. Mercer and J. Woollacott (eds), *Culture, Ideology and Social Process: A Reader*, London, Open University Press.

McRobbie, A. (1989) '*Jackie*: An Ideology of Adolescent Femininity', in B. Waites, T. Bennett and G. Martin (eds), *Popular Culture: Past and Present*, London, Routledge.

McRobbie, A. (1991) *Feminism and Youth Culture From Jackie to Just Seventeen*, London, Macmillan.

McRobbie, A. (1994) *Postmodernism and Popular Culture*, London, Routledge.

Mead, G.H. (1934) *Mind, Self and Society*, Chicago, Chicago University Press.

Mead, L. (1986) *Beyond Entitlement: The Social Obligations of Citizenship*, New York, Free Press.

Mead, M. (1928) *Coming of Age in Samoa: A Psychological Study of Primitive Youth for Western Civilization*, New York, Morrow.

Meek, R.L. (1973) *Studies in the Labour Theory of Value*, second edn, London, Lawrence & Wishart.

Mehlman, J. (ed.) (1972) *French Freud: Structural Studies in Psychoanalysis*, YFS 48.

Meja, V. and Stehr, N. (eds) (1990) *Knowledge and Politics: The Sociology of Knowledge Dispute*, London, Routledge.

Meltzer, D. (ed.) (1993) *Reading Jazz*, San Francisco, Mercury House.

Meltzer, F. (1987) *The Trials of Psychoanalysis*, Chicago and London, The University of Chicago Press.

Mepham, J. and Ruben, D-K. (eds) (1979) *Issues in Marxist Philosophy*, Volume 1, *Dialectics and Method*, Brighton, Harvester.

Merleau-Ponty, M. (1962) (*1945*) *Phenomenology of Perception*, London, Routledge & Kegan Paul.

Merrell, F. (1993) *Sign, Intertextuality, World*, Bloomington and Indianapolis, Indiana University Press.

Merton, R.K. (1968) (*1949*) *Social Theory and Social Structure*, New York, Free Press.

Mészáros, I. (1986) *Marx's Theory of Alienation*, fourth edn, London, Merlin Press.

Metz, C. (1974) (*1971/1972*) *Film Language: A Semiotics of the Cinema*, New York, Oxford University Press.

Metz, C. (1982) *Psychoanalysis and the Cinema: The Imaginary Signifier*, London, Macmillan.

Meynell. H. (1975) 'Science, the Truth, and Thomas Kuhn', *Mind*, 84: 79–93.

Mies, M. (1986) *Patriarchy and Accumulation on a World Scale: Women in the International Division of Labour*, London, Zed Books.

Miles, R. (1989) *Racism*, London, Routledge.

Mill, J.S. (1984) (*1859*) *On Liberty*, Harmondsworth, Penguin.

Mill, J.S. (1988) *The Subjection of Women*, ed. S.M. Okuri, Indianapolis, Hackett.

Miller, D. (ed.) (1995) *Acknowledging Consumption: A Review of New Studies*, London, Routledge.

Miller, F. (1986) *Batman: The Dark Knight Returns*, London, Titan Books.

Miller, J.-A. (1988) 'Another Lacan', tr. Ralph Chipman, *Lacan Study Notes: Hystoria* 6/9, Paris/New York, Published by the New York Lacan Study Group.

Miller, S.M. (1965) 'The "New" Working Class', in A.B. Shostak and W. Gomberg (eds), *Blue-Collar World*, Englewood Cliffs, NJ, Prentice Hall.

Miller, W. (1958) 'Lower Class Culture as a Generating Milieu of Gang Delinquency', *Journal of Social Issues*, 14: 5–19.

Mills, C.W. (1956) *The Power Elite*, London, Oxford University Press.

Milner, A. (1994) *Contemporary Cultural Theory*, London, UCL Press.

Minson, G. (1985) *Genealogies of Morals: Nietzsche, Foucault, Donzelot and the Eccentricity of Ethics*, Basingstoke, Macmillan.

Moerman, M. (1988) *Talking Culture: Ethnography and Conversation Analysis*, Philadelphia, University of Pennsylvania Press.

Moi T. (ed.) (1986) *The Kristeva Reader*, Oxford, Blackwell.

Mommsen, W. J. (1974) *The Age of Bureaucracy: Perspectives on the Political Sociology of Max Weber*, Oxford, Blackwell.

Moore, M. (1993) *Foundations of Liberalism*, Oxford, Clarendon Press.

Moore, A. and Gibbons, D. (1987) *Watchmen*, London, Titan Books.

Moreno, A.O.P. (1974) *Jung, Gods and Modern Man*, London, Sheldon Press.

Moriarty, M. (1991) *Roland Barthes*, Cambridge, Polity Press.

Morley, D. (1980) *The 'Nationwide' Audience*, London, British Film Institute.

Morley, D. (1992) *Television, Audiences and Cultural Studies*, London, Routledge.

Morris, B. (1991) *Western Conceptions of the Individual*, New York, St Martin's Press.

Morris, M. (1988) 'Feminism, Reading, Postmodernism', in J. Storey (ed.), *Cultural Theory and Popular Culture*, Hemel Hempstead, Prentice Hall.

Morris, M. (1993) 'Things to do with Shopping Centres', in S. During (ed.), *The Cultural Studies Reader*, London, Routledge.

Morrow, G.R. (1973) *The Ethical and Economic Theories of Adam Smith*, Clifton, NJ, A.M. Kelly.

Morson, G.S. (1986) 'Dialogue, Monologue, and the Social: A Reply to Ken Hirschkop', in G.S. Morson (ed.), *Bakhtin: Essays and Dialogues on His Work*, Chicago, University of Chicago Press.

Morson, G.S. and Emerson, C. (1990) *Mikhail Bakhtin: Creation of a Prosaics*, Stanford, CA, Stanford University Press.

Morton, D. (ed.) (1997) *A LesBiGay Cultural Studies Reader*, London, Westview Press.

Mosca, G. (1939) *The Ruling Class*, New York, McGraw-Hill.

Mosser, M. and Teyssot, G. (eds) (1991) *The History of Garden Design: The Western Tradition from the Renaissance to the Present Day*, London, Thames & Hudson.

Mounce, H.O. (1997) *The Two Pragmatisms: From Peirce to Rorty*, London and New York, Routledge.

Mulhall, S. (1996) *Heidegger and Being and Time*, London: Routledge.

Mulhall S. and Swift, A. (1996) *Liberals and Communitarians*, Oxford, Blackwell.

Mulhern, F. (1979) *The Moment of Scrutiny*, London, NLB.

Mulhern, F. (1995) 'Culture and Authority', *Critical Quarterly*, 37(1): 77–89.

Mulvey, L. (1975) 'Visual Pleasure and Narrative Cinema', *Screen*, 16(3): 6–18.

Mulvey, L. (1993) 'Afterthoughts on "Visual Pleasure and Narrative Cinema", inspired by King Vidor's *Duel in the Sun* (1946)', in A. Easthope (ed.), *Contemporary Film Theory*, London and New York, Longman.

Mungham, G. and Pearson, G. (eds) (1976) *Working Class Youth Cultures*, London, Routledge & Kegan Paul.

Murdock, G. and Golding, P. (1977) 'Capitalism, Communication and Class Relations', in J. Curran, M. Gurevitch and J. Woolacott (eds), *Mass Communication and Society*, London, Edward Arnold in association with the Open University Press.

Murphey, M.G. (1993) *The Development of Peirce's Philosophy*, Indianapolis, Hackett.

Neighbour O.W., Griffiths, P. and Perle, G. (1983) *The New Grove Second Viennese School: Schoenberg, Webern, Berg*, London, Macmillan.

Neocleous, M. (1997) *Fascism*, Philadelphia, Open University Press.

Newby, H. (1988) *The Countryside in Question*, London, Hutchinson.

Newhall, B. (1982) (*1937*) *The History of Photography*, New York, Museum of Modern Art.

Nietzsche, F.W. (1968a) *The Birth of Tragedy* (*1872*); *Beyond Good and Evil* (*1886*); *On the Genealogy of Morals* (*1887*), all in *Basic Writings of Nietzsche*, ed. and tr. Walter Kaufmann, New York, Basic Books.

Nietzsche, F.W. (1968b) *The Will to Power*, tr. Walter Kaufmann and R.J. Hollingdale, New York, Viking.

Nietzsche, F.W. (1974) *The Gay Science*, tr. Walter Kaufmann, New York, Vintage.

Nietzsche, F.W. (1982) (*1881*) *Daybreak*, tr. R.J. Hollingdale, Cambridge, Cambridge University Press.

Nietzsche, F.W. (1983) (*1873–6*) *Untimely Meditations*, tr. R.J. Hollingdale, Cambridge, Cambridge University Press.

Nietzsche, F.W. (1986) (*1878–80*) *Human, All-Too-Human*, tr. R.J. Hollingdale, Cambridge, Cambridge University Press.

Nietzsche, F.W. (1995) *Thus Spoke Zarathustra* (*1883–92*); *Twilight of the Idols* (*1889*); *The Antichrist* (*1888/95*), all in *The Portable Nietzsche*, ed. and tr. Walter Kaufmann, New York, Penguin.

Nisbet, R. (1980) *History of the Idea of Progress*, London, Heinemann.

Norman, R. (1980) *Hegel, Marx and Dialectic*, Hassocks, Harvester.

Norris, C. (1985) *The Contest of Faculties: Philosophy and Theory after Deconstruction*, London, Methuen.

Norris, C. (1986) *Deconstruction: Theory and Practice*, revised edition, London, Routledge.

Norris, C. (1987) *Derrida*, London, Fontana.

Norris, C. (1992) *Uncritical Theory: Postmodernism, Intellectuals and the Gulf War*, London, Lawrence and Wishart.

Nozick, R. (1974) *Anarchy, State and Utopia*, Oxford, Blackwell.

Oakes, P.J., Haslam, S.A. and Turner, J.C. (1994) *Stereotyping and Social Reality*, Oxford, Blackwell.

Oakeshott, M (1975) *On Human Conduct*, Oxford, Blackwell.

O'Connor, A. (1989) *Raymond Williams: Writing, Culture, Politics*, Oxford, Blackwell.

Ogden, S. (1979) *Faith and Freedom: Toward a Theology of Liberation*, Belfast, Ontario, Christian Journals Ltd.

Ogden, S. (1996) *Doing Theology Today*, Valley Forge, PA, Trinity Press International.

Orrù, M. (1987) *Anomie: History and Meanings*, London, Allen & Unwin.

Outhwaite, W. (1994) *Habermas: A Critical Introduction*, Oxford, Polity.

Page, R. M. (1984) *Stigma*, London, Routledge & Kegan Paul.

Pahl, R. (ed.) (1968) *Readings in Urban Sociology*, Oxford, Pergamon.

Palisca, C.V. (1991) *Baroque Music*, third edn, Englewood Cliffs, NJ, Prentice Hall.

Pareto, V. (1963) *The Mind and Society*, New York, Dover.

Parsons, T. (1937) *The Structure of Social Action*, New York, McGraw-Hill.

Parsons, T. (1951) *The Social System*, Glencoe, IL, Free Press.

Pascal, R. (1973) *From Naturalism to Expressionism: German Literature and Society 1880–1918*, London, Weidenfeld & Nicolson.

Patton, P. (ed.) (1993) *Nietzsche, Feminism and Political Theory*, London and New York, Routledge.

Pearce, F. (1989) *The Radical Durkheim*, London, Unwin Hyman.

Pears, D. (1985) *Wittgenstein*, London, Fontana.

Pearson, R.E. and Uricchio, W. (eds) (1991) *The Many Lives of the Batman*, New York, Routledge.

Peck, J. (ed.) (1987) *The Chomsky Reader*, New York, Pantheon.

Peirce, C.S. (1931–58) *Collected Papers of Charles Sanders Peirce*, 8 volumes, ed. C. Hartshorn and P. Weiss (volumes 1–6) A.W. Burks (volumes 7–8), Cambridge, MA, Harvard University Press.

Peirce, C.S. (1982) 'Definition and Description of Pragmatism' and 'The Fixation of Belief', in H.S. Thayer (ed.), *Pragmatism: The Classic Writings*, Indianapolis, Hackett.

Peirce, C.S. (1986) 'Logic as Semiotic: The Theory of Signs', in R.E. Innis (ed.), *Semiotics: An Introductory Reader*, London, Hutchinson.

Perkins, S. (1993) *Marxism and the Proletariat: A Lukácsian Perspective*, London, Pluto.

Pettit, P. (1975) *The Concept of Structuralism: A Critical Analysis*, Dublin, Gill and Macmillan.

Plamenatz, J. (1958) *The English Utilitarians*, Oxford, Blackwell.

Plato (1975) *Phaedo*, tr. David Gallop, Oxford, Clarendon Press.

Plekhanov, G.V. (1974) *Art and Society, and Other Papers in Historical Materialism*, New York, Oriole.

Pocock, J.G.A. (1975) *The Machiavellian Moment: Florentine Political Thought and the Atlantic Republican Tradition*, Princeton and London, Princeton University Press.

Poe, E.A. (1982) 'The Man of the Crowd', in *The Complete Tales and Poems of Edgar Allan Poe*, Harmondsworth, Penguin.

Polcari, S. (1991) *Abstract Expressionism and the Modern Experience*, Cambridge, Cambridge University Press.

Pollock, John L. (1987) *Contemporary Theories of Knowledge*, London, Hutchinson.

Ponzio, A. (1993) *Signs, Dialogue and Ideology*, Amsterdam, John Benjamins.

Popper, K. (1959) *The Logic of Scientific Discovery*, London, Hutchinson.

Popper, K. (1963) *Conjectures and Refutations*, New York, Harper & Row.

Popper, K. (1972) 'Conjectural Knowledge: My Solution to the Problem of Induction', in *Objective Knowledge*, Oxford, Oxford University Press.

Praz, M. (1970) *The Romantic Agony*, London, Oxford University Press.

Priest, S. (1990) *The British Empiricists: Hobbes to Ayer*, London, Penguin.

Putnam, H. (1981) *Reason, Truth and History*, Cambridge, Cambridge University Press.

Putnam, H. (1995) *Pragmatism: An Open Question*, Oxford, UK and Cambridge, MA, Blackwell.

Qualter, T.H. (1962) *Propaganda and Psychological Warfare*, New York, Random House.

Qualter, T.H. (1985) *Opinion Control in the Democracies*, London, Macmillan.

Quine, W.V.O. (1960) *Word and Object*, Cambridge, MA, MIT Press.

Quine, W.V.O. (1980) (1953) 'Two Dogmas of Empiricism', in *From a Logical Point of View*, second edn, Cambridge, MA and London, Harvard University Press, pp. 20–46.

Quine, W.V.O. (1991) 'Two Dogmas in Retrospect', *Canadian Journal of Philosophy*, 21(3): 265–74.

Radcliffe-Brown, A.R. (1952) *Structure and Function in Primitive Society*, New York, Free Press.

Radcliffe-Brown, A.R. (1977) *The Social Anthropology of Radcliffe-Brown*, ed. A. Kuper, London, Routledge & Kegan Paul.

Ragland-Sullivan, E. (1986) *Jacques Lacan and the Philosophy of Psychoanalysis*, London and Canberra, Croom Helm.

Rand, E. (1995) *Barbie's Queer Accessories*, London, Duke University Press.

Raphael, D.D. (1985) *Adam Smith*, Oxford, Oxford University Press.

Rawls, J. (1972) *A Theory of Justice*, Oxford, Clarendon Press.

Readings, B. (1991) *Introducing Lyotard: Art and Politics*, London and New York, Routledge.

Ricardo, D. (1951) (*1817*) *Principles of Political Economy*, Cambridge, Cambridge University Press.

Rice, P. and Waugh, P. (1989) *Modern Literary Theory: A Reader*, London, Edward Arnold.

Richards, I.A. (1938) *Interpretation in Teaching*, New York, Harcourt Brace.

Richardson, D. (ed.) (1996) *Theorising Heterosexuality: Telling it Straight*, Buckingham, Open University Press.

Richter, H. (1965) *Dada: Art and Anti-Art*, London, Thames & Hudson.

Ricoeur, P. (1981) *Hermeneutics and the Human Sciences*, tr. and ed. J.B. Thompson, Cambridge, Cambridge University Press.

Ricoeur, P. (1984–8) (*1983–5*) *Time and Narrative*, tr. Kathleen McLaughlin and David Pellaner, 3 volumes, Chicago and London, University of Chicago Press.

Rockmore, T. (1992) *Irrationalism: Lukács and the Marxist View of Reason*, Philadelphia, PA, Temple University Press.

Rorty, R. (1972) 'The World Well Lost', *Journal of Philosophy*, 69: 649–65.

Rorty, R. (1978) 'Philosophy as a Kind of Writing: An Essay on Derrida', *New Literary History*, 10(1); 141–60.

Rorty, R. (1982) *Consequences of Pragmatism: Essays, 1972–1980*, Brighton, Harvester.

Rorty, R. (1991) *Objectivity, Relativism and Truth: Philosophical Papers*, Cambridge, Cambridge University Press.

Rorty, Richard (1998) *Truth and Progress*, Cambridge, Cambridge University Press.

Rose, G. (1978) *The Melancholy Science: An Introduction to the Thought of Theodor W. Adorno*, London, Macmillan.

Rose, G. (1993) 'Architecture to Philosophy – the Post-Modern Complicity', in *Judaism and Modernity: Philosophical Essays*, Oxford, Blackwell.

Rosen C. and Zerner, H. (1984) *Romanticism and Realism: The Mythology of Nineteenth Century Art*, London, Faber & Faber.

Rosen, M. (1982) *Hegel's Dialectic and Its Criticism*, Cambridge, Cambridge University Press.

Rosselson, L. (1979) 'Pop Music: Mobilizer or Opiate', in C. Gardner (ed.) *Media, Politics and Culture*, London, Macmillan.

Rossi-Landi, F. (1990) *Marxism and Ideology*, Oxford, Clarendon Press.

Roszak, T. (1971) *(1968), The Making of a Counter Culture: Reflections on the Technocratic Society and Its Youthful Opposition*, London, Faber & Faber.

Rotenstreich, N. (1989) *Alienation: The Concept and its Reception*, Leiden, Brill.

Roudinesco, E. (1990) *Jacques Lacan and Co.: A History of Psychoanalysis in France 1925–1985* tr. Jeffrey Mehlman, Chicago, University of Chicago Press.

Rousseau, J.J. (1984) *(1754) A Discourse on Inequality*, tr. Maurice Cranston, Harmondsworth, Penguin.

Ruben, D. (1979) *Marxism and Materialism*, Brighton, Harvester.

Russell, B. (1905) 'On Denoting', *Mind*, 14: 479–93.

Russell, B. (1924) 'Logical Atomism', in R.C. Marsh (ed.) (1988) *Logic and Knowledge*, London, Hyman.

Russell, B. (1946) *History of Western Philosophy*, London, Allen & Unwin.

Russell, B. (1988) *(1912) The Problems of Philosophy*, Oxford, Oxford University Press.

Russell, B. (1988) *(1918)* 'The Philosophy of Logical Atomism', in R.C. Marsh (ed.), *Logic and Knowledge*, London, Hyman.

Russell, B. and Whitehead, A.N. (1910) *Principia Mathematica*, Cambridge, Cambridge University Press.

Ryan, M. (1982) *Marxism and Deconstruction: A Critical Articulation*, Baltimore, Johns Hopkins University Press.

Ryle, G. (1949) *The Concept of Mind*, London, Hutchinson.

Sabin, R. (1993) *Adult Comics: An Introduction*, London, Routledge.

Sacks, H. (1992) *Lectures on Conversation*, 2 volumes, Oxford, Blackwell.

Bibliography

Sadler, T. (1996) *Heidegger and Aristotle: The Question of Being*, London and Atlantic Highlands, NJ, Athlone.

Said, E. (1978a) *Orientalism*, New York, Random House.

Said, E. (1978b) 'The Problem of Textuality: Two Exemplary Positions', *Critical Inquiry*, 4: 673–714.

Sandel, M.J. (1982) *Liberalism and the Limits of Justice*, Cambridge, Cambridge University Press.

Sandel, M.J. (ed.) (1984) *Liberalism and its Critics*, Oxford, Blackwell.

Sartre, J.-P. (1958) (*1943*) *Being and Nothingness*, London, Methuen.

Sartre, J.-P. (1990) (*1946*) *Existentialism and Humanism*, tr. Philip Mairet, London, Methuen.

Sassoon, A.S. (1987) *Gramsci's Politics*, second edn, London, Hutchinson.

Saunders, P. (1981) *Social Theory and the Urban Question*, London, Hutchinson.

de Saussure, F. (1983) (*1916*) *Course in General Linguistics*, ed. C. Bally and A. Sechehaye, tr. Roy Harris, London, Duckworth.

Sayer, D. (1991) *Capitalism and Modernity: An Excursus on Max Weber*, London, Routledge.

Scarre, G. (1996) *Utilitarianism*, London and New York, Routledge.

Scheler, M. (1980) (*1926*) *Problems of a Sociology of Knowledge*, London, Routledge & Kegan Paul.

Schiffrin, D. (1993) *Approaches to Discourse*, Oxford, Blackwell.

Schmidt, W. (*1935*) *The Origin and Growth of Religion*, London, Methuen.

Schneiderman, S. (1983) *Jacques Lacan: The Death of an Intellectual Hero*, Cambridge, MA and London, Harvard University Press.

Schuller, G. (1968) *Early Jazz: Its Roots and Musical Development*, New York, Oxford University Press.

Schuller, G. (1989) *The Swing Era: The Development of Jazz 1930–1945*, New York, Oxford University Press.

Schutz, A. (1962) *Collected Papers*, volume 1, The Hague, Martinus Nijhoff.

Schutz, A. (1964) *Collected Papers*, volume 2, The Hague, Martinus Nijhoff.

Schutz, A. (1967) (*1932*) *The Phenomenology of the Social World*, London, Heinemann.

Schutz, A. and Luckmann, T. (1974) *The Structures of the Lifeworld*, London, Heinemann.

Scott, J. (1990) *The Sociology of Elites*, 3 volumes, Aldershot, Edward Elgar.

Scott, J. (1996) *Stratification and Power: Structures of Class, Status and Command*, Cambridge, Polity Press.

Scruton, R. (1984) *The Meaning of Conservatism*, London, Macmillan.

Searle, J. (1969), *Speech Acts*, Cambridge, Cambridge University Press.

Sedgwick, E.K. (1994) *Epistemology of the Closet*, London, Penguin.

Sedgwick, E.K. (ed.) (1997) *Novel Gazing: Queer Reading in Fiction*, Durham, NC, Duke University Press.

Sedgwick, P. (ed.) (1995) *Nietzsche: A Critical Reader*, Oxford, Blackwell.

Sedgwick, P. (1998) 'Politics as Antagonism and Diversity: Mill and Lyotard', in G. Day (ed.), *Varieties of Victorianism*, Basingstoke, Macmillan.

Sen, A. and Williams, B. (eds) (1982) *Utilitarianism and Beyond*, Cambridge, Cambridge University Press.

Shapiro, D. and Shapiro, C. (eds) (1990) *Abstract Expressionism: A Critical Reader*, Cambridge, Cambridge University Press.

Shepherd, J. (1991) *Music as Social Text*, Cambridge, Polity Press.

Shepherd, J. *et al.* (1977) *Whose Music? A Sociology of Musical Languages*, London, Latimer New Dimensions.

Shiach, M. (1991) *Hélène Cixous: A Politics of Writing*, London, Routledge.

Shope, R.A. (1983) *The Analysis of Knowing*, Princeton, NJ, Princeton University Press.

Silverman, H.J. and Welton, D. (eds) (1988) *Postmodernism and Continental Philosophy*, Albany, State University of New York Press.

Silverman, K. (1983) *The Subject of Semiotics*, Oxford, Oxford University Press.

Simmel, G. (1950a) *The Sociology of Georg Simmel*, ed. and tr. Kurt H. Wolff, Glencoe, IL, Free Press.

Simmel, G. (1950b) (*1903*) 'The Metropolis and Mental Life', in *The Sociology of Georg Simmel*, Glencoe, IL, Free Press.

Simmel, G. (1950c) (*1908*) 'The Stranger', in *The Sociology of Georg Simmel*, Glencoe, IL, Free Press.

Simmel, G. (1957) (*1904*) 'Fashion', *American Journal of Sociology*, 62(6): 541–58.

Simmel, G. (1959a) *Georg Simmel 1858–1918: A Collection of Essays with Translations and a Bibliography*, ed. Kurt H. Wolff, Columbus, Ohio University Press.

Simmel, G. (1959b) (*1908*) 'How is Society Possible?', in *Georg Simmel 1858–1918: A Collection of Essays with Translations and a Bibliography*, Columbus, Ohio University Press.

Simmel, G. (1968) (*1911*) 'On the Concept and Tragedy of Culture', in *Conflict in Modern Culture and Other Essays*, New York, Teachers College.

Simmel, G. (1978) (*1907*) *The Philosophy of Money*, London, Routledge & Kegan Paul.

Simmel, G. (1997) *Essays on Culture: Selected Writings*, ed. D. Frisby and M. Featherstone, London, Sage.

Simpson, D. (ed.) (1988) *The Origins of Modern Critical Thought: German Aesthetic and Literary Criticism from Lessing to Hegel*, Cambridge, Cambridge University Press.

Singer, P. (1993) *Practical Ethics*, Cambridge and New York, Cambridge University Press.

Skinner, B.F. (1973) *Beyond Freedom and Dignity*, Harmondsworth, Penguin.

Skinner, B.F. (1974) *About Behaviourism*, London, Jonathan Cape.

Skinner, B.F. (1976) *Waldon Two*, London, Macmillan.

Skirbekk, G. (1993) *Rationality and Modernity: Essays in Philosophical Pragmatics*, Oslo, Scandavian University Press.

Smart, B. (1984) *Foucault, Marxism and Critique*, London, Routledge.

Smart, N. (1960) *A Dialogue of Religions*, London, SCM Press.

Smart, N. (1971) *The Religious Experience of Mankind*, London, Fontana.

Smart, N. (1972) *The Concept of Worship*, London, Macmillan.

Smart, N. (1973) *The Phenomenon of Religion*, New York, Herder and Herder.

Smith, A. (1976) (*1776*) *The Wealth of Nations*, ed. R.H. Campbell, A.S. Skinner and W.B. Todd, Oxford, Clarendon Press.

Smith, A. (1986) *The Essential Adam Smith*, ed. Robert L. Heilbroner, Oxford, Oxford University Press.

Smith, G. (ed.) (1988) *On Walter Benjamin: Critical Essays and Recollections*, Cambridge, MA, MIT Press.

Smith, S. (1984) *Reading Althusser: An Essay on Structural Marxism*, Ithaca, NY, Cornell University Press.

Soja, E. (1989) *Postmodern Geographies*, London, Verso.

Solomon, R.C. (1983) *In the Spirit of Hegel*, New York, Oxford University Press.

Sontag, S. (1973) *On Photography*, New York, Farrar, Struas, and Giroux.

Sorel, G. (1972) (*1907*) *Reflections on Violence*, London, Macmillan.

Spector, J. (1997) *Surrealist Art and Writing 1919–1939: The Gold of Time*, Cambridge, Cambridge University Press.

Spencer, H. (1971) *Structure, Function and Evolution*, ed. Stanislav Andrewski, London, Thomas Nelson and Sons.

Spiegelman, A. (1987) *Maus: A Survivor's Tale*, Harmondsworth, Penguin.

Spiegelman, A. (1992) *Maus II: A Survivor's Tale: And Here My Troubles Began*, Harmondsworth, Penguin.

Spivak, G. (1987) *In Other Worlds: Essays in Cultural Politics*, New York, Methuen.

Spradley, J.P. (1980) *Participant Observation*, New York, Holt, Rinehart & Winston.

Sprigge, T.L.S. (1984) *Theories of Existence*, Harmondsworth, Penguin.

Squires, J. (ed.) (1993) *Principled Positions: Postmodernism and the Rediscovery of Value*, London, Lawrence & Wishart.

Stacey, J. (1994) *Star Gazing: Hollywood, Cinema and Female Spectatorship*, London, Routledge.

Stanley, L. and Roland, F. (1988) *Doing Feminist Ethnography in Rochdale*, Manchester, Manchester University Press.

Stanton, E.C. (1990) *The Woman's Bible*, Seattle, Coalition on Women and Religion.

Stearns, M.W. (1956) *The Story of Jazz*, London, Oxford University Press.

Sternhell, Z., Sznajder, M. and Asheri, M. (1994) *The Birth of Fascist Ideology: From Cultural Rebellion to Political Revolution*, tr. David Maisel, Princeton, NJ, Princeton University Press.

Stevens, A. (1994) *Jung*, Oxford, Oxford University Press.

Stevenson, N. (1995) *Understanding Media Cultures: Social Theory and Mass Communication*, London, Sage.

Storey, J. (1996) *Cultural Studies and the Study of Popular Culture: Theories and Methods*, Edinburgh, Edinburgh University Press.

Storey, J. (ed.) (1997) *Cultural Theory and Popular Culture: A Reader*, London, Routledge.

Strathern, M. (ed.) (1995) *Shifting Contexts: Transformations in Anthropological Knowledge*, London, Routledge.

Strauss, L. (1965) (*1949*) *Natural Right and History*, Chicago, University of Chicago Press.

Strawson, P. (1959) *Individuals: An Essay in Descriptive Metaphysics*, London, Methuen.

Strawson, P.F. (1966) *The Bounds of Sense: An Essay on Kant's Critique of Pure Reason*, London, Methuen.

Strianti, D. (1995) *An Introduction to Theories of Popular Culture*, London, Routledge.

Stroud, B. (1984) *The Significance of Philosophical Scepticism*, Oxford, Clarendon Press.

Sturrock, J. (ed.) (1979) *Structuralism and Since: From Lévi-Strauss to Derrida*, Oxford, Oxford University Press.

Sweezy, P.M. *et al.* (1978) *The Transition from Feudalism to Capitalism*, London, Verso.

Swift, F. (1996) (*1729*) 'A Modest Proposal for Preventing the Children of Ireland from being a Burden to their Parents or Country', in *A Modest Proposal and other Satires*, New York, Dover.

Swiss, T., Sloop, J.M. and Harmon, A. (eds) (1997) *Mapping the Beat*, Malden, MA, Blackwell.

Sztompka, P. (ed.) (1993) *Agency and Structure: Reorienting Social Theory*, Reading, Gordon and Breach.

Tarski, A. (1949) (*1944*) 'The Semantic Conception of Truth and the Foundations of Semantics', in H. Feigl and W. Sellars (eds), *Readings in Philosophical Analysis*, New York, Appleton-Century-Crofts.

Taylor, C. (1975) *Hegel*, Cambridge, Cambridge University Press.

Taylor, C. (1990) *Sources of the Self*, Cambridge, Cambridge University Press.

Taylor, C. (1997) *Philosophical Arguments*, Cambridge, MA, Harvard University Press.

Taylor, F.W. (1964) (*1947*) *Scientific Management*, New York, Harper.

Taylor, T.D. (1997) *Global Pop: World Music, World Markets*, New York, Routledge.

Thomas, H. (ed.) (1993) *Dance, Gender and Culture*, Basingstoke, Macmillan.

Thomason, B.C. (1982) *Making Sense of Reification: Alfred Schutz and Constructionist Theory*, London, Macmillan.

Thompson, E.P. (1963) *The Making of the English Working Class*, London, Gollancz.

Thomson, P. and Sacks, G. (eds) (1993) *The Cambridge Companion to Brecht*, Cambridge, Cambridge University Press.

Tiles, M. (1984) *Bachelard: Science and Objectivity*, Cambridge, Cambridge University Press.

Tivey, L. (ed.) (1981) *The Nation-State: The Formation of Modern Politics*, Oxford, Martin Robertson.

Tomlinson, G. (1984) 'The Web of Culture: A Context for Musicology', *Nineteenth Century Music*, 7: 350–62.

Touraine, A. (1971) (*1968*) *The Post-Industrial Society*, New York, Random House.

Treichler, P. (eds) (1992) *Cultural Studies*, London, Routledge.

Treitler, L. (1989) *Music and the Historical Imagination*, Cambridge, MA, Harvard University Press.

Turner, B.S. (1981) *For Weber: Essays on the Sociology of Fate*, London, Routledge & Kegan Paul.

Turner, B.S. (1984) *The Body and Society: Explorations in Social Theory*, Oxford, Blackwell.

Turner, B.S. (1986) *Citizenship and Capitalism: The Debate Over Reformism*, London, Allen & Unwin.

Turner, B.S. (1988) *Status*, Minneapolis, University of Minnesota Press.

Turner, B.S. and Hamilton, P. (eds) (1994) *Citizenship: Critical Concepts*, London, Routledge.

Turner, G. (1996) *British Cultural Studies*, second edn, London, Routledge.

Turner, R. (ed.) (1974) *Ethnomethology*, Harmondsworth, Penguin.

Van Inwagen, P. (1993) *Metaphysics*, Oxford, Oxford University Press.

Van Pelt, R.J. and Dwork, D. (1996) *Auschwitz: 1270 to the Present*, London and New Haven, Yale University Press.

Vattimo, G. (1988) *The End of Modernity: Nihilism and Hermeneutics in Postmodern Culture*, tr. Jon R. Snyder, Cambridge, Polity Press.

Vaughan Williams, R. (1963) *National Music and Other Essays*, Oxford, Oxford University Press.

Veblen, T. (1953) *The Theory of the Leisure Class*, New York, Mentor Books.

Veeser, H.A. (ed.) (1989) *The New Historicism*, London and New York, Routledge.

Venturi, R., Scott Brown, D. and Izenour, S. (1977) *Learning from Las Vegas: The Forgotten Symbolism of Architectural Form*, Cambridge, MA, MIT Press.

Voloshinov, V.N. (1973) *Marxism and the Philosophy of Language*, New York and London, Seminar Press.

Voloshinov, V.N. (1976) *Freudianism: A Marxist Critique*, New York, Academic Press.

Voloshinov, V.N. (1988) 'Discourse in Life and Discourse in Poetry', in A. Shukman (ed.), *Bakhtin School Papers*, Oxford, RTP.

Waites, B., Bennett, T. and Martin, G. (eds) (1989) *Popular Culture: Past and Present*, London, Routledge in association with the Open University Press.

Walby, S. (1986) *Patriarchy at Work*, Cambridge, Polity Press.

Walby, S. (1990) *Theorising Patriarchy*, Oxford, Blackwell.

Walsh, W.H. (1963) *Metaphysics*, London, Hutchinson.

Walzer, M. (1983) *Spheres of Justice*, New York, Basic Books.

Watkin, D. (1977) *Morality and Architecture: The Development of a Theme in Architectural History and Theory from the Gothic Revival to the Modern Movement*, Oxford, Clarendon Press.

Watkin, D. (1992) *A History of Western Architecture*, London, Laurence King.
Waugh, L. (1976) *Roman Jakobson's Science of Language*, Bloomington, IN, P. de Ridder.
Weber, M. (1930) (*1904–5*) *The Protestant Ethic and the Spirit of Capitalism*, London, George Allen & Unwin.
Weber, M. (1946a) *From Max Weber: Essays in Sociology*, ed. H.H. Gerth and C.W. Mills, London, Routledge & Kegan Paul.
Weber, M. (1946b) (*1921*) 'Bureaucracy', in *From Max Weber: Essays in Sociology*, London, Routledge & Kegan Paul.
Weber, M. (1946c) (*1921*) 'Class, Status, Party', in *From Max Weber: Essays in Sociology*, London, Routledge & Kegan Paul.
Weber, M. (1946d) 'India: The Brahman and the Castes', in *From Max Weber: Essays in Sociology*, London, Routledge & Kegan Paul.
Weber M. (1958) (*1922*) 'Three Types of Legitimate Rule', tr. H.H. Gerth, *Berkeley Publications in Society and Institutions*.
Weber, M. (1964) (*1922*) *The Theory of Social and Economic Organisation*, tr. A. M. Henderson and T. Parsons, New York, Free Press.
Weber, M. (1978) (*1921*) *Economy and Society*, ed. Guenther Roth and Claus Wittich, Berkeley, Los Angeles and London, University of California Press.
Weber, M. (1979) (*1923*) *General Economic History*, New Brunswick, NJ, Transaction Books.
Weber, M. (1994) (*1895*) 'The Freidberg Address', in *Political Writings*, Cambridge, Cambridge University Press.
Weber, R.P. (1990) *Basic Content Analysis*, second edn, Newbury Park, CA, Sage.
Weber, S.M. (1985) 'The Intersection: Marxism and the Philosophy of Language', *Diacritics*, 15(4): 94–112.
Weider, D.L. (1974) 'Telling the Code', in R. Turner (ed.), *Ethnomethodology*, Harmondsworth, Penguin.
Welford, A.T. *et al.* (eds) (1967) *Society: Problems and Methods of Study*, London, Routledge & Kegan Paul.
Wellek, R. (1986) *A History of Modern Criticism*, 6 volumes, New Haven, CT, Yale University Press.
West, D. (1996) *An Introduction to Continental Philosophy*, Cambridge, Polity Press.
White, H. (1987) *The Content of the Form: Narrative Discourse and Historical Representation*, Baltimore and London, Johns Hopkins University Press.
White, S.K. (1988) *The Recent Work of Jürgen Habermas: Reason, Justice and Modernity*, Cambridge, Cambridge University Press.

Bibliography

Whiteley, S. (ed.) (1997) *Sexing the Groove: Popular Music and Gender*, London, Routledge.

Whitford, F. (1984) *Bauhaus*, London, Thames & Hudson.

Whitford, M. (1991) *Luce Irigaray: Philosophy in the Feminine*, London, Routledge.

Wiggerthaus, R. (1994) (*1986*) *The Frankfurt School: Its History, Theories and Political Significance*, Cambridge, Polity Press.

Wilcox, H. (ed.) (1990) *The Body and the Text: Hélène Cixous, Reading and Teaching*, Hemel Hempstead, Harvester.

Willett, J. (1970) *Expressionism*, London, Weidenfeld & Nicolson.

Willett, J. (1984) *Brecht in Context: Comparative Approaches*, London, Methuen.

Williams, R. (1958) *Culture and Society 1780–1950*, London, Chatto & Windus.

Williams, R. (1961) *The Long Revolution*, London, Chatto & Windus.

Williams, R. (1962) *Communications*, Harmondsworth, Penguin.

Williams, R. (1968), *Drama from Ibsen to Brecht*, revised edn, London, Chatto & Windus.

Williams, R. (1973) *The Country and the City*, London, Chatto & Windus.

Williams, R. (1974) *Television: Technology and Cultural Form*, London, Fontana.

Willams, R. (1976) *Keywords*, London, Fontana.

Williams, R. (1977) *Marxism and Literature*, Oxford, Oxford University Press.

Williams, R. (1983) *Keywords*, second edn, London, Fontana.

Williams, R. (1986) *Culture*, London, Fontana.

Willis, P. (1977) *Learning to Labour: How Working Class Kids Get Working Class Jobs*, London, Saxon House.

Willis, P. (1978) *Profane Culture*, London, Routledge & Kegan Paul.

Willis, P. (1990) *Common Culture*, Milton Keynes, Open University Press.

Wilmer, V. (1992) *As Serious as Your Life: The Story of the New Jazz*, London, Serpent's Tail.

Wilson, E. (1991) *The Sphinx in the City*, London, Virago.

Wilson, E.O. (1975) *Sociobiology: The New Synthesis*, Cambridge, MA, Harvard University Press.

Wilson, E.O. (1994) *Naturalist*, London, Allen Lane.

Winch, P. (1958) *The Idea of a Social Science and Its Relation to Philosophy*, London, Routledge & Kegan Paul.

Wirth, L. (1938) 'Urbanism as a Way of Life', *American Journal of Sociology*, 44: 1–24.

Wittgenstein, L. (1961) (*1921*) *Tractatus Logico-Philosophicus*, tr. D.F. Pears and B.F. McGuinness, London, Routledge & Kegan Paul.

Wittgenstein, L. (1967) (*1953*) *Philosophical Investigations*, tr. G.E.M. Anscombe, Oxford, Blackwell.

Wittgenstein, L. (1956) *Remarks on the Foundations of Mathematics*, tr, G.E.M. Anscombe, Oxford, Blackwell.

Wittgenstein, L. (1958) *Philosophical Investigations*, second edn, tr. G.E.M. Anscombe, Oxford, Blackwell.

Wolfe, T. (1989) *From Bauhaus to Our House*, London, Cardinal.

Wolff, J. (1981) *The Social Production of Art*, London, Macmillan.

Wollstonecraft, M. (1992) *Vindication of the Rights of Woman*, ed. M. Brody, Harmondworth, Penguin.

Wood, J.C. (ed.) (1984) *Adam Smith: Critical Assessments*, London, Croom Helm.

Woolhouse, R.S. (1988) *The Empiricists*, Oxford, Oxford University Press.

Wright, E.O. (1985) *Classes*, London, Verso.

Wright, W. (1975) *Six Guns and Society: A Structural Study of the Western*, Berkeley, University of California Press.

Wrong, D (1980) (*1961*) 'The Oversocialised Conception of Man in Modern Sociology', in R. Bocock, P. Hamilton, K. Thompson and A. Walton (eds), *An Introduction to Sociology*, London, Fontana in association with the Open University Press.

Wu, D. (ed.) (1994) *Romanticism: An Anthology*, Oxford, Blackwell.

Yates, F.A. (1975) *Astraea: The Imperial Theme in the Sixteenth Century*, London, Routledge & Kegan Paul.

Yinger, J.M. (1982) *Countercultures: The Promise and Peril of a World Turned Upside Down*, New York, Free Press.

Young, I.M. (1990) *Justice and the Politics of Difference*, Princeton, NJ, Princeton University Press.

Young, M. (1958) *The Rise of Meritocracy*, London, Thames & Hudson.

Young, R.E. (ed.) (1981) *Untying the Text: A Post-Structuralist Reader*, London, Routledge & Kegan Paul.

Young-Eisendrath, P. and Dawson, T. (eds) (1997) *The Cambridge Companion to Jung*, Cambridge, Cambridge University Press.

Zizek, S. (1989) *The Sublime Object of Ideology*, London and New York, Verso.

Zizek, S. (1992) *Enjoy Your Symptom! Jacques Lacan in Hollywood and Out*, New York and London, Routledge.

Zuriff, G.E. (1985) *Behaviourism: A Conceptual Reconstruction*, New York, Columbia University Press.

NAME INDEX

SUBJECT INDEX

496